Due to a chance event several years ago, I began visiting the ocean regularly. However, since the series started, I've been having trouble putting aside the time for that. Sitting at my desk, I find myself in a bad situation, where I'm not as productive as I want to be.

I'd like to become a mature adult, who can handle both work and play properly.
— Koji Inada

Author Riku Sanjo and artist Koji Inada were both born in Tokyo in 1964. Sanjo began his career writing a radio-controlled car manga for the comic **Bonbon**. Inada debuted with **Kussotare Daze!!** in **Weekly Shonen Jump**. Sanjo and Inada first worked together on the highly successful **Dragon Quest–Dai's Big Adventure. Beet the Vandel Buster,** their latest collaboration, debuted in **Monthly Shonen Jump** in 2002 and was an immediate hit, inspiring an action-packed video game and an animated series on Japanese TV.

BEET THE VANDEL BUSTER
VOL. 5
The SHONEN JUMP Graphic Novel Edition

STORY BY RIKU SANJO
ART BY KOJI INADA

English Adaptation/Shaenon K. Garrity
Translation/Naomi Kokubo
Touch-Up & Lettering/Mark McMurray
Graphics & Cover Design/Andrea Rice
Editor/Pancha Diaz

Managing Editor/Elizabeth Kawasaki
Director of Production/Noboru Watanabe
Vice President of Publishing/Alvin Lu
Vice President & Editor in Chief/ Yumi Hoashi
Sr. Director of Acquisitions/Rika Inouye
Vice President of Sales & Marketing/Liza Coppola
Publisher/Hyoe Narita

Printed in the U.S.A.

Published by VIZ, LLC
P.O. Box 77064
San Francisco, CA 94107

SHONEN JUMP Graphic Novel Edition
10 9 8 7 6 5 4 3 2 1
First printing, May 2005

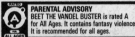

www.viz.com

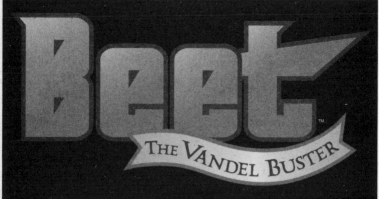

SHONEN JUMP GRAPHIC NOVEL

Beet™ THE VANDEL BUSTER

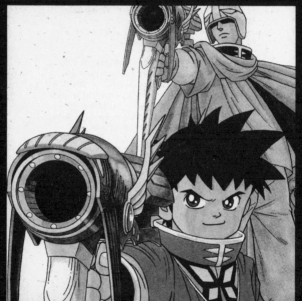

Volume 5

Story by **Riku Sanjo**

Art by **Koji Inada**

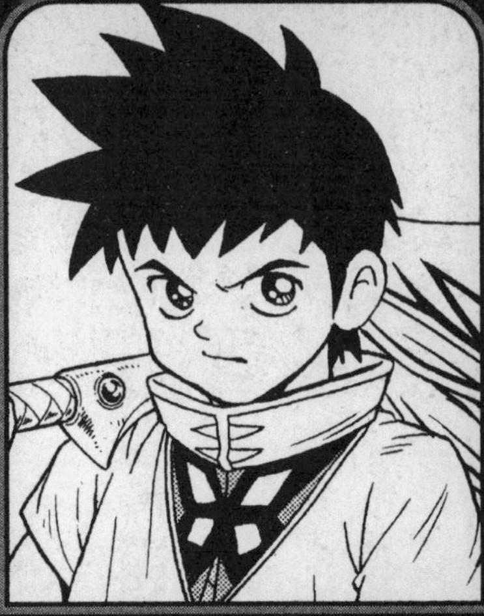

BEET

The hero of this story.
Believing in justice, he sets out on a journey to save the world. He received five Saiga weapons from the Zenon Warriors.

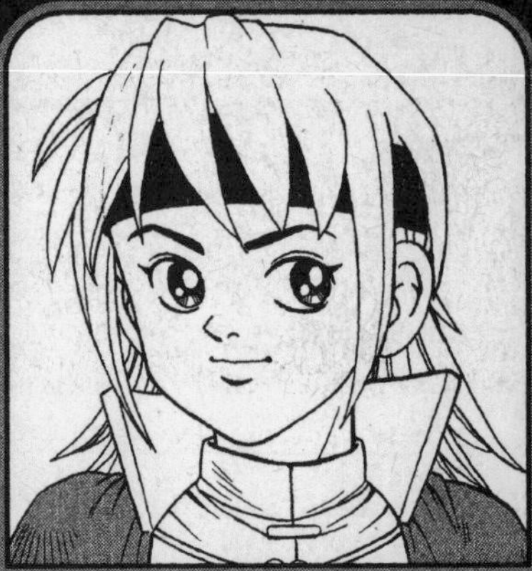

POALA

Beet's childhood friend.
She has an unyielding spirit. Poala joins Beet in his journey as the second of the Beet Warriors. She is skilled at attacking enemies using her Divine Attack.

STORY

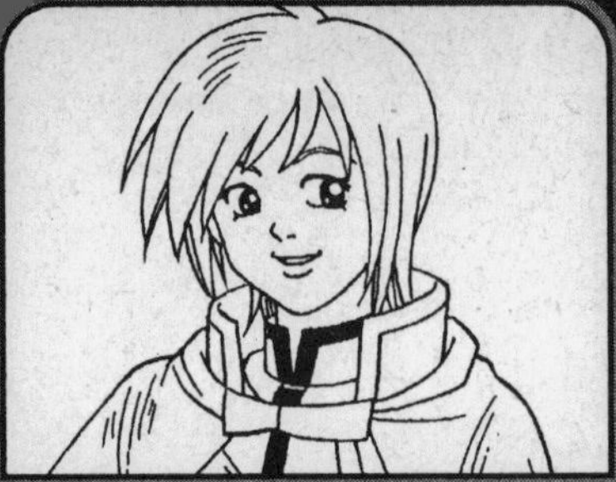

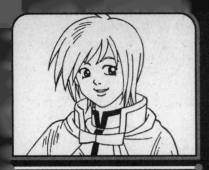

KISSU

An old friend of Beet's, he is skilled at the Divine Attack. After being betrayed by humans, he became a servant of Grineed.

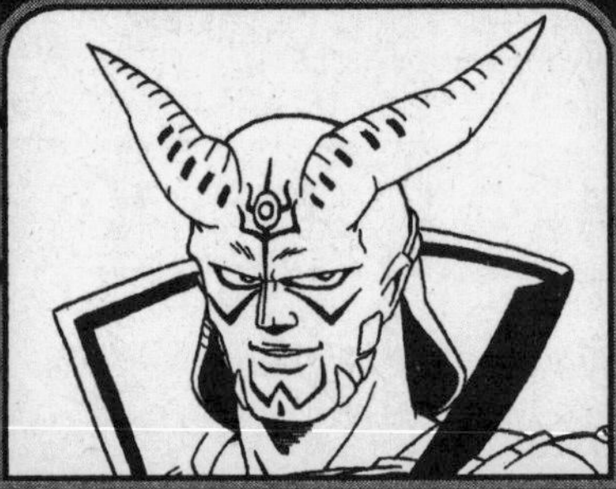

BELTORZE

Known as the "King of Tragedy," he is a seven-star Vandel widely feared by humans.

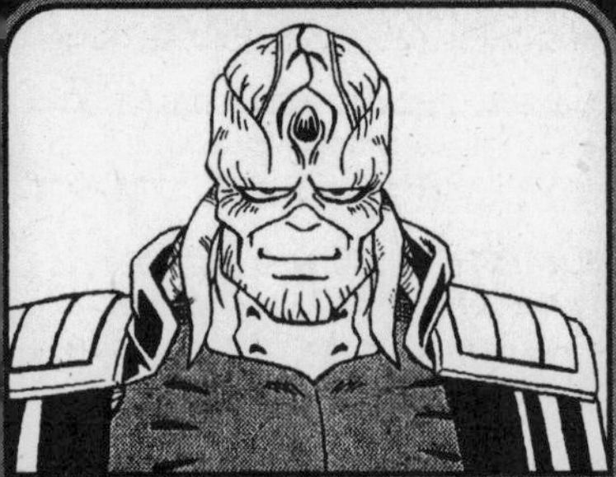

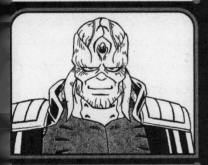

GRINEED

He is a Vandel who believes in being emotionless and cool at all times. Despite this, he has immense brutality inside him.

CHARACTERS

ROZZGOAT

As Grineed's faithful right-hand man, this five-star Vandel has the authority to command in place of Grineed.

FRAUSKY

This assassin is the strongest of Grineed's minions. He has biological firearms hidden all over his body and uses them to cruelly kill his targets.

VENTURA

One of Grineed's flunkies, he's a coward with oversized ambitions. He has spider-like abilities, and his main duty is gathering intelligence.

"Vandels"... In this story, that's what we call evil creatures with magical powers. One day they appeared on the surface of the Earth, releasing monsters and destroying whole nations. People called this seemingly endless era "The Dark Age."

Beet, a young boy who believes in justice, binds himself with a contract to become a Vandel Buster and conquer Vandels for a living. However, Beet stumbles into a battle between Beltorze and the Zenon Warriors, where he suffers a fatal injury. He miraculously survives by receiving the Saiga of the Zenon Warriors.

Three years later, Beet sets out on a journey with his friend Poala to carry on the Zenon Warriors' mission. They land in the "Black Horizon," an area controlled by a powerful Vandel named Grineed, in search of a third teammate. There, they clash violently with the Vandels who work for Grineed. In the midst of this conflict, Beet encounters an old friend, Kissu. But Kissu betrays their friendship and buries Beet alive beneath ancient ruins...

Beet™ THE VANDEL BUSTER

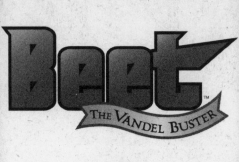

5

Chapter 15: Roar, Cyclone Bullet!!

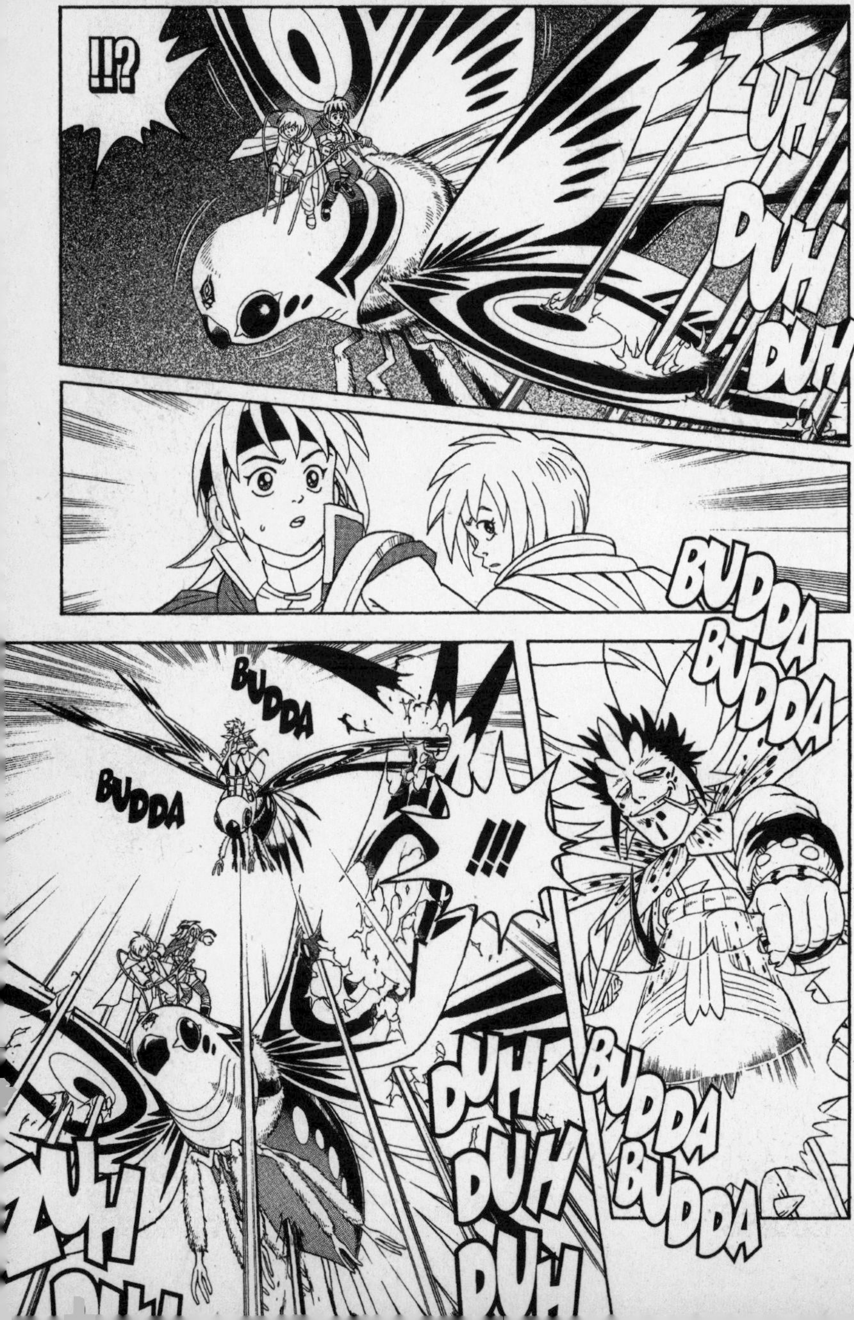
ZUH DUH DUH
!!?
BUDDA BUDDA BUDDA
BUDDA
!!!
BUDDA
BUDDA BUDDA BUDDA
DUH DUH DUH
ZUH

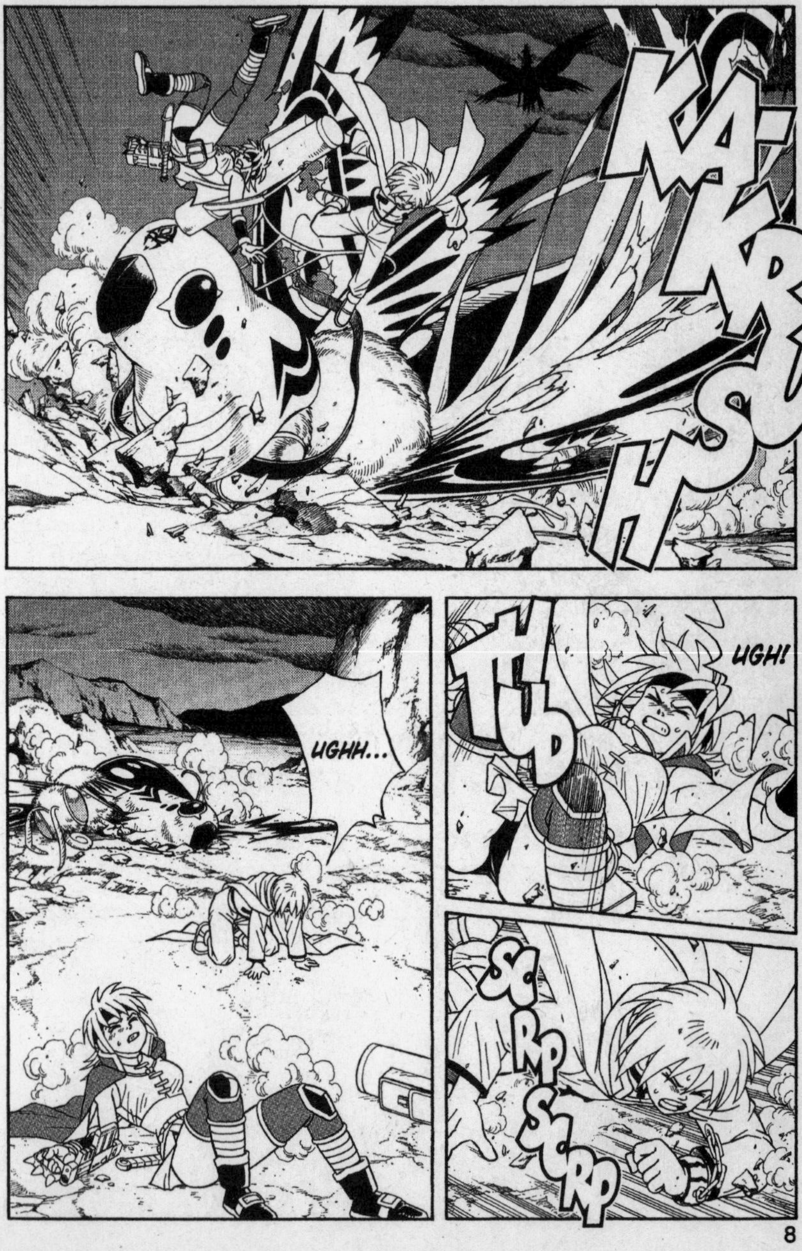
KA-KRUSH
THUD
UGH!
SCRP
SCRP
UGHH...

READ THIS WAY

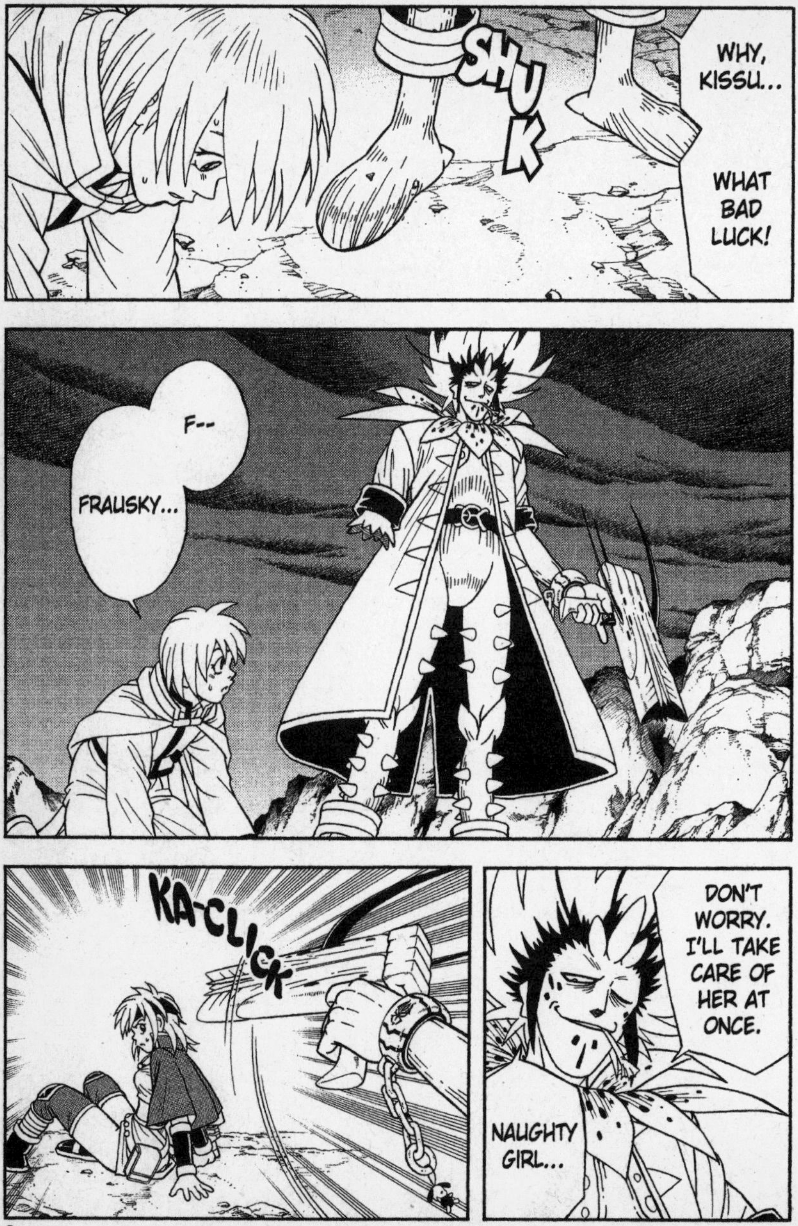
WHY, KISSU...
WHAT BAD LUCK!
SHUK
F--
FRAUSKY...
DON'T WORRY. I'LL TAKE CARE OF HER AT ONCE.
NAUGHTY GIRL...
KA-CLICK

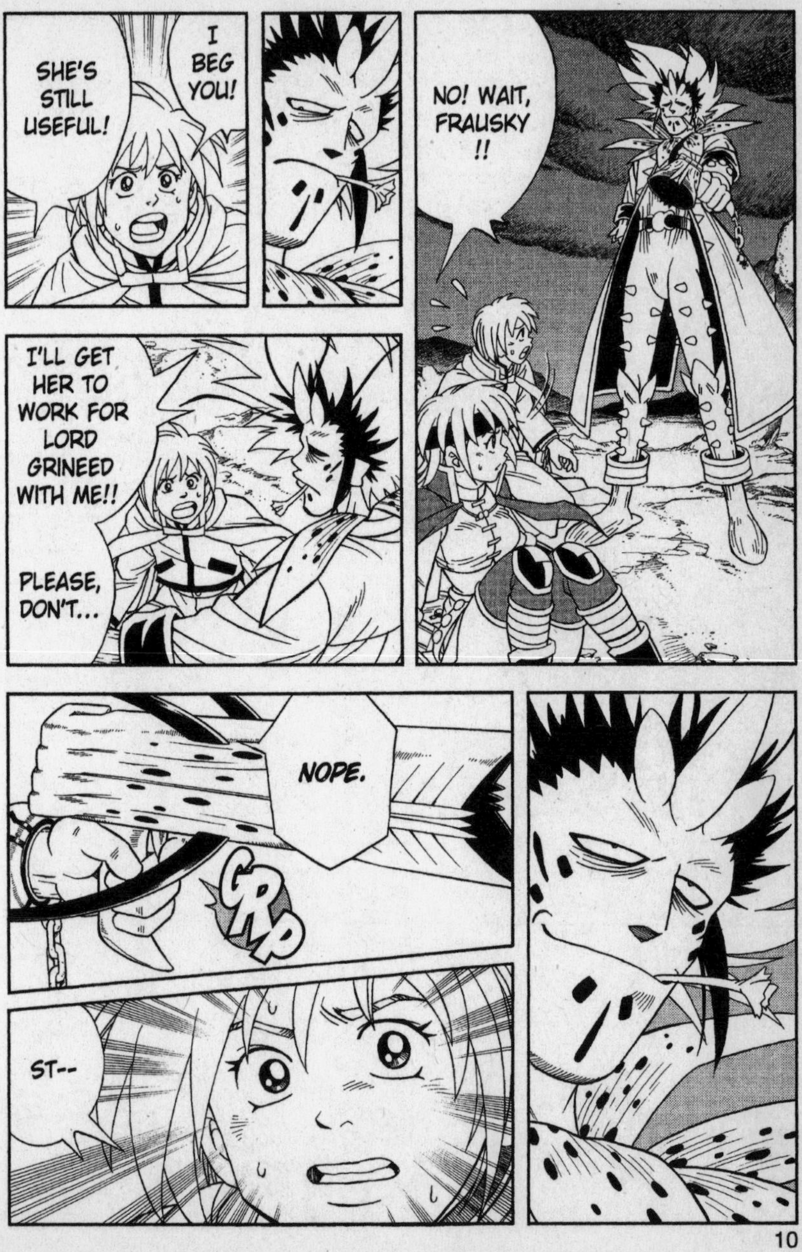
NO! WAIT, FRAUSKY !!
I BEG YOU!
SHE'S STILL USEFUL!
I'LL GET HER TO WORK FOR LORD GRINEED WITH ME!!
PLEASE, DON'T...
NOPE.
GRIP
ST--

READ THIS WAY

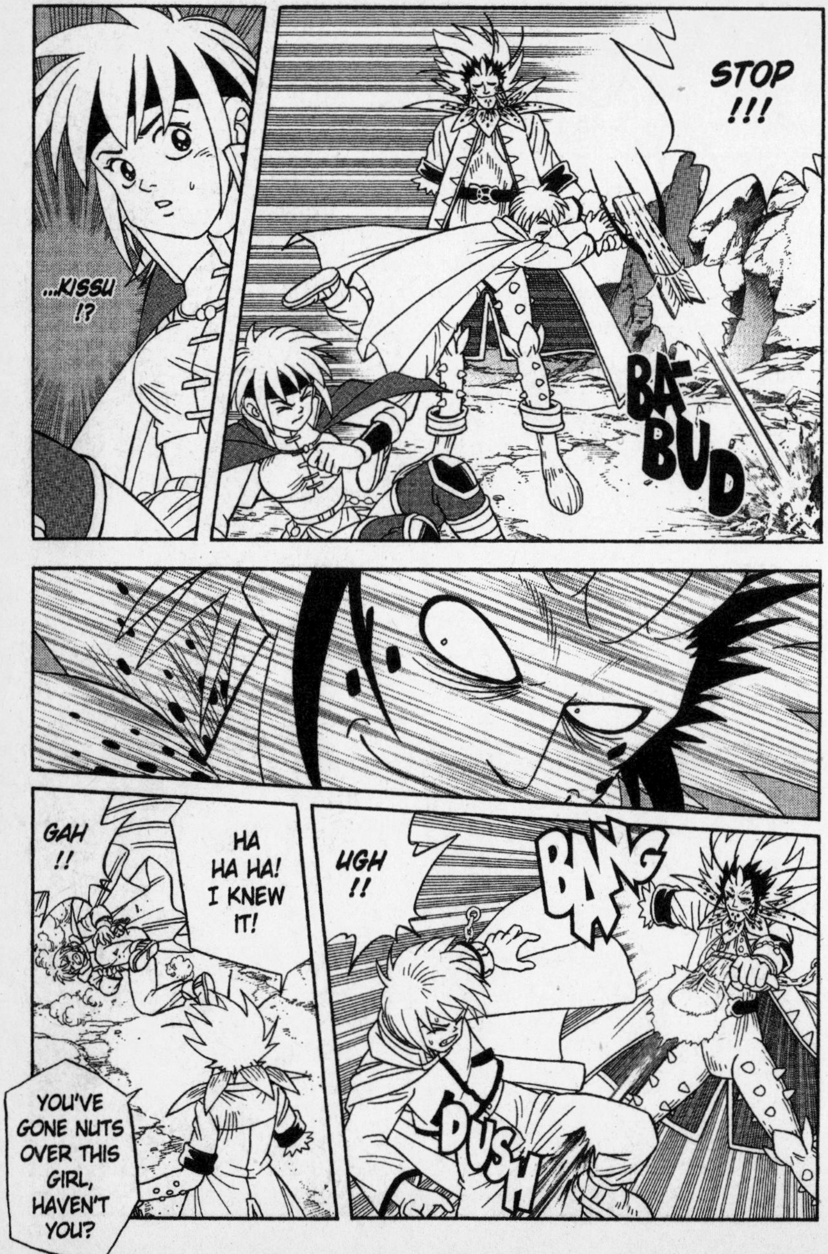
STOP !!!
BA-BUD
...KISSU !?
BANG
UGH !!
DUSH
HA HA HA! I KNEW IT!
GAH !!
YOU'VE GONE NUTS OVER THIS GIRL, HAVEN'T YOU?

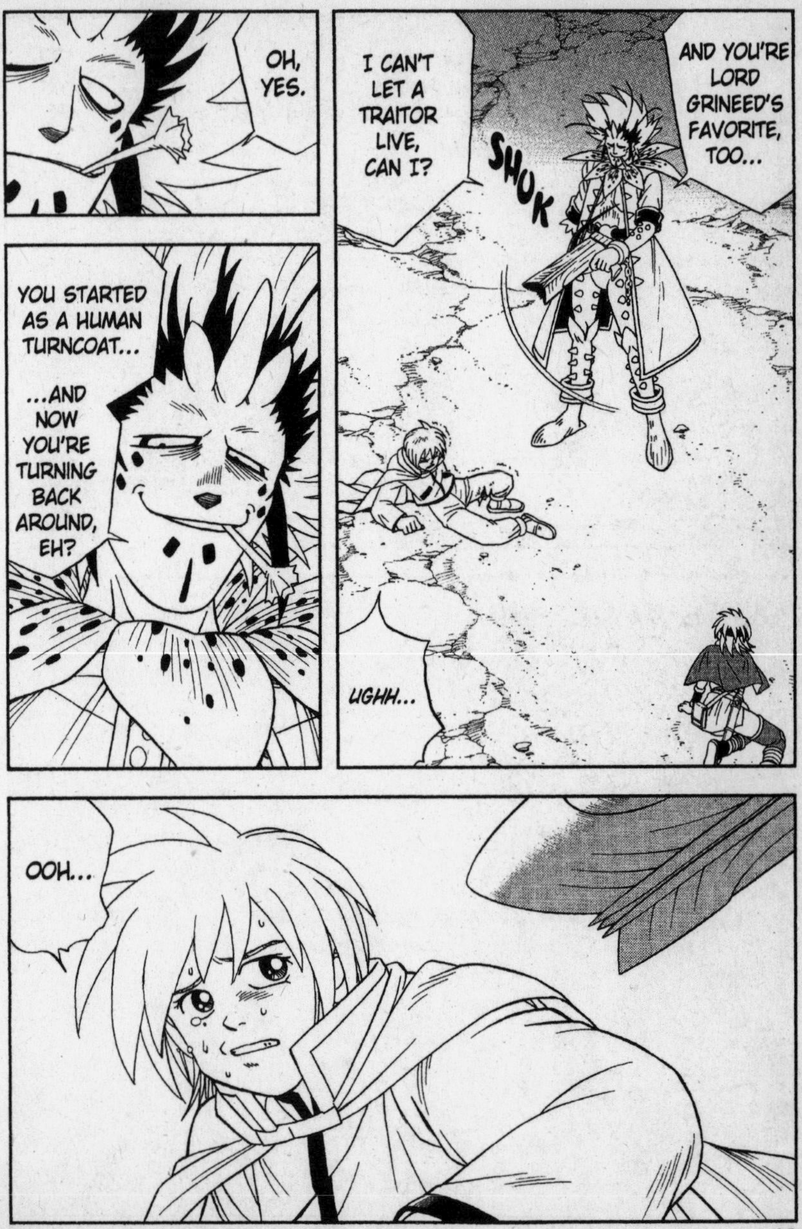
AND YOU'RE LORD GRINEED'S FAVORITE, TOO...
I CAN'T LET A TRAITOR LIVE, CAN I?
SHOK
UGHH...
OH, YES.
YOU STARTED AS A HUMAN TURNCOAT...
...AND NOW YOU'RE TURNING BACK AROUND, EH?
OOH...

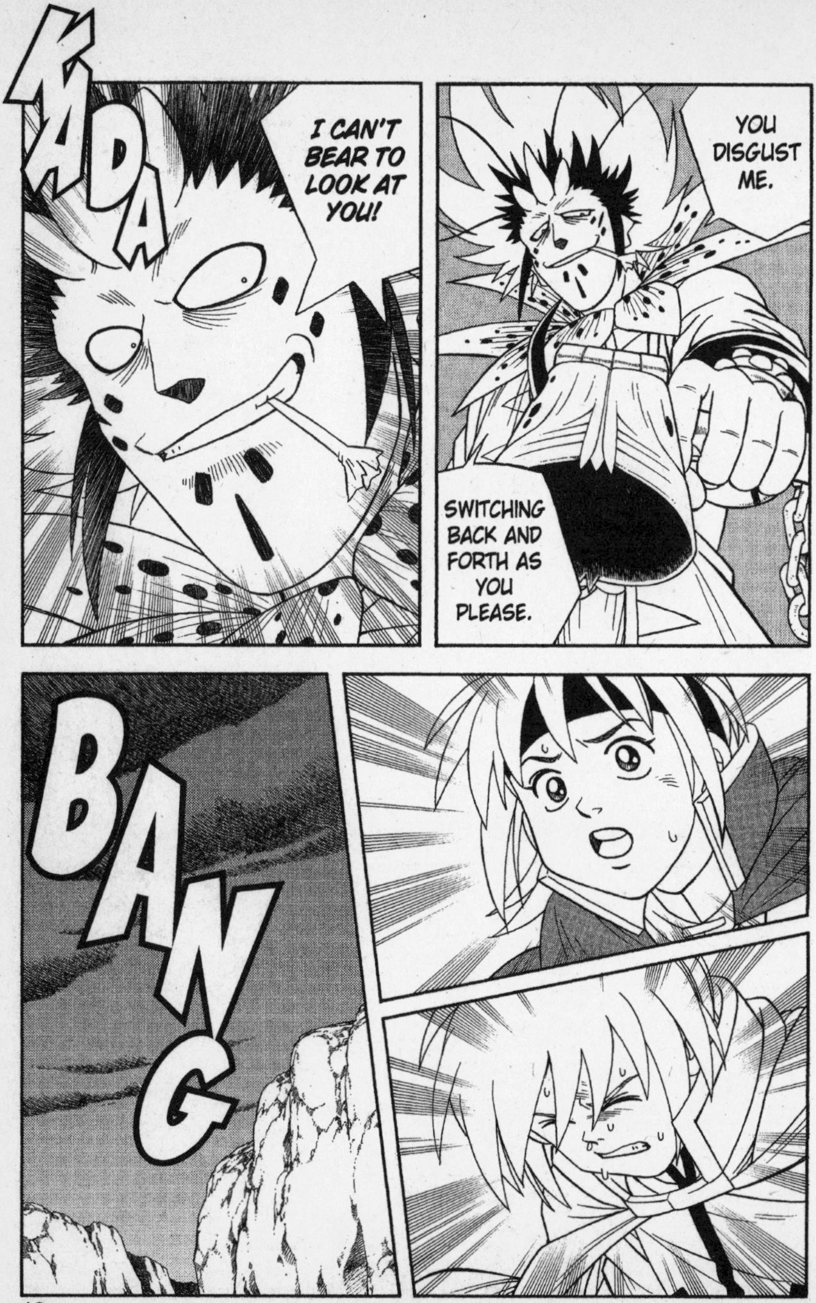
YOU DISGUST ME.
SWITCHING BACK AND FORTH AS YOU PLEASE.
KADA
I CAN'T BEAR TO LOOK AT YOU!
BANG

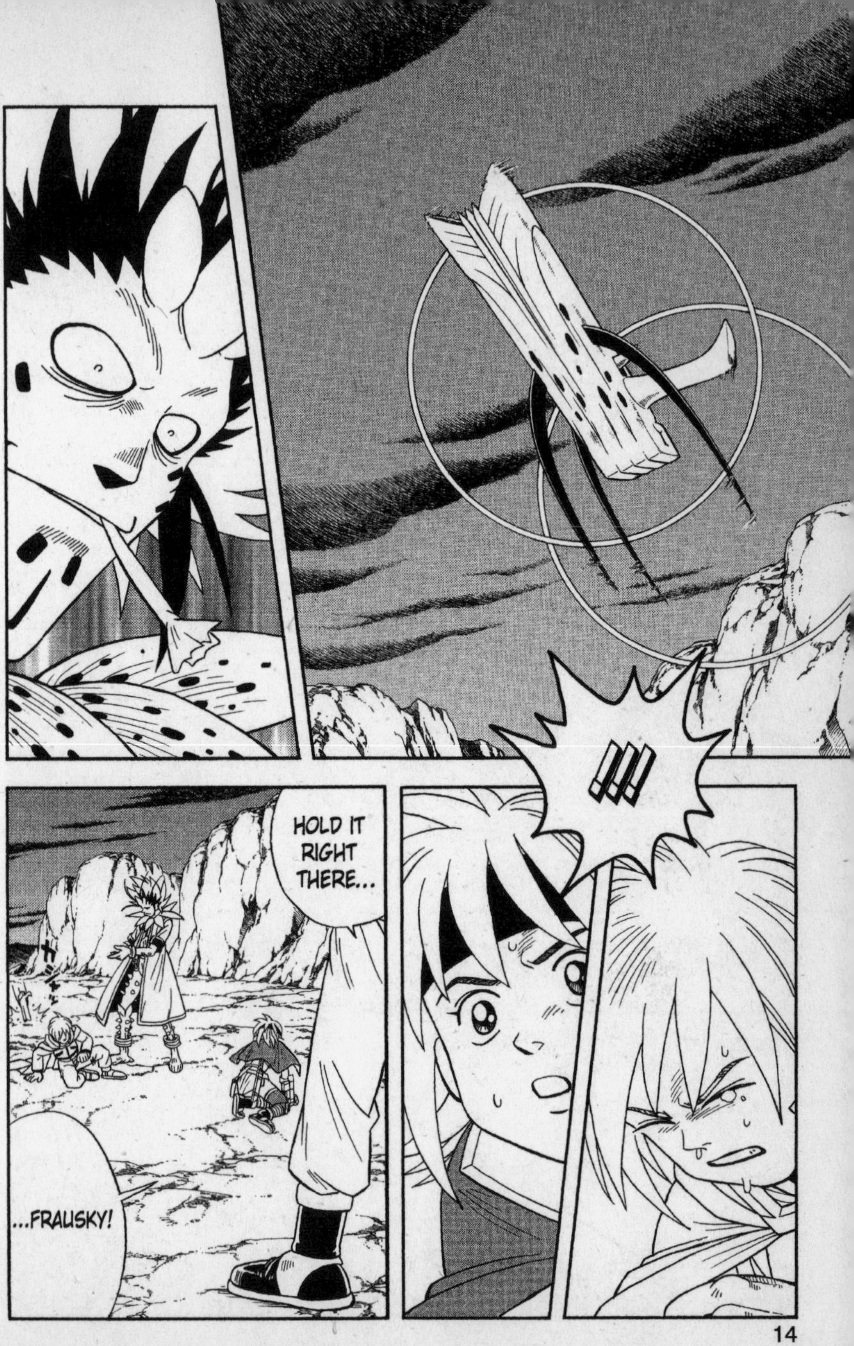
!!!!
HOLD IT RIGHT THERE...
...FRAUSKY!

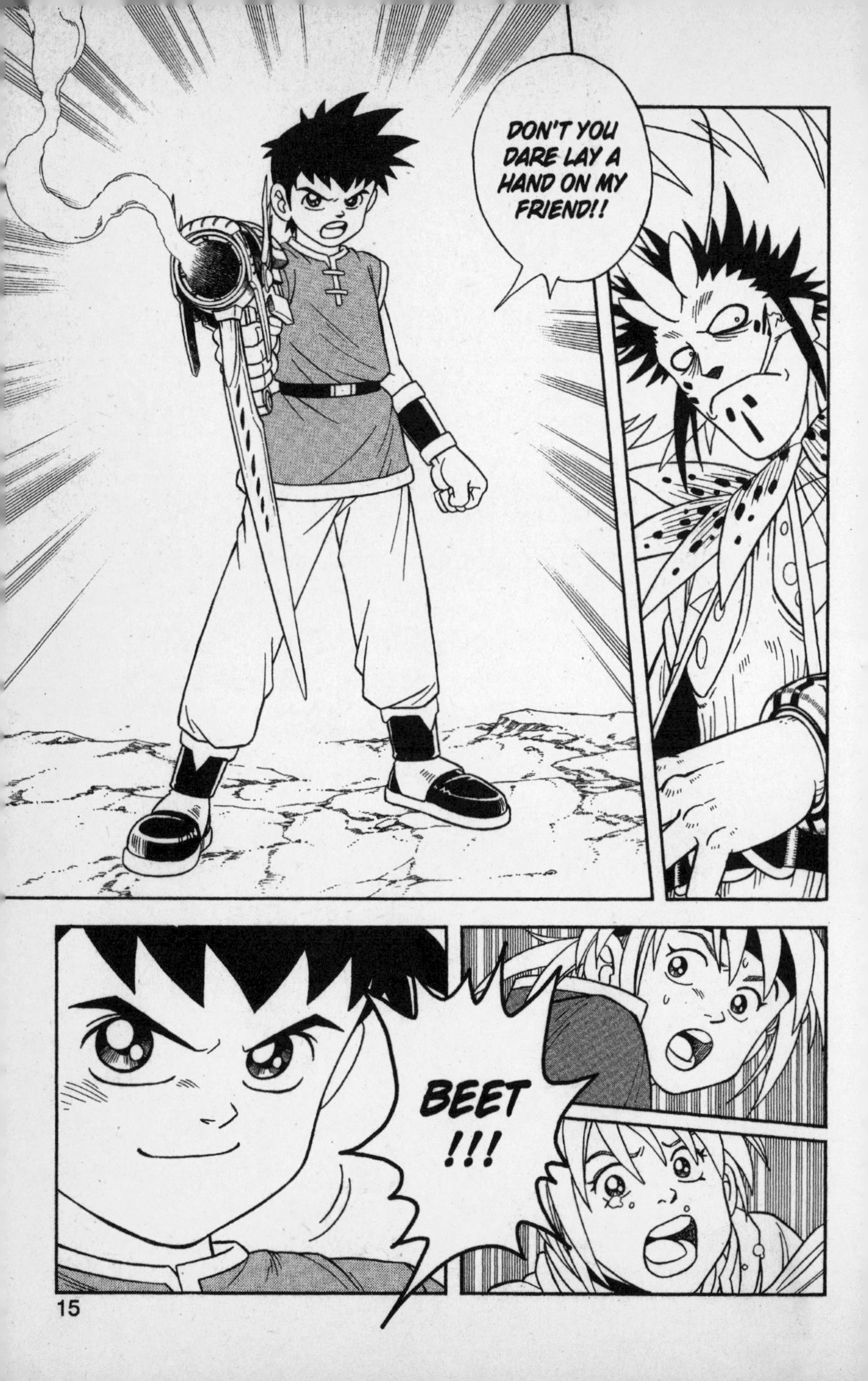
DON'T YOU DARE LAY A HAND ON MY FRIEND!!
BEET !!!

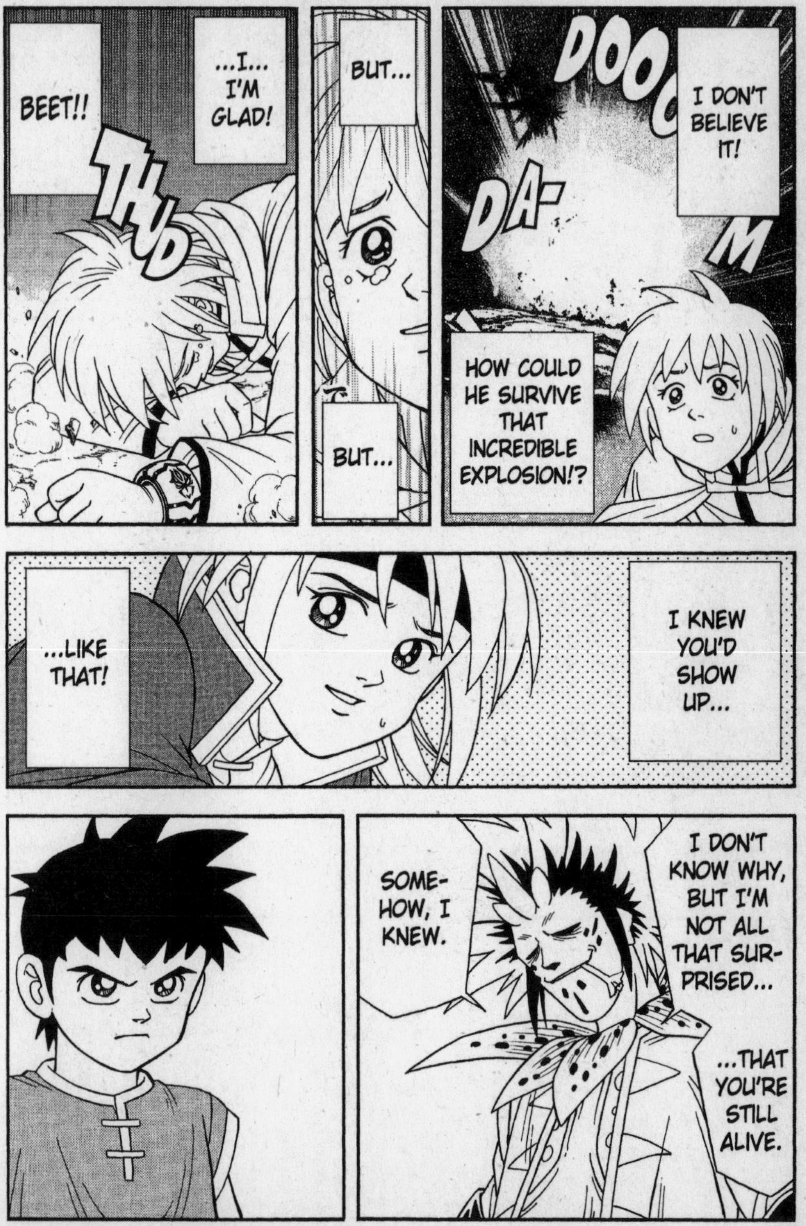
DOOO
M
DA-
I DON'T BELIEVE IT!
HOW COULD HE SURVIVE THAT INCREDIBLE EXPLOSION!?
BUT...
BUT...
...I... I'M GLAD!
BEET!!
THUD
I KNEW YOU'D SHOW UP...
...LIKE THAT!
I DON'T KNOW WHY, BUT I'M NOT ALL THAT SUR-PRISED...
SOME-HOW, I KNEW.
...THAT YOU'RE STILL ALIVE.

READ THIS WAY

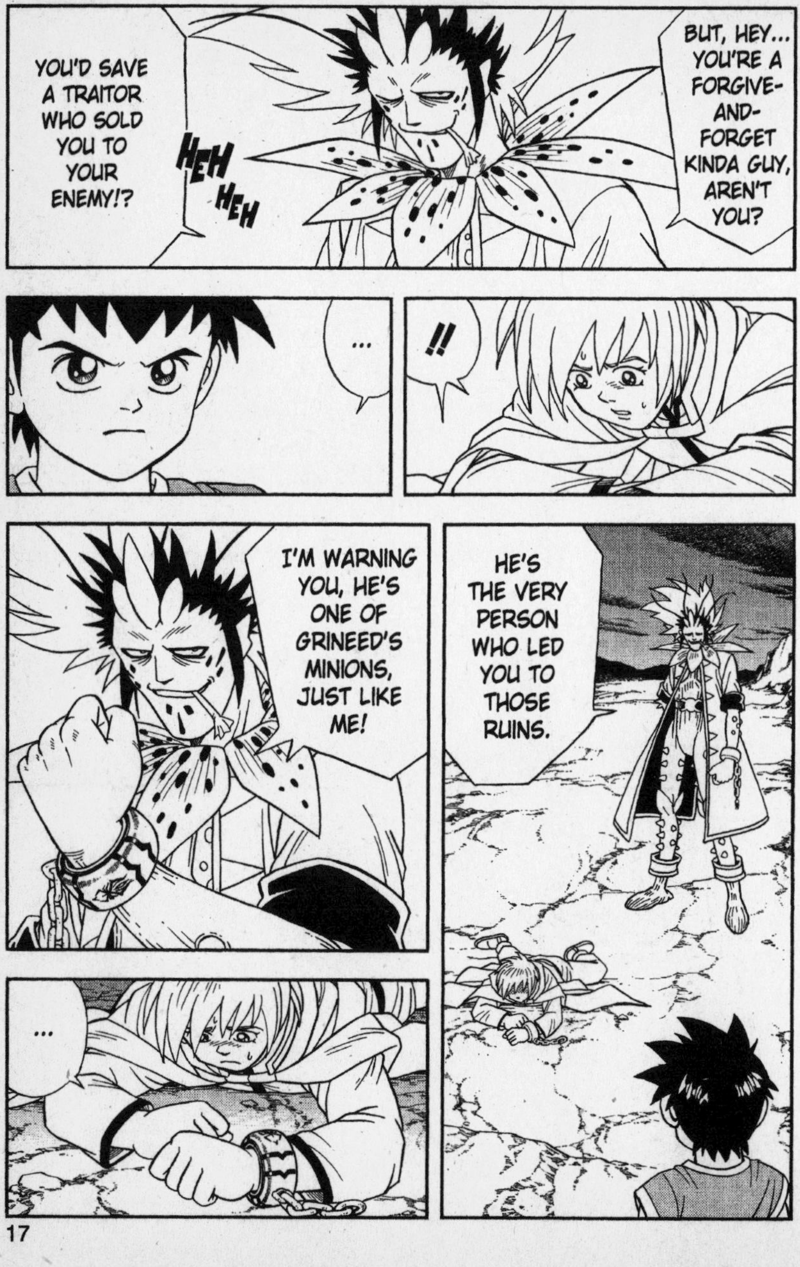
BUT, HEY... YOU'RE A FORGIVE-AND-FORGET KINDA GUY, AREN'T YOU?
HEH HEH
YOU'D SAVE A TRAITOR WHO SOLD YOU TO YOUR ENEMY!?
!!
...
HE'S THE VERY PERSON WHO LED YOU TO THOSE RUINS.
I'M WARNING YOU, HE'S ONE OF GRINEED'S MINIONS, JUST LIKE ME!
...

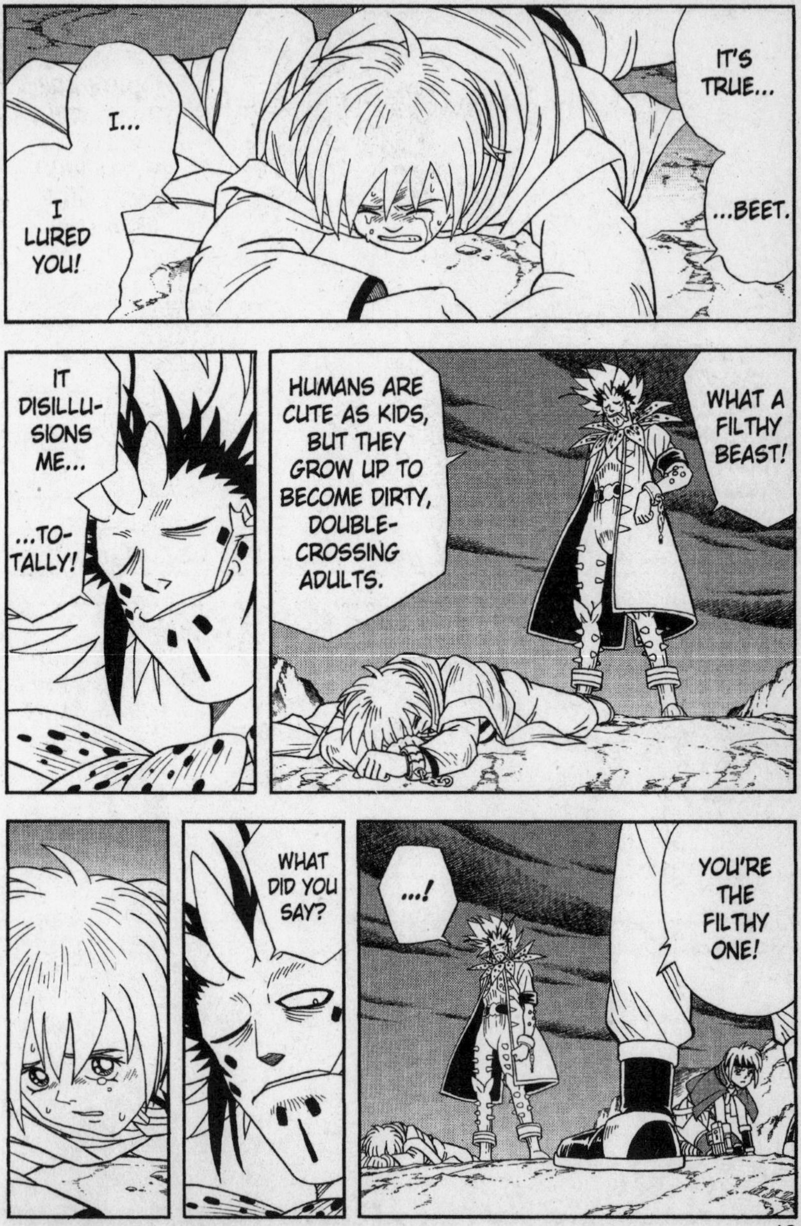
IT'S TRUE...
...BEET.
I...
I LURED YOU!
WHAT A FILTHY BEAST!
HUMANS ARE CUTE AS KIDS, BUT THEY GROW UP TO BECOME DIRTY, DOUBLE-CROSSING ADULTS.
IT DISILLU-SIONS ME...
...TO-TALLY!
YOU'RE THE FILTHY ONE!
...!
WHAT DID YOU SAY?

READ THIS WAY

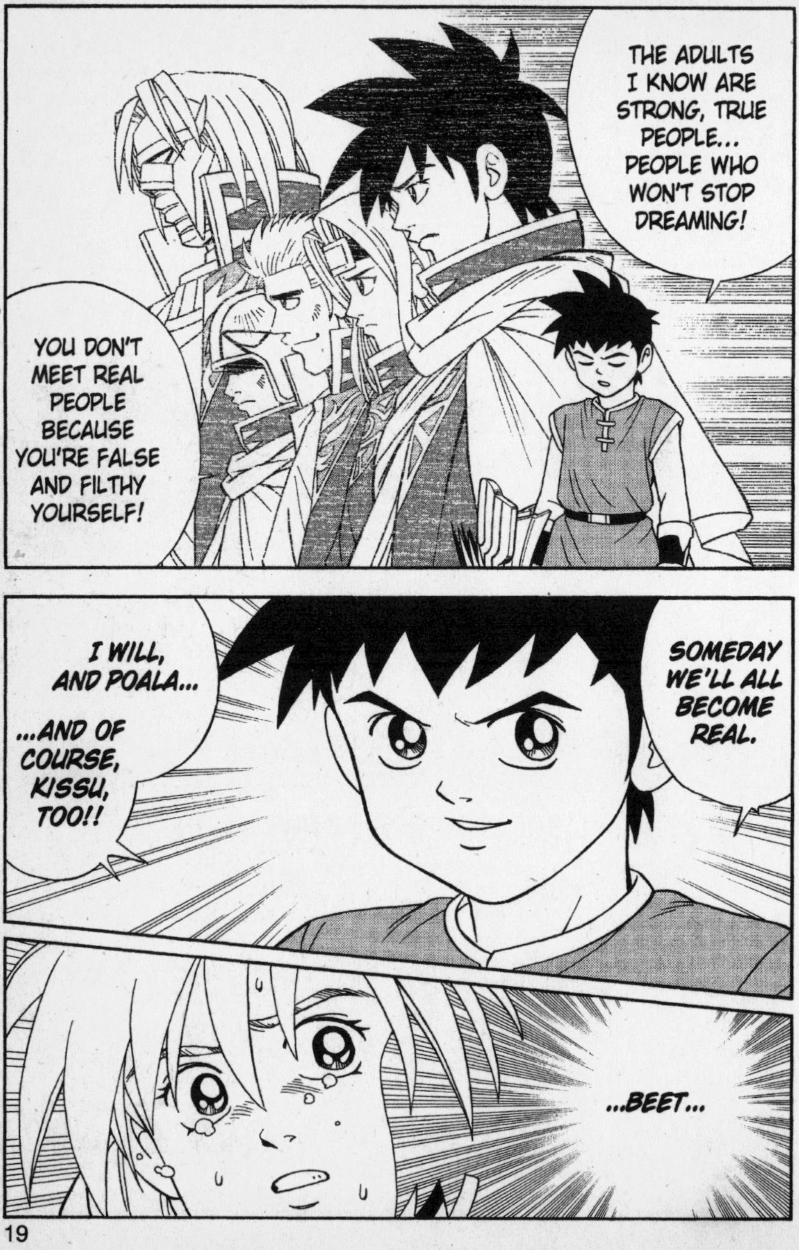
THE ADULTS I KNOW ARE STRONG, TRUE PEOPLE... PEOPLE WHO WON'T STOP DREAMING!
YOU DON'T MEET REAL PEOPLE BECAUSE YOU'RE FALSE AND FILTHY YOURSELF!
SOMEDAY WE'LL ALL BECOME REAL.
I WILL, AND POALA...
...AND OF COURSE, KISSU, TOO!!
...BEET...

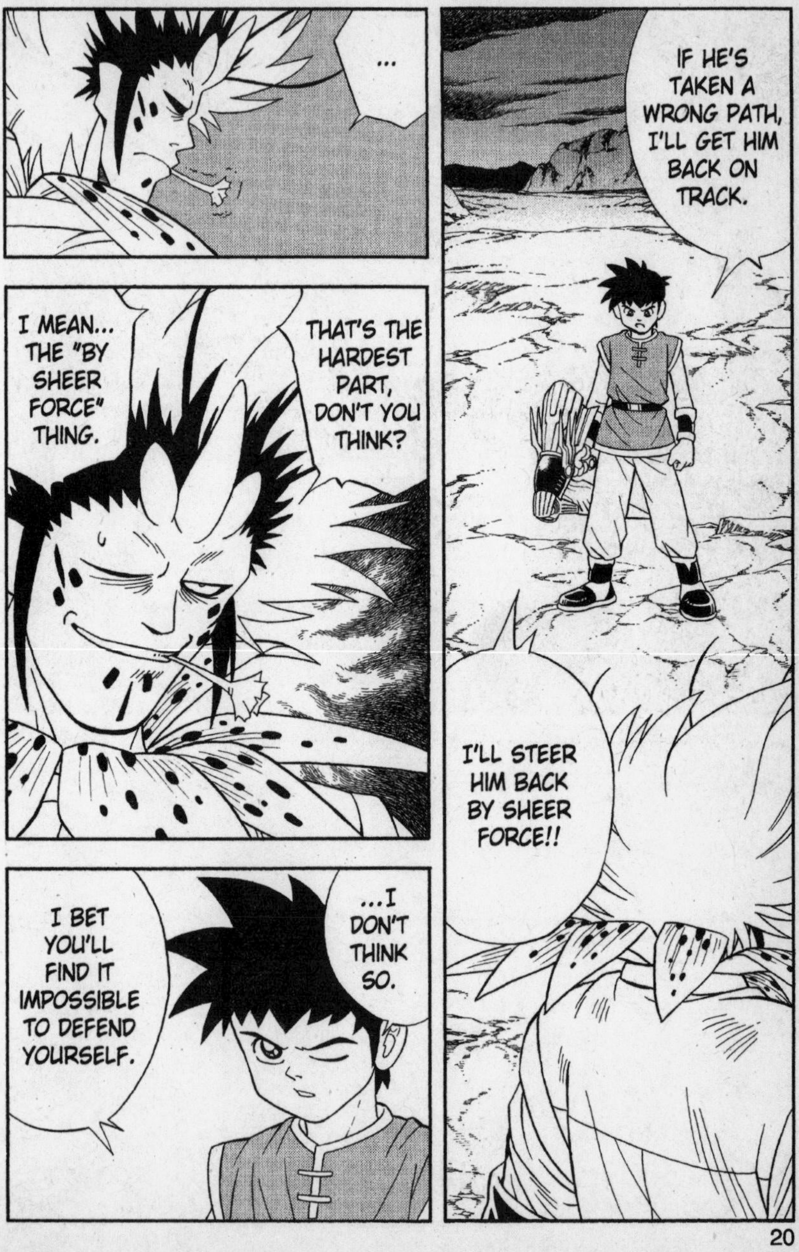
IF HE'S TAKEN A WRONG PATH, I'LL GET HIM BACK ON TRACK.
I'LL STEER HIM BACK BY SHEER FORCE!!
...
THAT'S THE HARDEST PART, DON'T YOU THINK?
I MEAN... THE "BY SHEER FORCE" THING.
...I DON'T THINK SO.
I BET YOU'LL FIND IT IMPOSSIBLE TO DEFEND YOURSELF.

READ THIS WAY

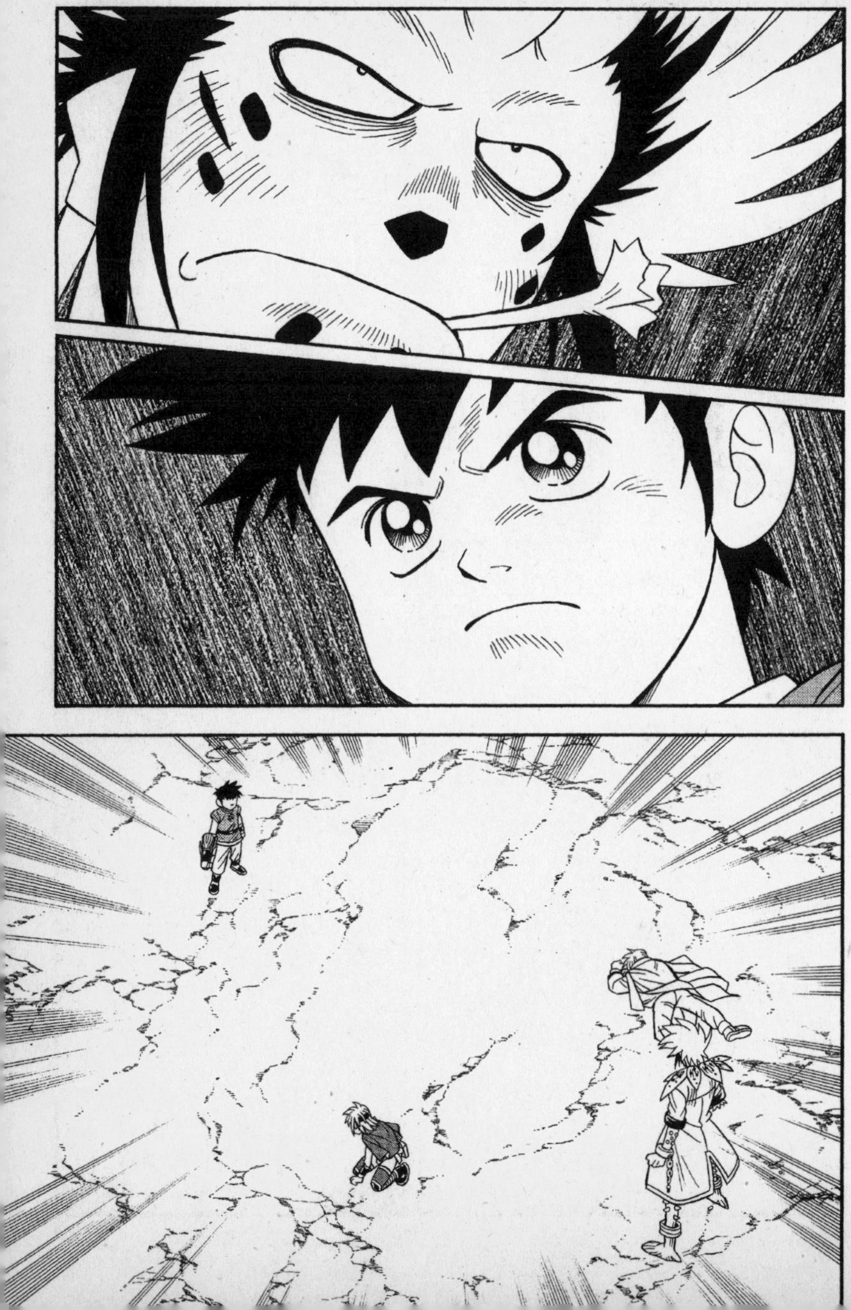

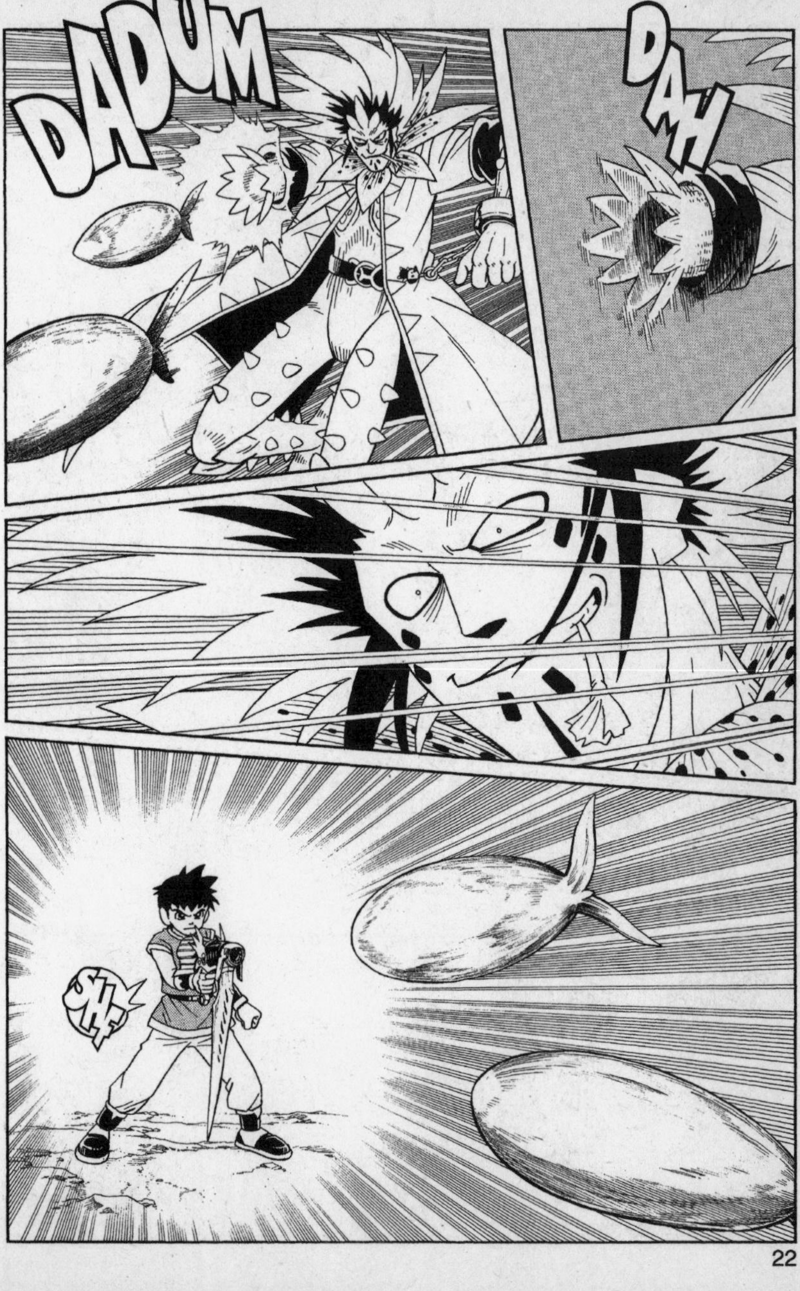
DAH
DADUM
SHF

READ THIS WAY

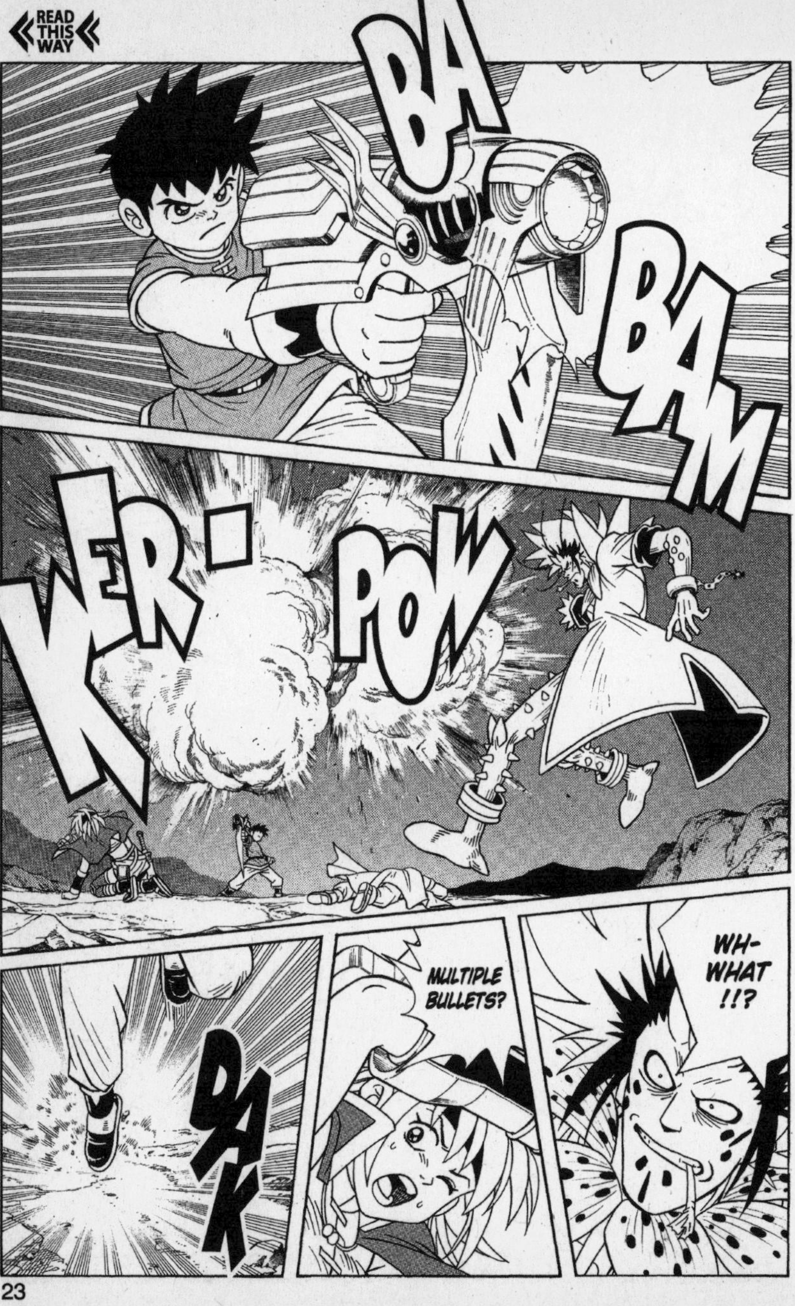
BA
BAM
KER-POW
WH-WHAT!!?
MULTIPLE BULLETS?
DAK

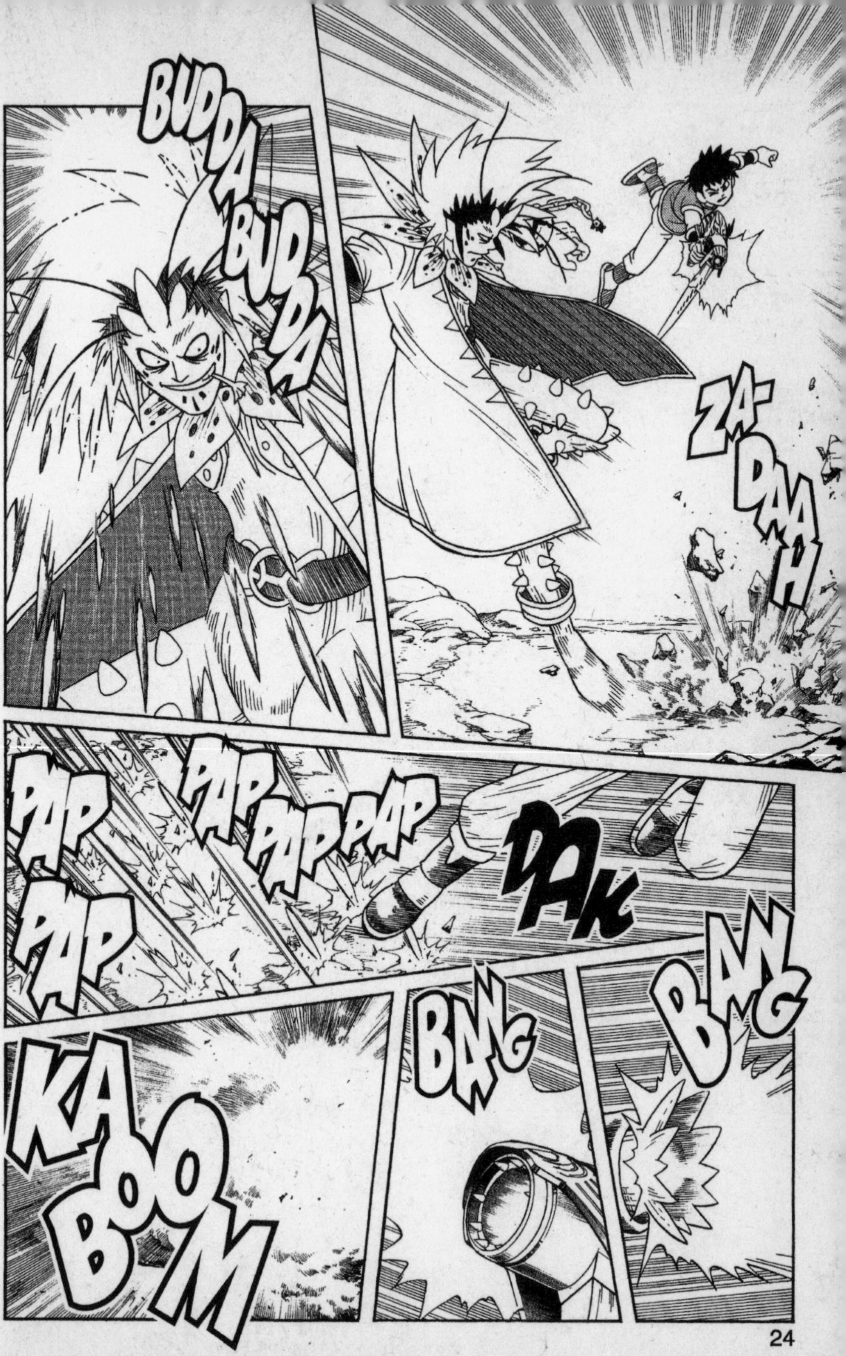
ZA-DAAAH
BUDDA BUDDA BUDDA
DAK
PAP PAP PAP
PAP
PAP
BANG
BANG
KABOOM

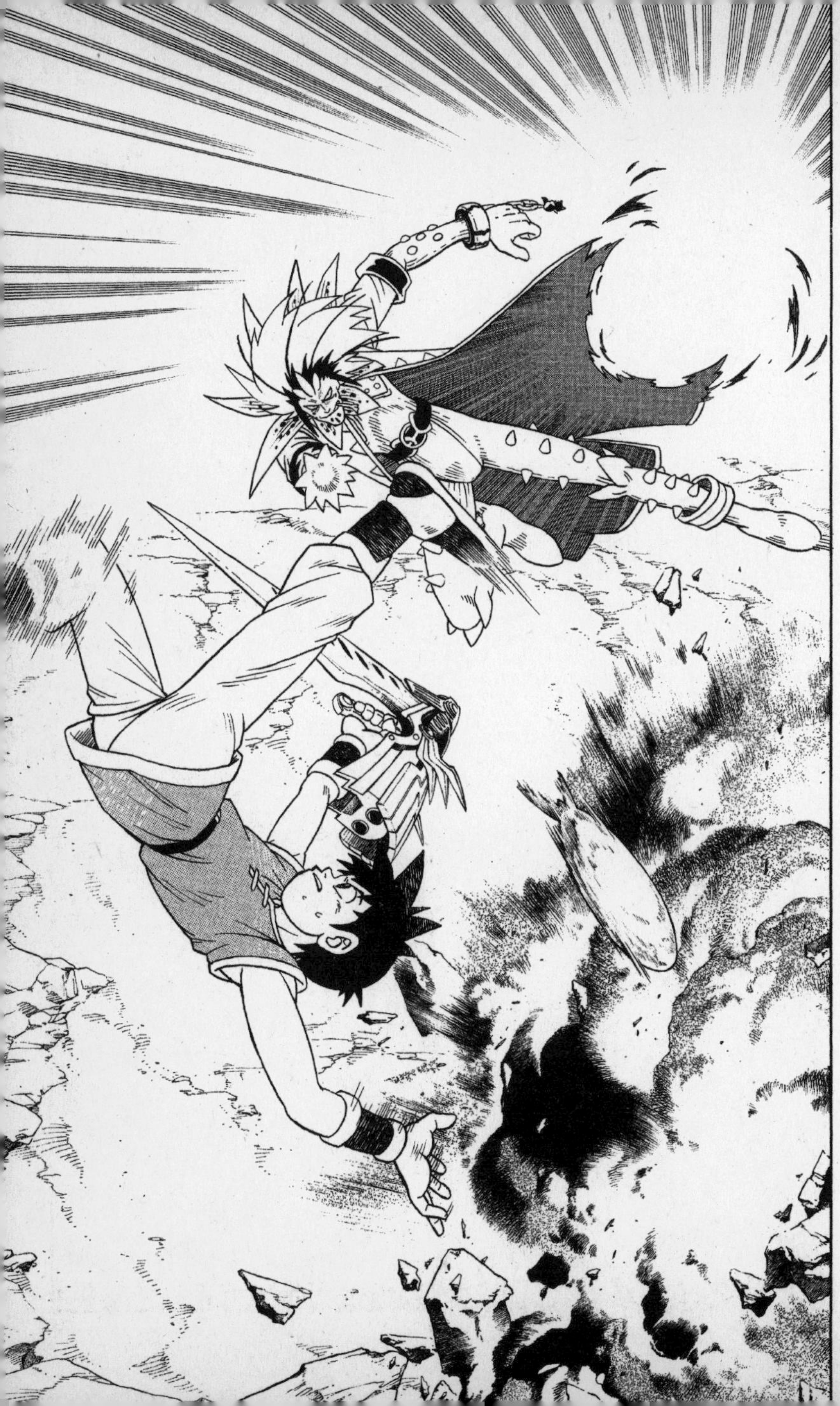

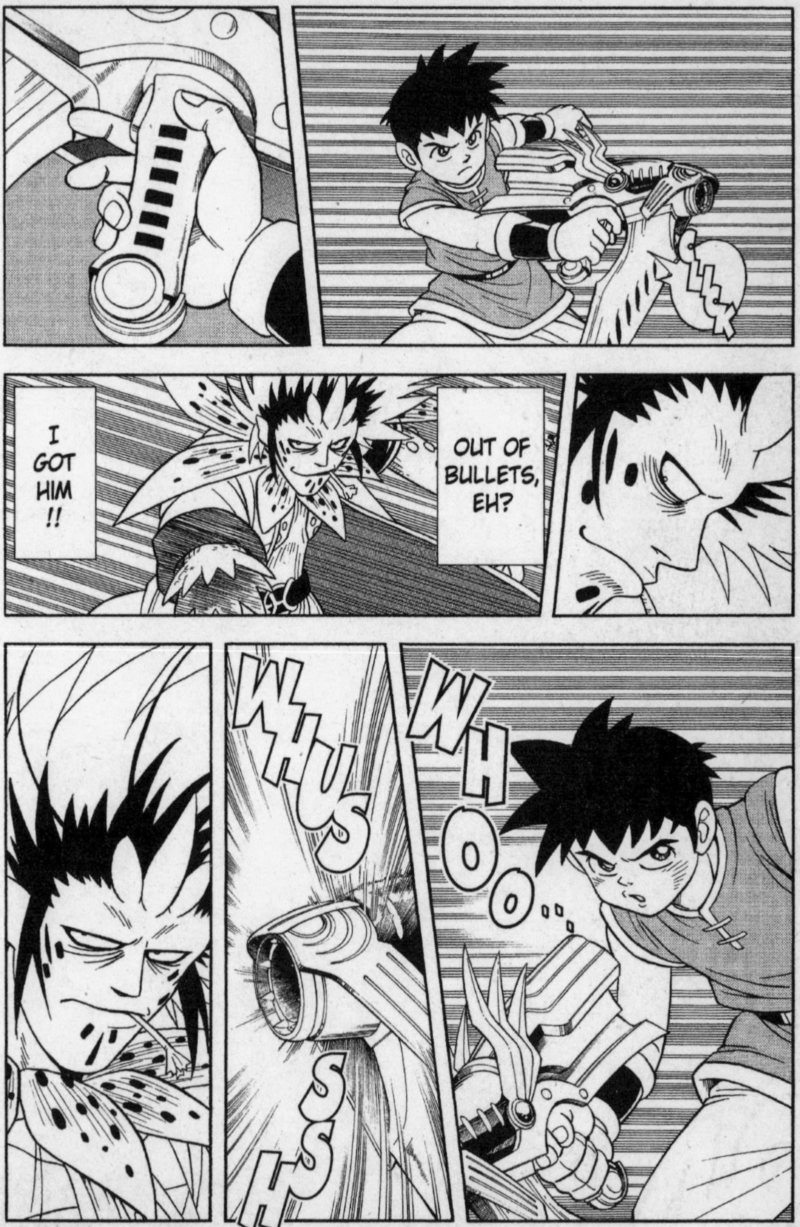
CLICK
OUT OF BULLETS, EH?
I GOT HIM !!
WHOOO...
WHUSSSH

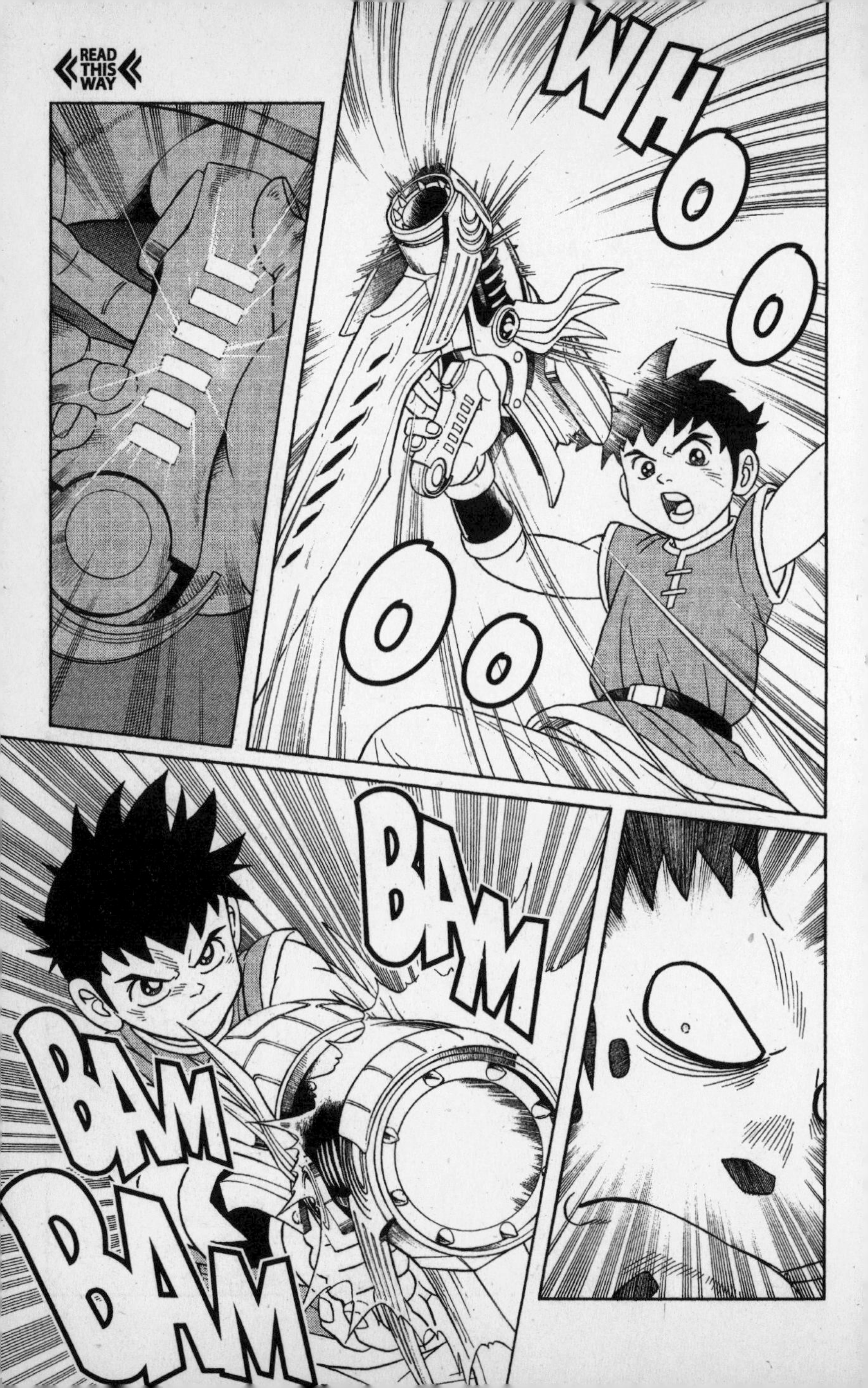
READ THIS WAY
WHOOOOOOO
BAM
BAM
BAM

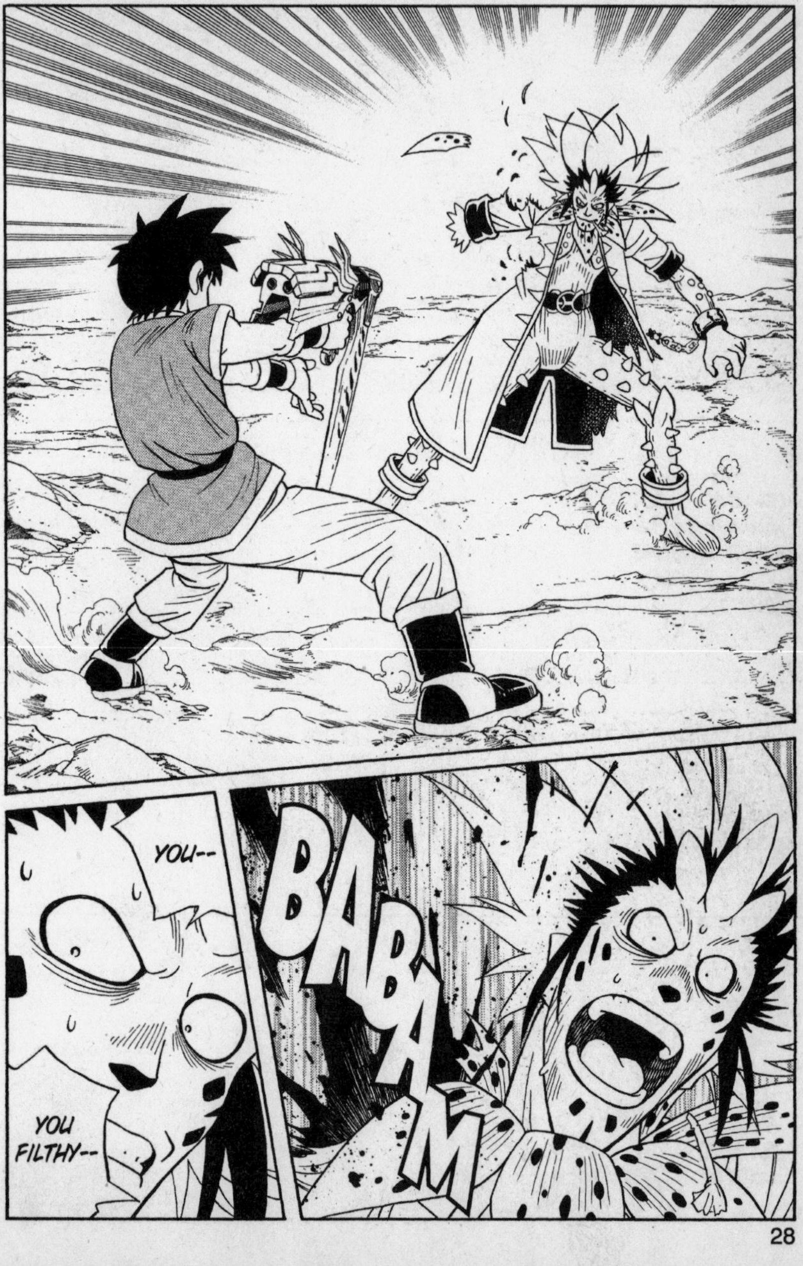
BABAM
YOU--
YOU FILTHY--

READ THIS WAY

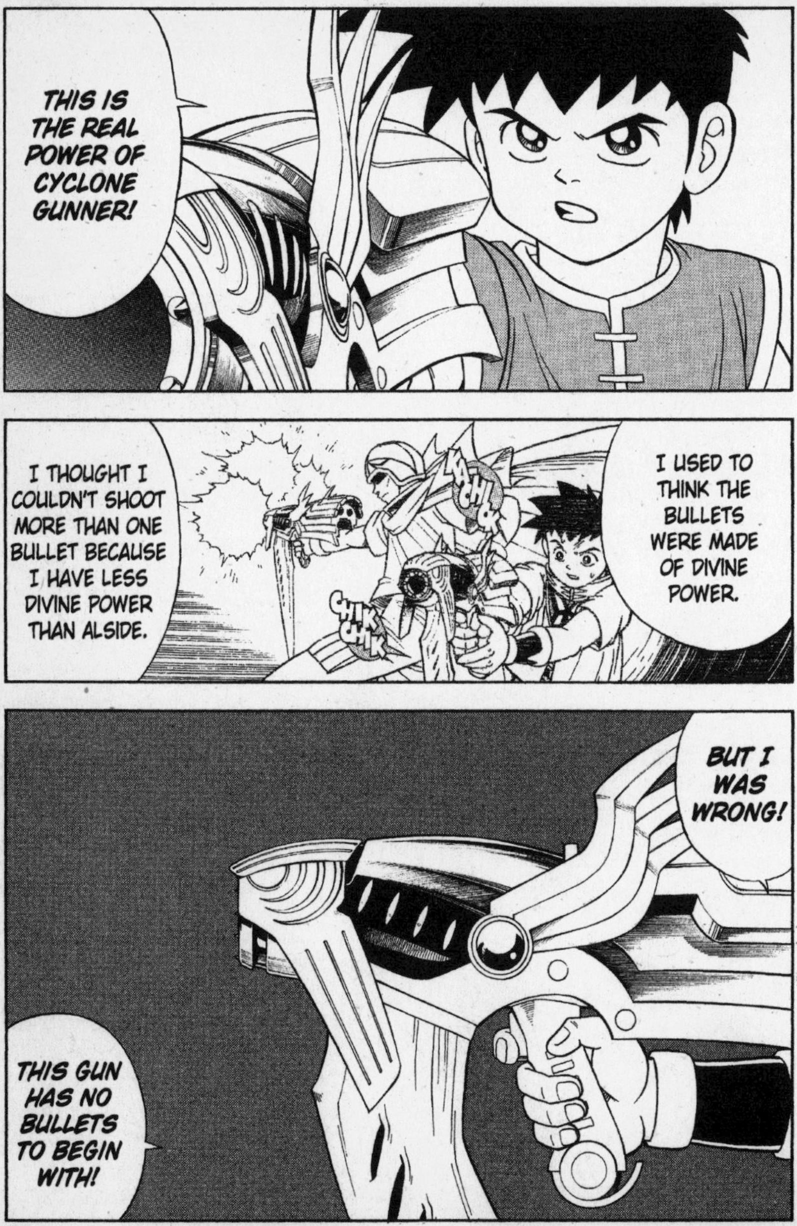
THIS IS THE REAL POWER OF CYCLONE GUNNER!
I USED TO THINK THE BULLETS WERE MADE OF DIVINE POWER.
KACHIK
I THOUGHT I COULDN'T SHOOT MORE THAN ONE BULLET BECAUSE I HAVE LESS DIVINE POWER THAN ALSIDE.
CHIK CHIK
BUT I WAS WRONG!
THIS GUN HAS NO BULLETS TO BEGIN WITH!

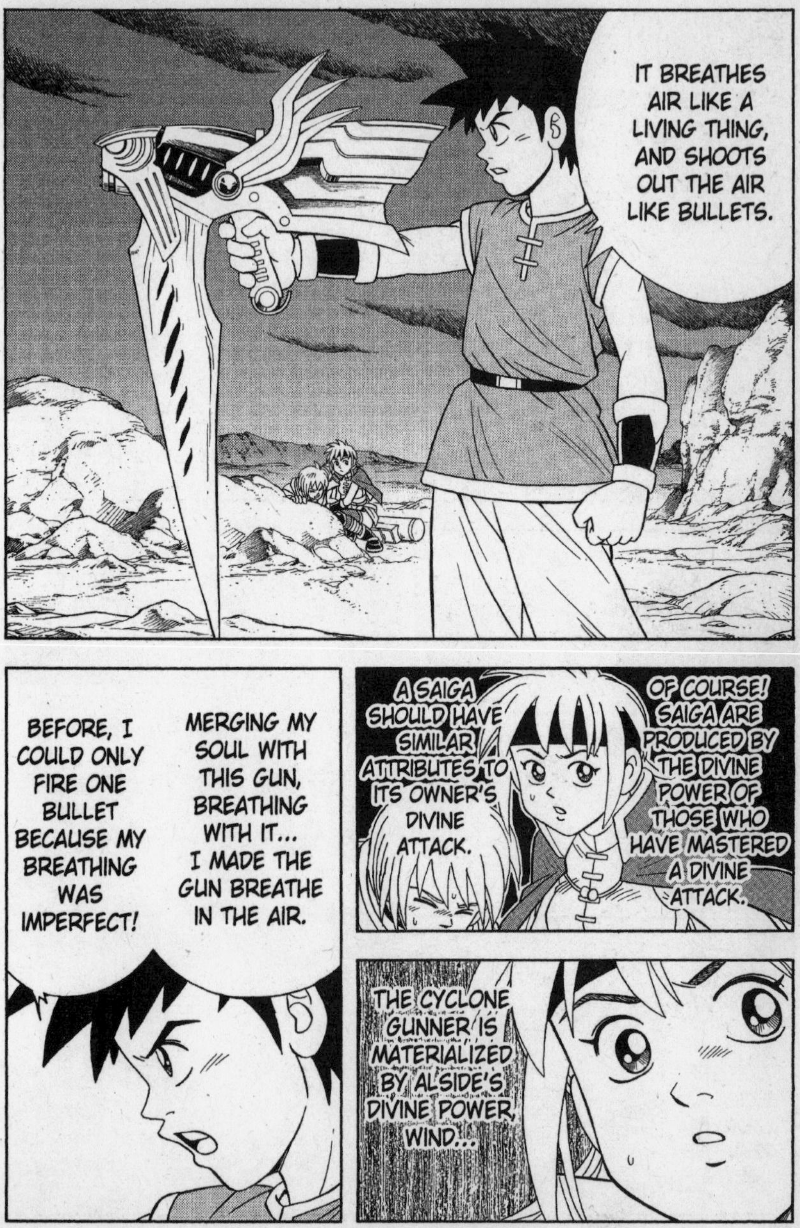
IT BREATHES AIR LIKE A LIVING THING, AND SHOOTS OUT THE AIR LIKE BULLETS.
OF COURSE! SAIGA ARE PRODUCED BY THE DIVINE POWER OF THOSE WHO HAVE MASTERED A DIVINE ATTACK.
A SAIGA SHOULD HAVE SIMILAR ATTRIBUTES TO ITS OWNER'S DIVINE ATTACK.
THE CYCLONE GUNNER IS MATERIALIZED BY ALSIDE'S DIVINE POWER, WIND...
BEFORE, I COULD ONLY FIRE ONE BULLET BECAUSE MY BREATHING WAS IMPERFECT!
MERGING MY SOUL WITH THIS GUN, BREATHING WITH IT... I MADE THE GUN BREATHE IN THE AIR.

READ THIS WAY

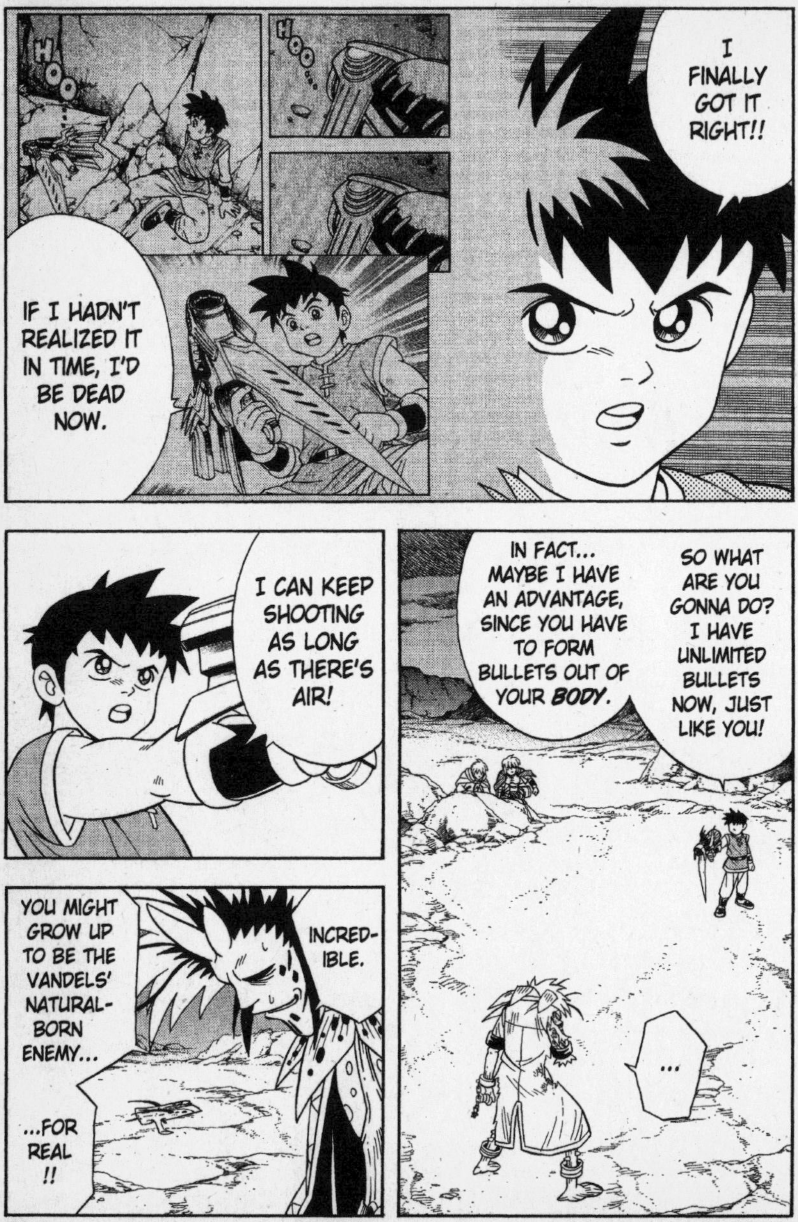
I FINALLY GOT IT RIGHT!!
HOO...
HOO
IF I HADN'T REALIZED IT IN TIME, I'D BE DEAD NOW.
SO WHAT ARE YOU GONNA DO? I HAVE UNLIMITED BULLETS NOW, JUST LIKE YOU!
IN FACT... MAYBE I HAVE AN ADVANTAGE, SINCE YOU HAVE TO FORM BULLETS OUT OF YOUR *BODY*.
...
I CAN KEEP SHOOTING AS LONG AS THERE'S AIR!
INCRED-IBLE.
YOU MIGHT GROW UP TO BE THE VANDELS' NATURAL-BORN ENEMY...
...FOR REAL !!

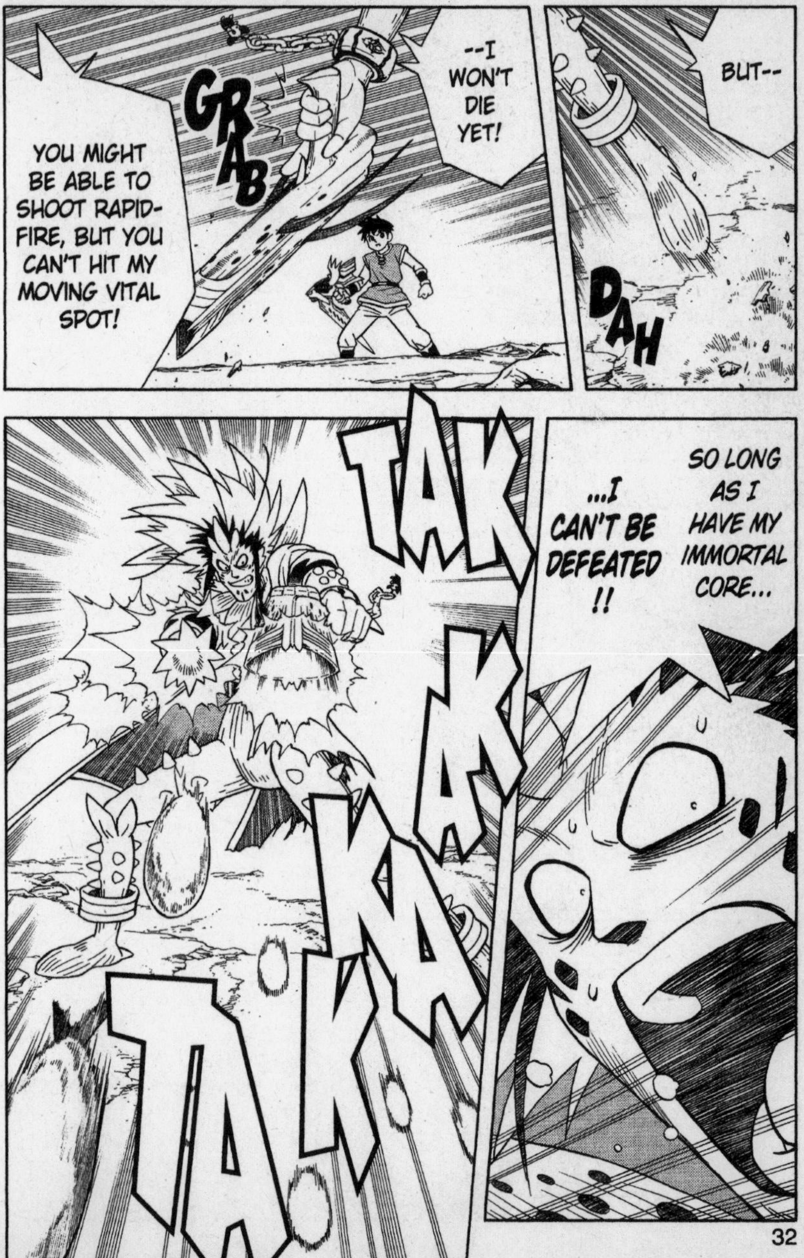
BUT--
DAH
--I WON'T DIE YET!
GRAB
YOU MIGHT BE ABLE TO SHOOT RAPID-FIRE, BUT YOU CAN'T HIT MY MOVING VITAL SPOT!
SO LONG AS I HAVE MY IMMORTAL CORE...
...I CAN'T BE DEFEATED!!
TAK
KAK
KAK
TAK

READ THIS WAY

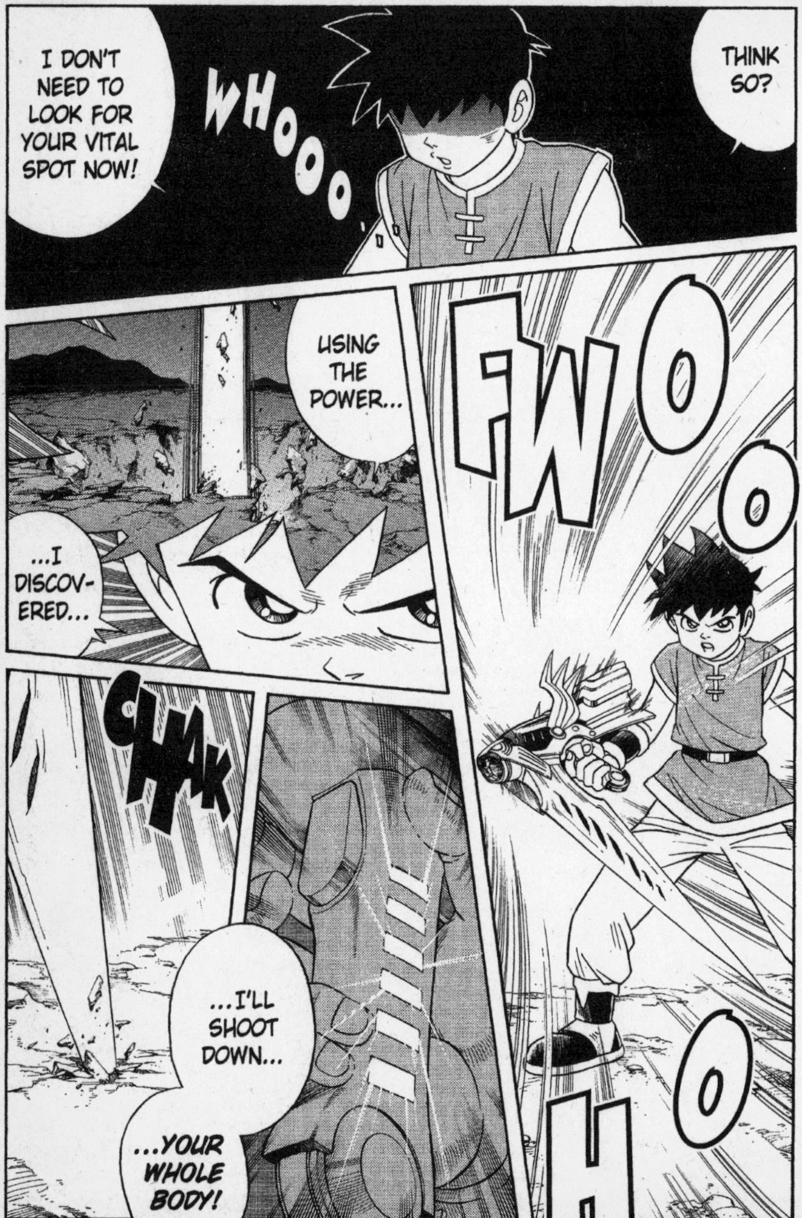
THINK SO?
WHOOOO
I DON'T NEED TO LOOK FOR YOUR VITAL SPOT NOW!
FWOOOH
USING THE POWER...
...I DISCOVERED...
CHAK
...I'LL SHOOT DOWN...
...YOUR WHOLE BODY!

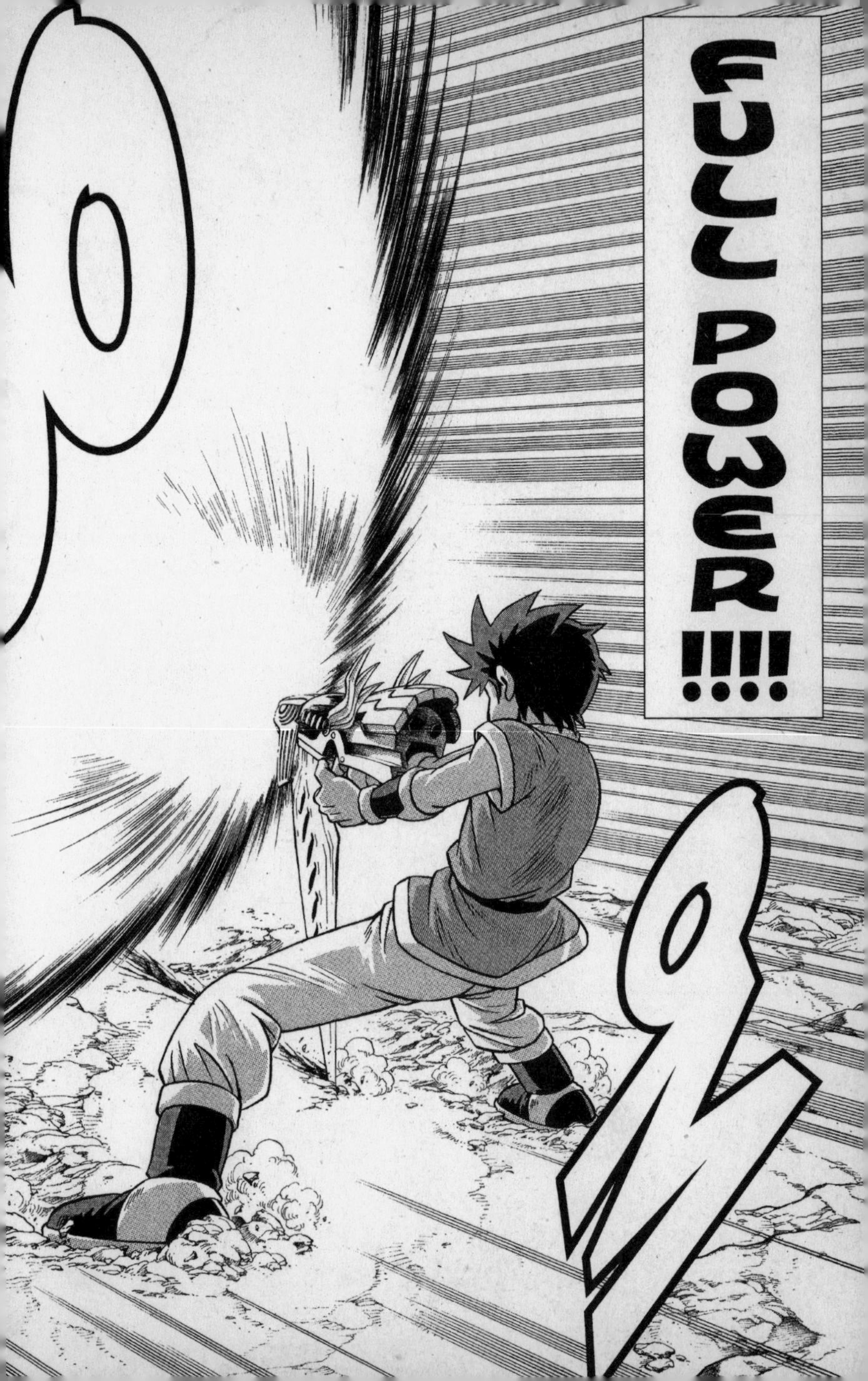
FULL POWER!!!!

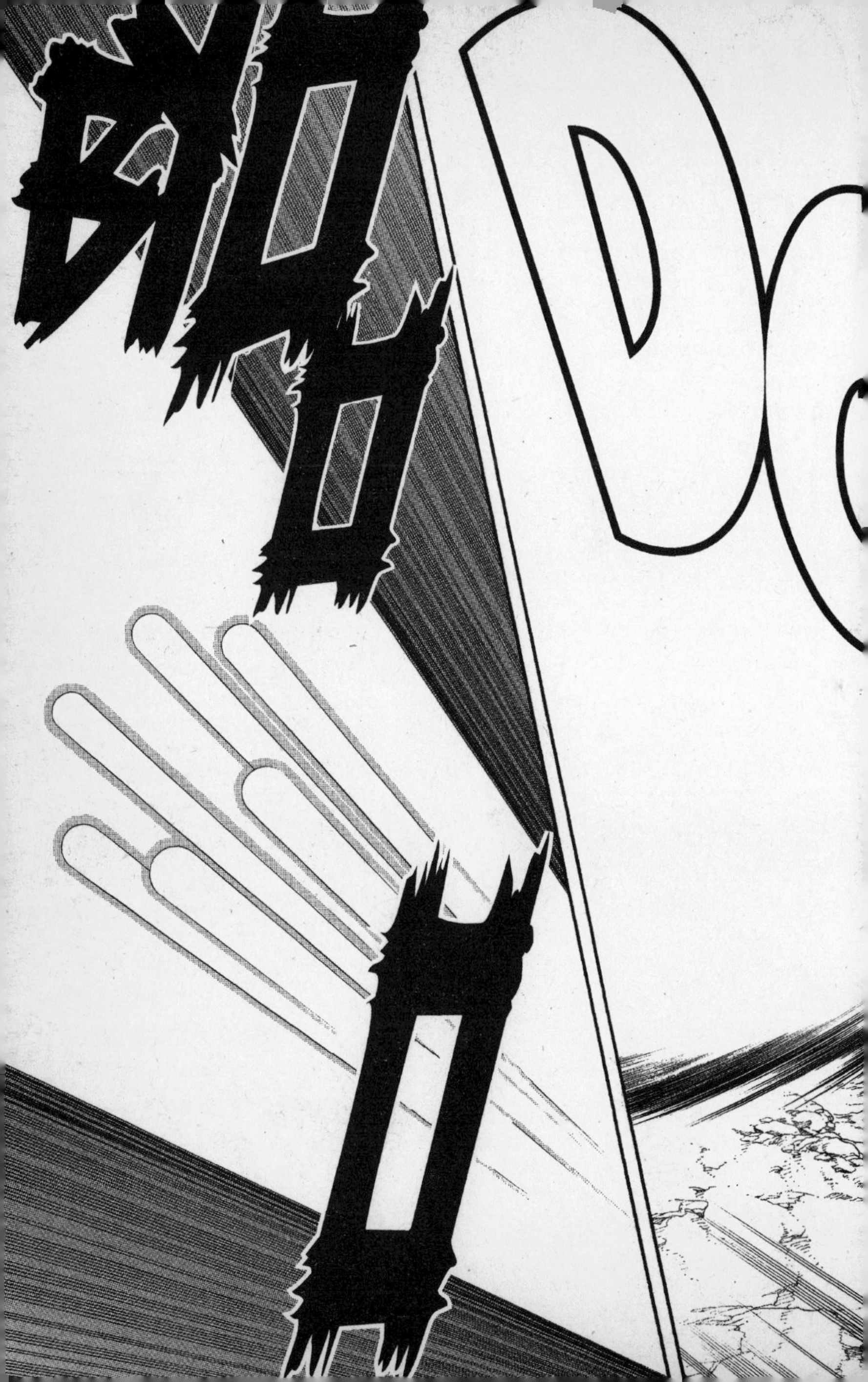

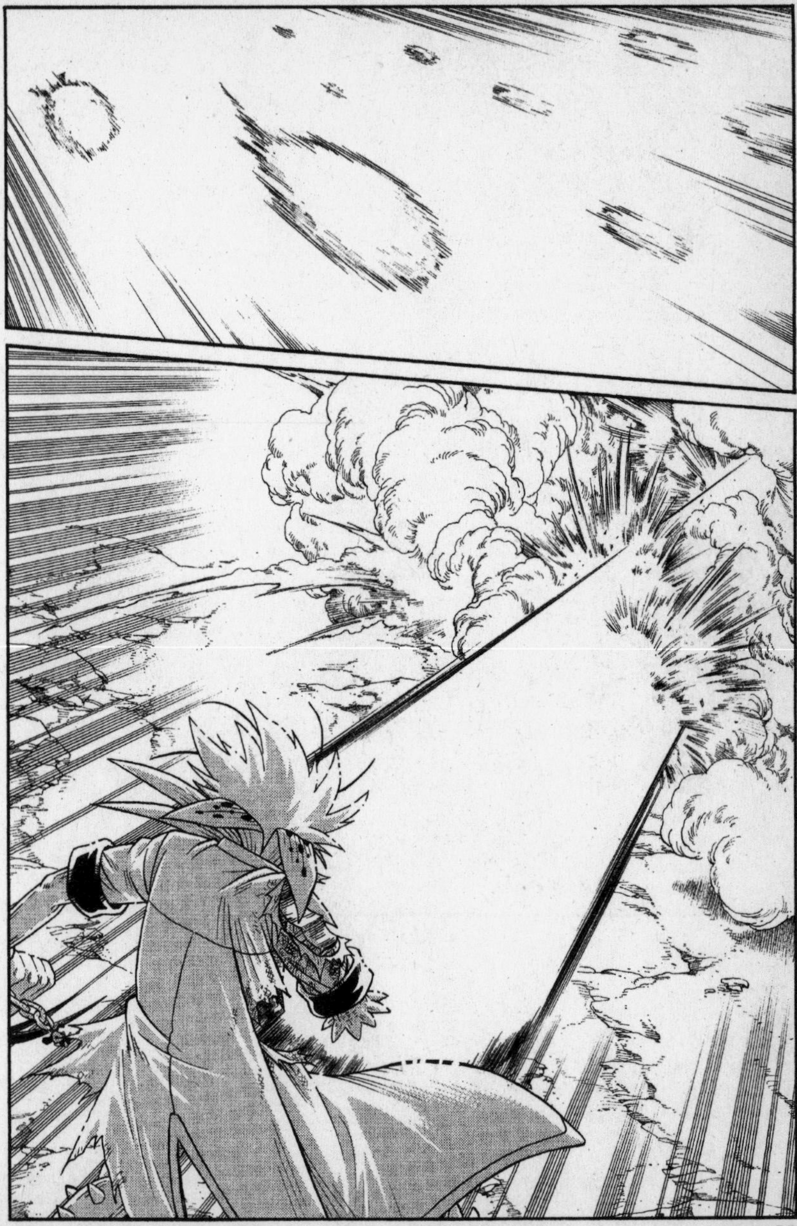

READ THIS WAY

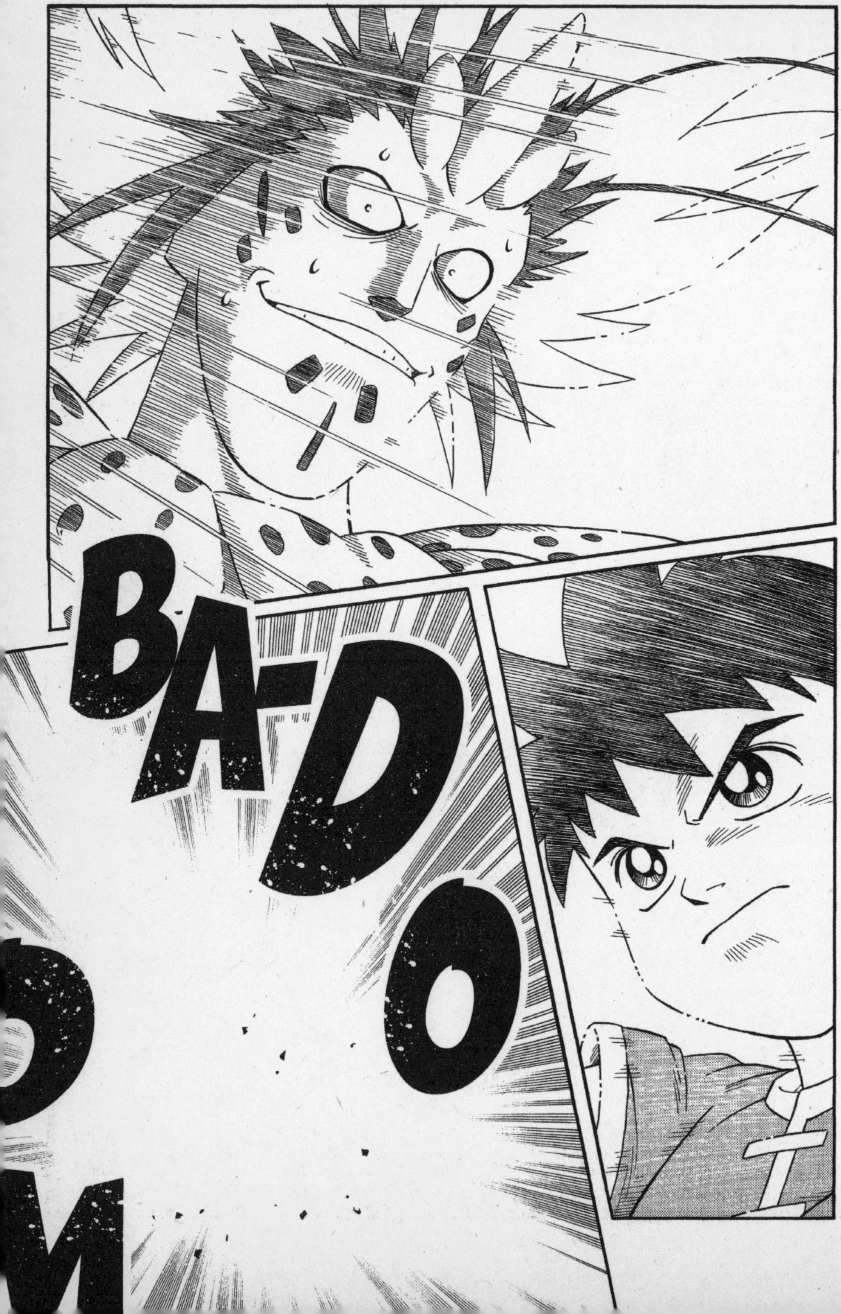
BA-DO

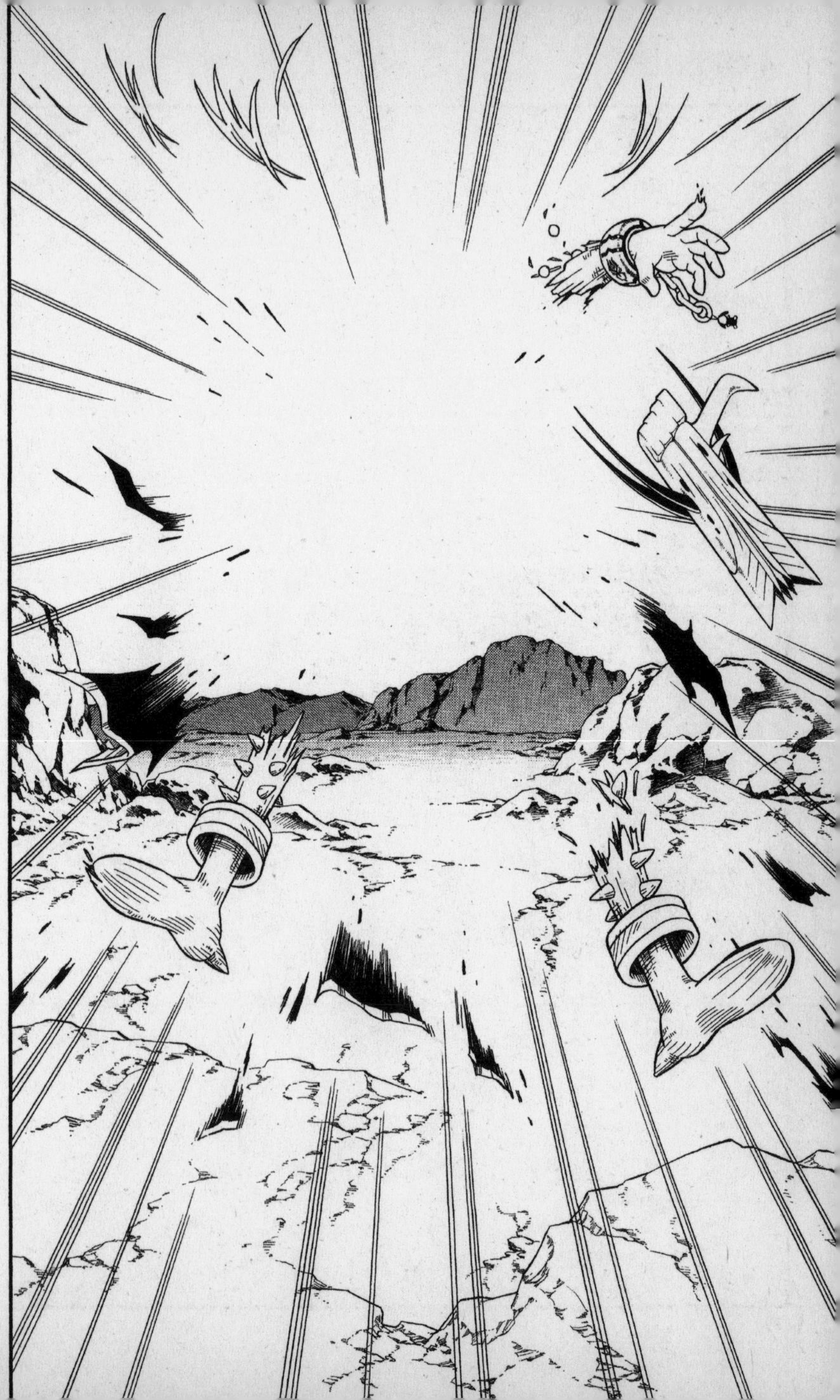

READ THIS WAY

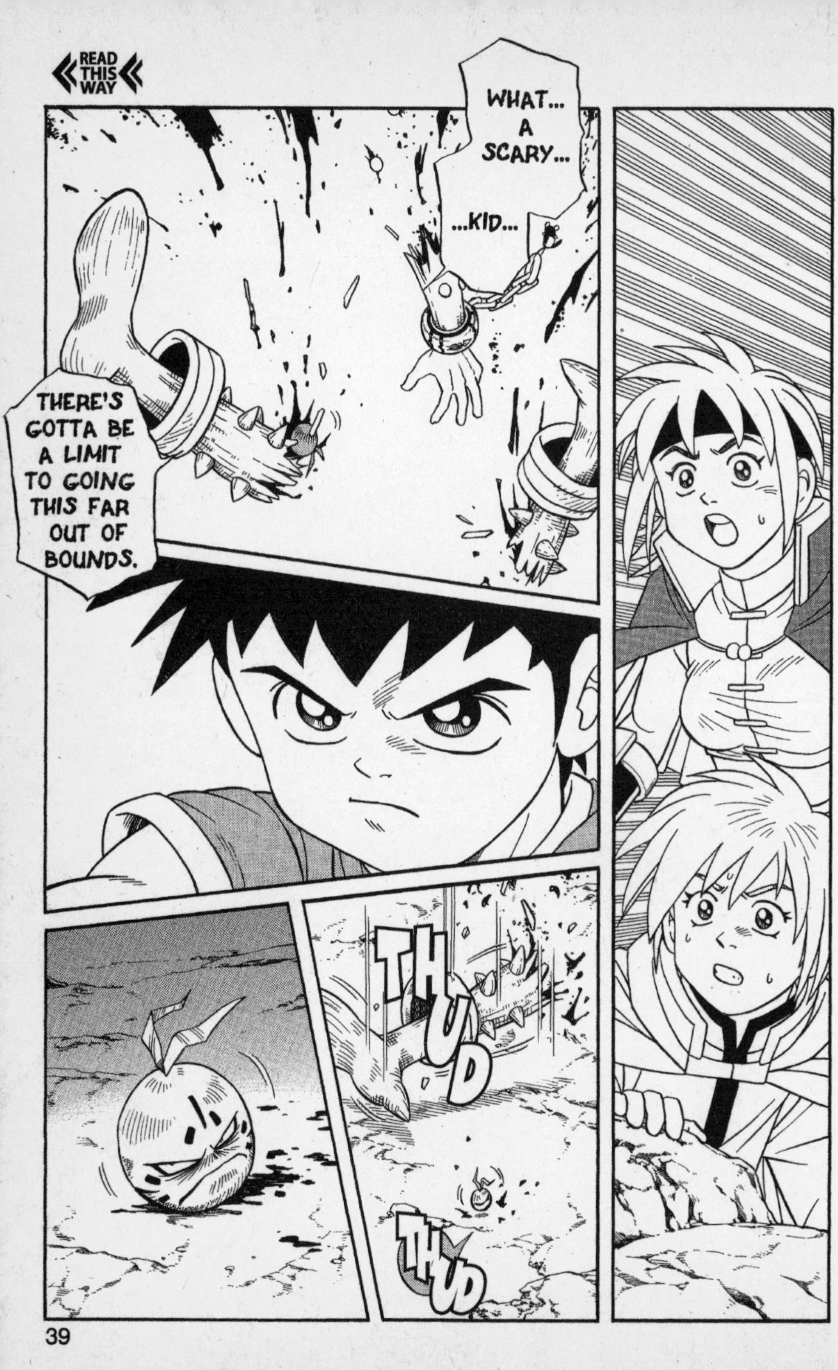
WHAT... A SCARY...
...KID...
THERE'S GOTTA BE A LIMIT TO GOING THIS FAR OUT OF BOUNDS.
THUD
THUD

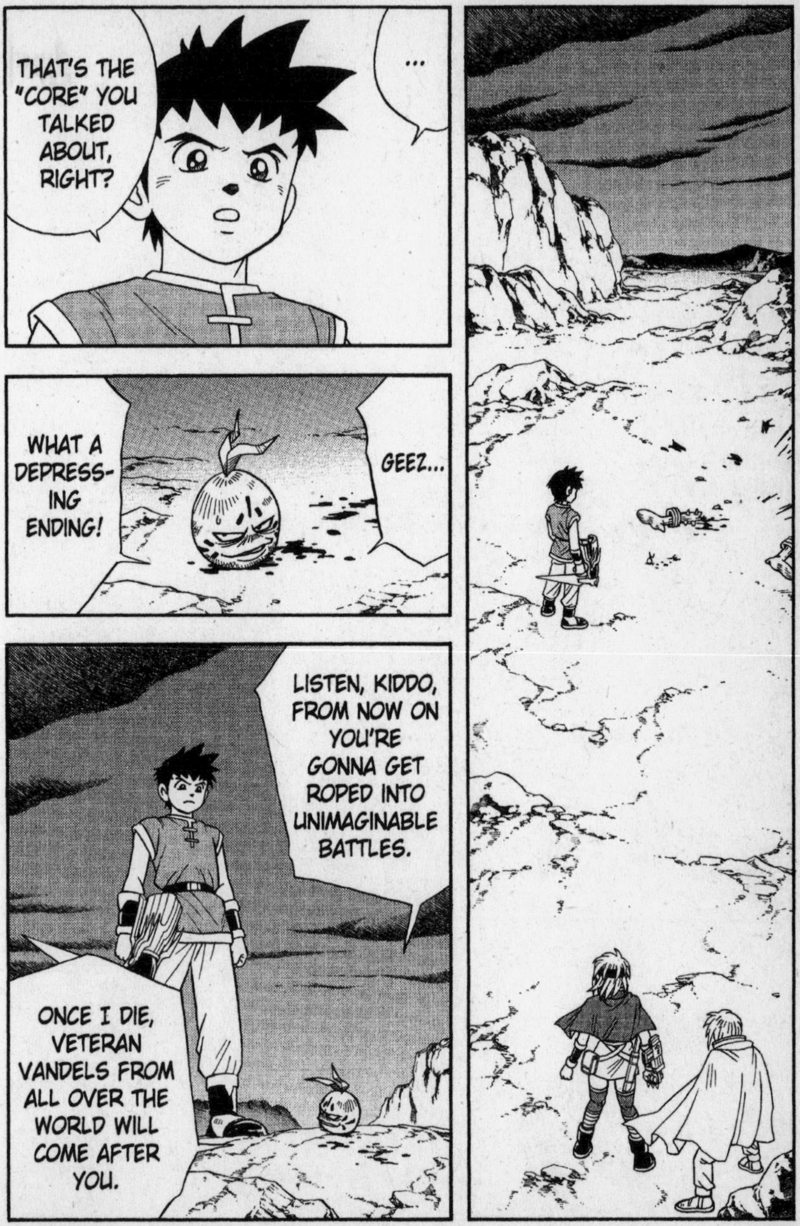
...
THAT'S THE "CORE" YOU TALKED ABOUT, RIGHT?
GEEZ...
WHAT A DEPRESS-ING ENDING!
LISTEN, KIDDO, FROM NOW ON YOU'RE GONNA GET ROPED INTO UNIMAGINABLE BATTLES.
ONCE I DIE, VETERAN VANDELS FROM ALL OVER THE WORLD WILL COME AFTER YOU.

READ THIS WAY

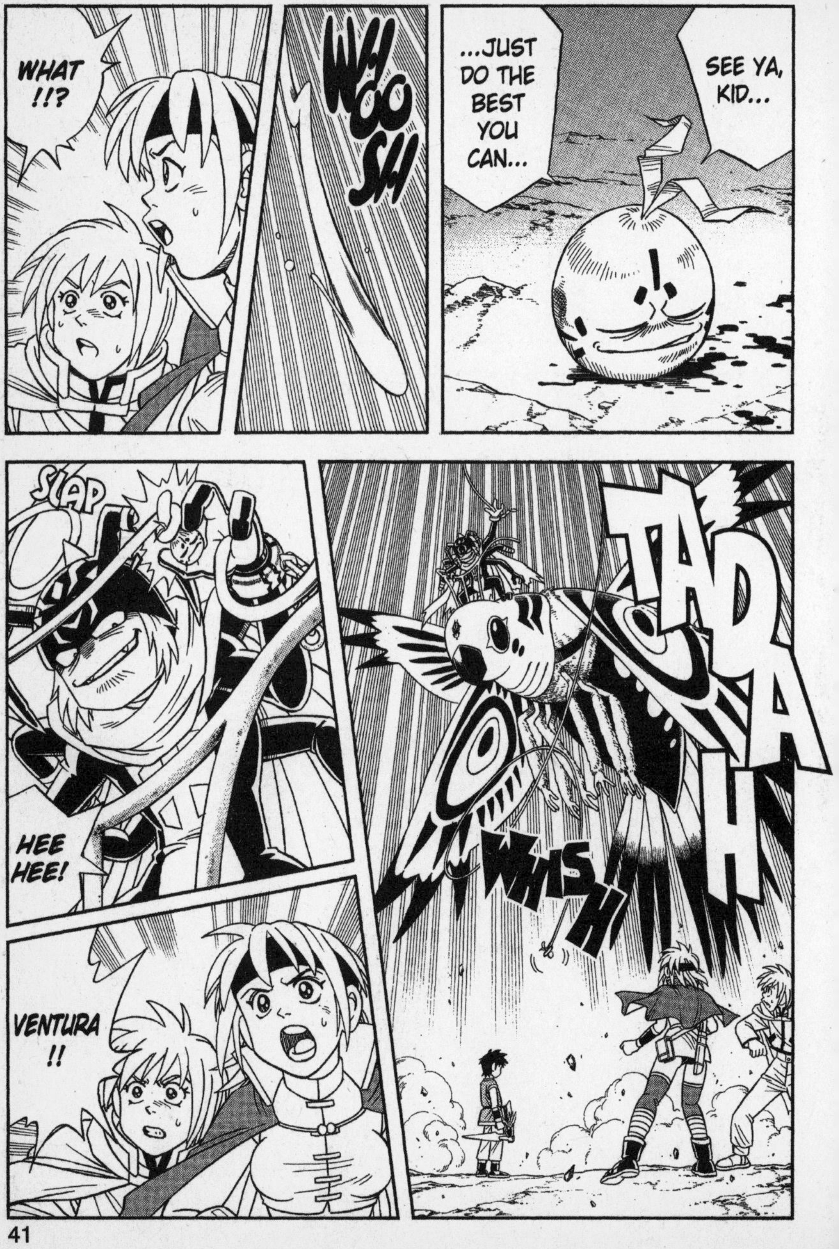
SEE YA, KID...
...JUST DO THE BEST YOU CAN...
WHOOSH
WHAT !!?
TADAH
WHISH
SLAP
HEE HEE!
VENTURA !!

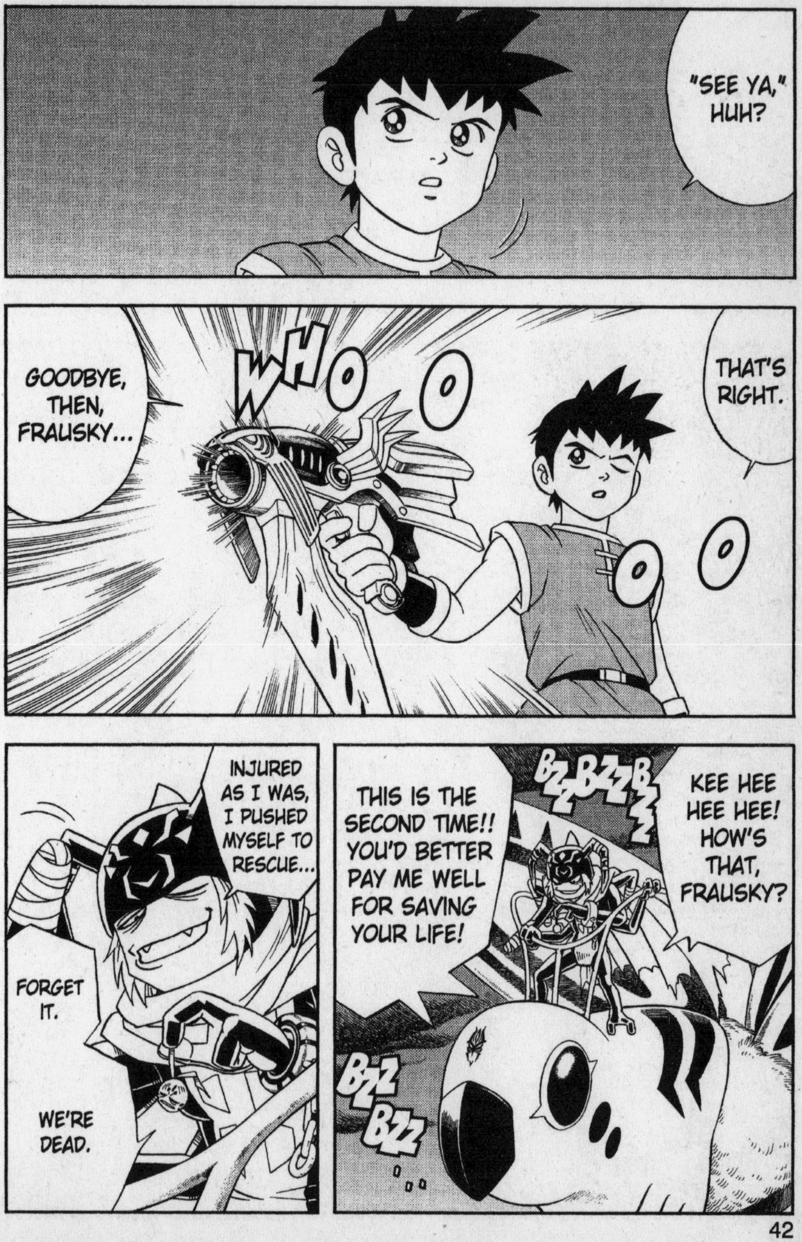
"SEE YA," HUH?
THAT'S RIGHT.
WHOOOO
GOODBYE, THEN, FRAUSKY...
BZZ BZZ BZZ
KEE HEE HEE HEE! HOW'S THAT, FRAUSKY?
THIS IS THE SECOND TIME!! YOU'D BETTER PAY ME WELL FOR SAVING YOUR LIFE!
BZZ BZZ
INJURED AS I WAS, I PUSHED MYSELF TO RESCUE...
FORGET IT.
WE'RE DEAD.

READ THIS WAY

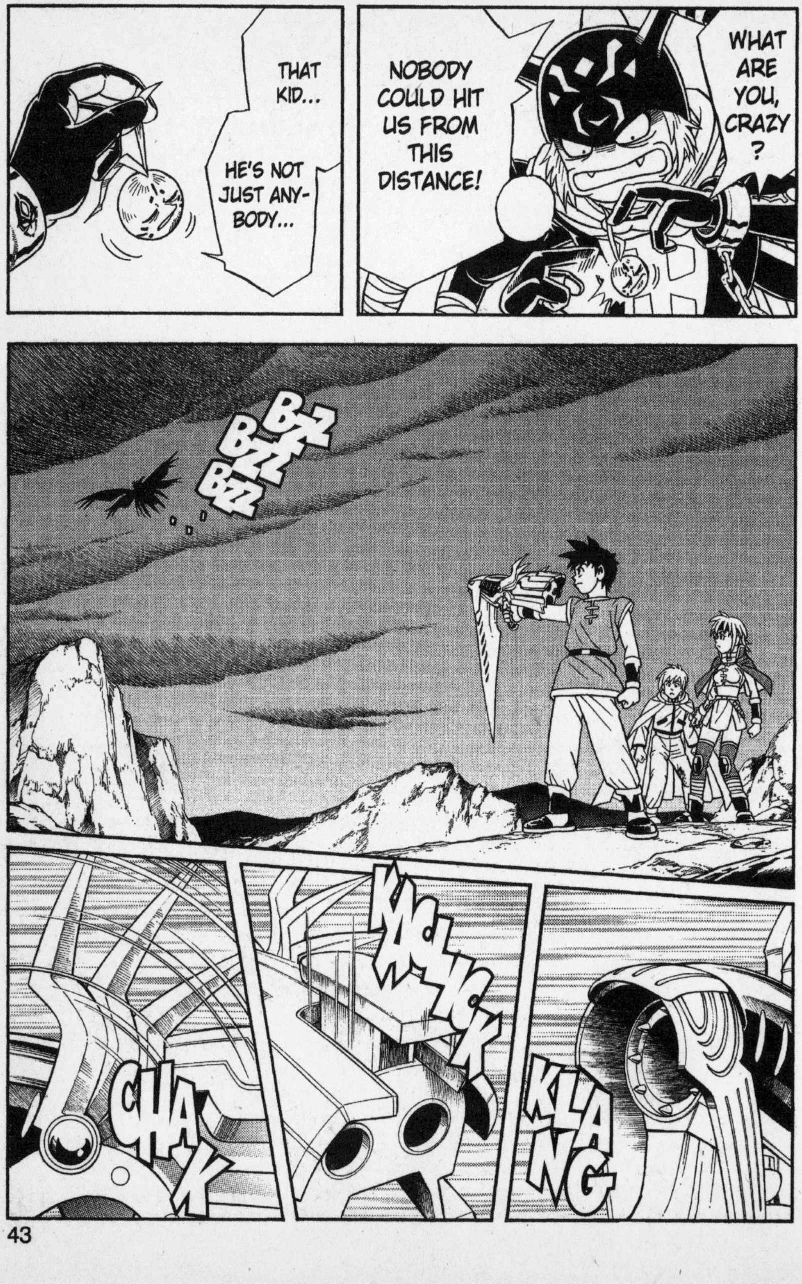
WHAT ARE YOU, CRAZY?
NOBODY COULD HIT US FROM THIS DISTANCE!
THAT KID...
HE'S NOT JUST ANYBODY...
BZZ BZZ BZZ
KLANG
KACLICK
CHA-K

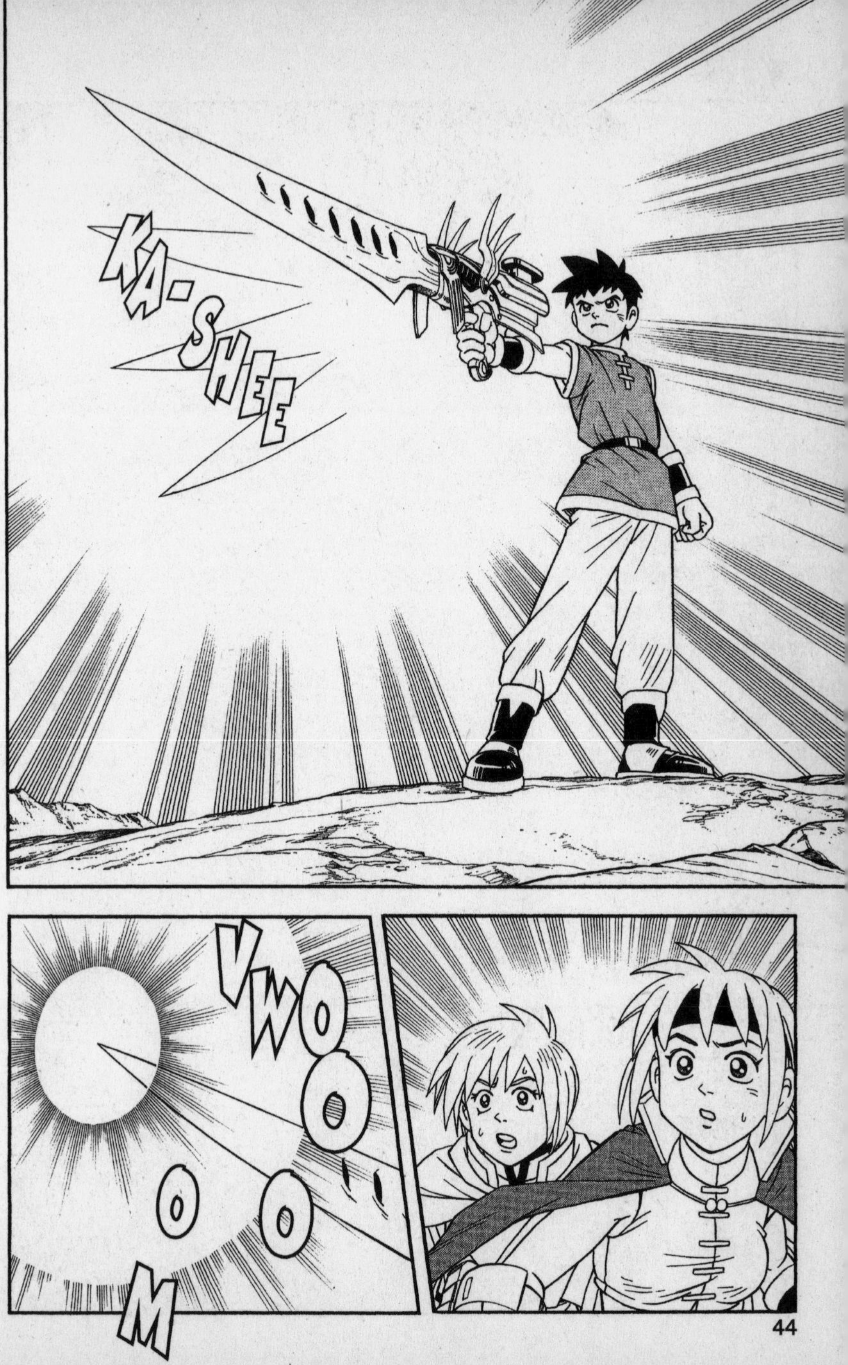
KA-SHEE
VWOOOOOM

« READ THIS WAY «

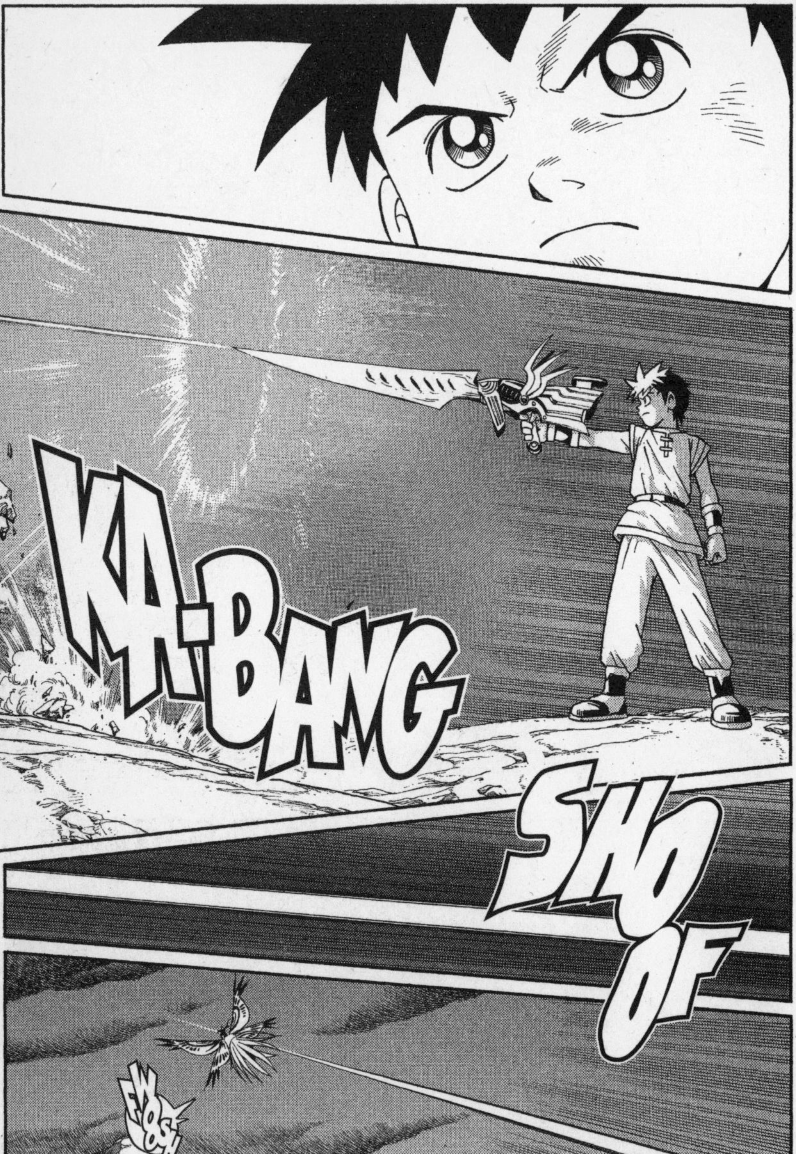
KA-BANG
SHOOF
FWOOSH

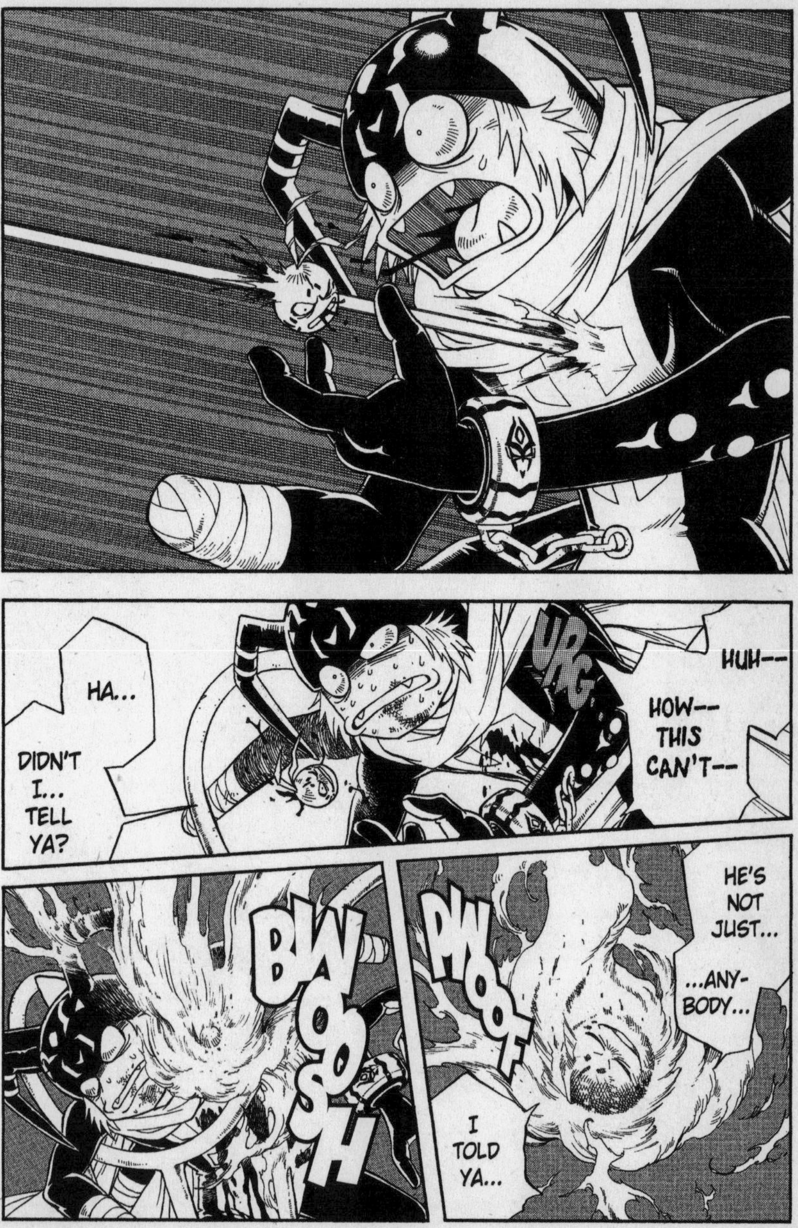
HUH--
HOW-- THIS CAN'T--
URG
HA...
DIDN'T I... TELL YA?
HE'S NOT JUST...
...ANY-BODY...
DWOOF
I TOLD YA...
BWOOSH

READ THIS WAY

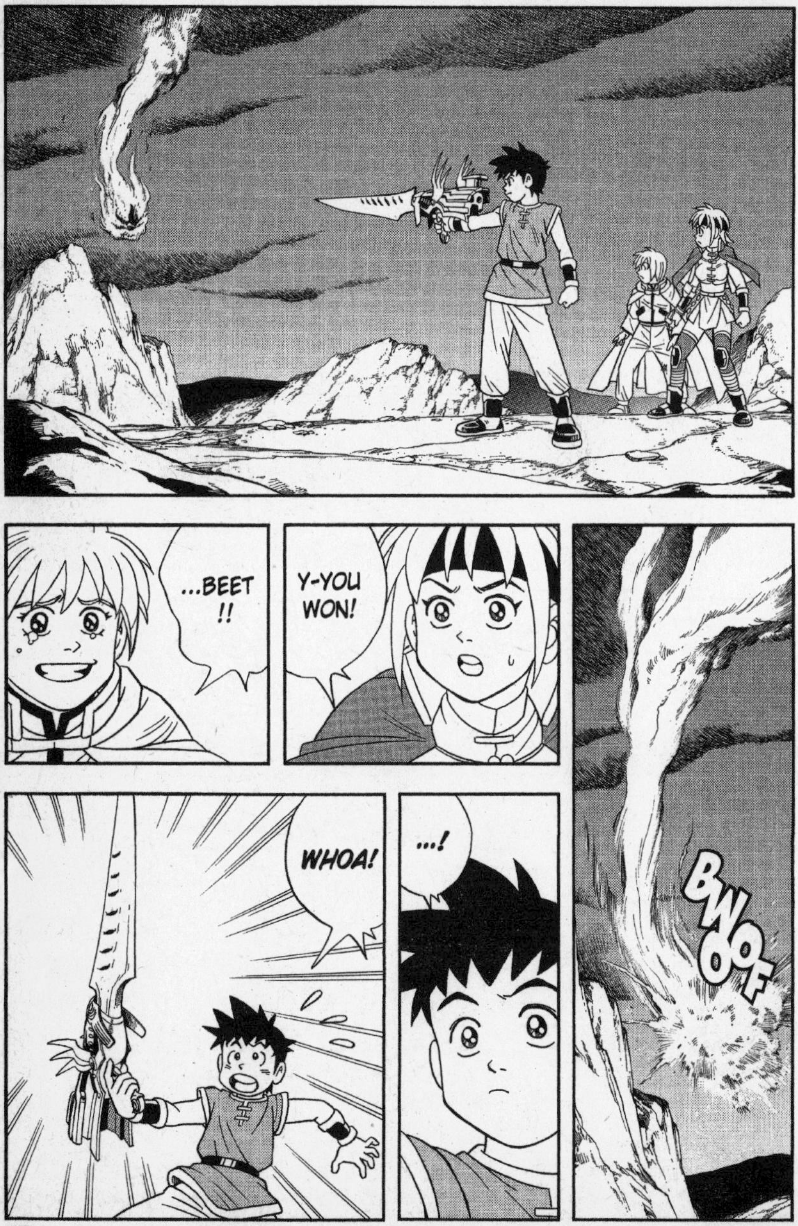
BWOOF
Y-YOU WON!
...BEET !!
...!
WHOA!

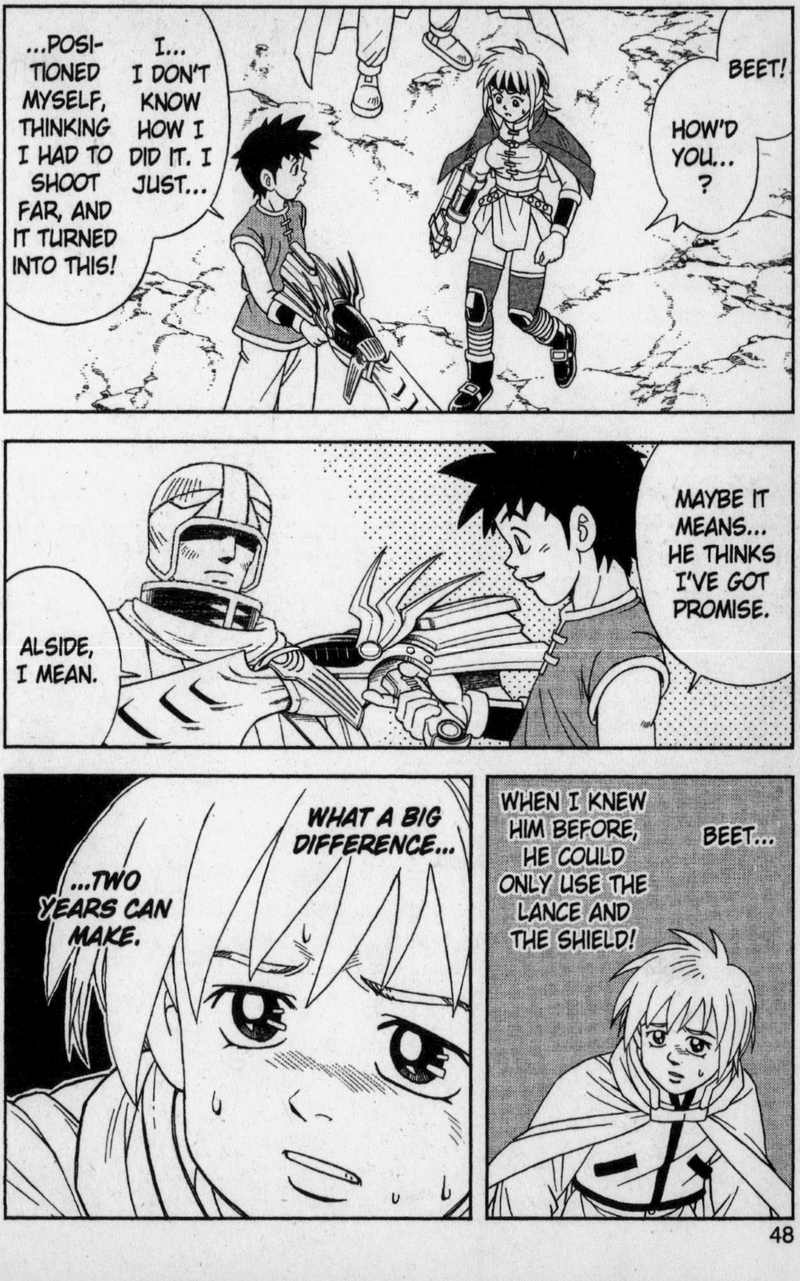
BEET! HOW'D YOU...?
I... I DON'T KNOW HOW I DID IT. I JUST...
...POSITIONED MYSELF, THINKING I HAD TO SHOOT FAR, AND IT TURNED INTO THIS!
MAYBE IT MEANS... HE THINKS I'VE GOT PROMISE.
ALSIDE, I MEAN.
BEET...
WHEN I KNEW HIM BEFORE, HE COULD ONLY USE THE LANCE AND THE SHIELD!
WHAT A BIG DIFFERENCE...
...TWO YEARS CAN MAKE.

READ THIS WAY

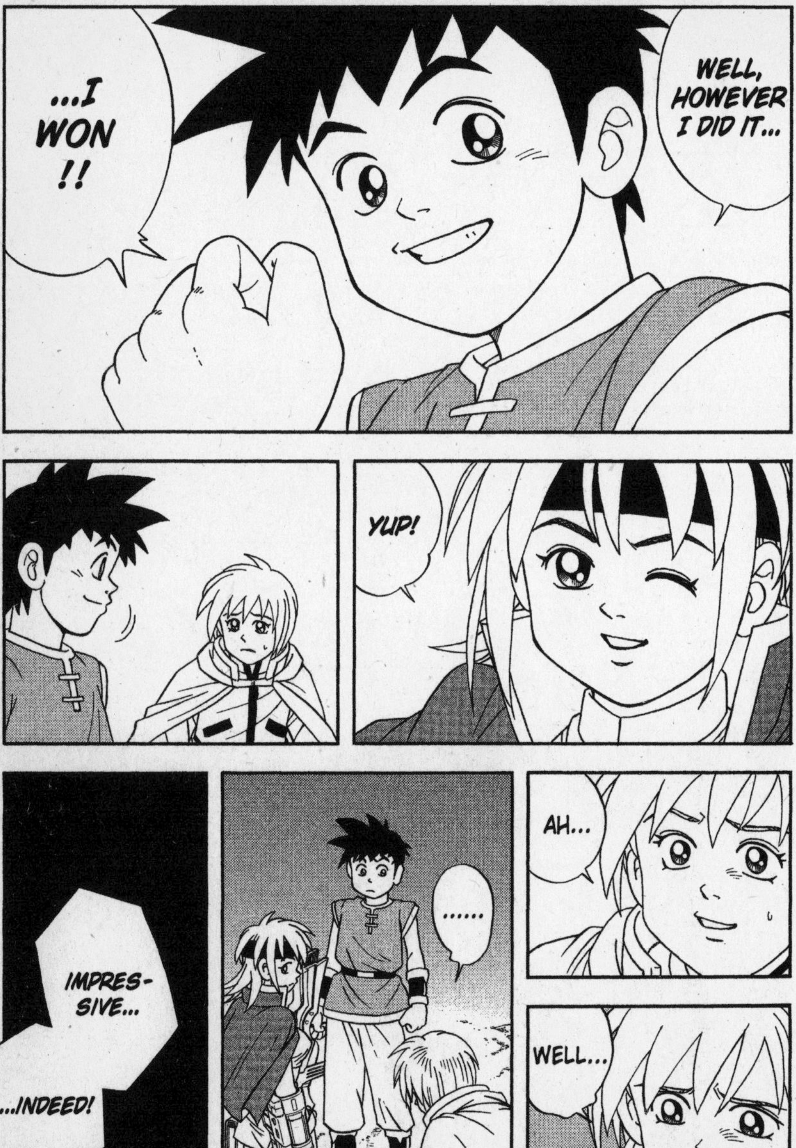
WELL, HOWEVER I DID IT...
...I WON !!
YUP!
AH...
WELL...
......
IMPRES-SIVE...
...INDEED!

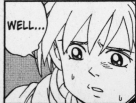

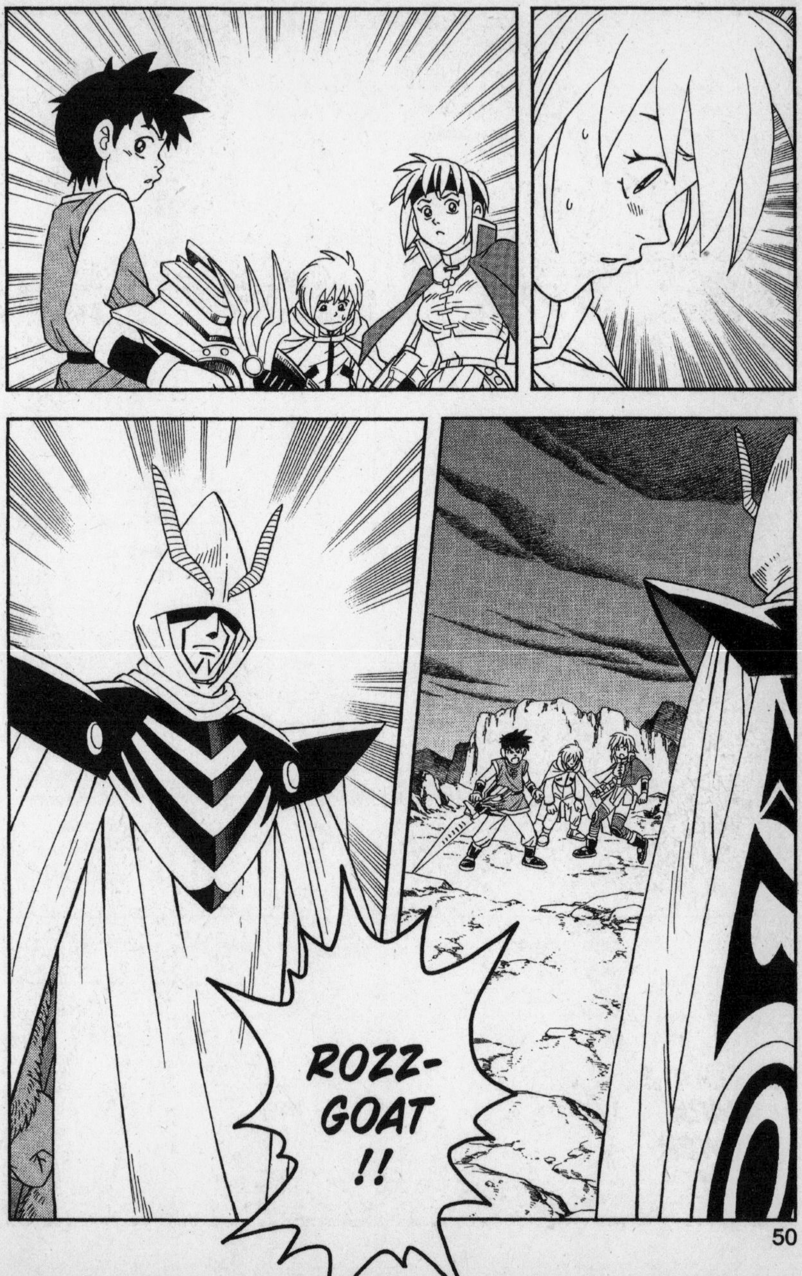
ROZZ-
GOAT
!!

READ THIS WAY

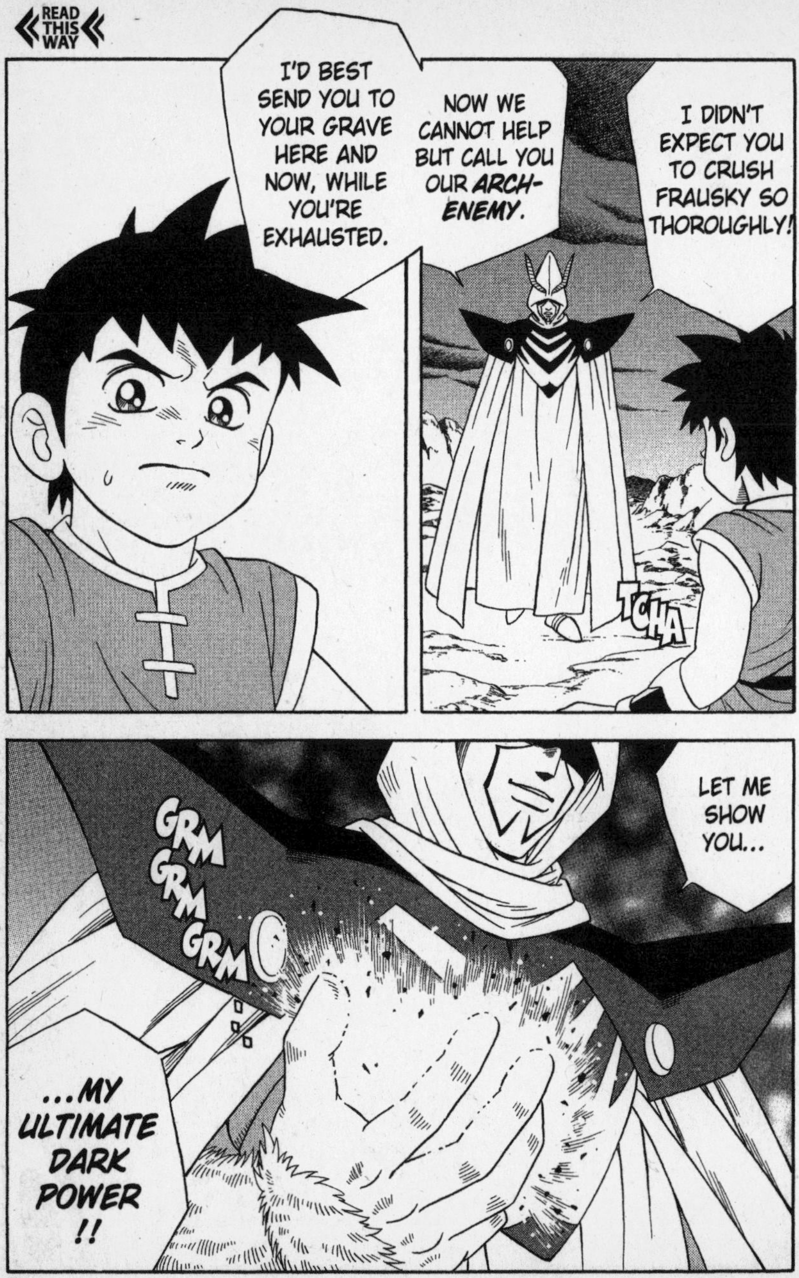

I DIDN'T EXPECT YOU TO CRUSH FRAUSKY SO THOROUGHLY!
NOW WE CANNOT HELP BUT CALL YOU OUR ***ARCH-ENEMY***.
I'D BEST SEND YOU TO YOUR GRAVE HERE AND NOW, WHILE YOU'RE EXHAUSTED.
TCHA
LET ME SHOW YOU...
GRM GRM GRM GRM
...MY ULTIMATE DARK POWER!!

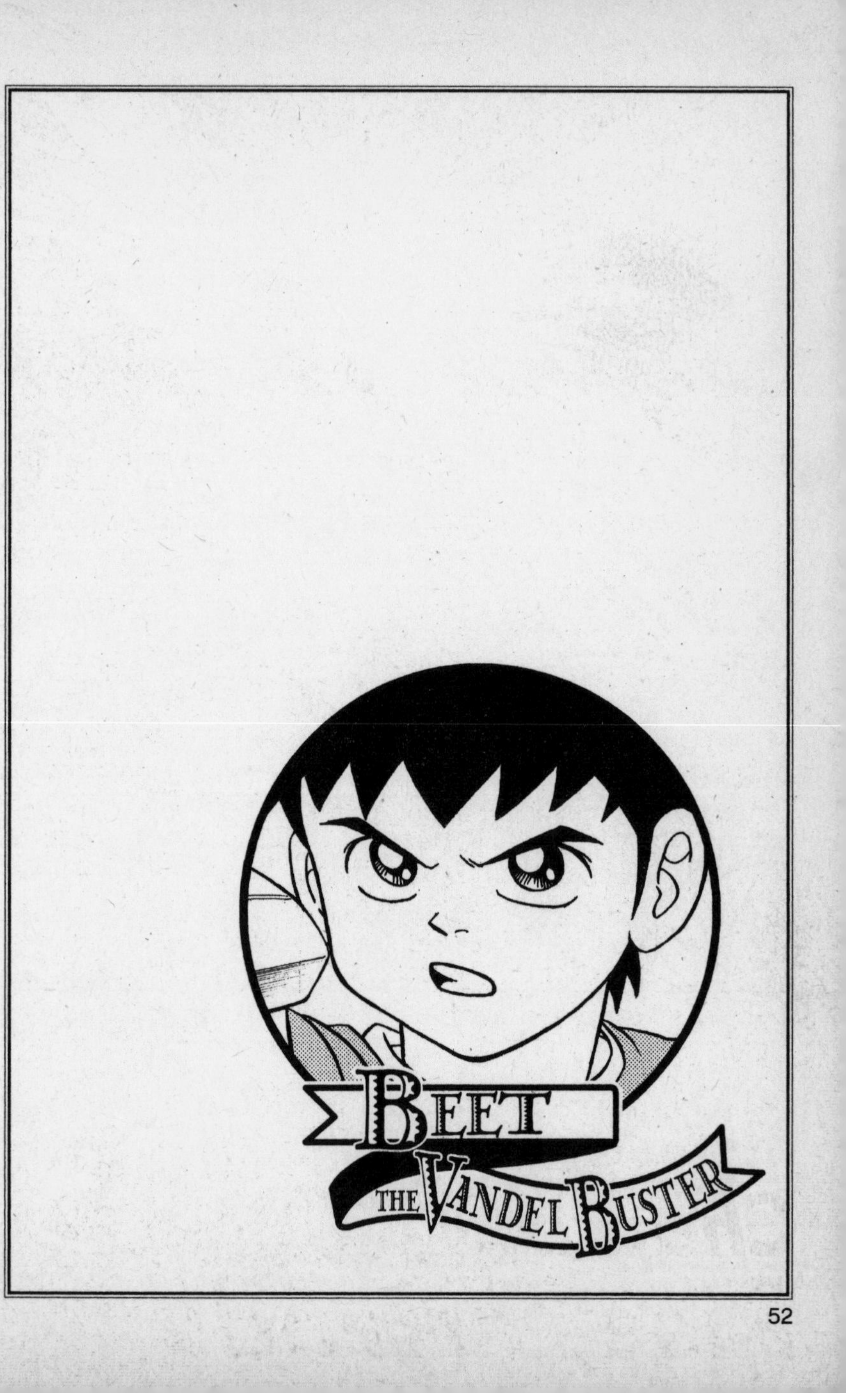
BEET
THE VANDEL BUSTER

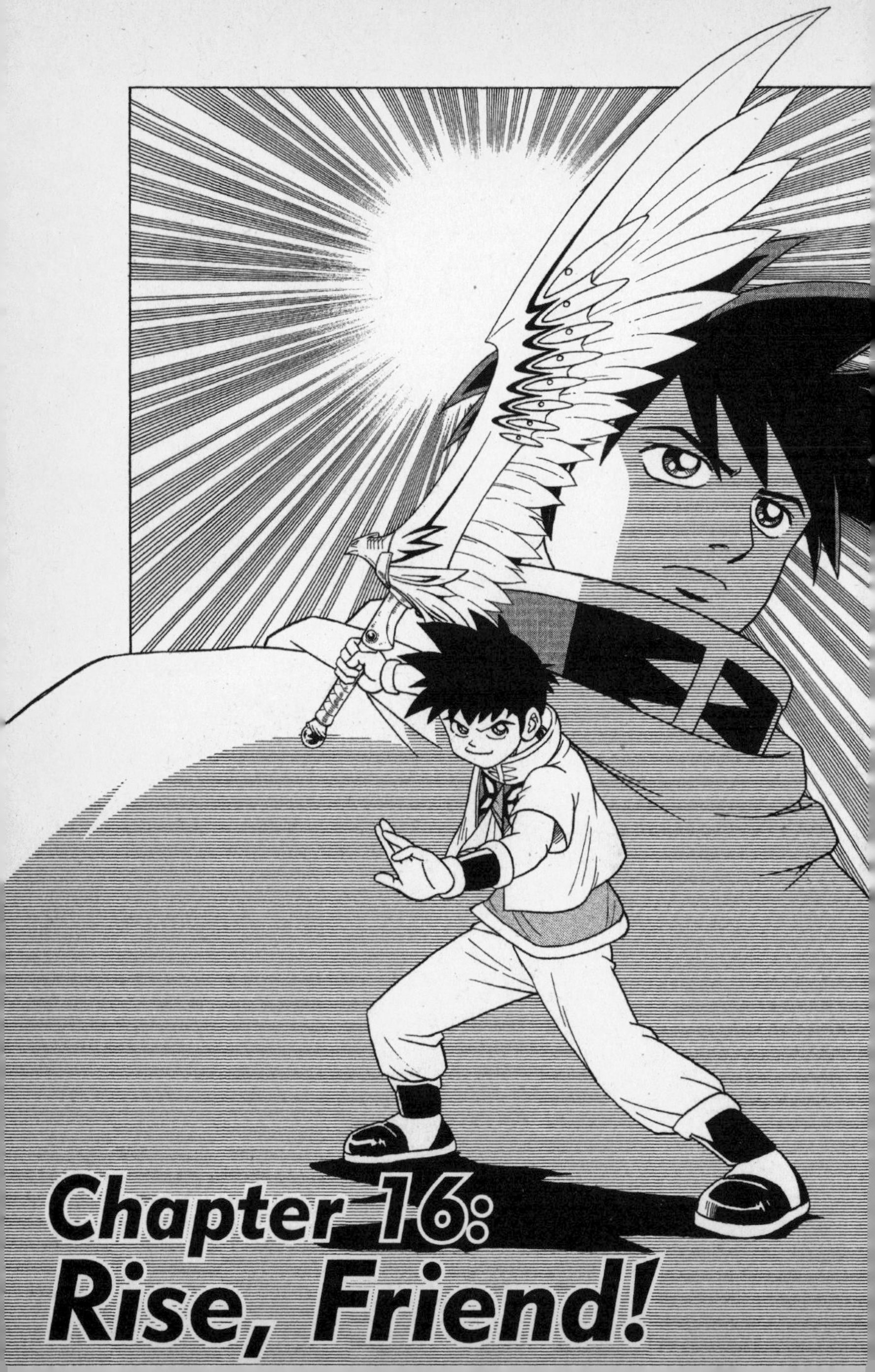
Chapter 16:
Rise, Friend!

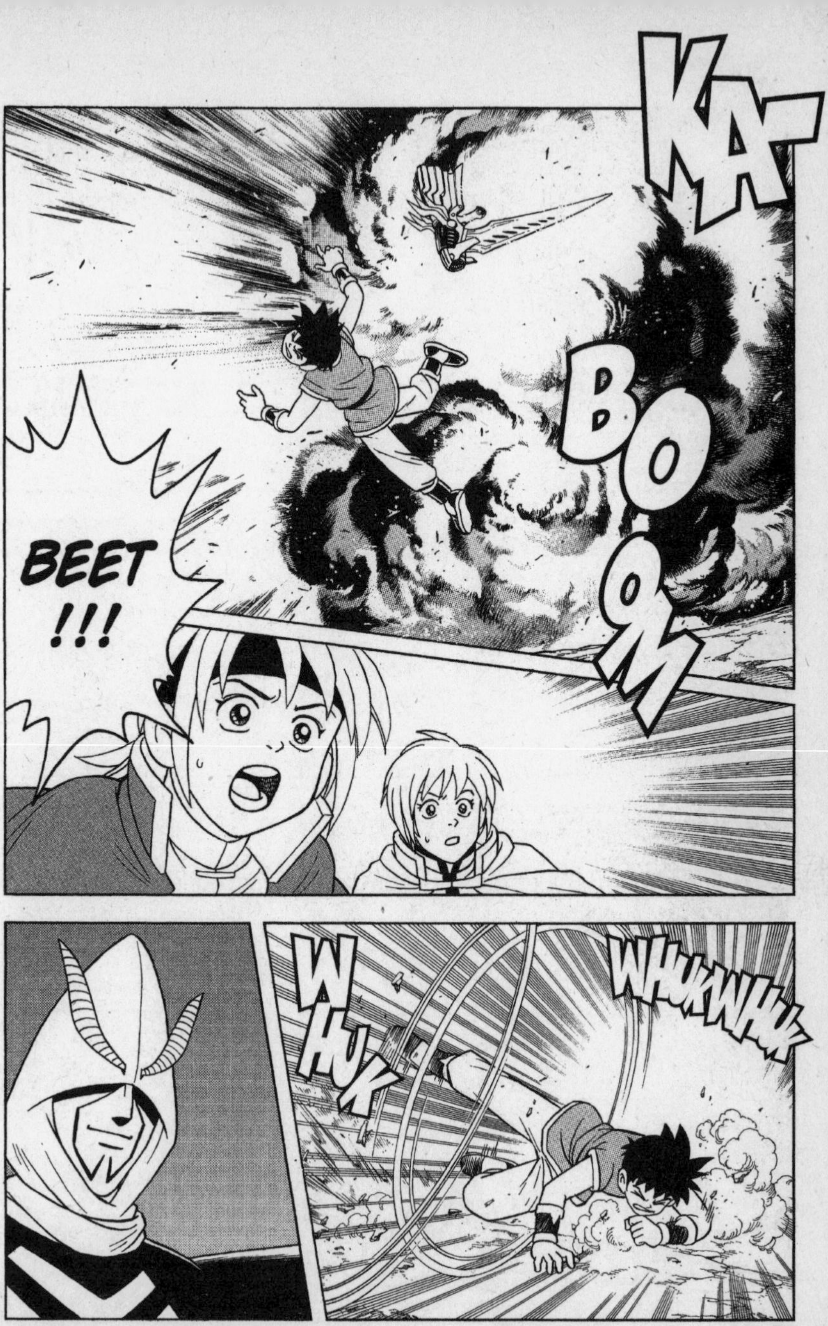
KA
BOOOM
BEET !!!
WHUKWHUK
WHUK

READ THIS WAY

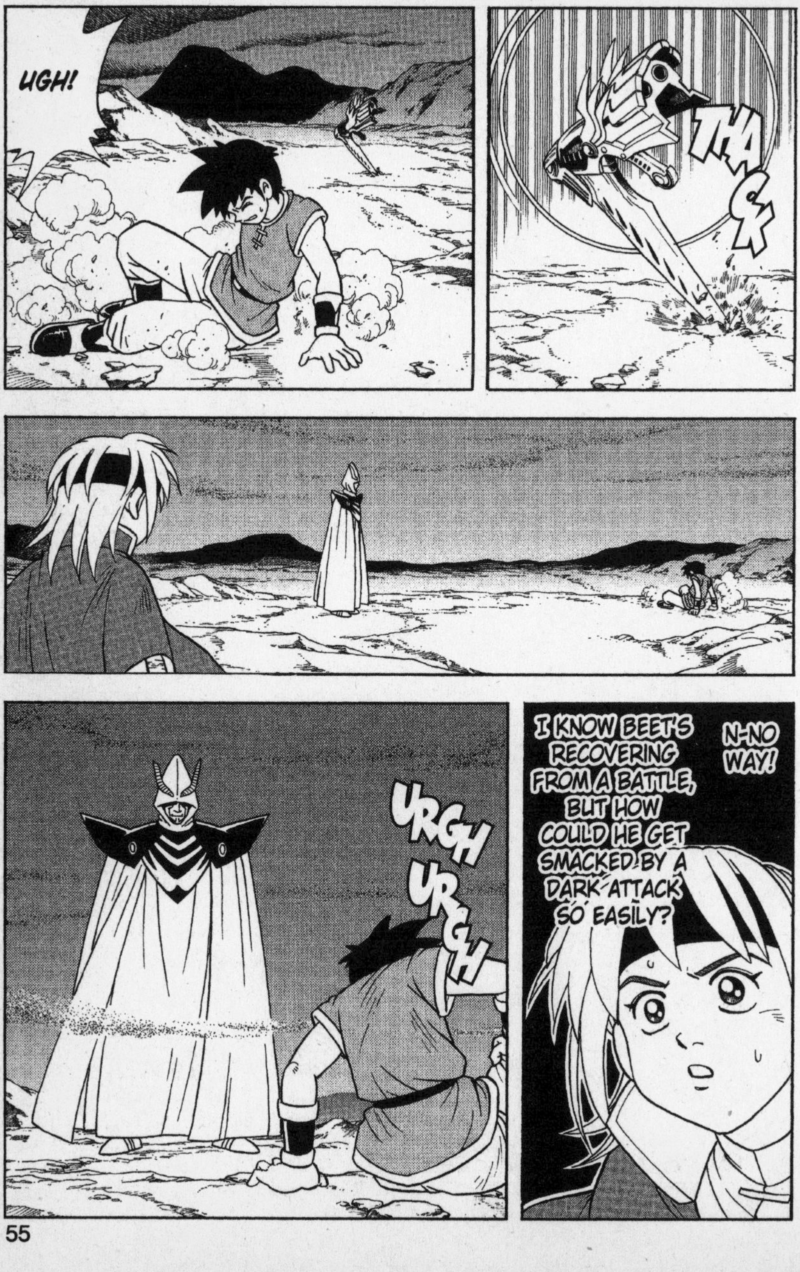
THACK
UGH!
N-NO WAY!
I KNOW BEET'S RECOVERING FROM A BATTLE, BUT HOW COULD HE GET SMACKED BY A DARK ATTACK SO EASILY?
URGH URGH

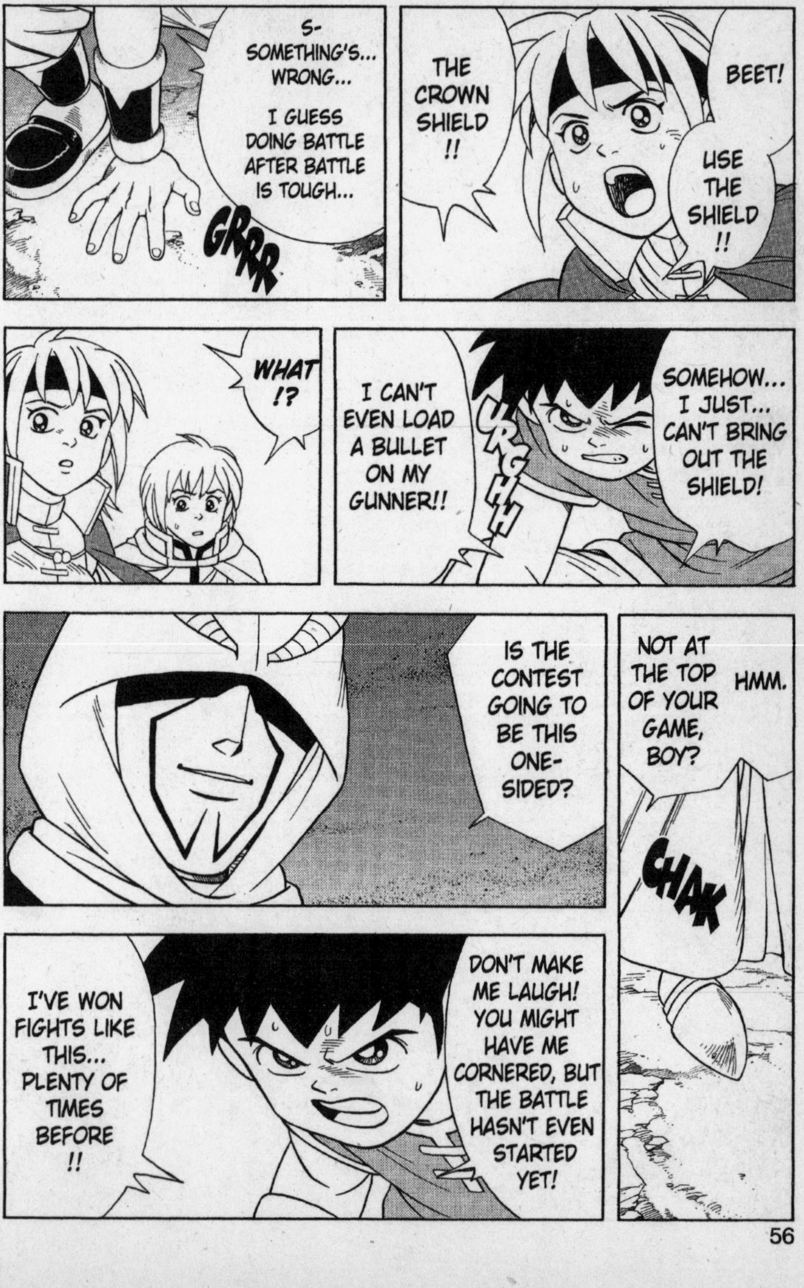

BEET!
USE THE SHIELD!!
THE CROWN SHIELD!!
S-SOMETHING'S... WRONG...
I GUESS DOING BATTLE AFTER BATTLE IS TOUGH...
GRRRR
SOMEHOW... I JUST... CAN'T BRING OUT THE SHIELD!
URGHHH
I CAN'T EVEN LOAD A BULLET ON MY GUNNER!!
WHAT!?
HMM.
NOT AT THE TOP OF YOUR GAME, BOY?
CHAK
IS THE CONTEST GOING TO BE THIS ONE-SIDED?
DON'T MAKE ME LAUGH! YOU MIGHT HAVE ME CORNERED, BUT THE BATTLE HASN'T EVEN STARTED YET!
I'VE WON FIGHTS LIKE THIS... PLENTY OF TIMES BEFORE!!

READ THIS WAY

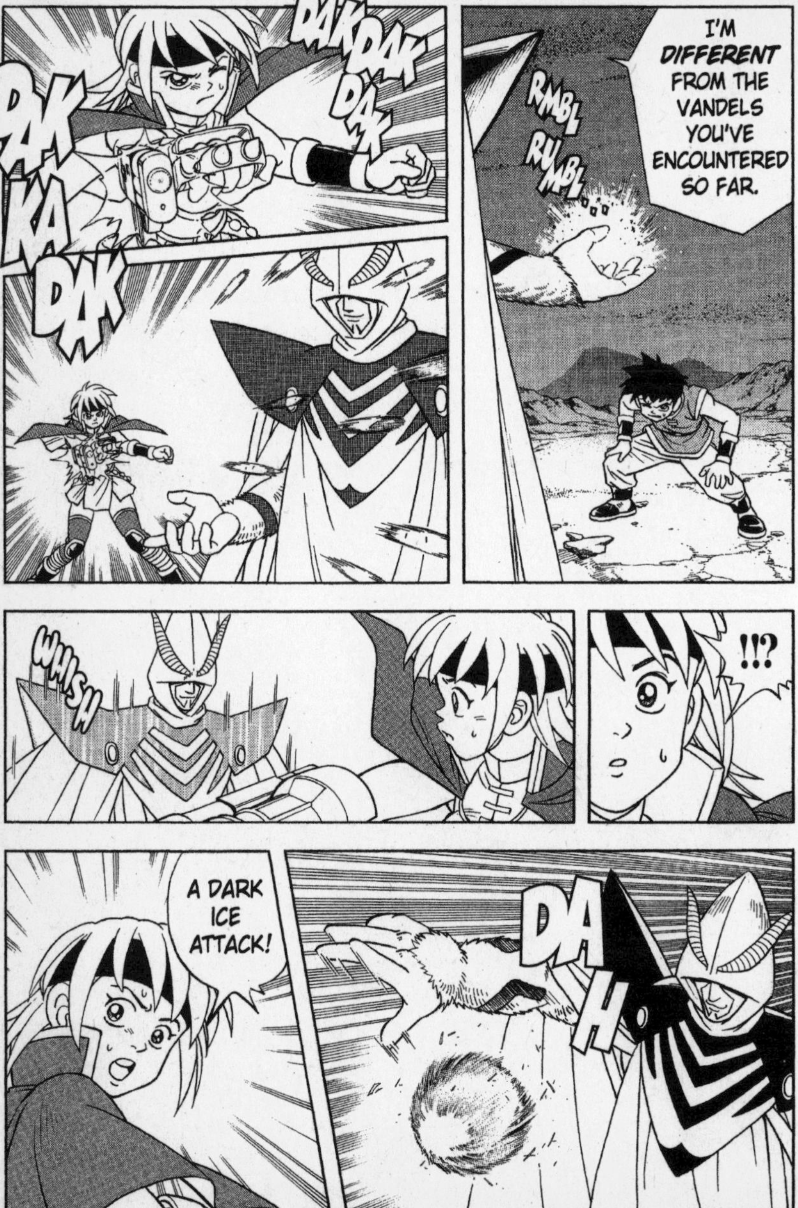
I'M DIFFERENT FROM THE VANDELS YOU'VE ENCOUNTERED SO FAR.
RMBL RUMBL...
DAKDAK DAK
DAK KA DAK
!!?
WHISH
DAH
A DARK ICE ATTACK!

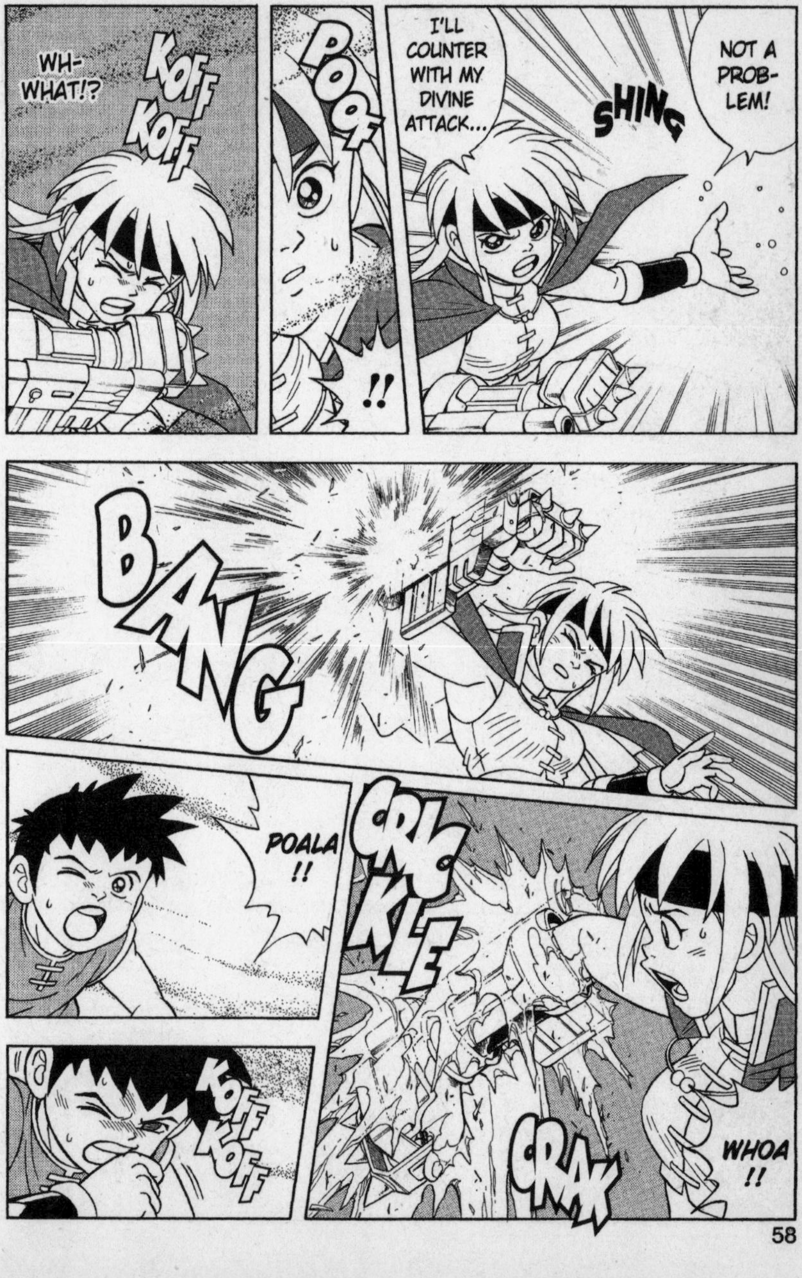
NOT A PROB-LEM!
I'LL COUNTER WITH MY DIVINE ATTACK...
SHING
POOF
!!
KOFF KOFF
WH-WHAT!?
BANG
CRACKLE
WHOA !!
CRAK
POALA !!
KOFF KOFF

READ THIS WAY

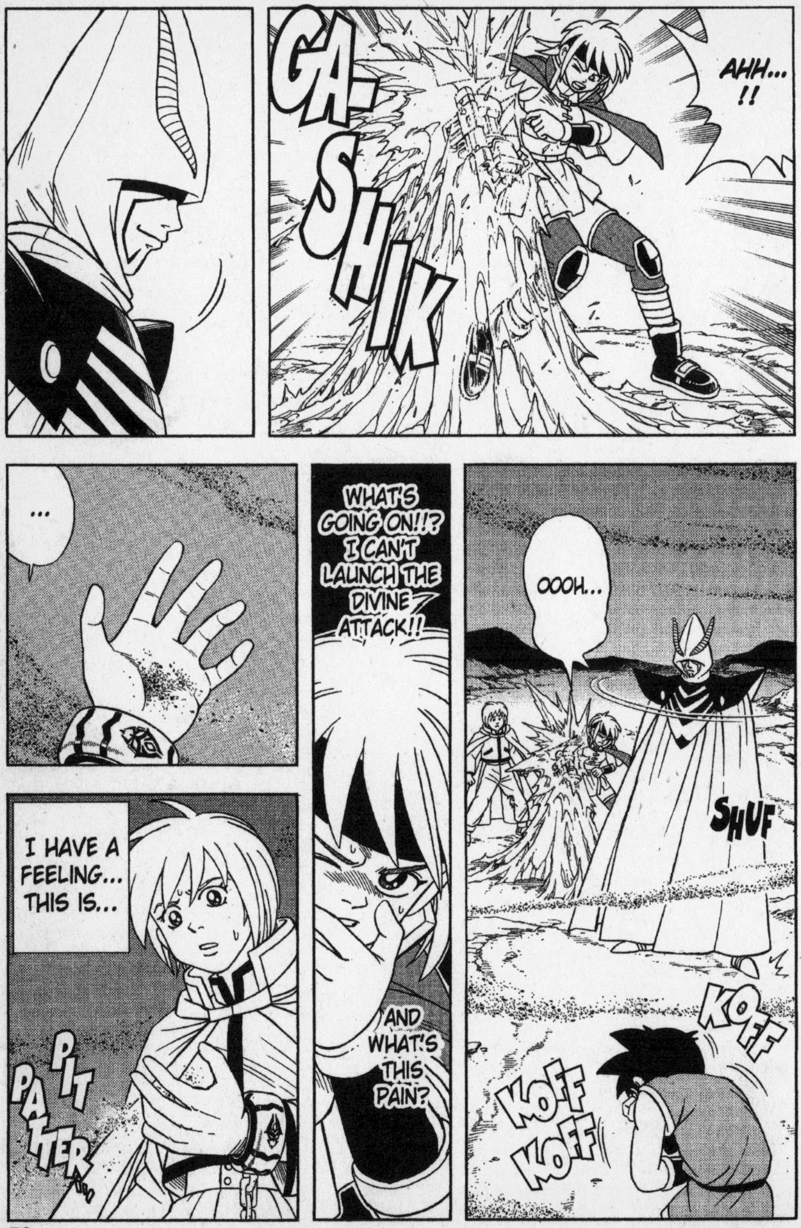
GA-SHIK
AHH... !!
OOOH...
SHUF
KOFF
KOFF KOFF
WHAT'S GOING ON!!? I CAN'T LAUNCH THE DIVINE ATTACK!!
AND WHAT'S THIS PAIN?
...
I HAVE A FEELING... THIS IS...
PIT PATTER

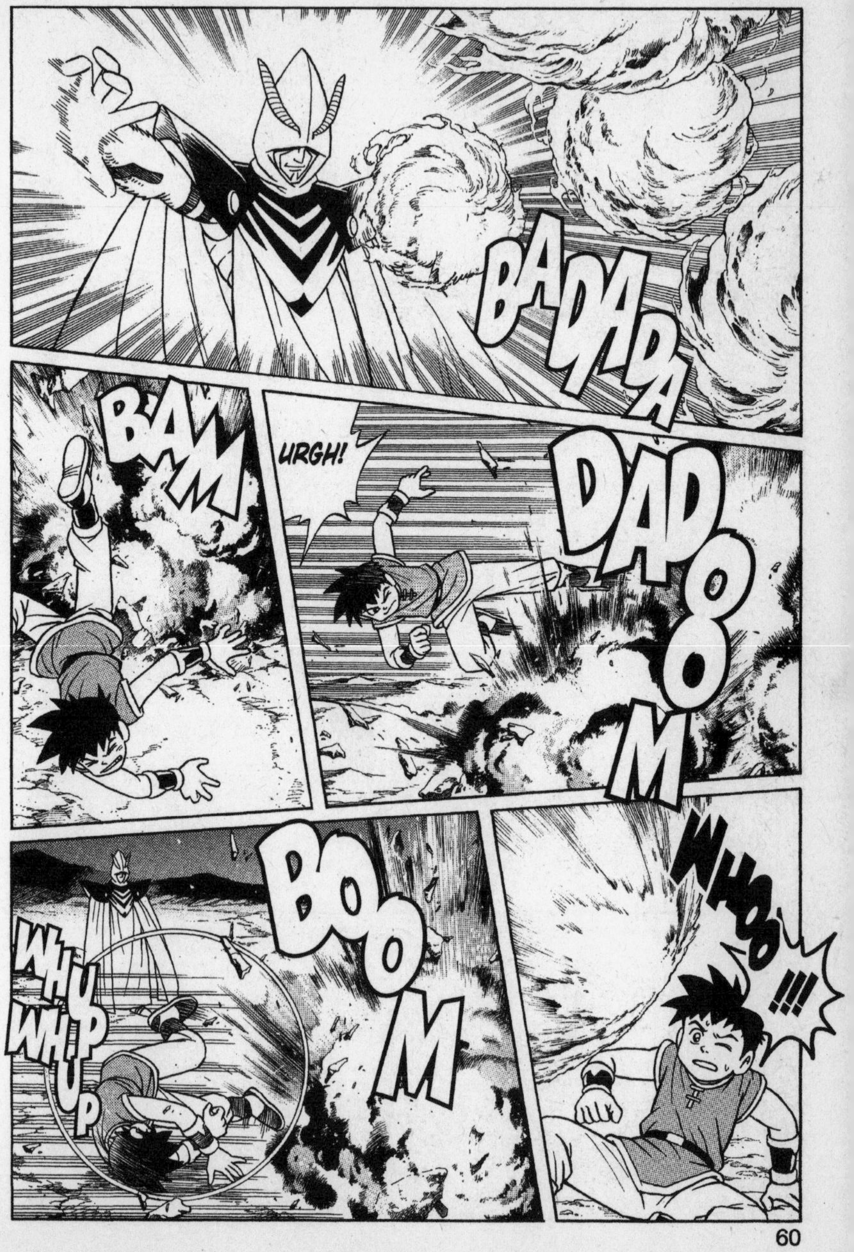
BADADADA
DADOOM
URGH!
BAM
WHOO!!!
BOOOM
WHUP
WHUP
WHUP

READ THIS WAY

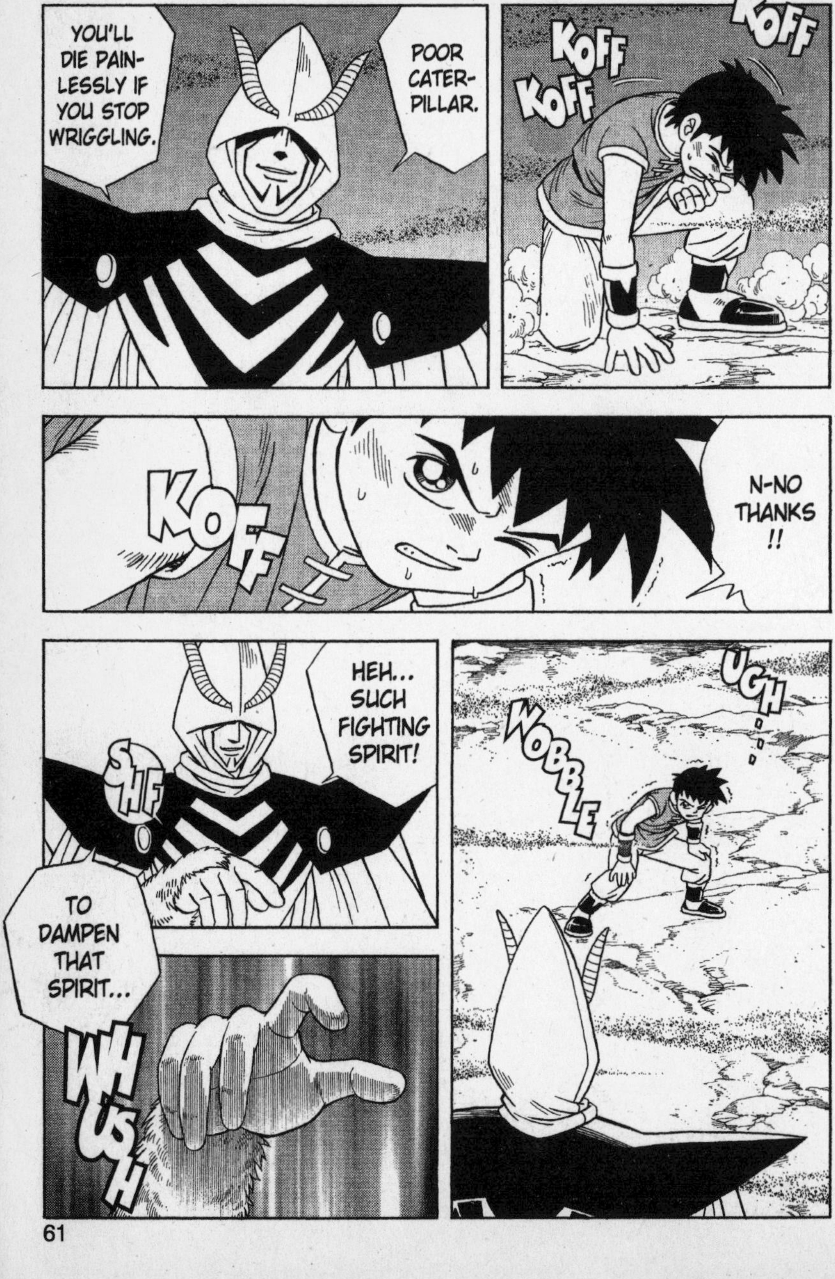
KOFF
KOFF
KOFF
POOR CATER-PILLAR.
YOU'LL DIE PAIN-LESSLY IF YOU STOP WRIGGLING.
N-NO THANKS !!
KOFF
UGH
WOBBLE
HEH... SUCH FIGHTING SPIRIT!
SHF
TO DAMPEN THAT SPIRIT...
WHUSH

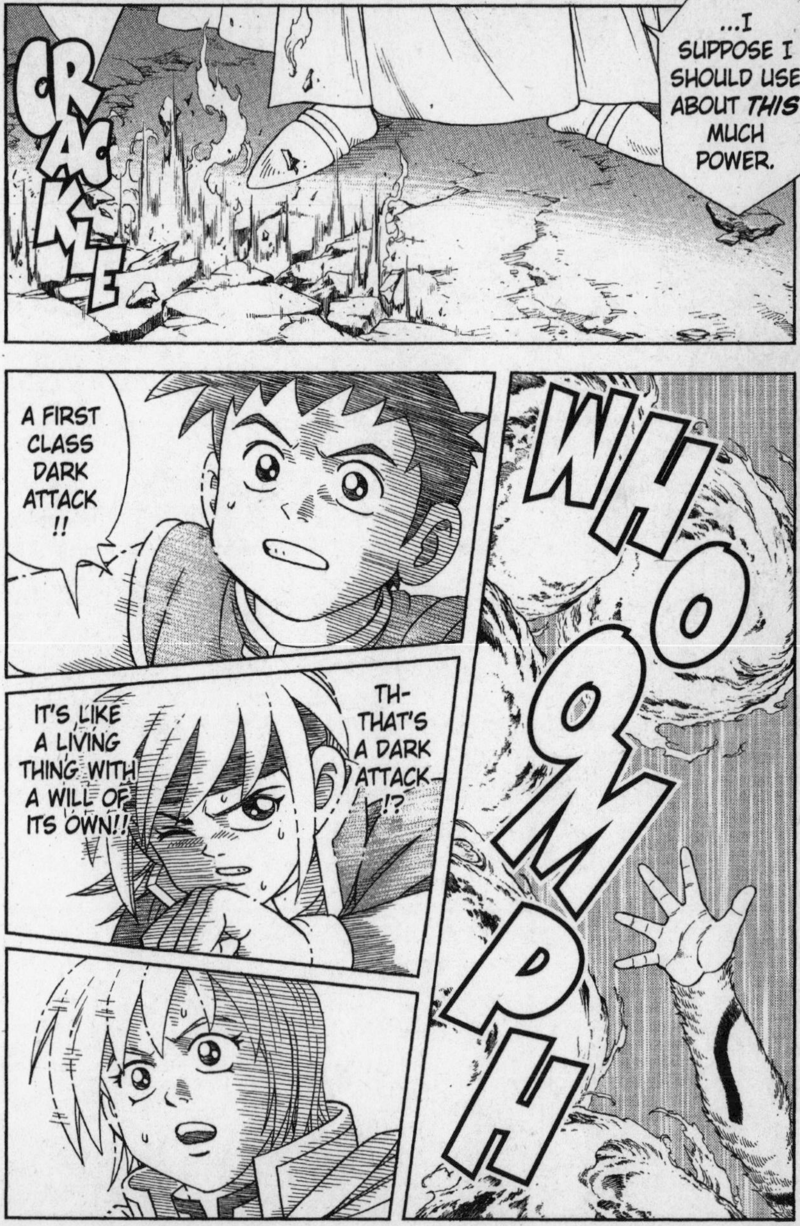
...I SUPPOSE I SHOULD USE ABOUT *THIS* MUCH POWER.
CRACKLE
WHOOOMPH
A FIRST CLASS DARK ATTACK !!
TH- THAT'S A DARK ATTACK !?
IT'S LIKE A LIVING THING WITH A WILL OF ITS OWN!!

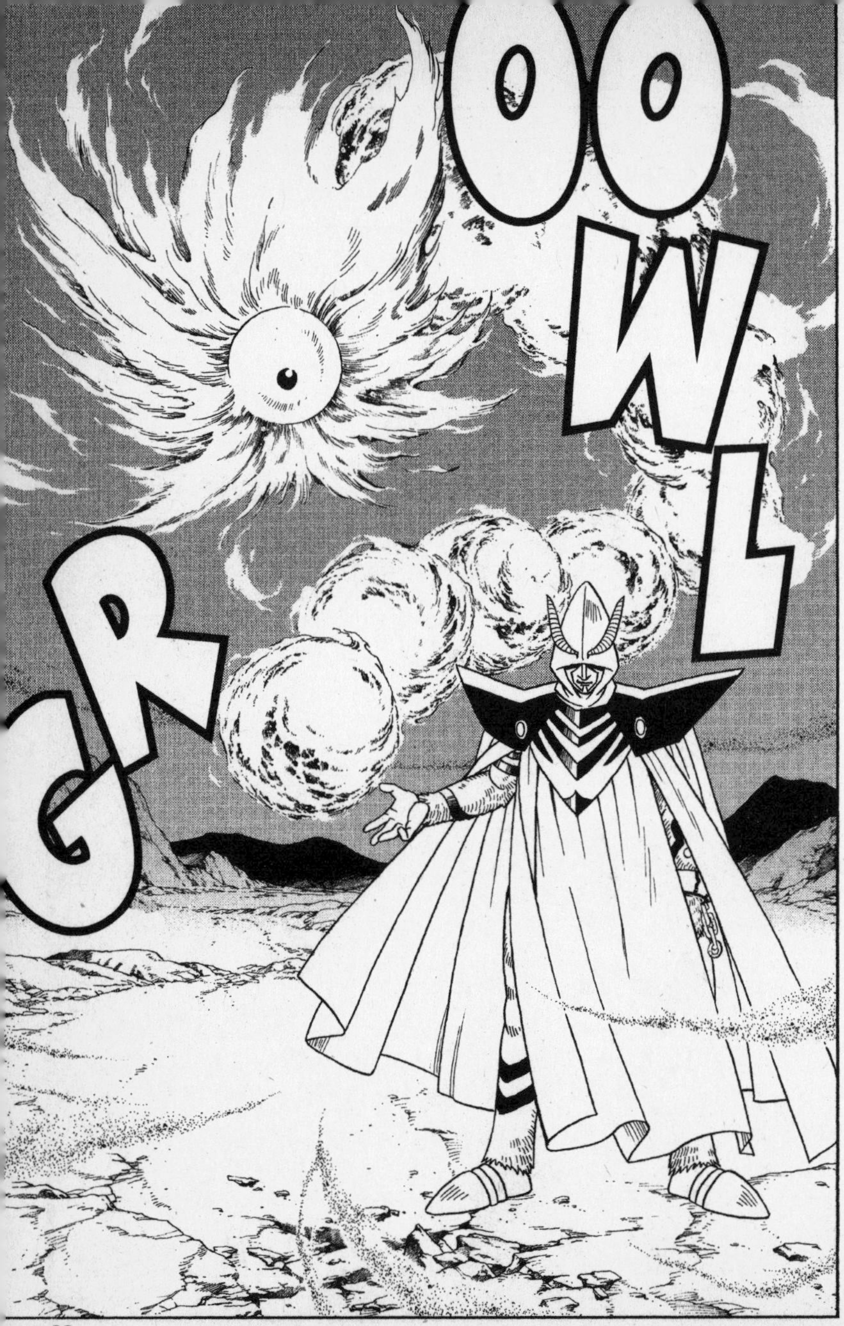
GROOWL

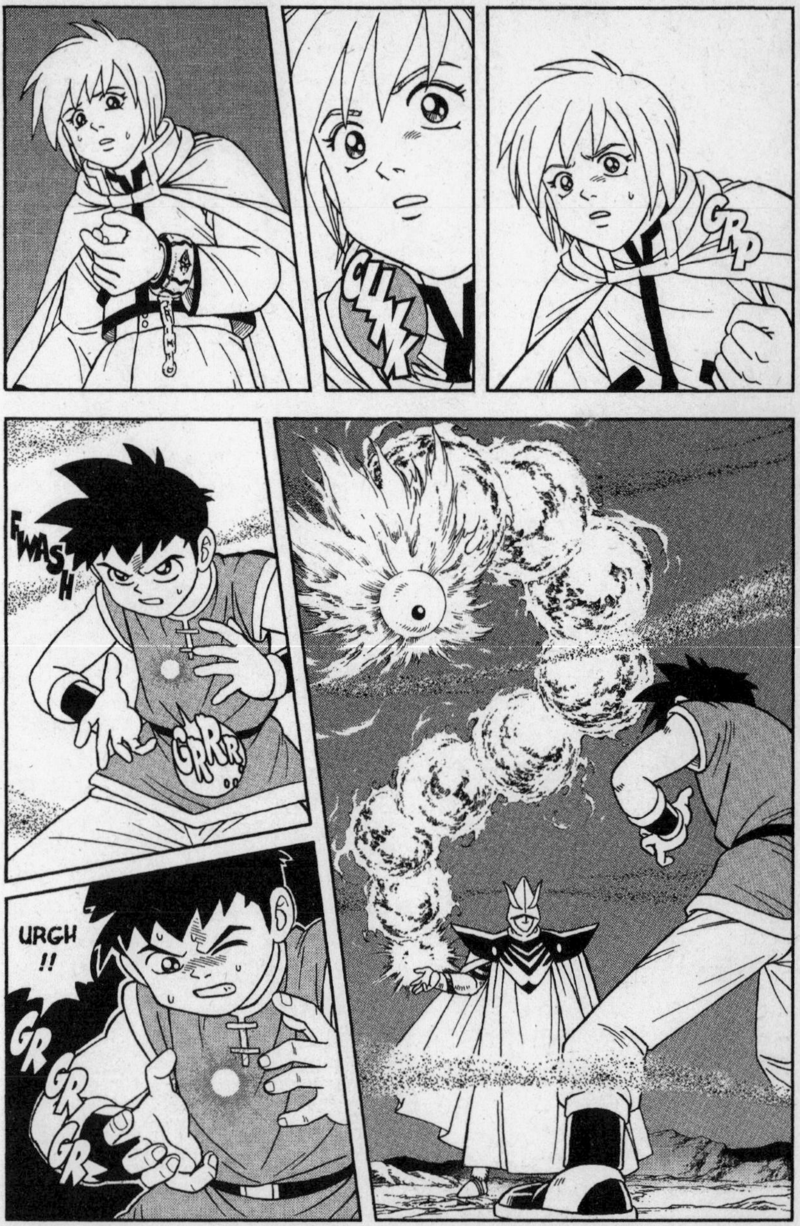
GRP
CLINK
FWASH
GRRR
URGH !!
GR GR GR GR

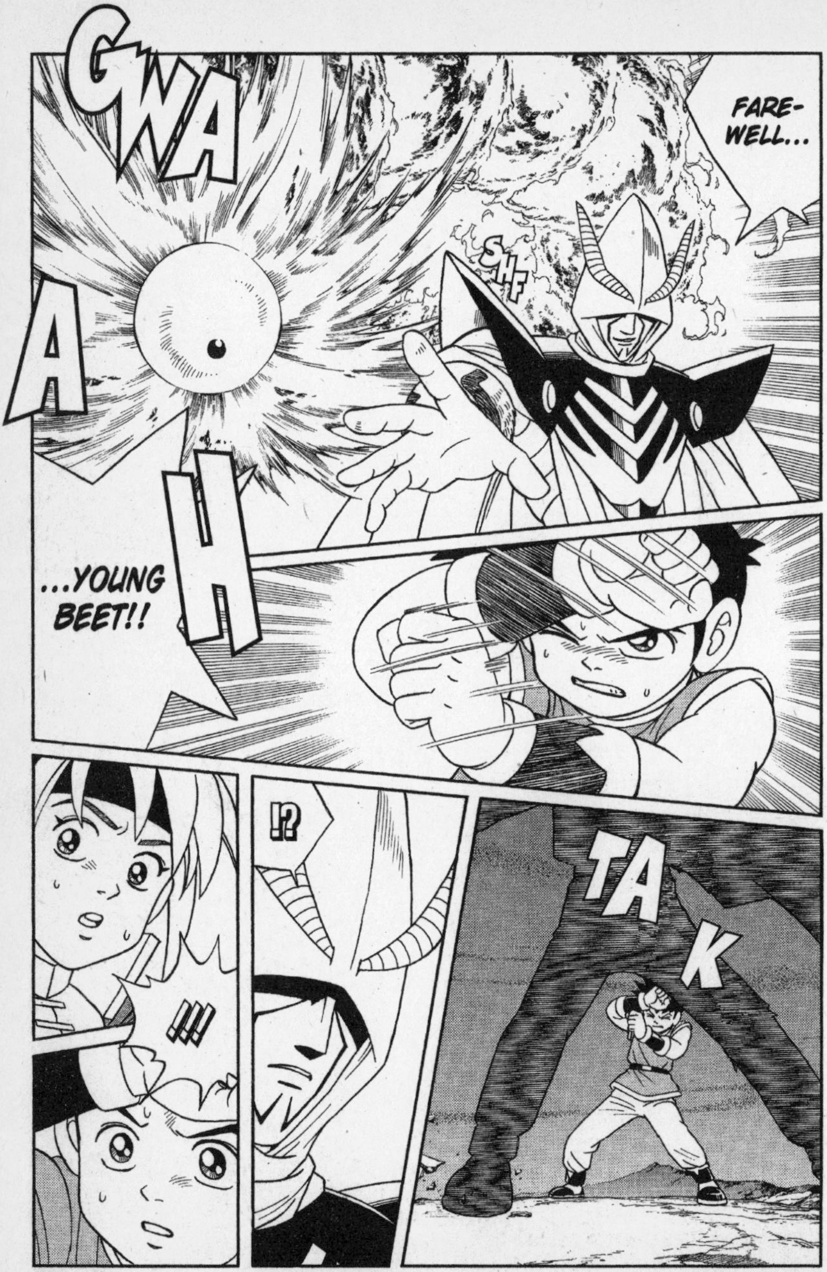
FARE-WELL...
SHF
GWAAH
...YOUNG BEET!!
TAK
!?
!!!

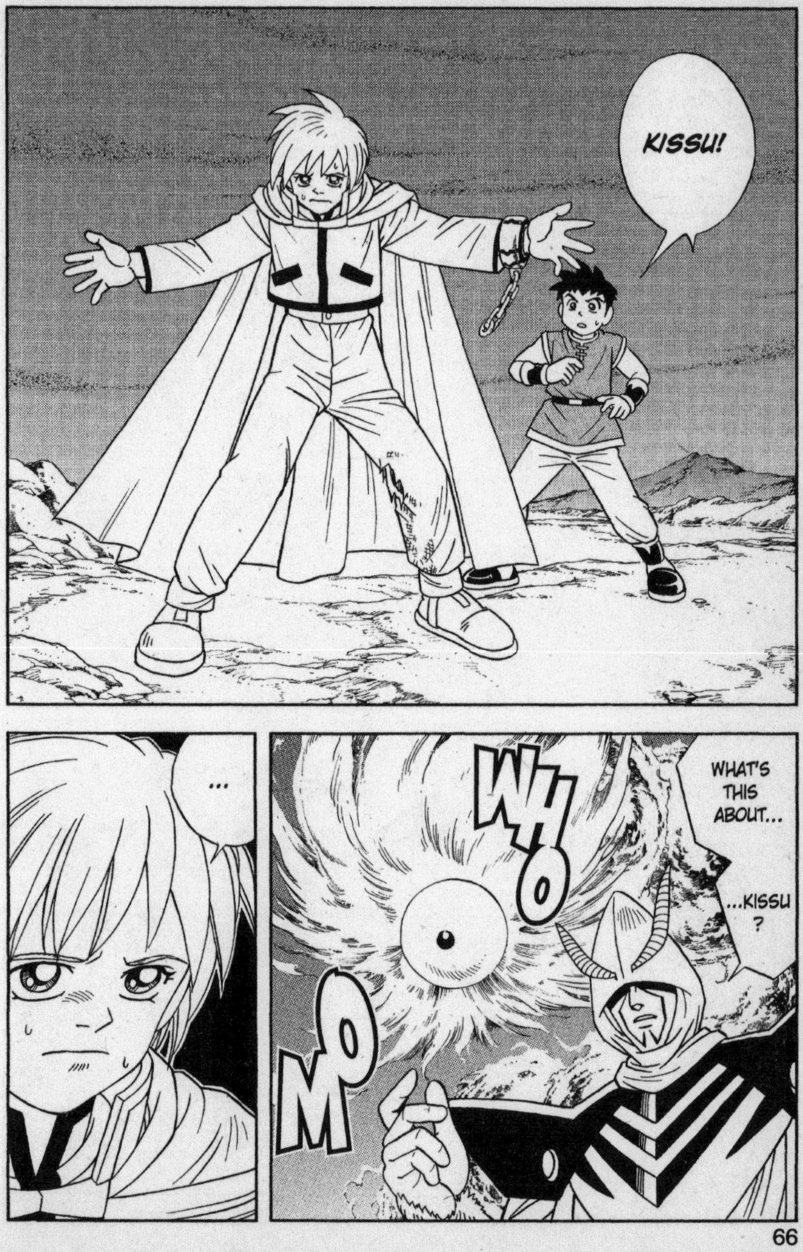
KISSU!
WHOOM
WHAT'S THIS ABOUT...
...KISSU ?
...

READ THIS WAY

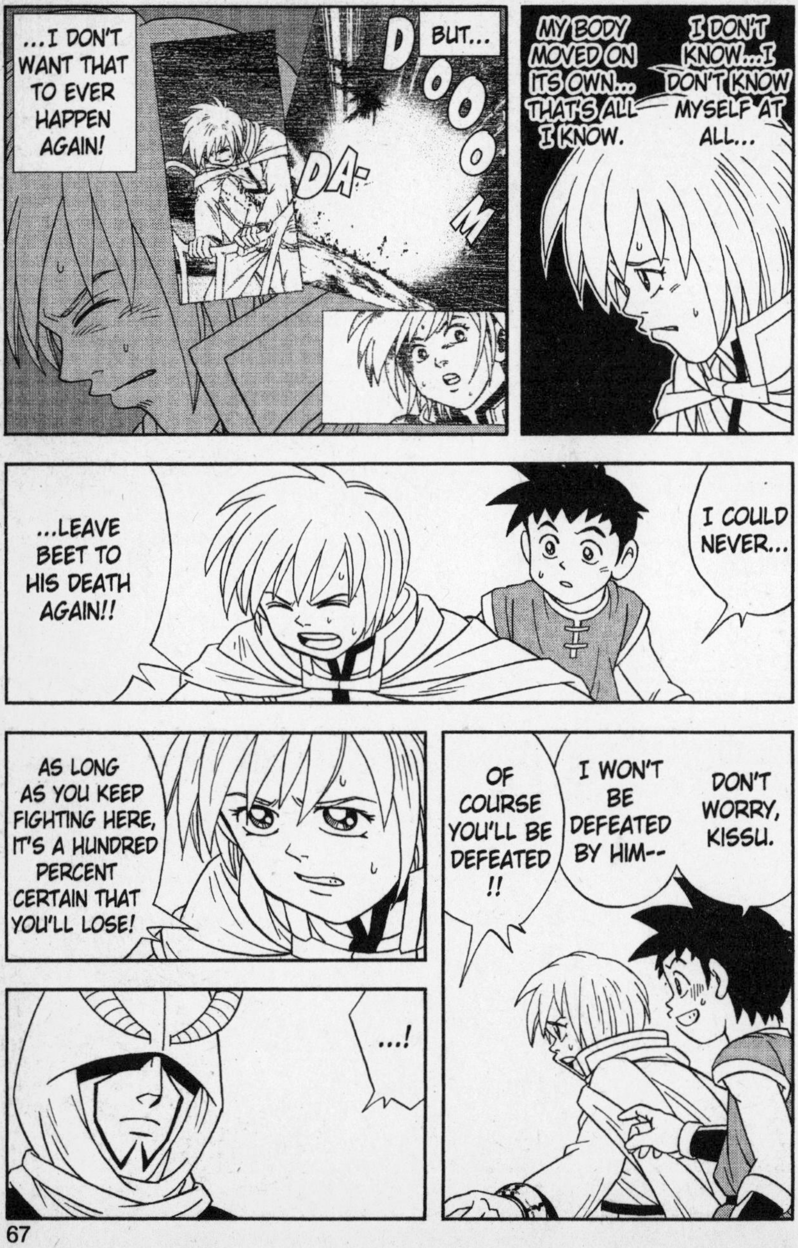
I DON'T KNOW...I DON'T KNOW MYSELF AT ALL...
MY BODY MOVED ON ITS OWN... THAT'S ALL I KNOW.
BUT...
DOOOM
DA-
...I DON'T WANT THAT TO EVER HAPPEN AGAIN!
I COULD NEVER...
...LEAVE BEET TO HIS DEATH AGAIN!!
DON'T WORRY, KISSU.
I WON'T BE DEFEATED BY HIM--
OF COURSE YOU'LL BE DEFEATED!!
AS LONG AS YOU KEEP FIGHTING HERE, IT'S A HUNDRED PERCENT CERTAIN THAT YOU'LL LOSE!
...!

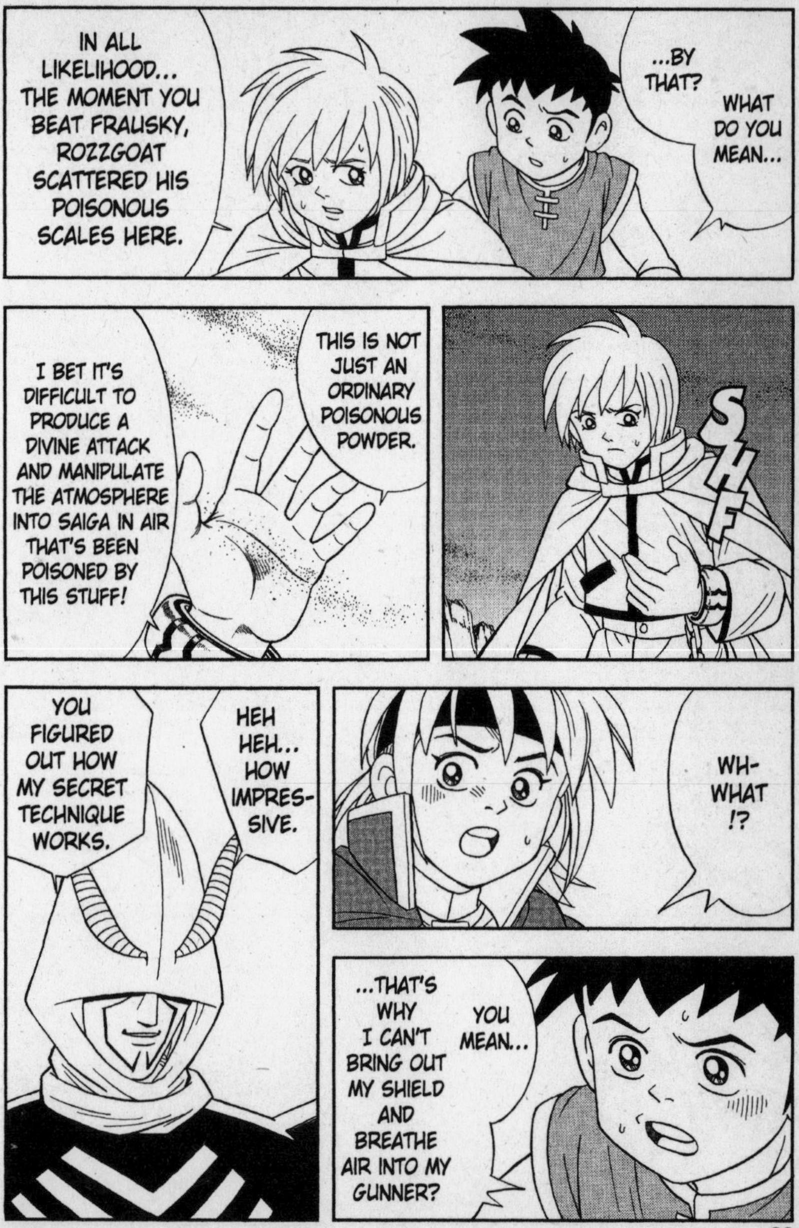
WHAT DO YOU MEAN... ...BY THAT?
IN ALL LIKELIHOOD... THE MOMENT YOU BEAT FRAUSKY, ROZZGOAT SCATTERED HIS POISONOUS SCALES HERE.
SHUF
THIS IS NOT JUST AN ORDINARY POISONOUS POWDER.
I BET IT'S DIFFICULT TO PRODUCE A DIVINE ATTACK AND MANIPULATE THE ATMOSPHERE INTO SAIGA IN AIR THAT'S BEEN POISONED BY THIS STUFF!
WH-WHAT!?
YOU MEAN...
...THAT'S WHY I CAN'T BRING OUT MY SHIELD AND BREATHE AIR INTO MY GUNNER?
HEH HEH... HOW IMPRES-SIVE.
YOU FIGURED OUT HOW MY SECRET TECHNIQUE WORKS.

READ THIS WAY

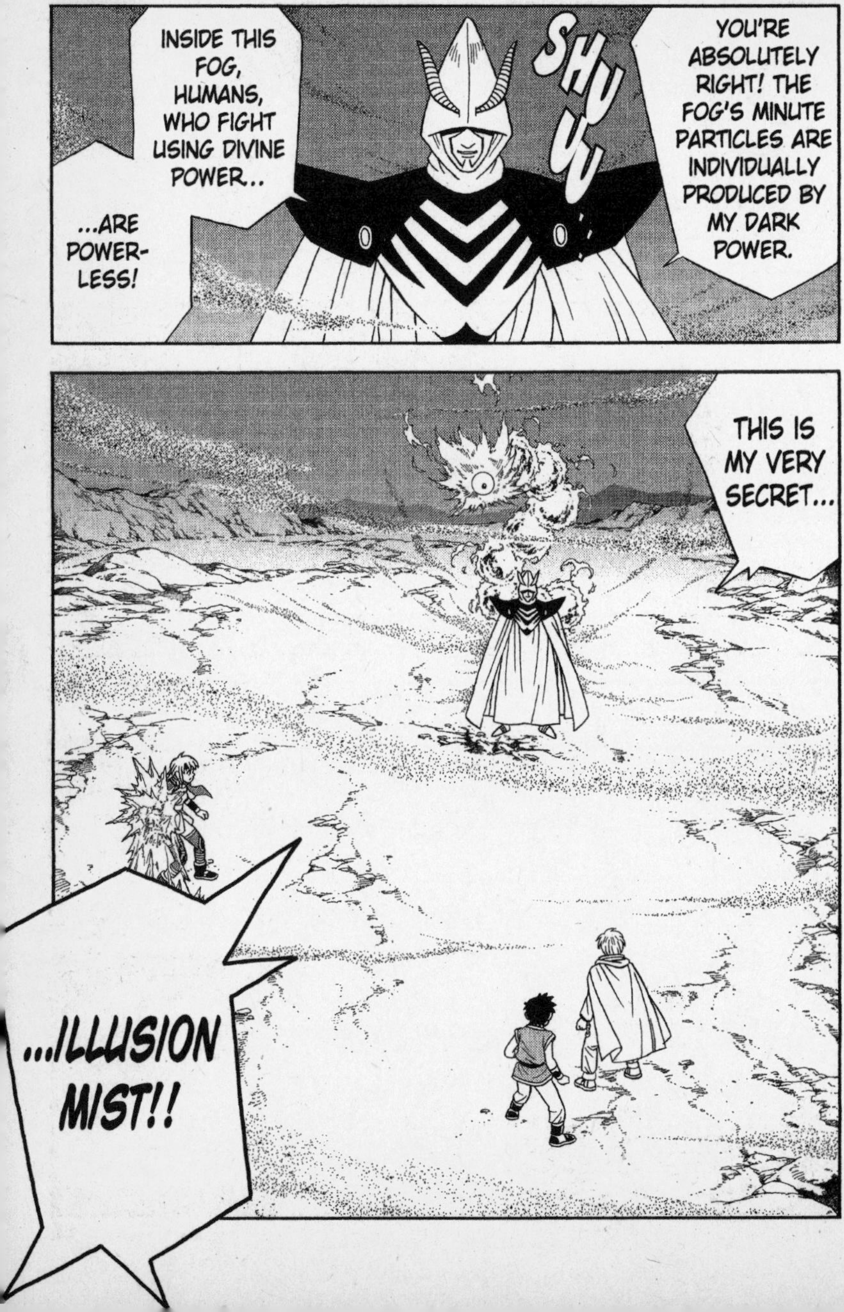
YOU'RE ABSOLUTELY RIGHT! THE FOG'S MINUTE PARTICLES ARE INDIVIDUALLY PRODUCED BY MY DARK POWER.
SHUUU
INSIDE THIS FOG, HUMANS, WHO FIGHT USING DIVINE POWER...
...ARE POWER-LESS!
THIS IS MY VERY SECRET...
...ILLUSION MIST!!

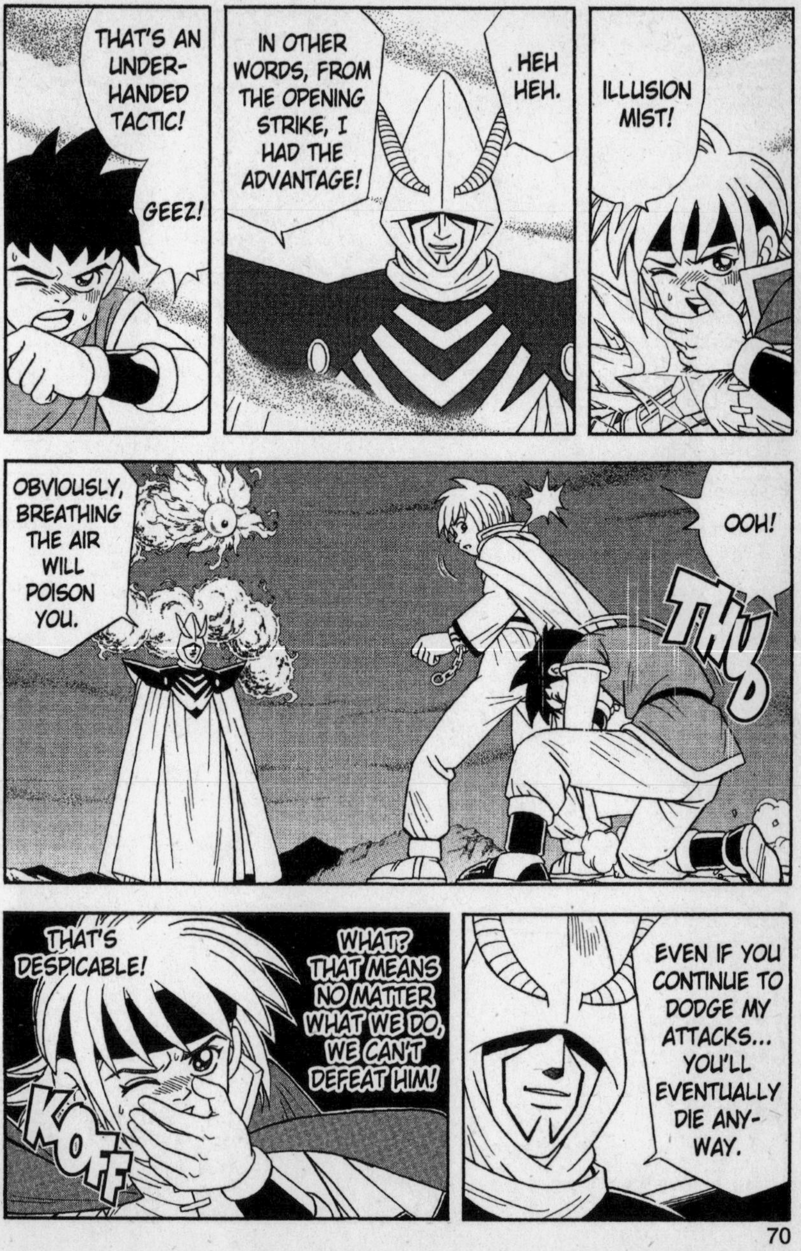
ILLUSION MIST!
HEH HEH.
IN OTHER WORDS, FROM THE OPENING STRIKE, I HAD THE ADVANTAGE!
THAT'S AN UNDER-HANDED TACTIC!
GEEZ!
OOH!
THUD
OBVIOUSLY, BREATHING THE AIR WILL POISON YOU.
EVEN IF YOU CONTINUE TO DODGE MY ATTACKS... YOU'LL EVENTUALLY DIE ANY-WAY.
WHAT? THAT MEANS NO MATTER WHAT WE DO, WE CAN'T DEFEAT HIM!
THAT'S DESPICABLE!
KOFF

READ THIS WAY

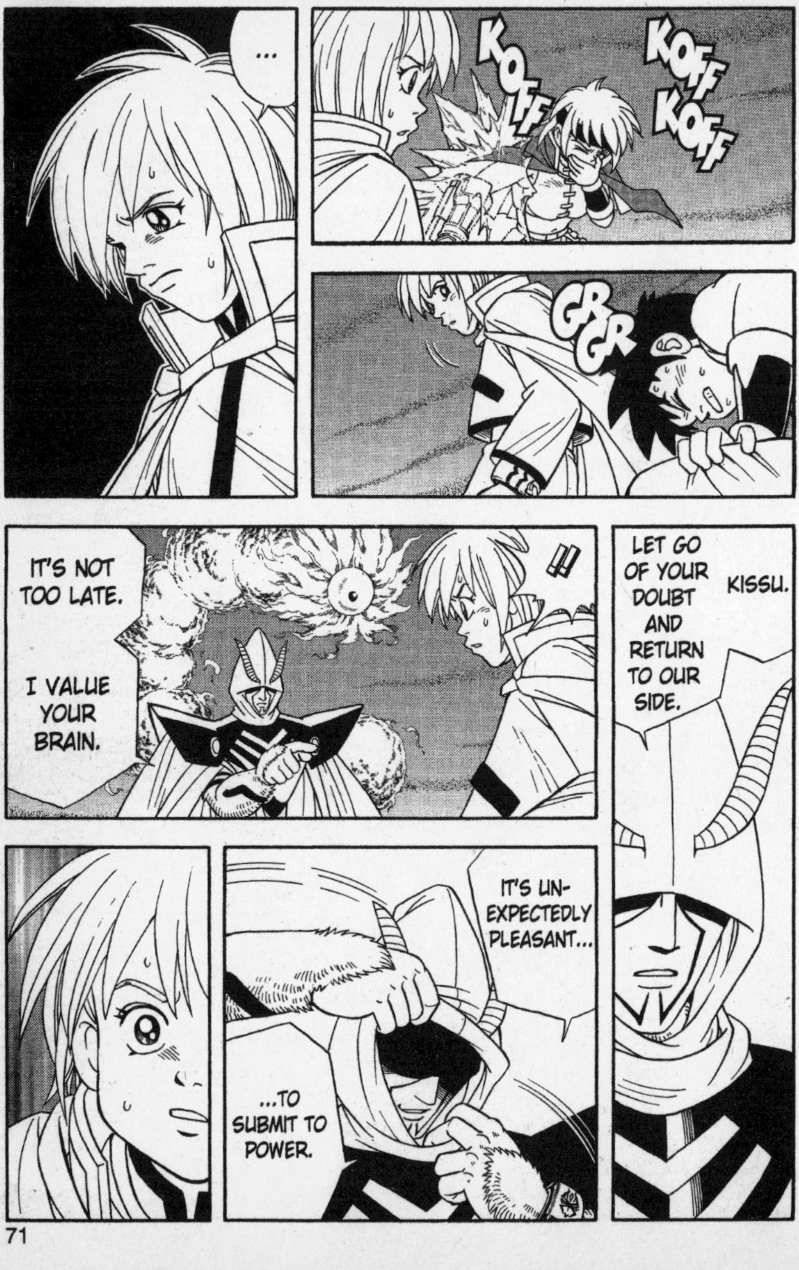
KOFF
KOFF KOFF
GRGR
...
KISSU.
LET GO OF YOUR DOUBT AND RETURN TO OUR SIDE.
!!
IT'S NOT TOO LATE.
I VALUE YOUR BRAIN.
IT'S UN-EXPECTEDLY PLEASANT...
...TO SUBMIT TO POWER.

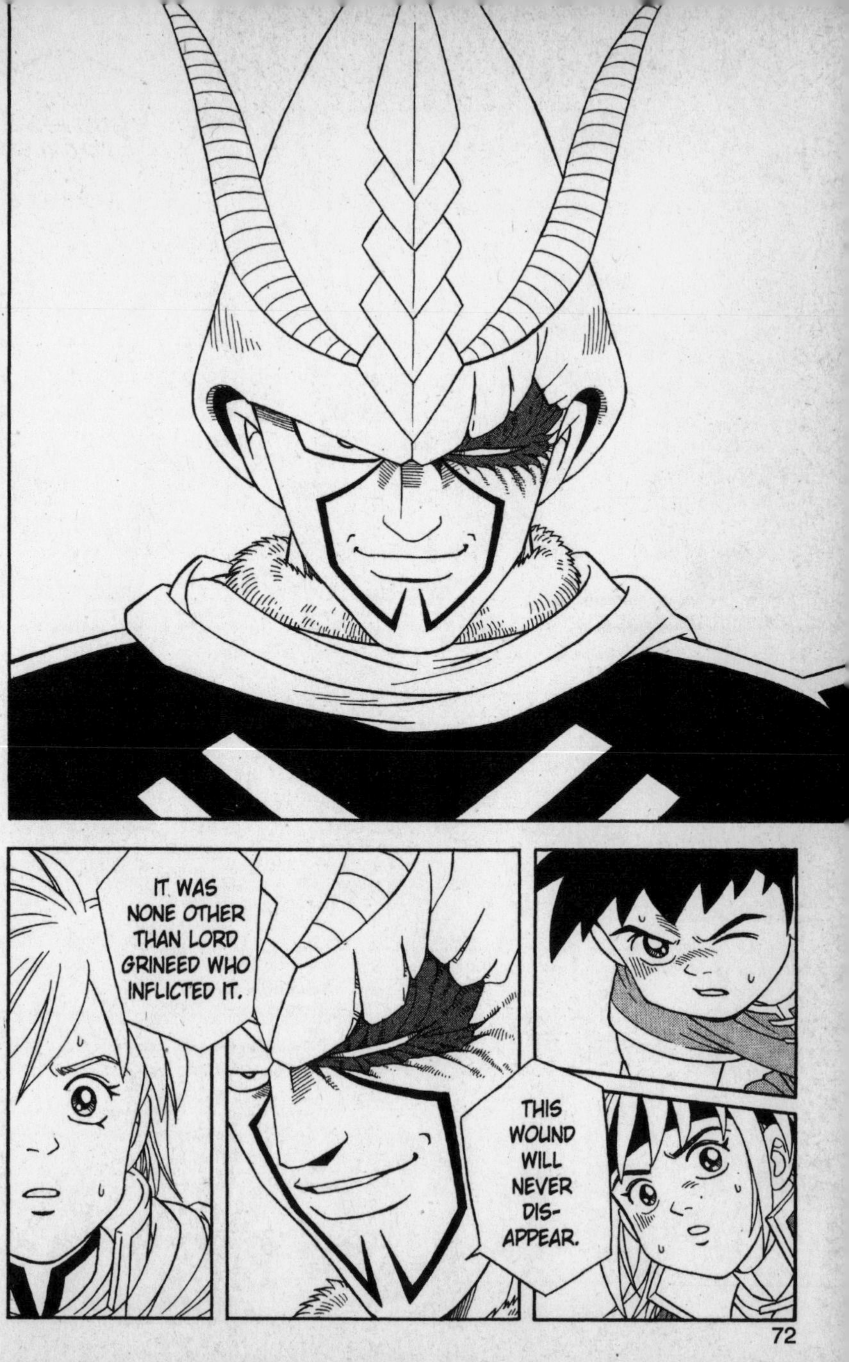
THIS WOUND WILL NEVER DIS- APPEAR.
IT WAS NONE OTHER THAN LORD GRINEED WHO INFLICTED IT.

READ THIS WAY

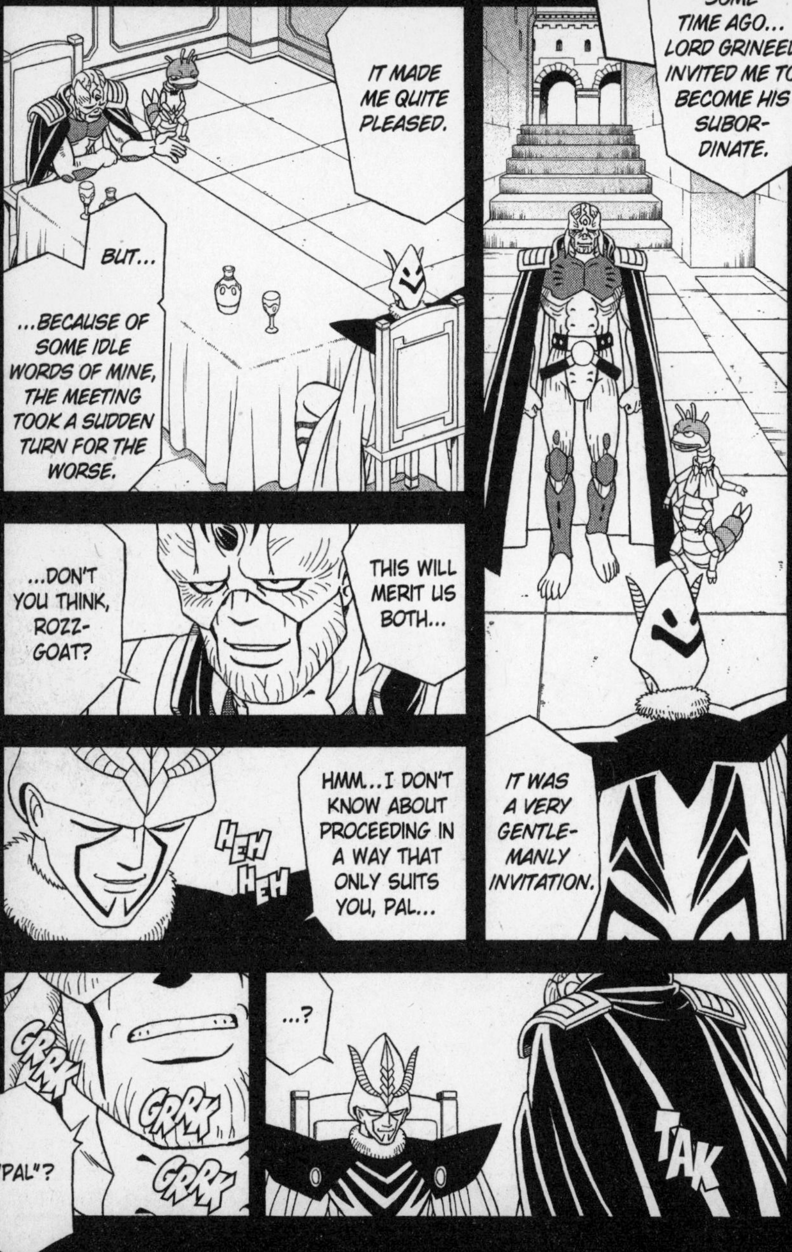
SOME TIME AGO... LORD GRINEED INVITED ME TO BECOME HIS SUBOR-DINATE.
IT WAS A VERY GENTLE-MANLY INVITATION.
IT MADE ME QUITE PLEASED.
BUT...
...BECAUSE OF SOME IDLE WORDS OF MINE, THE MEETING TOOK A SUDDEN TURN FOR THE WORSE.
THIS WILL MERIT US BOTH...
...DON'T YOU THINK, ROZZ-GOAT?
HMM...I DON'T KNOW ABOUT PROCEEDING IN A WAY THAT ONLY SUITS YOU, PAL...
HEH HEH
TAK
...?
GRRK
GRRK
GRRK
"PAL"?

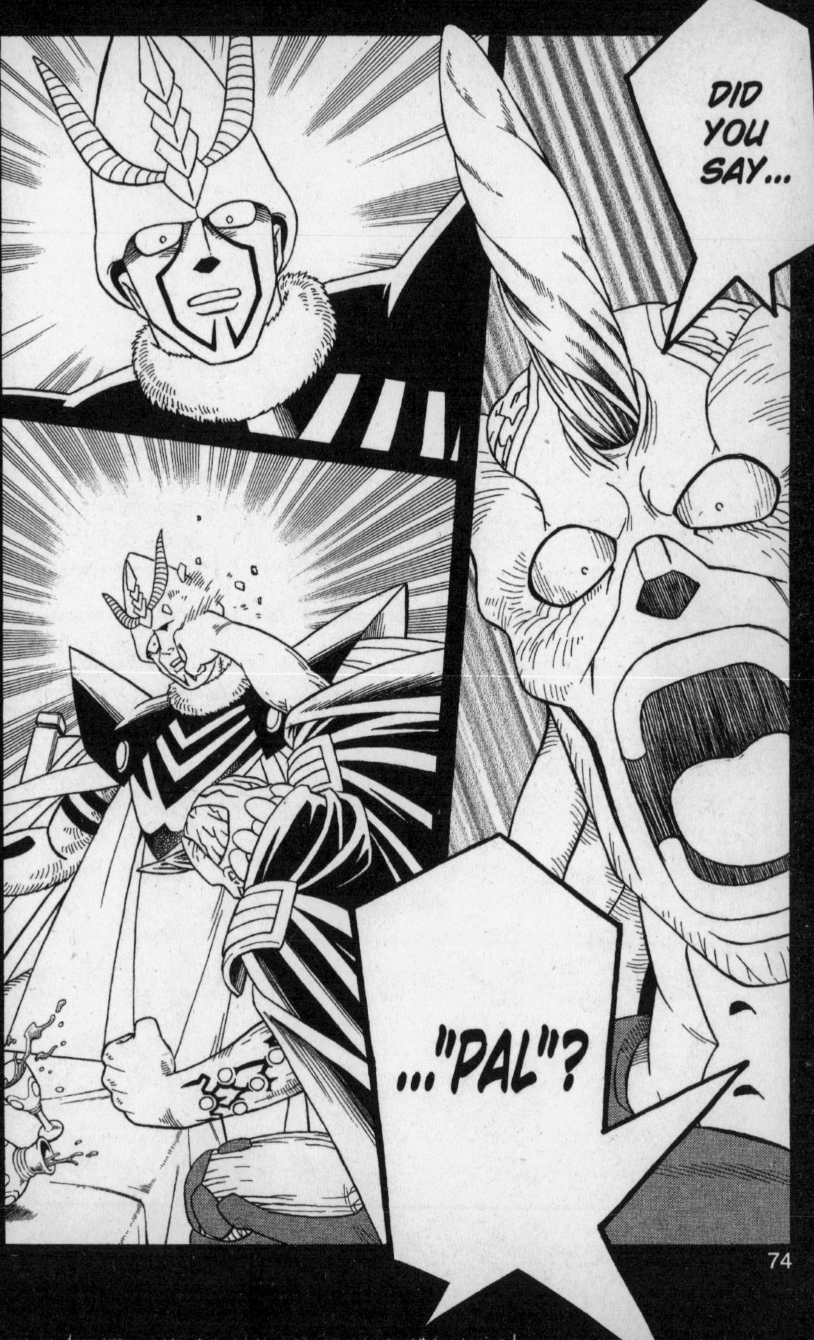
DID YOU SAY...
..."PAL"?

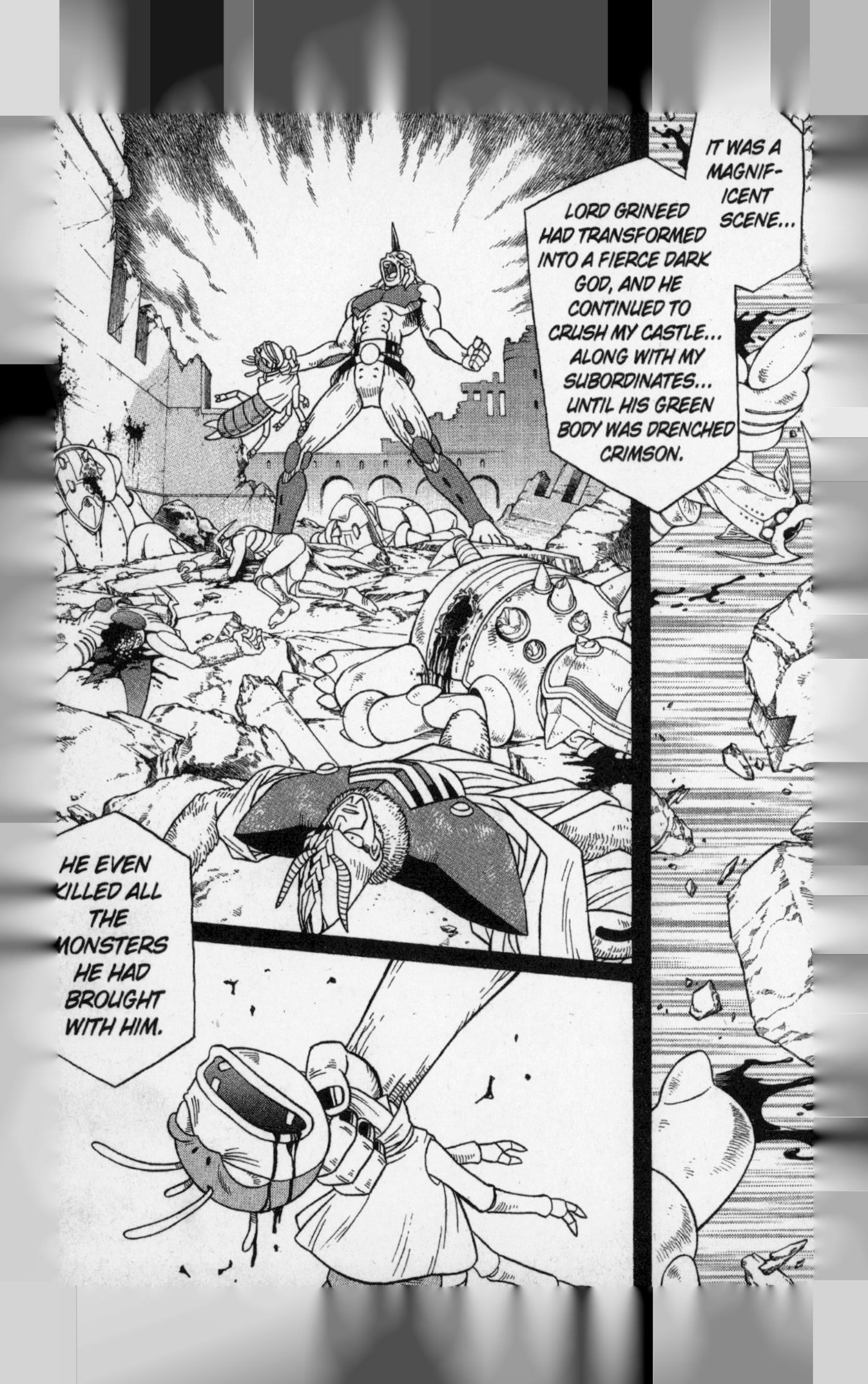
IT WAS A MAGNIFICENT SCENE...
LORD GRINEED HAD TRANSFORMED INTO A FIERCE DARK GOD, AND HE CONTINUED TO CRUSH MY CASTLE... ALONG WITH MY SUBORDINATES... UNTIL HIS GREEN BODY WAS DRENCHED CRIMSON.
HE EVEN KILLED ALL THE MONSTERS HE HAD BROUGHT WITH HIM.

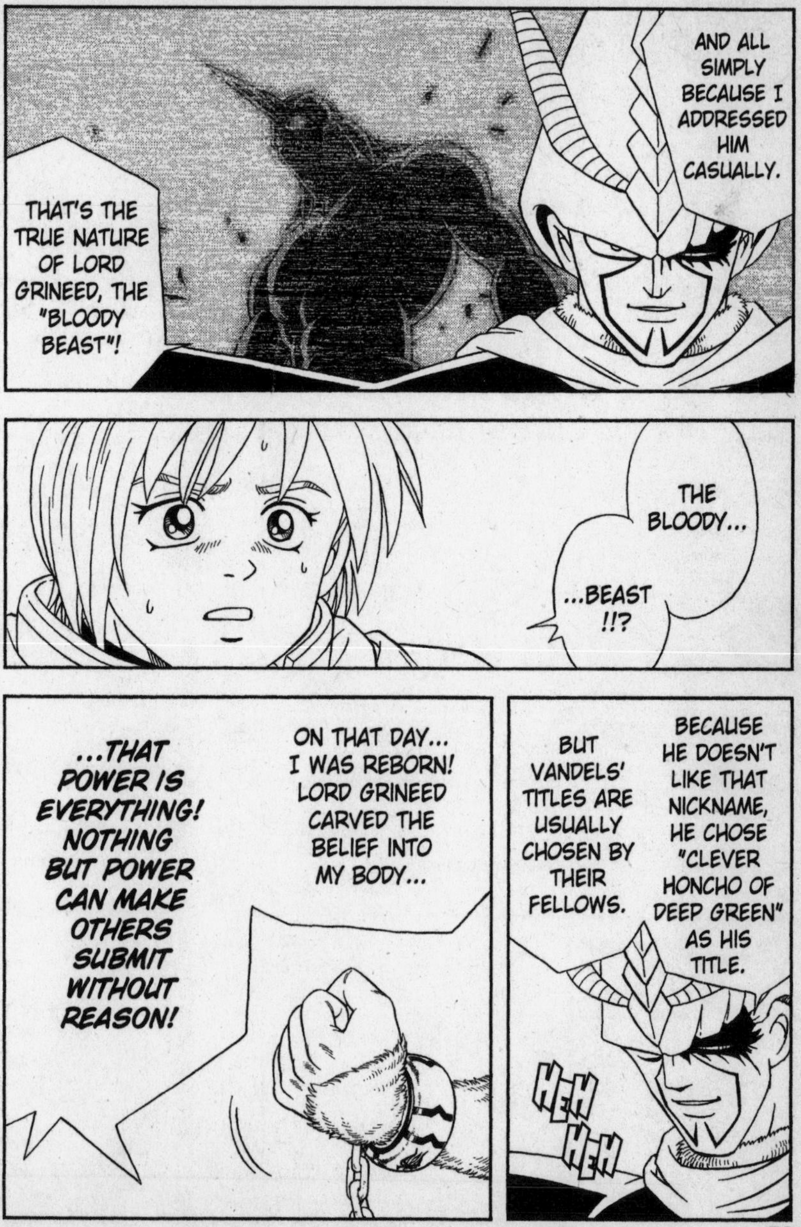
AND ALL SIMPLY BECAUSE I ADDRESSED HIM CASUALLY.
THAT'S THE TRUE NATURE OF LORD GRINEED, THE "BLOODY BEAST"!
THE BLOODY...
...BEAST !!?
BECAUSE HE DOESN'T LIKE THAT NICKNAME, HE CHOSE "CLEVER HONCHO OF DEEP GREEN" AS HIS TITLE.
BUT VANDELS' TITLES ARE USUALLY CHOSEN BY THEIR FELLOWS.
HEH HEH
ON THAT DAY... I WAS REBORN! LORD GRINEED CARVED THE BELIEF INTO MY BODY...
...THAT POWER IS EVERYTHING! NOTHING BUT POWER CAN MAKE OTHERS SUBMIT WITHOUT REASON!

READ THIS WAY

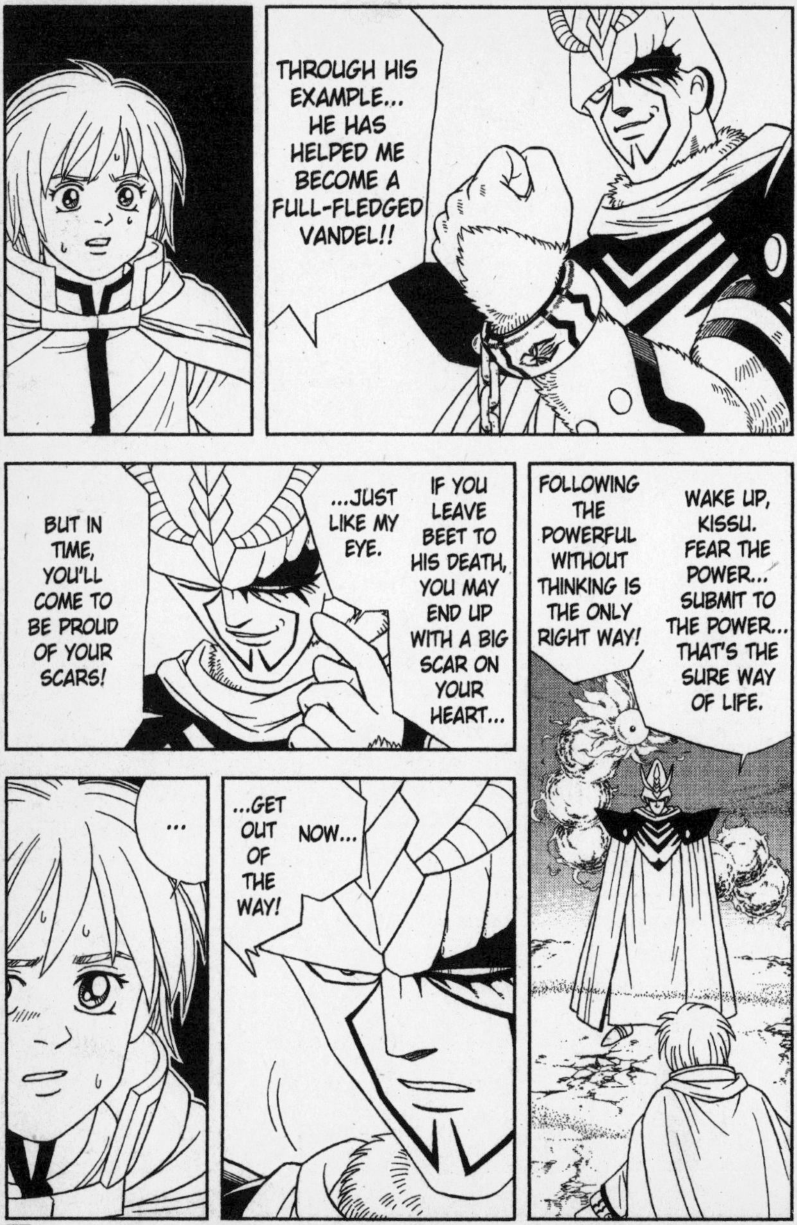
THROUGH HIS EXAMPLE... HE HAS HELPED ME BECOME A FULL-FLEDGED VANDEL!!
WAKE UP, KISSU. FEAR THE POWER... SUBMIT TO THE POWER... THAT'S THE SURE WAY OF LIFE.
FOLLOWING THE POWERFUL WITHOUT THINKING IS THE ONLY RIGHT WAY!
IF YOU LEAVE BEET TO HIS DEATH, YOU MAY END UP WITH A BIG SCAR ON YOUR HEART...
...JUST LIKE MY EYE.
BUT IN TIME, YOU'LL COME TO BE PROUD OF YOUR SCARS!
NOW...
...GET OUT OF THE WAY!
...

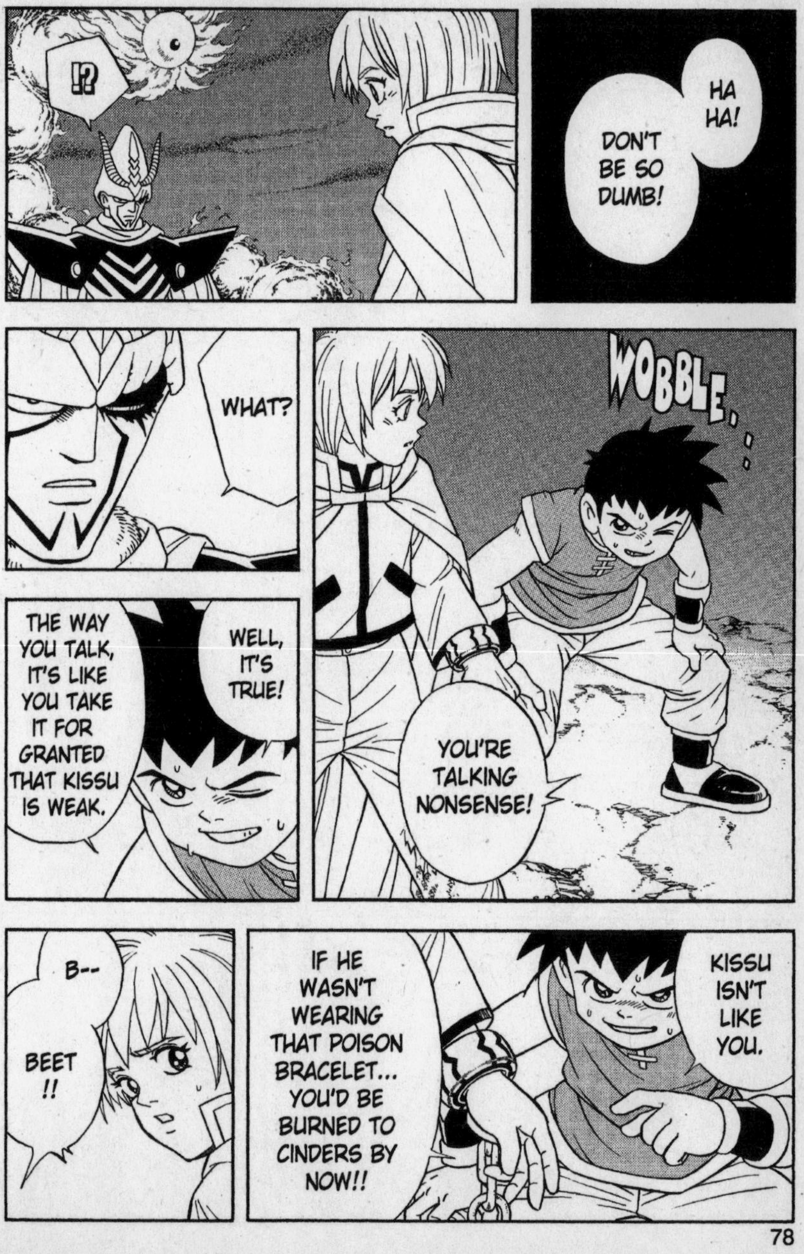
HA HA!
DON'T BE SO DUMB!
!?
WOBBLE...
YOU'RE TALKING NONSENSE!
WHAT?
WELL, IT'S TRUE!
THE WAY YOU TALK, IT'S LIKE YOU TAKE IT FOR GRANTED THAT KISSU IS WEAK.
KISSU ISN'T LIKE YOU.
IF HE WASN'T WEARING THAT POISON BRACELET... YOU'D BE BURNED TO CINDERS BY NOW!!
B--
BEET!!

READ THIS WAY

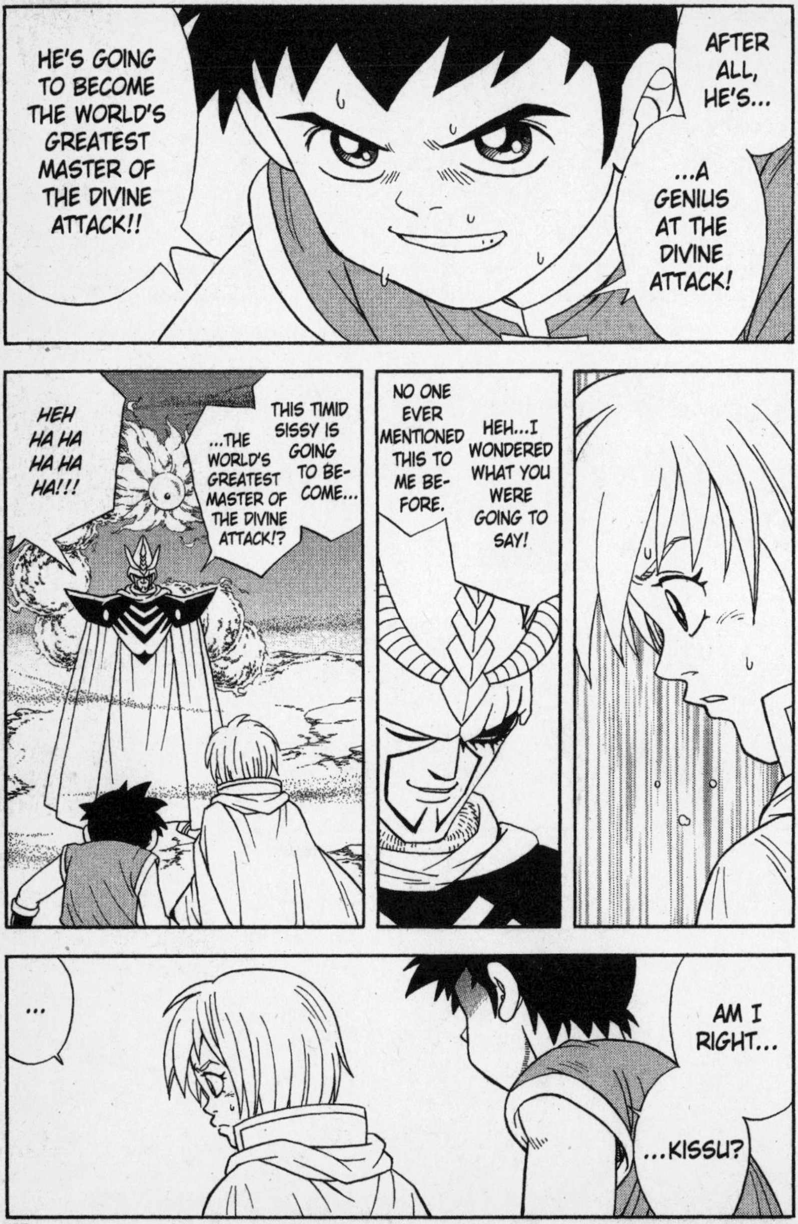
AFTER ALL, HE'S...
...A GENIUS AT THE DIVINE ATTACK!
HE'S GOING TO BECOME THE WORLD'S GREATEST MASTER OF THE DIVINE ATTACK!!
HEH...I WONDERED WHAT YOU WERE GOING TO SAY!
NO ONE EVER MENTIONED THIS TO ME BEFORE.
THIS TIMID SISSY IS GOING TO BECOME...
...THE WORLD'S GREATEST MASTER OF THE DIVINE ATTACK!?
HEH HA HA HA HA HA!!!
AM I RIGHT...
...KISSU?
...

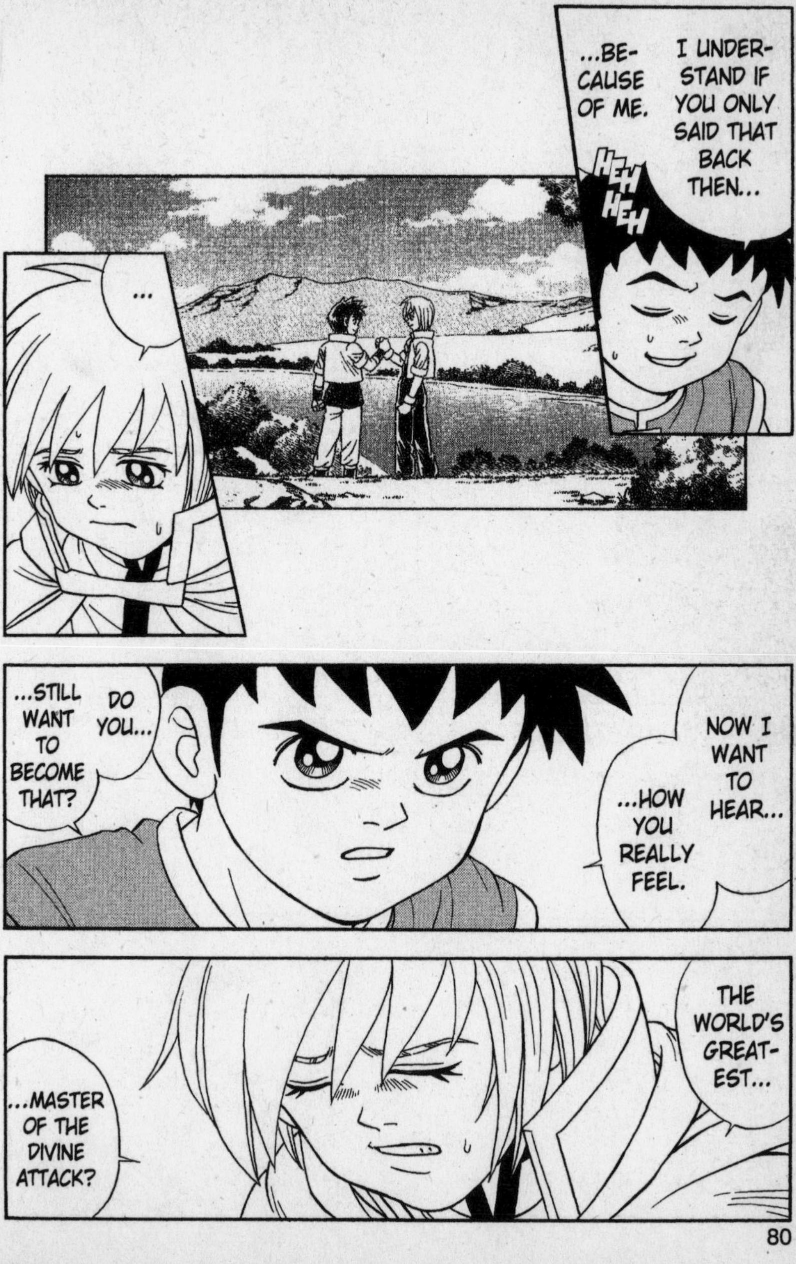
I UNDERSTAND IF YOU ONLY SAID THAT BACK THEN...
...BECAUSE OF ME.
HEH HEH
...
NOW I WANT TO HEAR...
...HOW YOU REALLY FEEL.
DO YOU...
...STILL WANT TO BECOME THAT?
THE WORLD'S GREATEST...
...MASTER OF THE DIVINE ATTACK?

READ THIS WAY

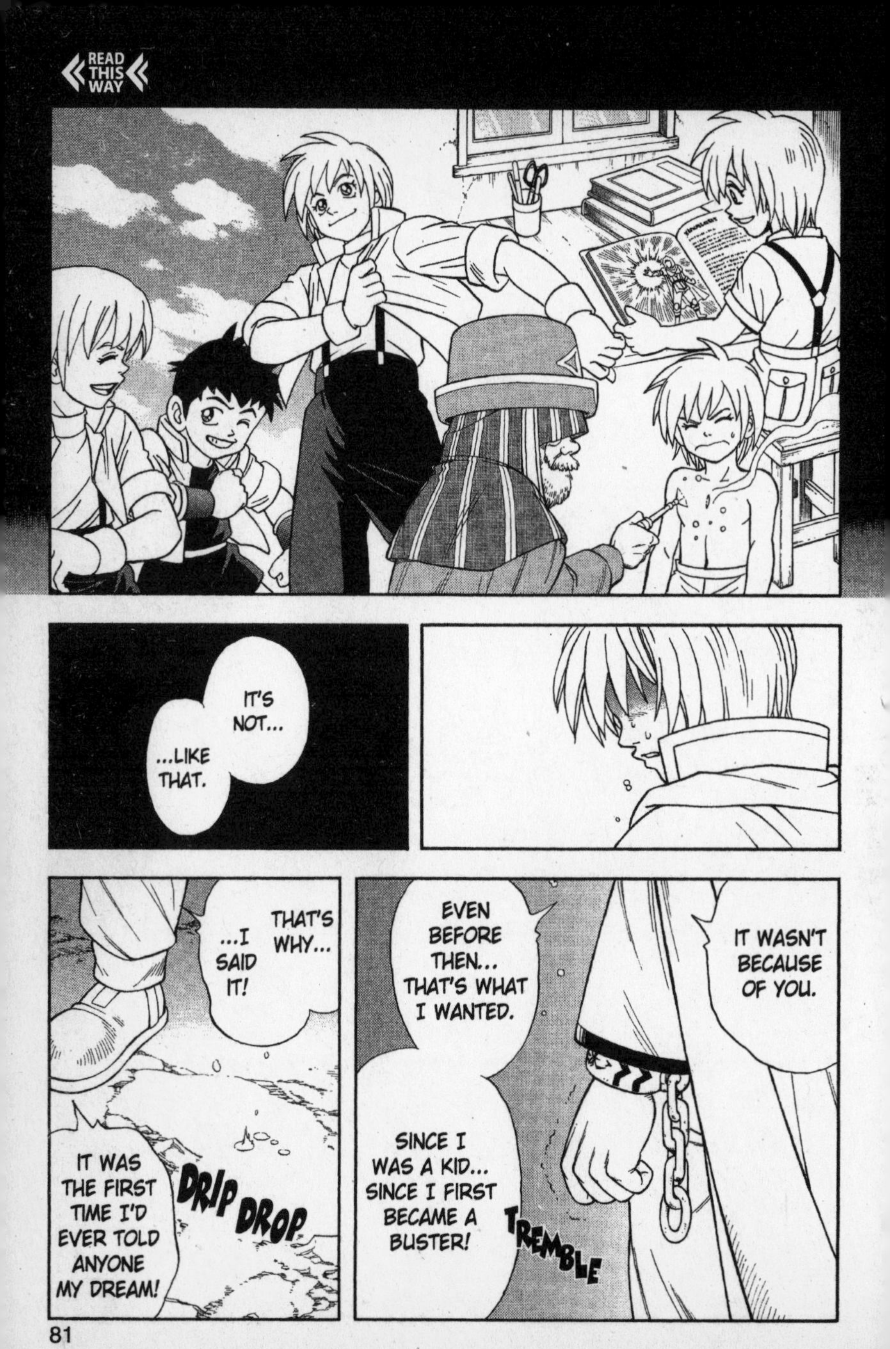
IT'S NOT...
...LIKE THAT.
IT WASN'T BECAUSE OF YOU.
EVEN BEFORE THEN... THAT'S WHAT I WANTED.
SINCE I WAS A KID... SINCE I FIRST BECAME A BUSTER!
TREMBLE
THAT'S WHY...
...I SAID IT!
DRIP DROP
IT WAS THE FIRST TIME I'D EVER TOLD ANYONE MY DREAM!

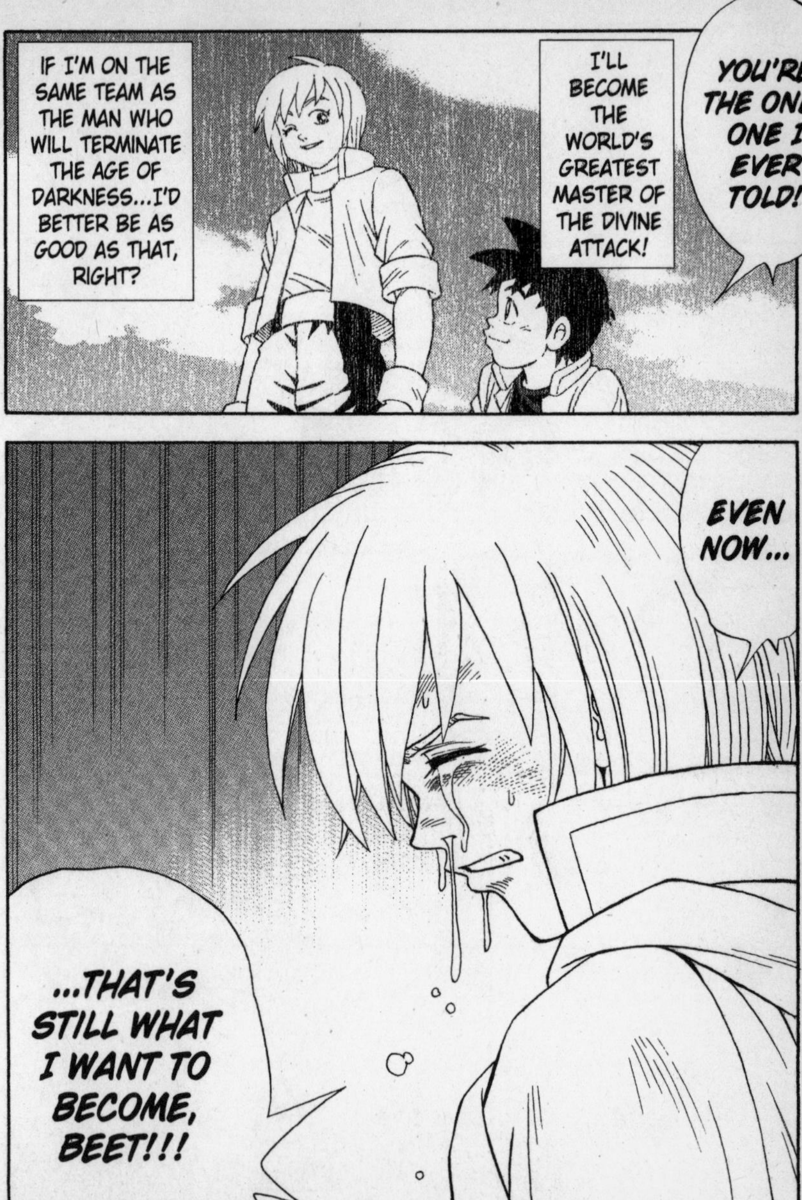
YOU'RE THE ONLY ONE I EVER TOLD!
I'LL BECOME THE WORLD'S GREATEST MASTER OF THE DIVINE ATTACK!
IF I'M ON THE SAME TEAM AS THE MAN WHO WILL TERMINATE THE AGE OF DARKNESS...I'D BETTER BE AS GOOD AS THAT, RIGHT?
EVEN NOW...
...THAT'S STILL WHAT I WANT TO BECOME, BEET!!!

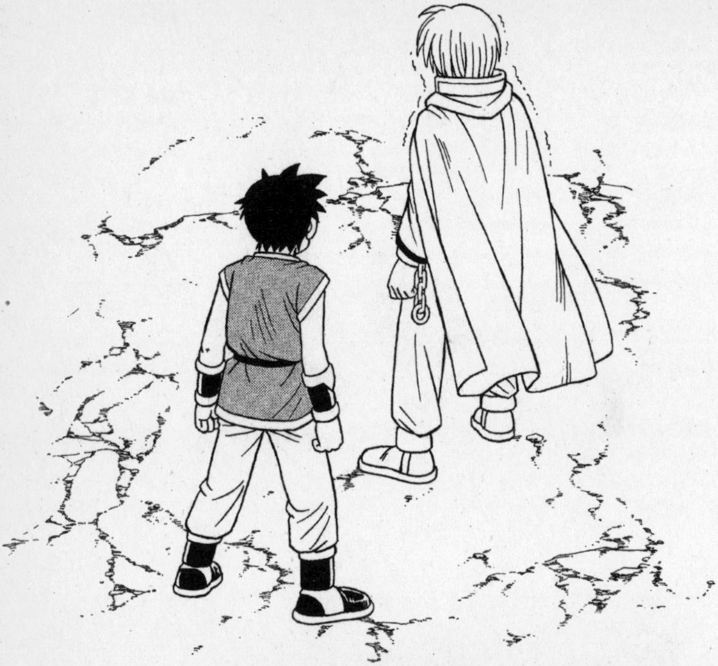

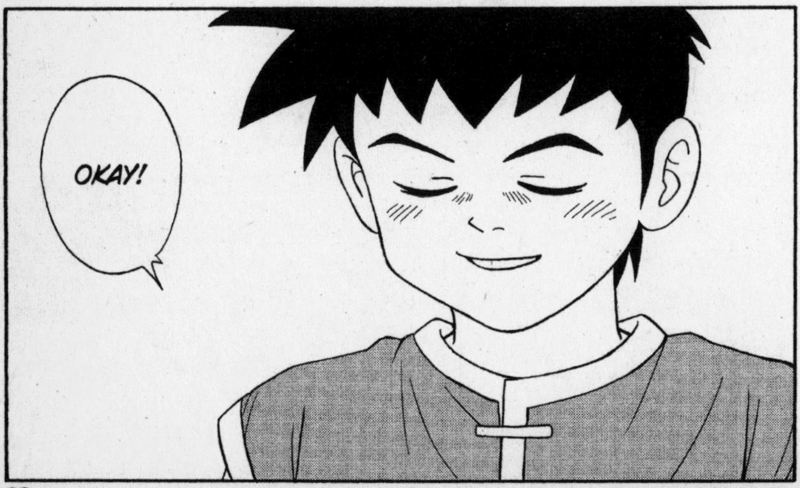
OKAY!

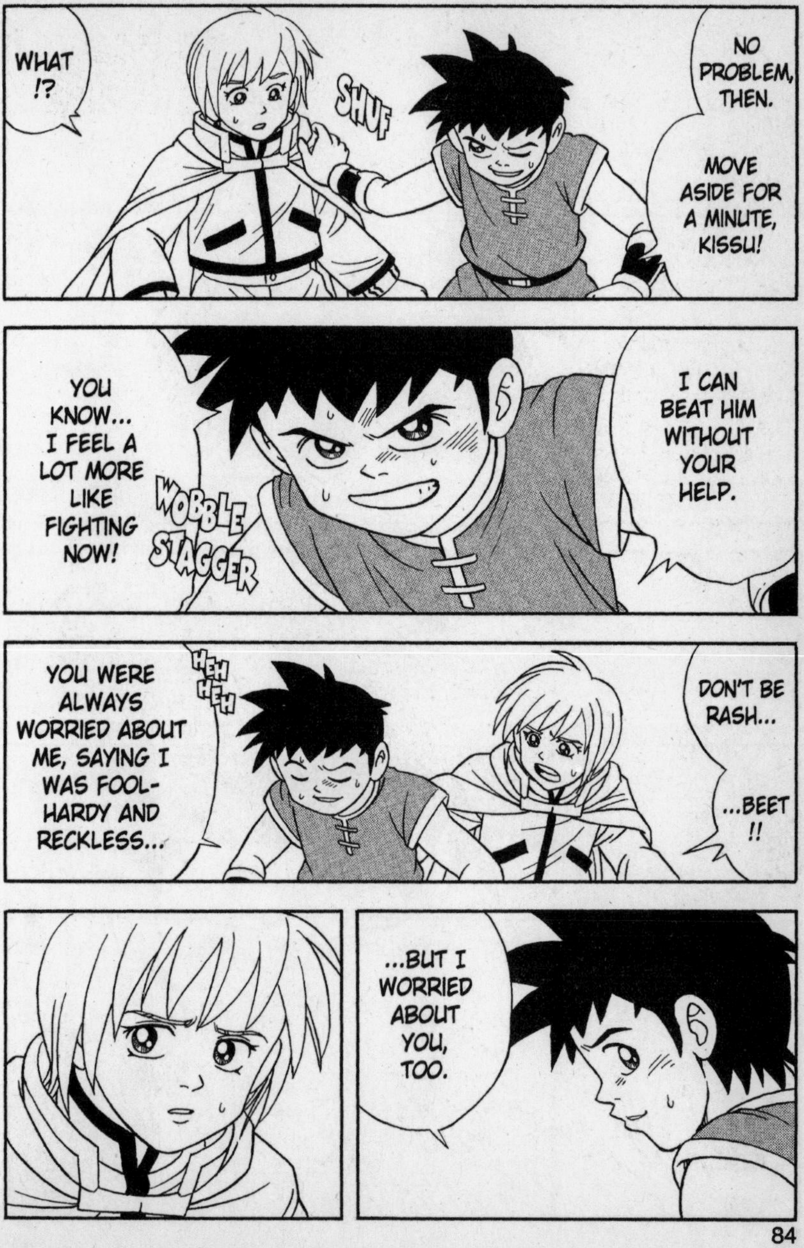
NO PROBLEM, THEN.
MOVE ASIDE FOR A MINUTE, KISSU!
SHUF
WHAT !?
I CAN BEAT HIM WITHOUT YOUR HELP.
WOBBLE STAGGER
YOU KNOW... I FEEL A LOT MORE LIKE FIGHTING NOW!
DON'T BE RASH...
...BEET !!
HEH HEH
YOU WERE ALWAYS WORRIED ABOUT ME, SAYING I WAS FOOL-HARDY AND RECKLESS...
...BUT I WORRIED ABOUT YOU, TOO.

READ THIS WAY

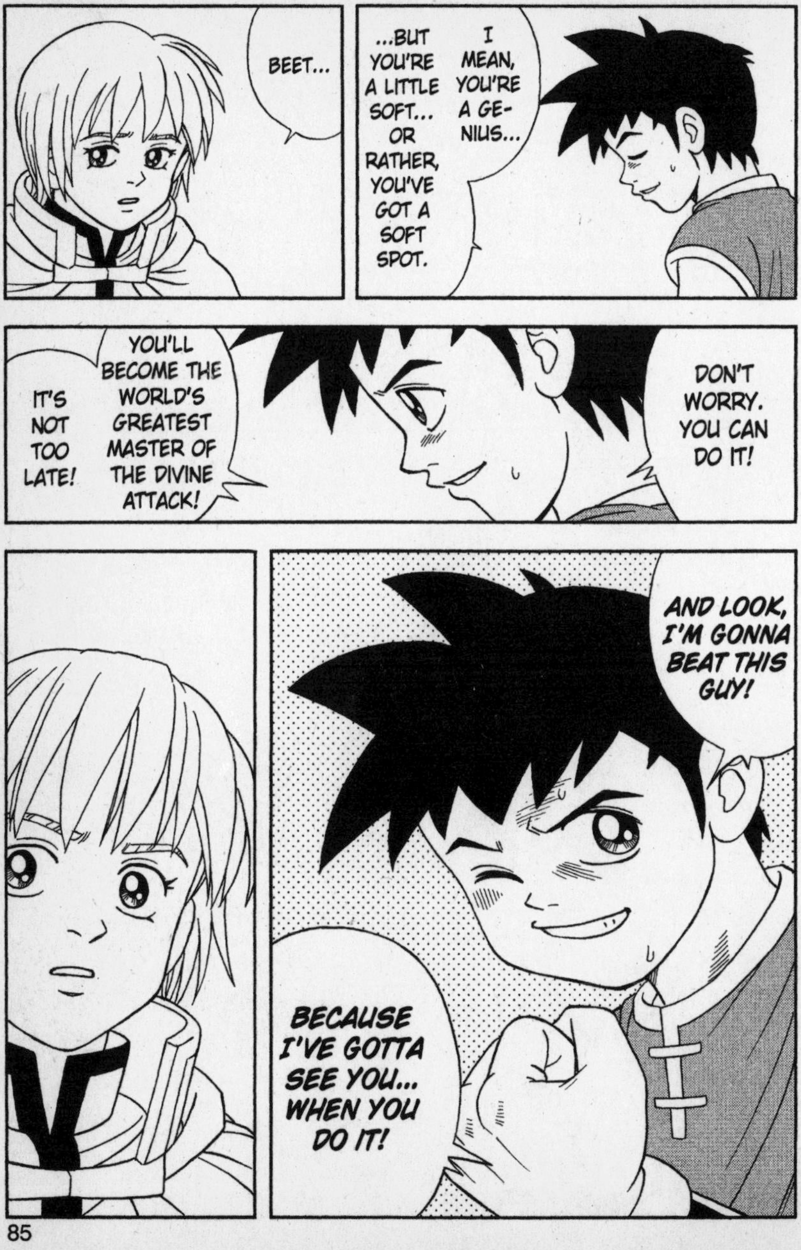
I MEAN, YOU'RE A GE-NIUS...
...BUT YOU'RE A LITTLE SOFT... OR RATHER, YOU'VE GOT A SOFT SPOT.
BEET...
DON'T WORRY. YOU CAN DO IT!
YOU'LL BECOME THE WORLD'S GREATEST MASTER OF THE DIVINE ATTACK!
IT'S NOT TOO LATE!
AND LOOK, I'M GONNA BEAT THIS GUY!
BECAUSE I'VE GOTTA SEE YOU... WHEN YOU DO IT!

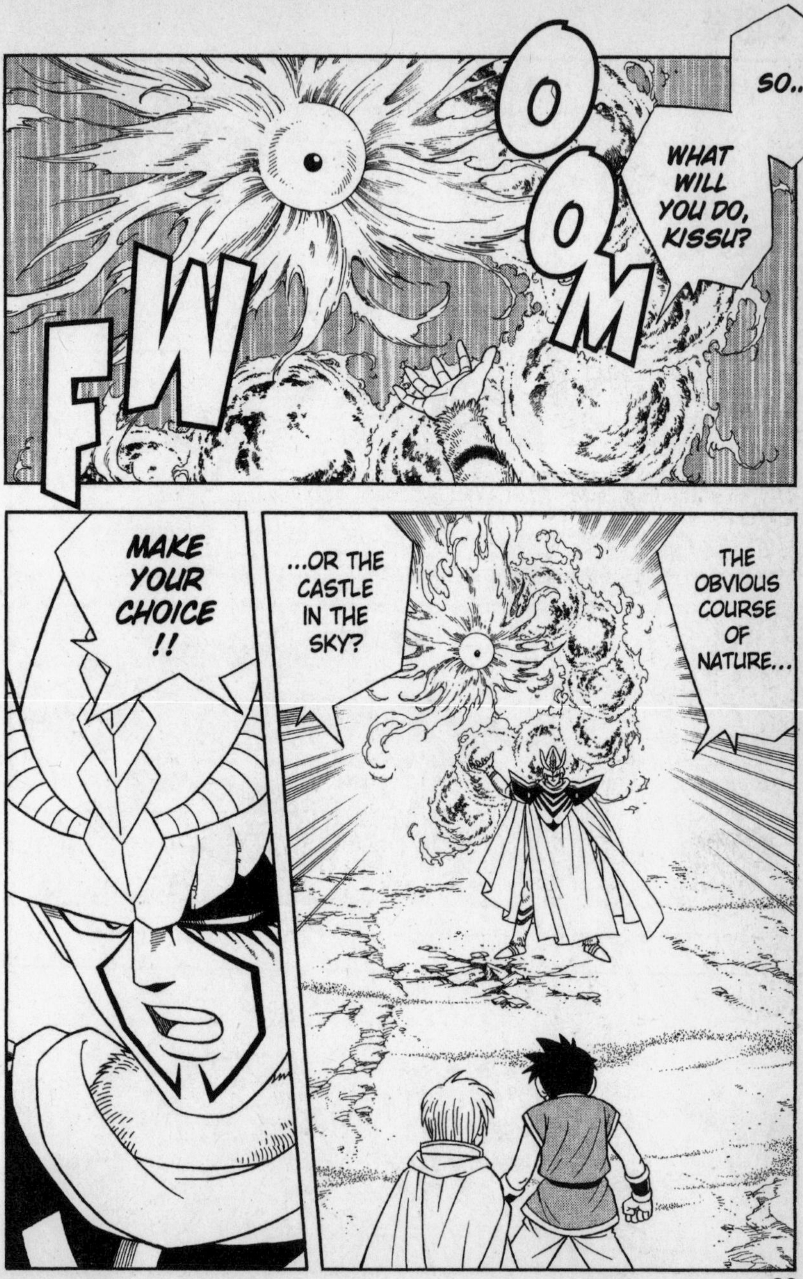
SO...
WHAT WILL YOU DO, KISSU?
FWOOM
THE OBVIOUS COURSE OF NATURE...
...OR THE CASTLE IN THE SKY?
MAKE YOUR CHOICE !!

READ THIS WAY

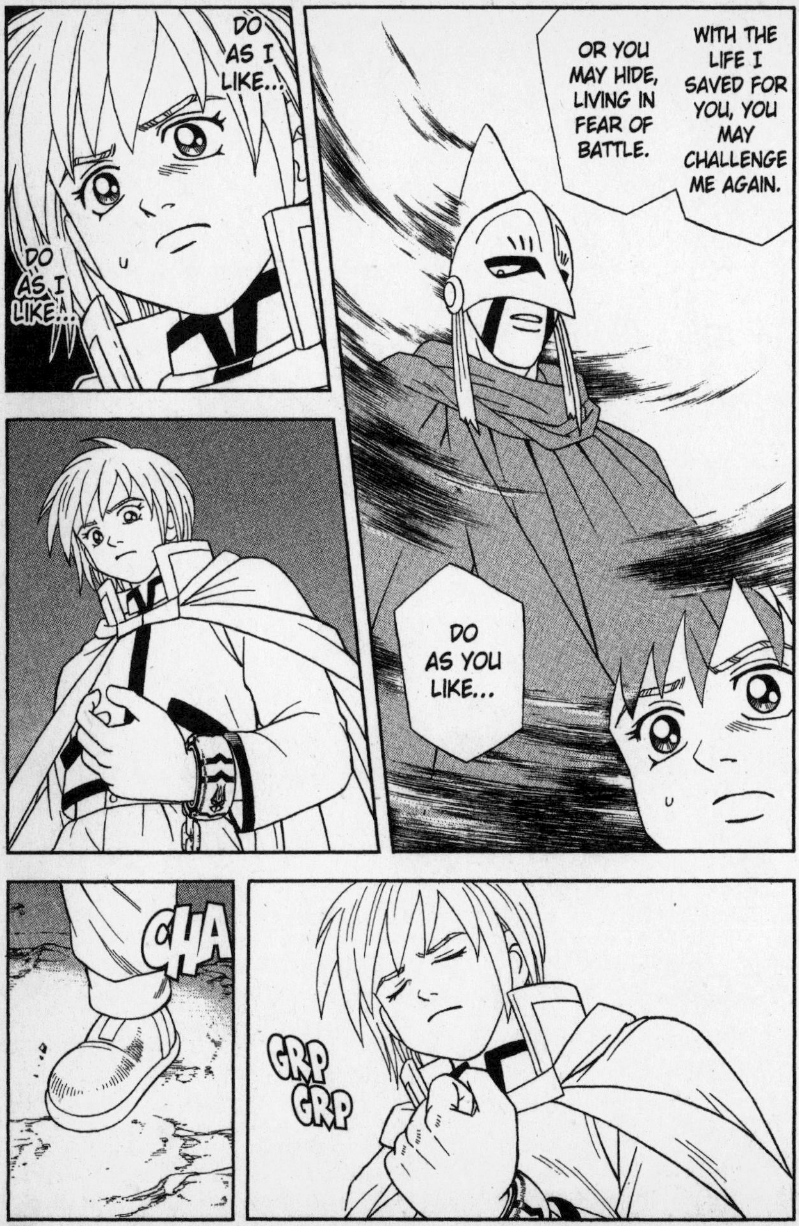
WITH THE LIFE I SAVED FOR YOU, YOU MAY CHALLENGE ME AGAIN.
OR YOU MAY HIDE, LIVING IN FEAR OF BATTLE.
DO AS YOU LIKE...
DO AS I LIKE...
DO AS I LIKE...
GRP GRP
CHA

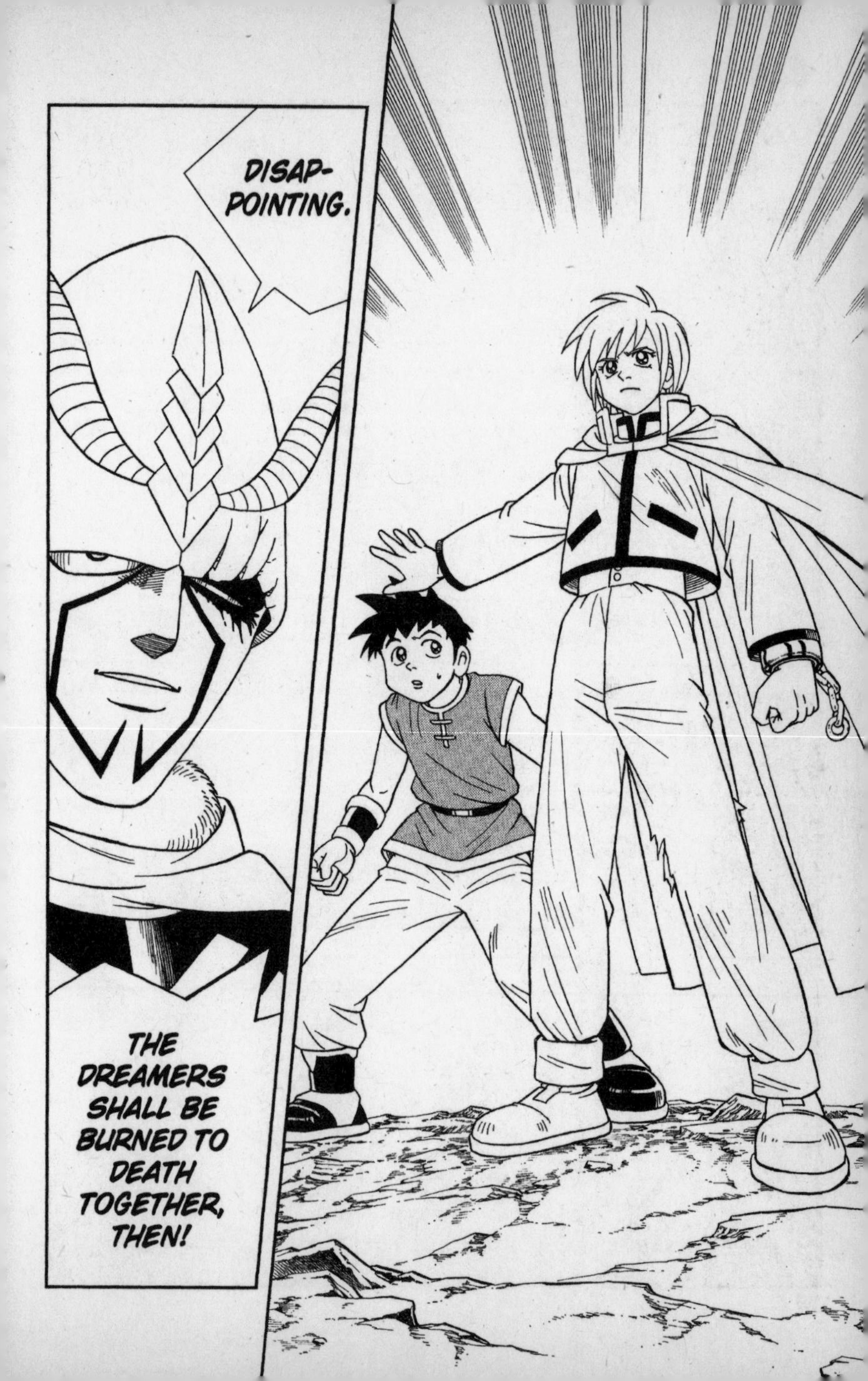
DISAP-POINTING.
THE DREAMERS SHALL BE BURNED TO DEATH TOGETHER, THEN!

READ THIS WAY

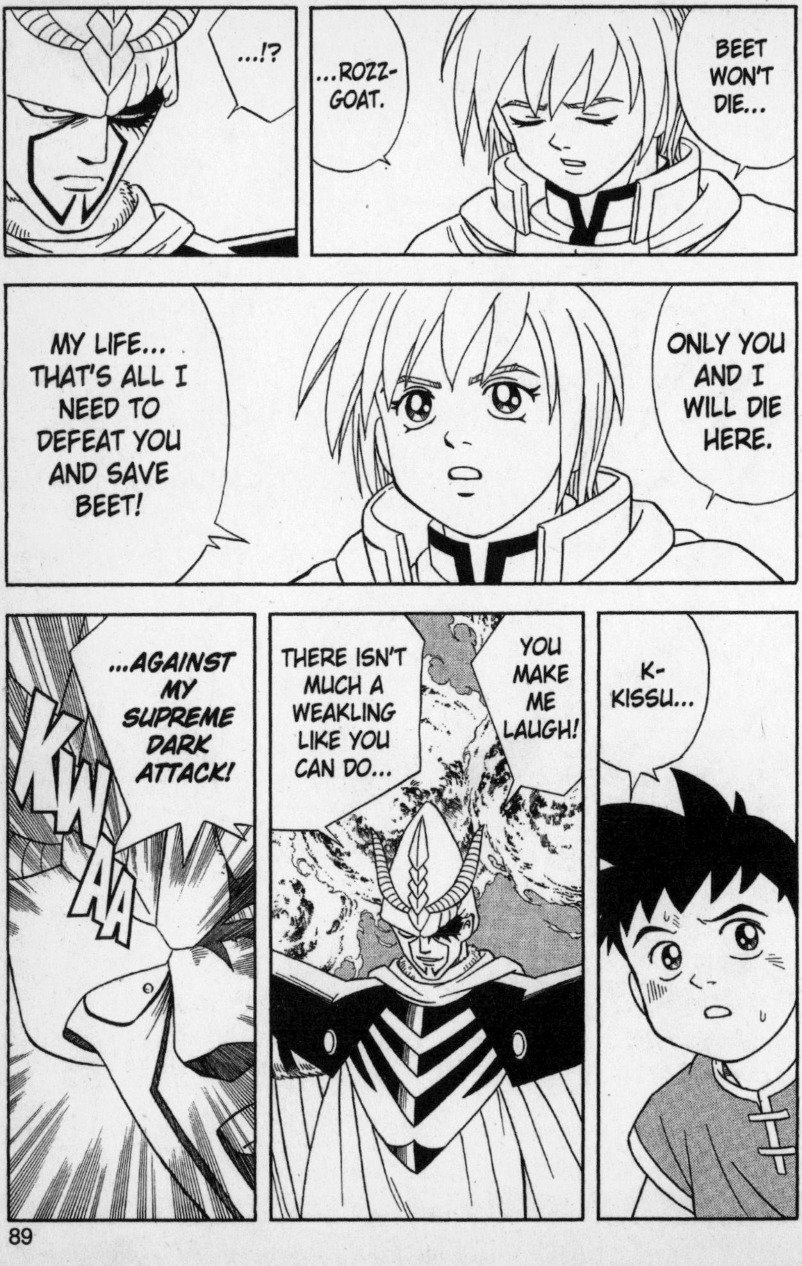

BEET WON'T DIE...
...ROZZ-GOAT.
...!?
ONLY YOU AND I WILL DIE HERE.
MY LIFE... THAT'S ALL I NEED TO DEFEAT YOU AND SAVE BEET!
K-KISSU...
YOU MAKE ME LAUGH!
THERE ISN'T MUCH A WEAKLING LIKE YOU CAN DO...
...AGAINST MY SUPREME DARK ATTACK!
KWAA

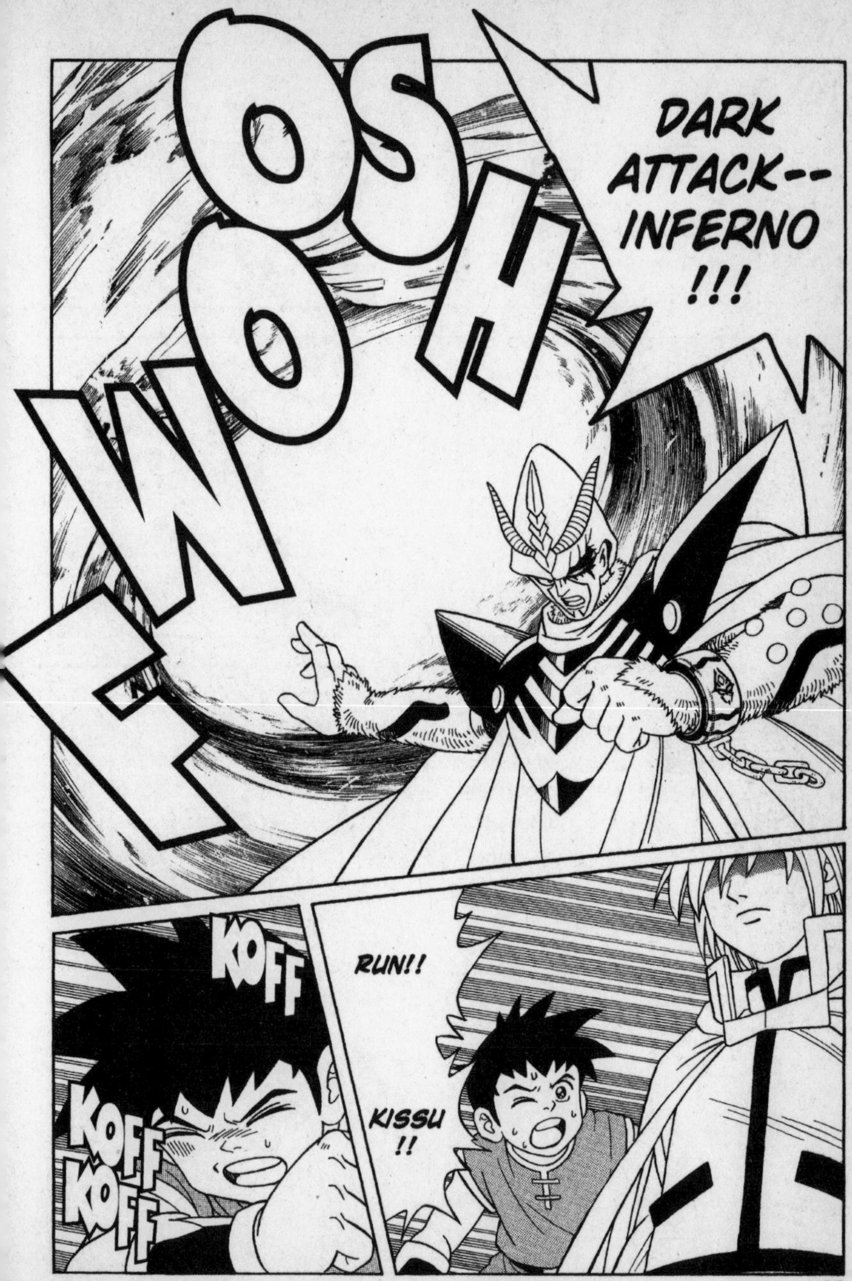
DARK ATTACK-- INFERNO !!!
WOOSH
RUN!!
KISSU !!
KOFF
KOFF KOFF

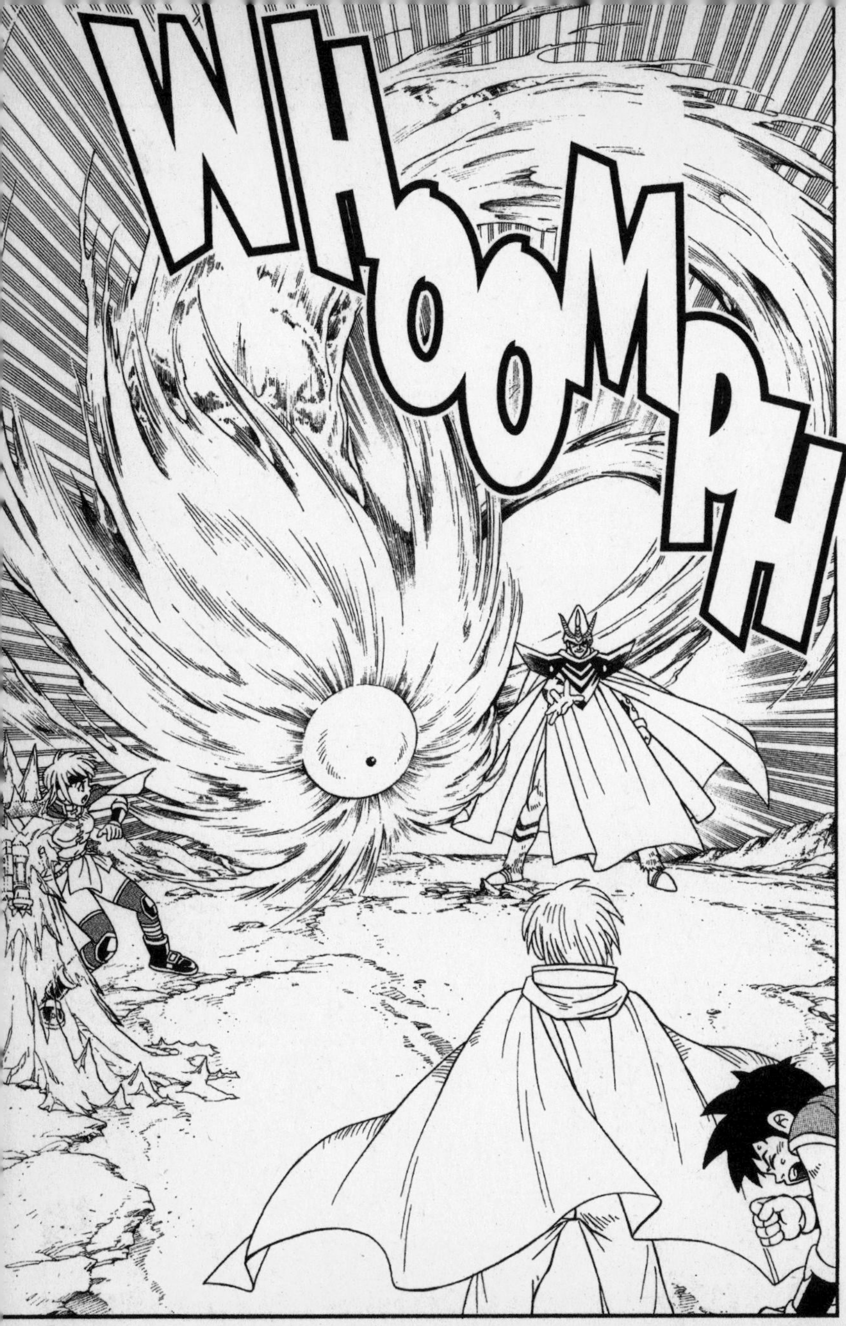
WHOOMPH

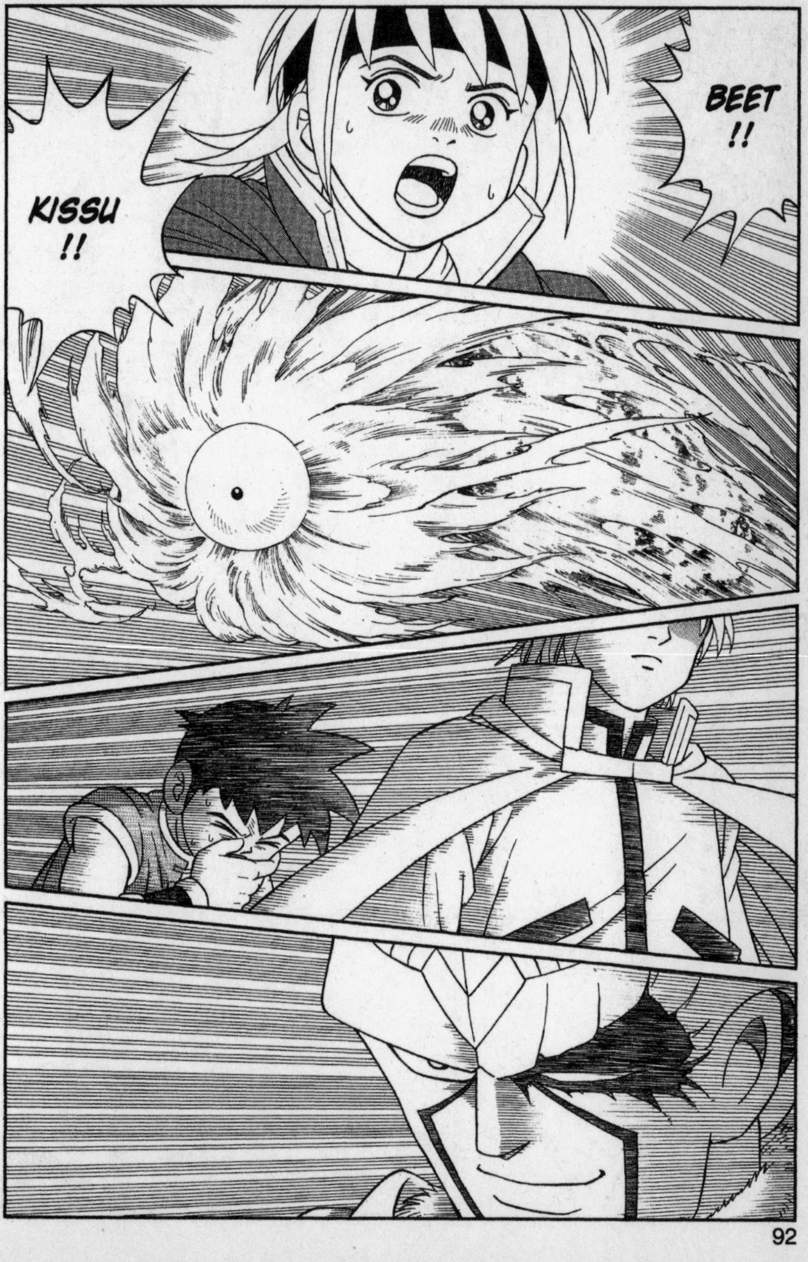
BEET !!
KISSU !!

READ THIS WAY

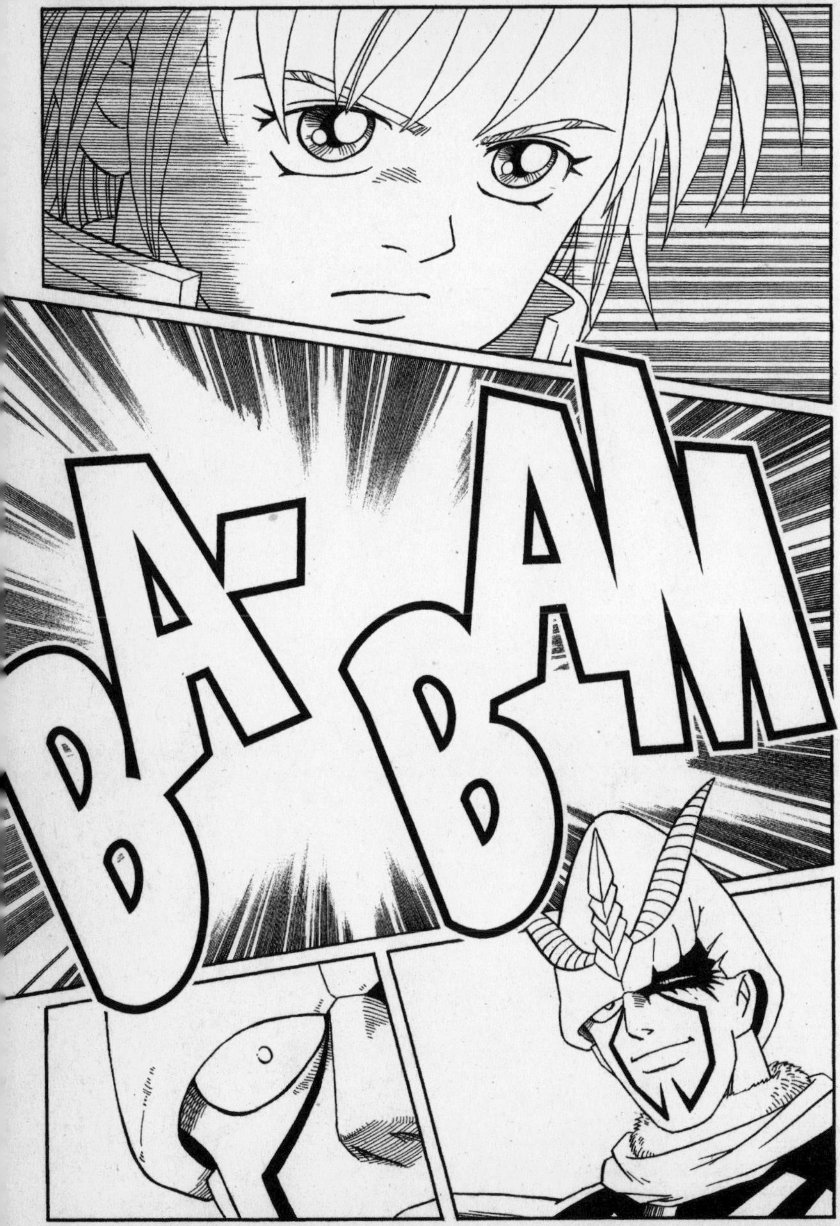
BA-BAM

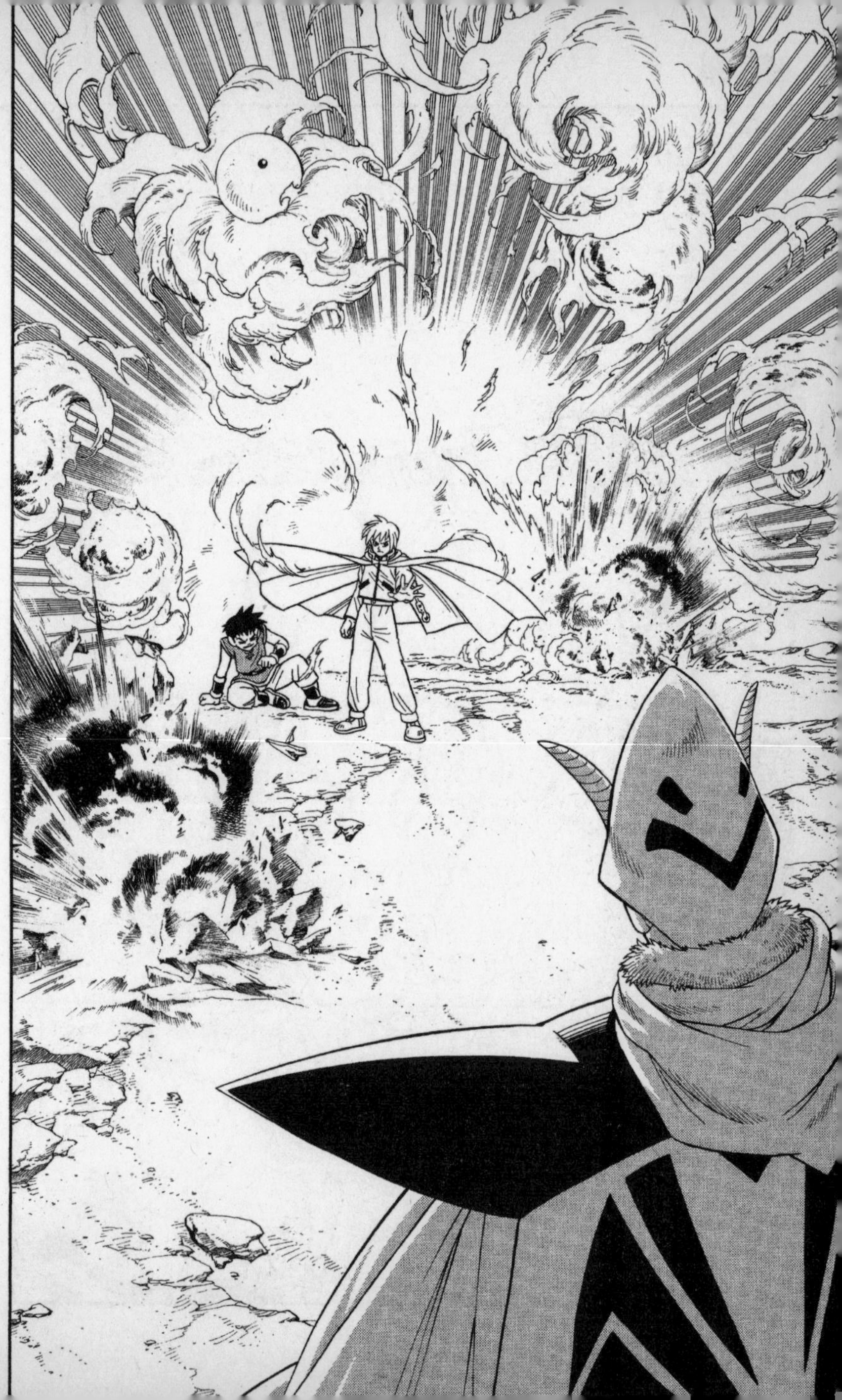

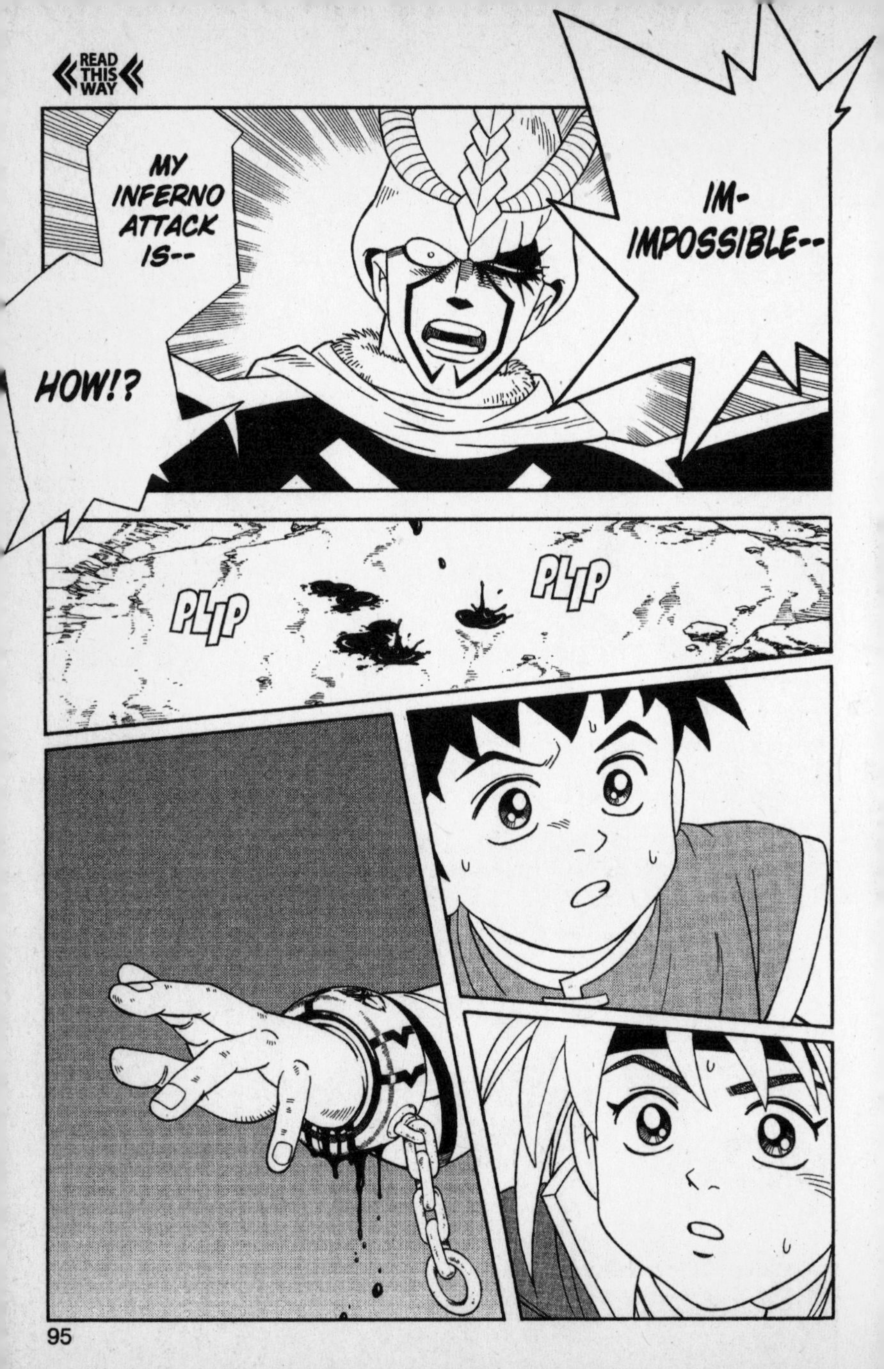
IM-IMPOSSIBLE--
MY INFERNO ATTACK IS--
HOW!?
PLIP
PLIP

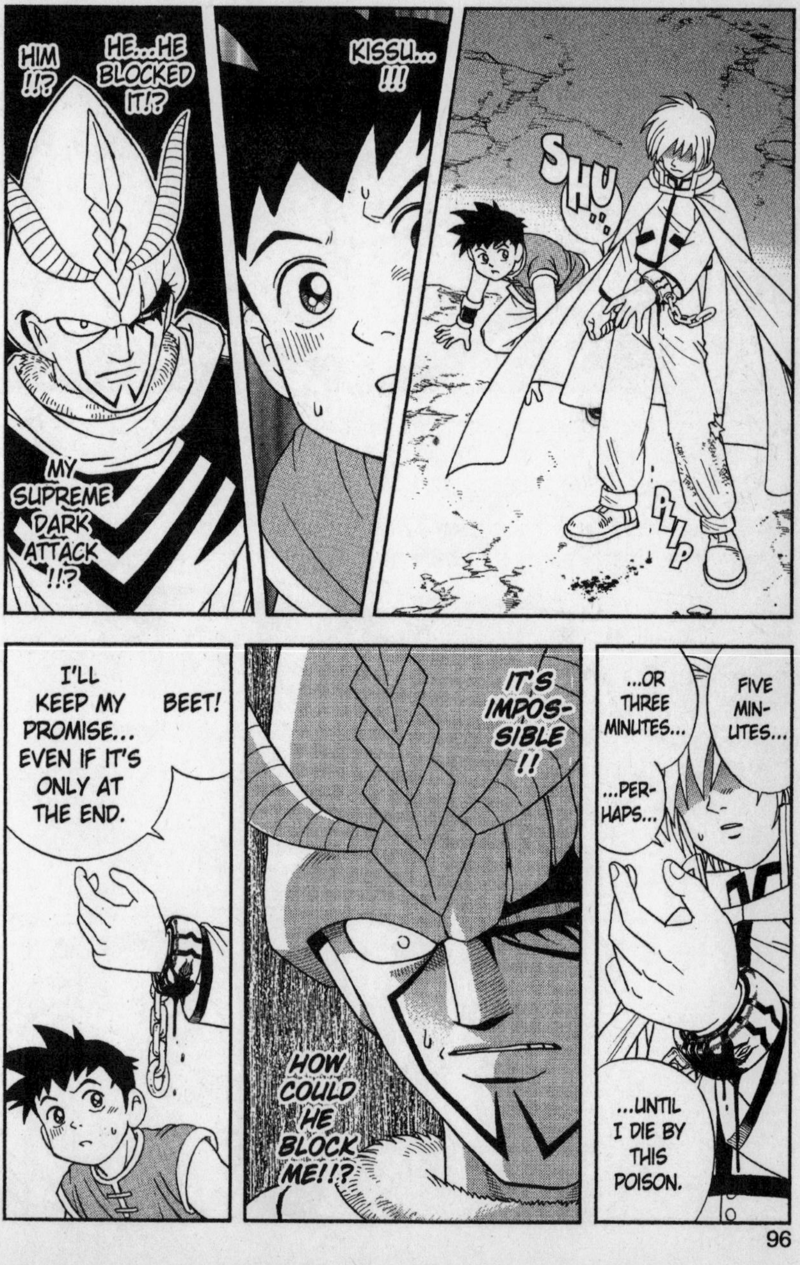
SHU...
PLIP
KISSU... !!!
HE...HE BLOCKED IT!?
HIM!!?
MY SUPREME DARK ATTACK!!?
FIVE MINUTES...
...OR THREE MINUTES...
...PERHAPS...
...UNTIL I DIE BY THIS POISON.
IT'S IMPOSSIBLE!!
HOW COULD HE BLOCK ME!!?
BEET!
I'LL KEEP MY PROMISE... EVEN IF IT'S ONLY AT THE END.

READ THIS WAY

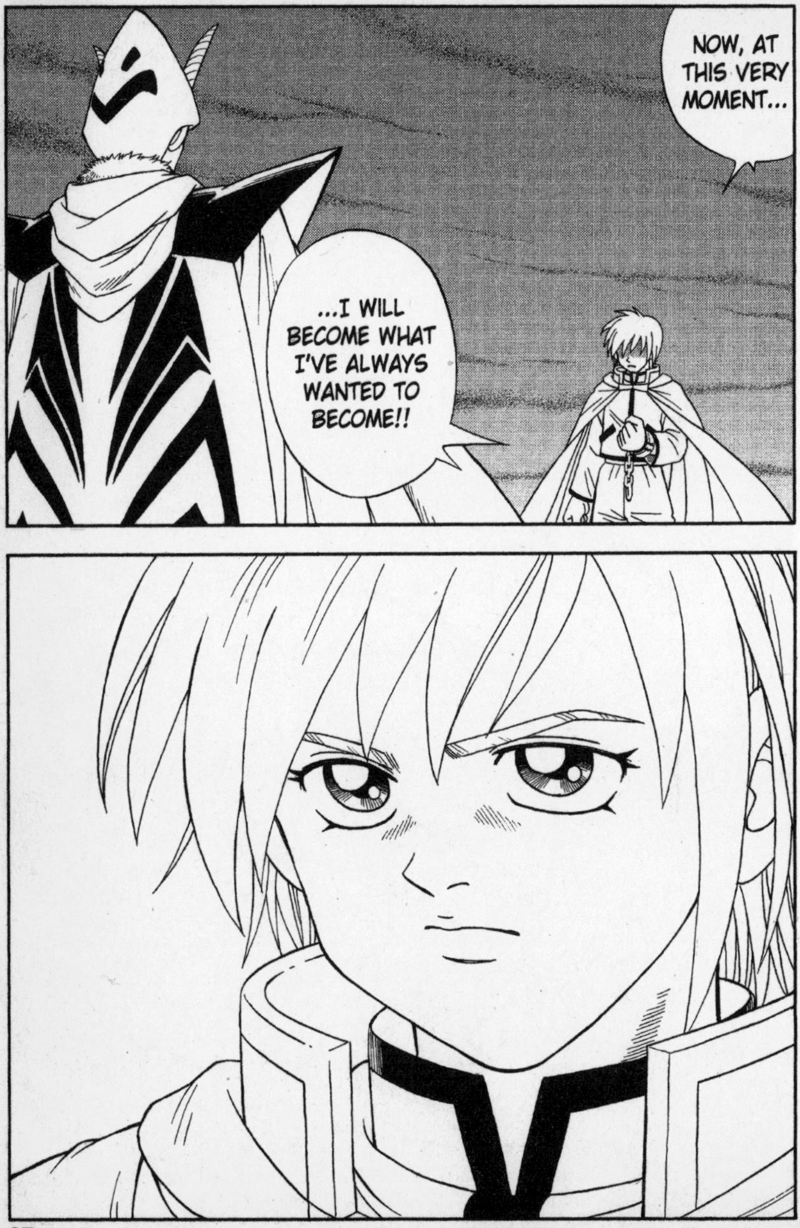
NOW, AT THIS VERY MOMENT...
...I WILL BECOME WHAT I'VE ALWAYS WANTED TO BECOME!!

BEET
THE VANDEL BUSTER

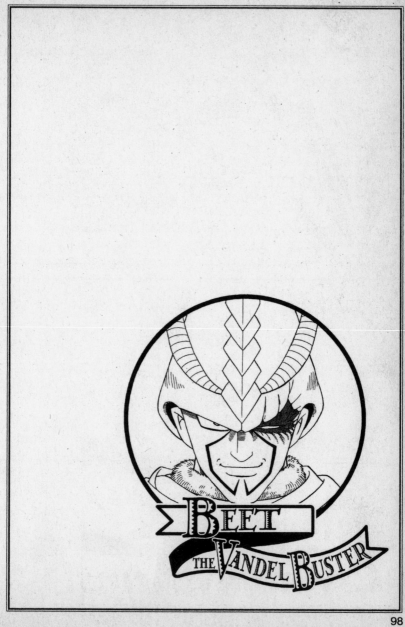

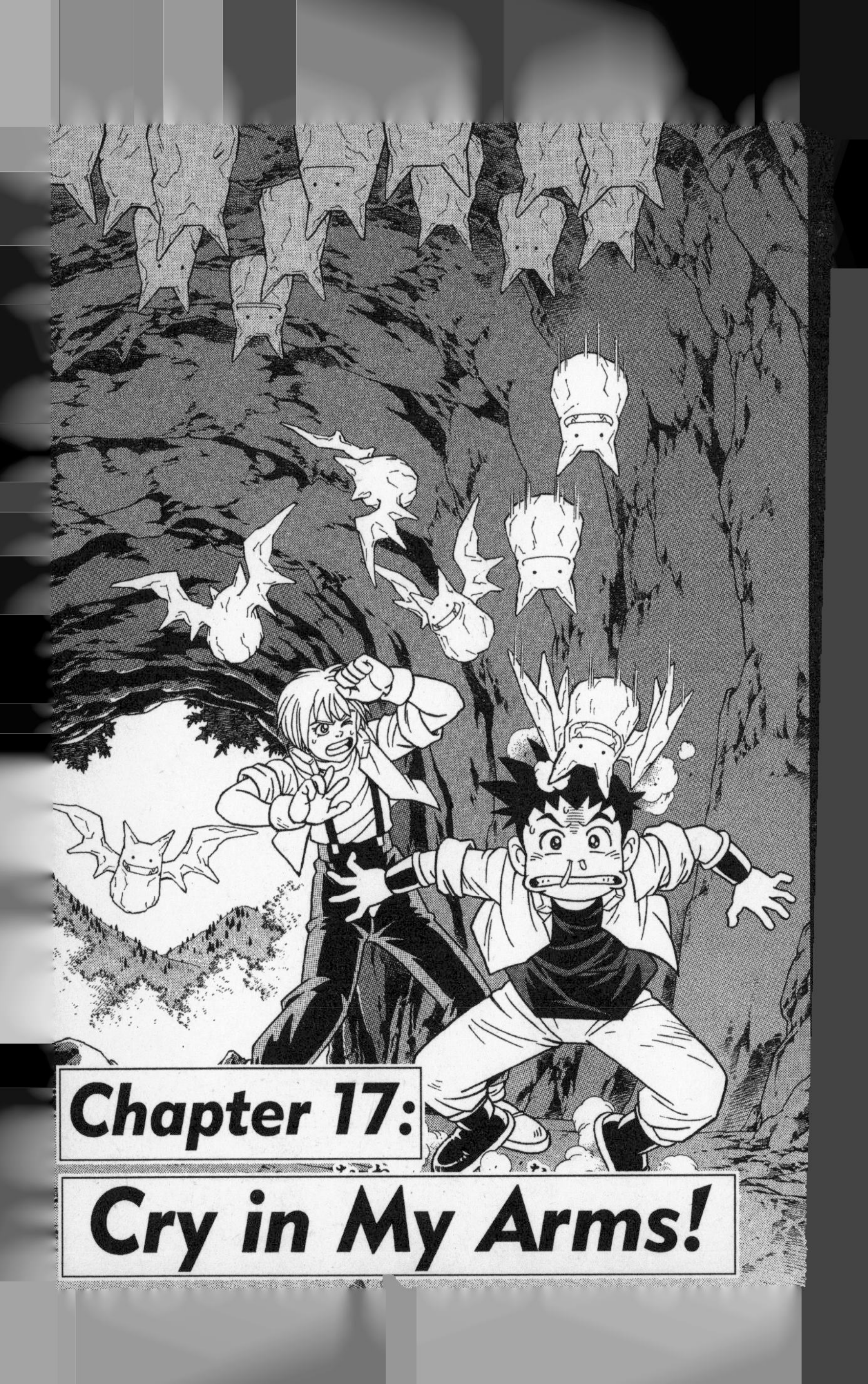
Chapter 17:
Cry in My Arms!

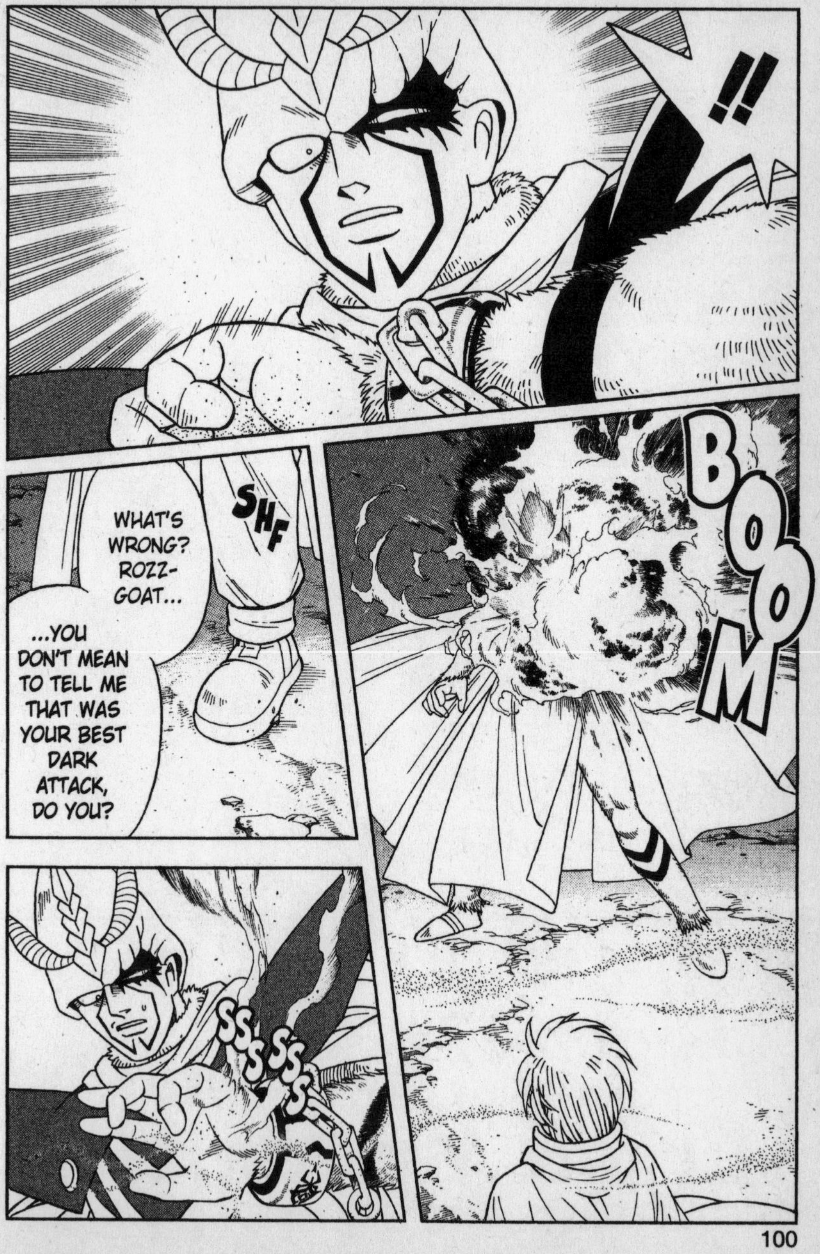
!!
BOOM
SHF
WHAT'S WRONG? ROZZ-GOAT...
...YOU DON'T MEAN TO TELL ME THAT WAS YOUR BEST DARK ATTACK, DO YOU?
SSSSSS

READ THIS WAY

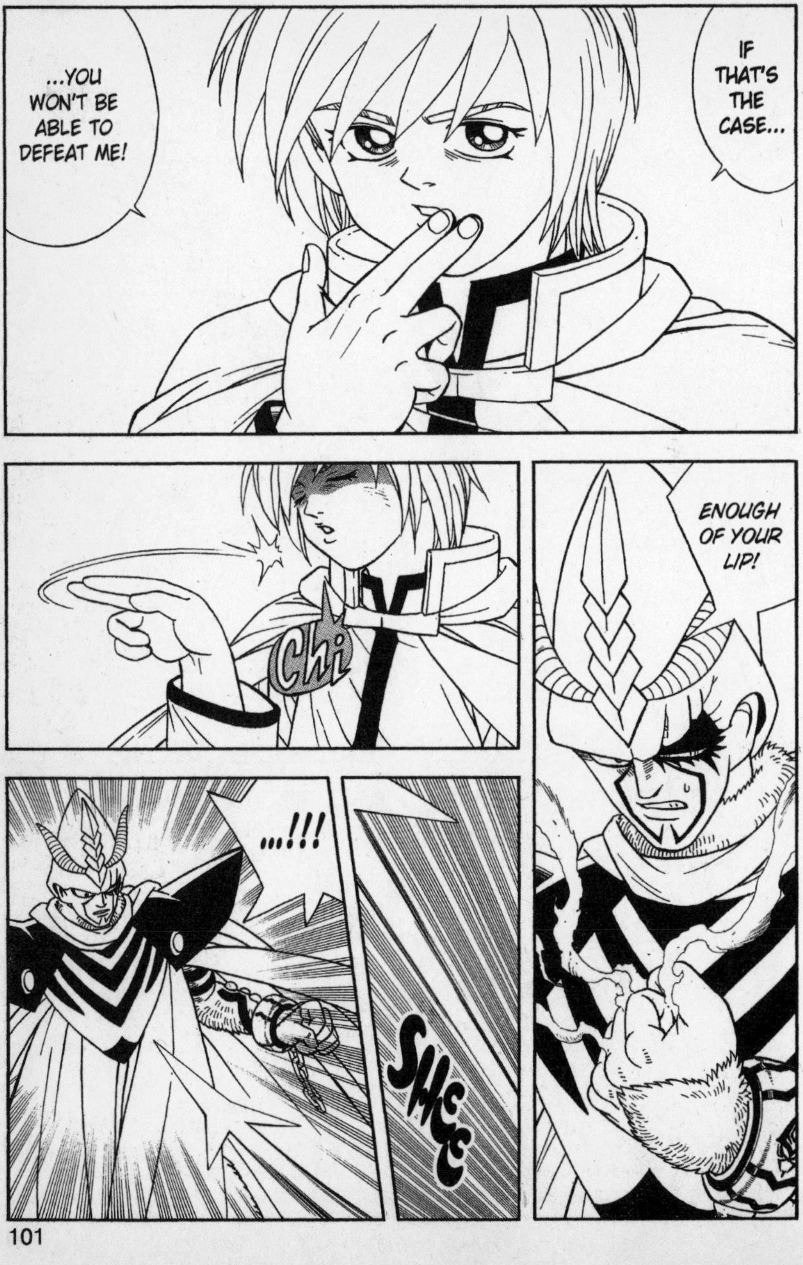
IF THAT'S THE CASE...
...YOU WON'T BE ABLE TO DEFEAT ME!
ENOUGH OF YOUR LIP!
Chi
SHEE
...!!!

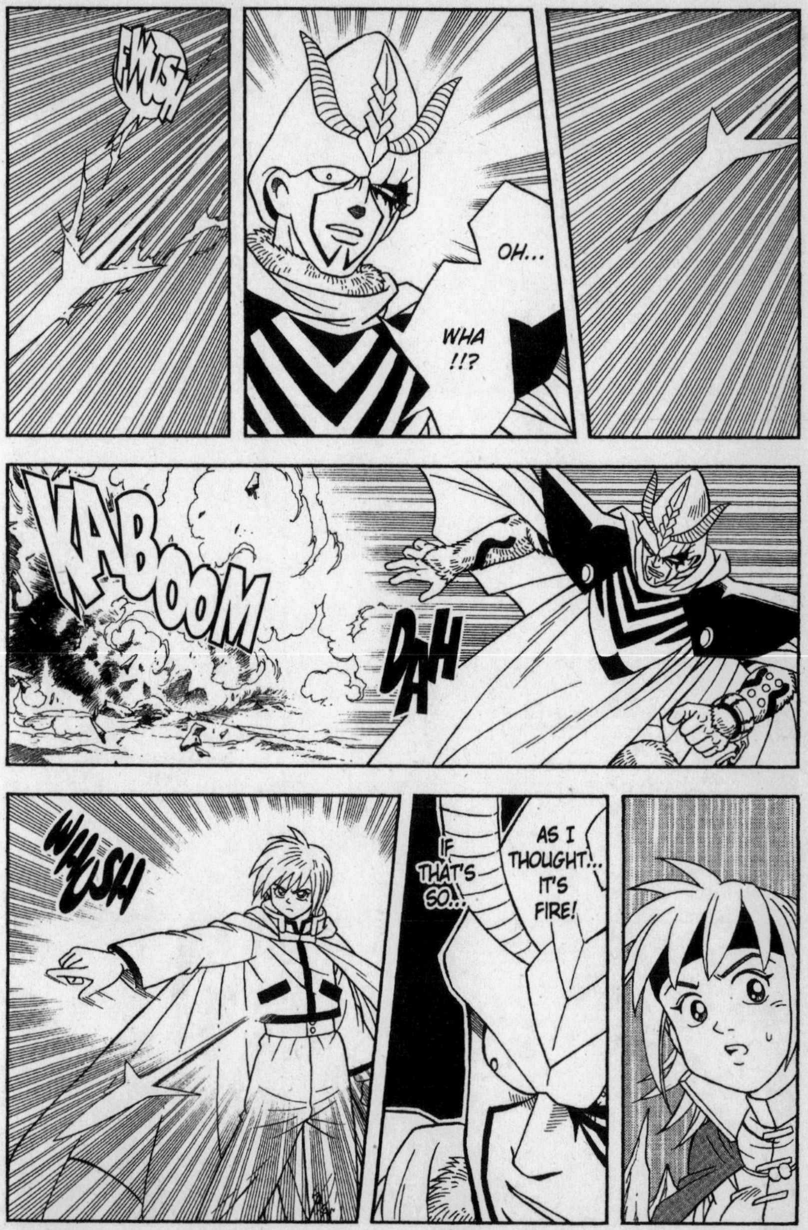
OH...
WHA !!?
FWUSH
DAH
KABOOM
AS I THOUGHT... IT'S FIRE!
IF THAT'S SO...
WHUSH

READ THIS WAY

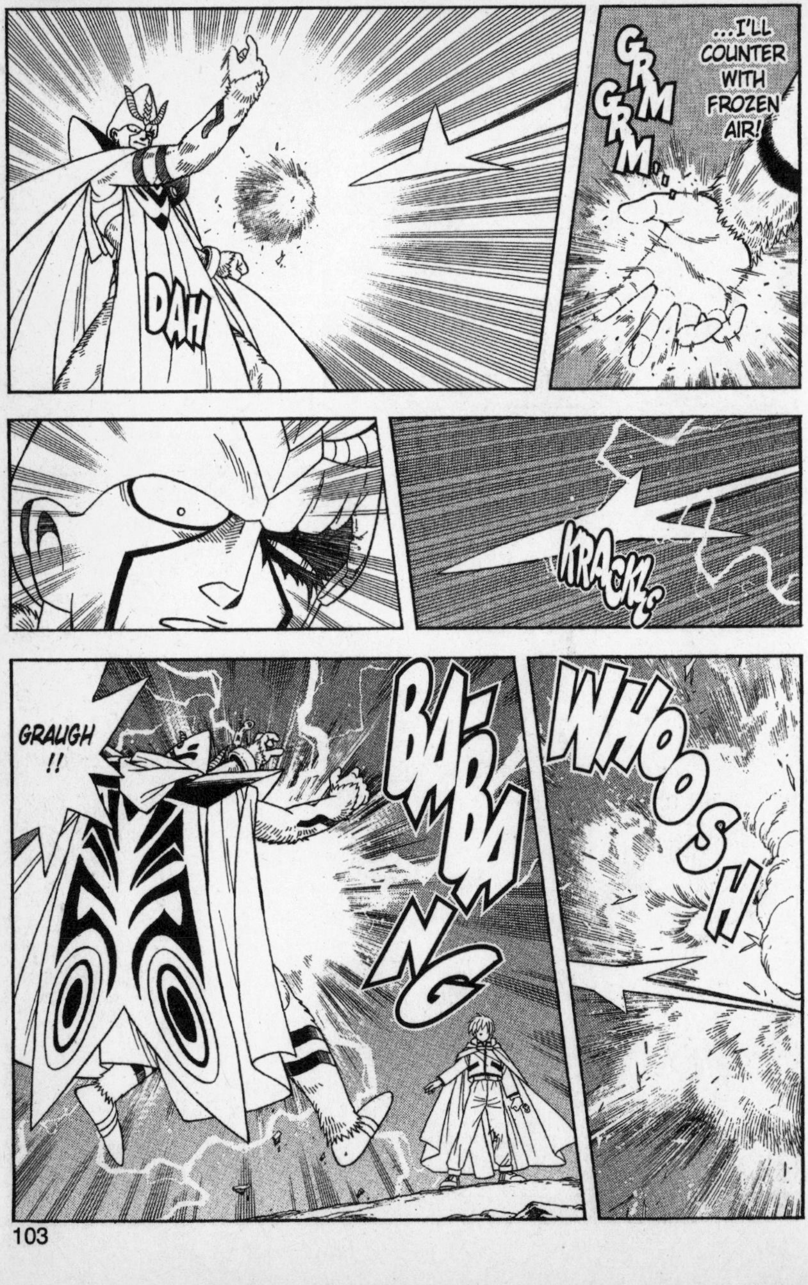
GRM GRM
...I'LL COUNTER WITH FROZEN AIR!
DAH
KRACKLE
WHOOSH
BA-BA-BANG
GRAUGH !!

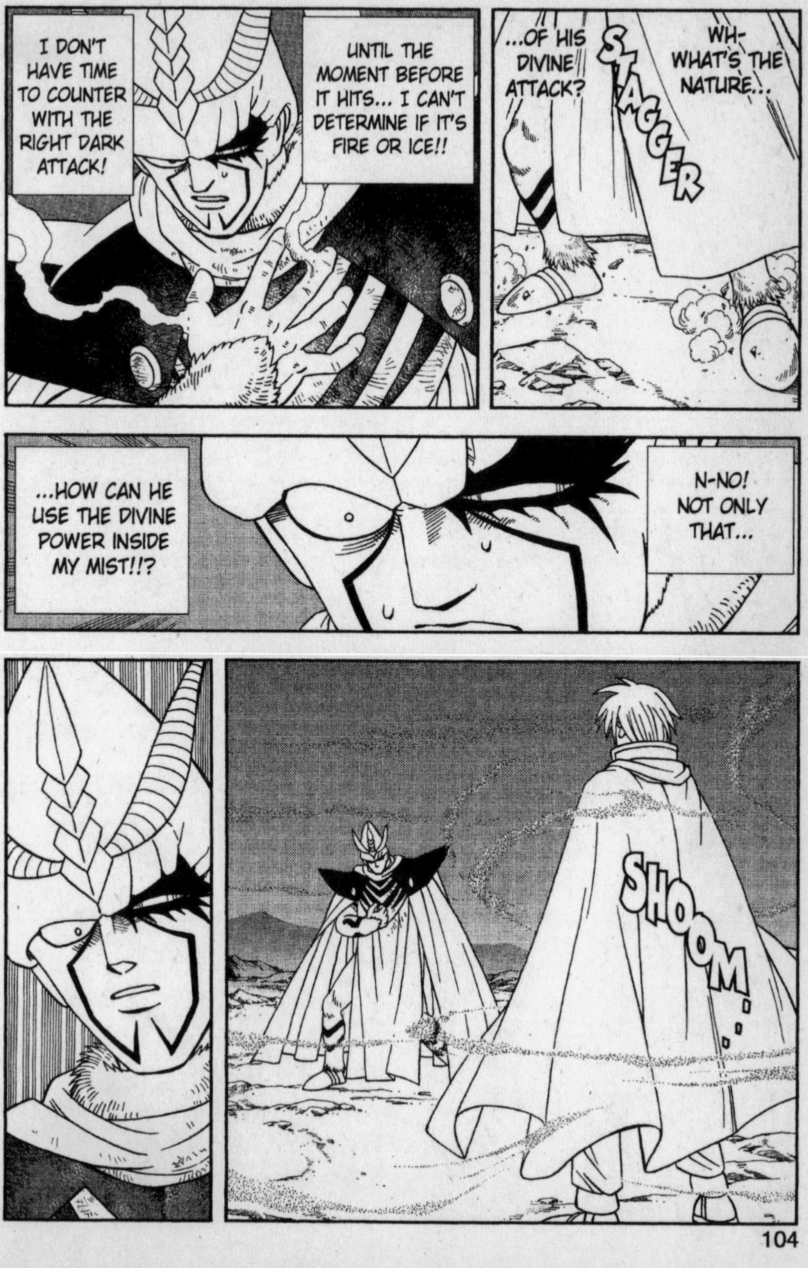
WH- WHAT'S THE NATURE...
...OF HIS DIVINE ATTACK?
STAGGER
UNTIL THE MOMENT BEFORE IT HITS... I CAN'T DETERMINE IF IT'S FIRE OR ICE!!
I DON'T HAVE TIME TO COUNTER WITH THE RIGHT DARK ATTACK!
N-NO! NOT ONLY THAT...
...HOW CAN HE USE THE DIVINE POWER INSIDE MY MIST!!?
SHOOM...

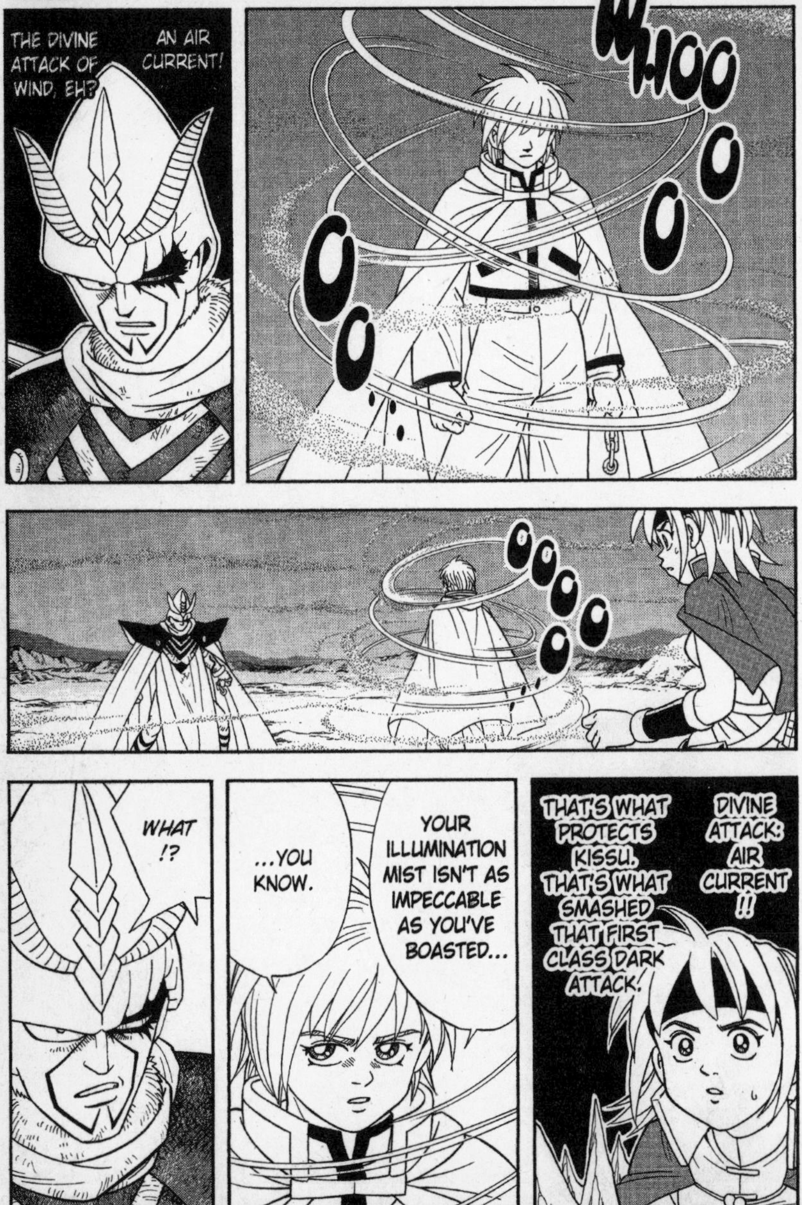
WHOOOOOO...
AN AIR CURRENT!
THE DIVINE ATTACK OF WIND, EH?
OOOOOO...
DIVINE ATTACK: AIR CURRENT !!
THAT'S WHAT PROTECTS KISSU. THAT'S WHAT SMASHED THAT FIRST CLASS DARK ATTACK.
YOUR ILLUMINATION MIST ISN'T AS IMPECCABLE AS YOU'VE BOASTED...
...YOU KNOW.
WHAT !?

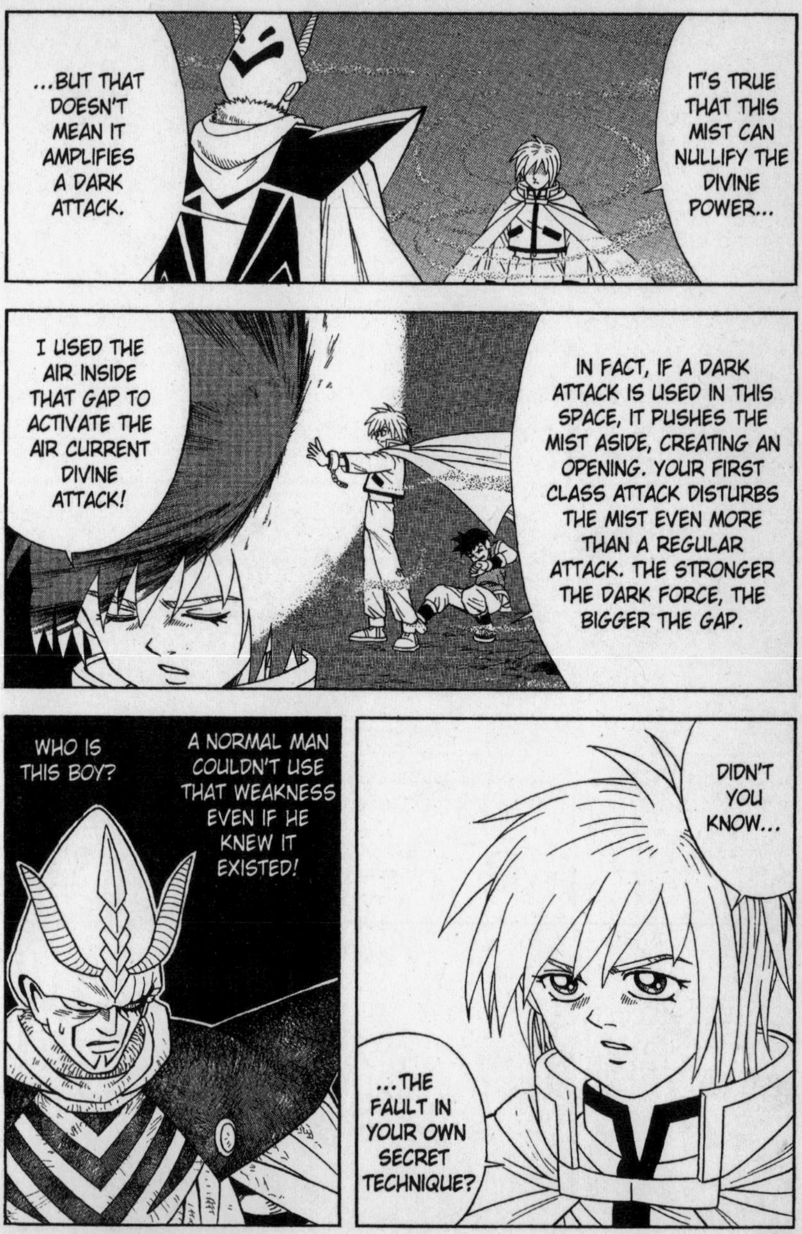
IT'S TRUE THAT THIS MIST CAN NULLIFY THE DIVINE POWER...
...BUT THAT DOESN'T MEAN IT AMPLIFIES A DARK ATTACK.
IN FACT, IF A DARK ATTACK IS USED IN THIS SPACE, IT PUSHES THE MIST ASIDE, CREATING AN OPENING. YOUR FIRST CLASS ATTACK DISTURBS THE MIST EVEN MORE THAN A REGULAR ATTACK. THE STRONGER THE DARK FORCE, THE BIGGER THE GAP.
I USED THE AIR INSIDE THAT GAP TO ACTIVATE THE AIR CURRENT DIVINE ATTACK!
DIDN'T YOU KNOW...
...THE FAULT IN YOUR OWN SECRET TECHNIQUE?
A NORMAL MAN COULDN'T USE THAT WEAKNESS EVEN IF HE KNEW IT EXISTED!
WHO IS THIS BOY?

READ THIS WAY

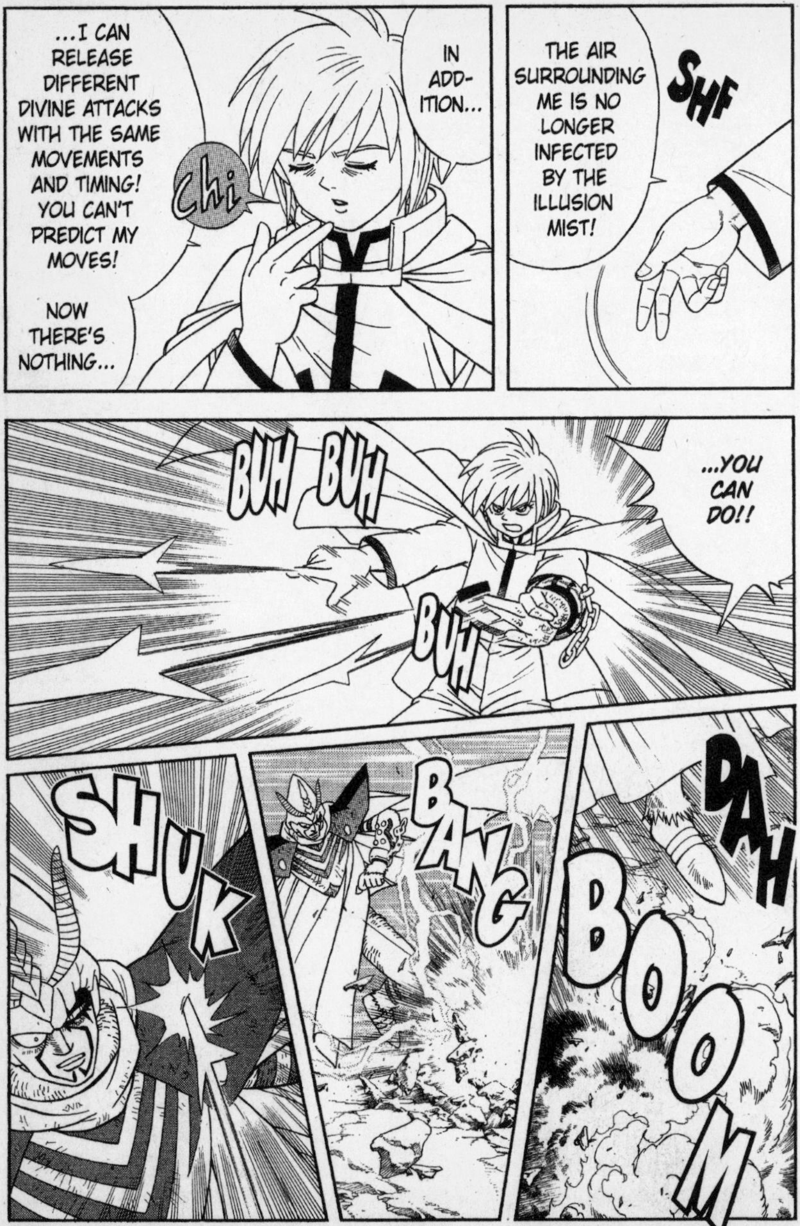

THE AIR SURROUNDING ME IS NO LONGER INFECTED BY THE ILLUSION MIST!
SHF
IN ADDITION...
...I CAN RELEASE DIFFERENT DIVINE ATTACKS WITH THE SAME MOVEMENTS AND TIMING! YOU CAN'T PREDICT MY MOVES!
Chi
NOW THERE'S NOTHING...
...YOU CAN DO!!
BUH BUH
BUH
DAH
BOOM
BANG
SHUK

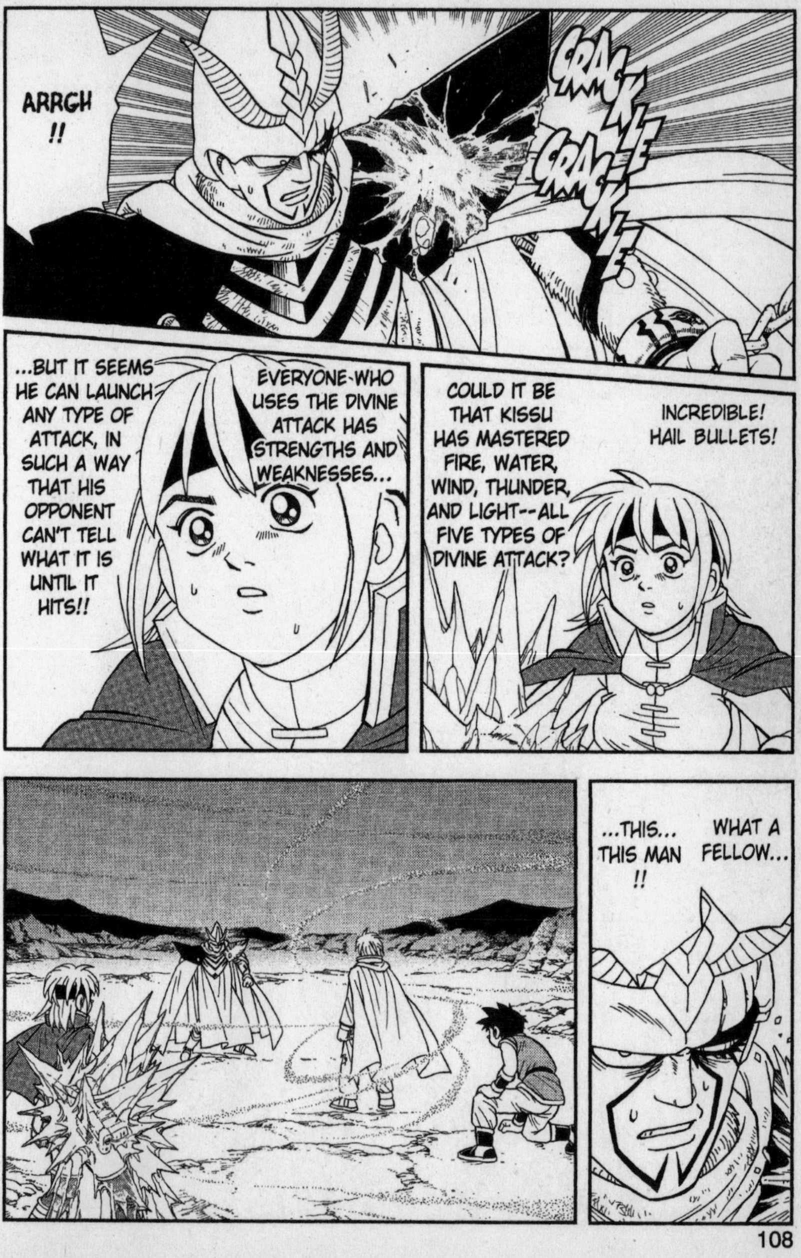
CRACKLE CRACKLE
ARRGH!!
INCREDIBLE! HAIL BULLETS!
COULD IT BE THAT KISSU HAS MASTERED FIRE, WATER, WIND, THUNDER, AND LIGHT--ALL FIVE TYPES OF DIVINE ATTACK?
EVERYONE WHO USES THE DIVINE ATTACK HAS STRENGTHS AND WEAKNESSES...
...BUT IT SEEMS HE CAN LAUNCH ANY TYPE OF ATTACK, IN SUCH A WAY THAT HIS OPPONENT CAN'T TELL WHAT IT IS UNTIL IT HITS!!
WHAT A FELLOW...
...THIS... THIS MAN!!

READ THIS WAY

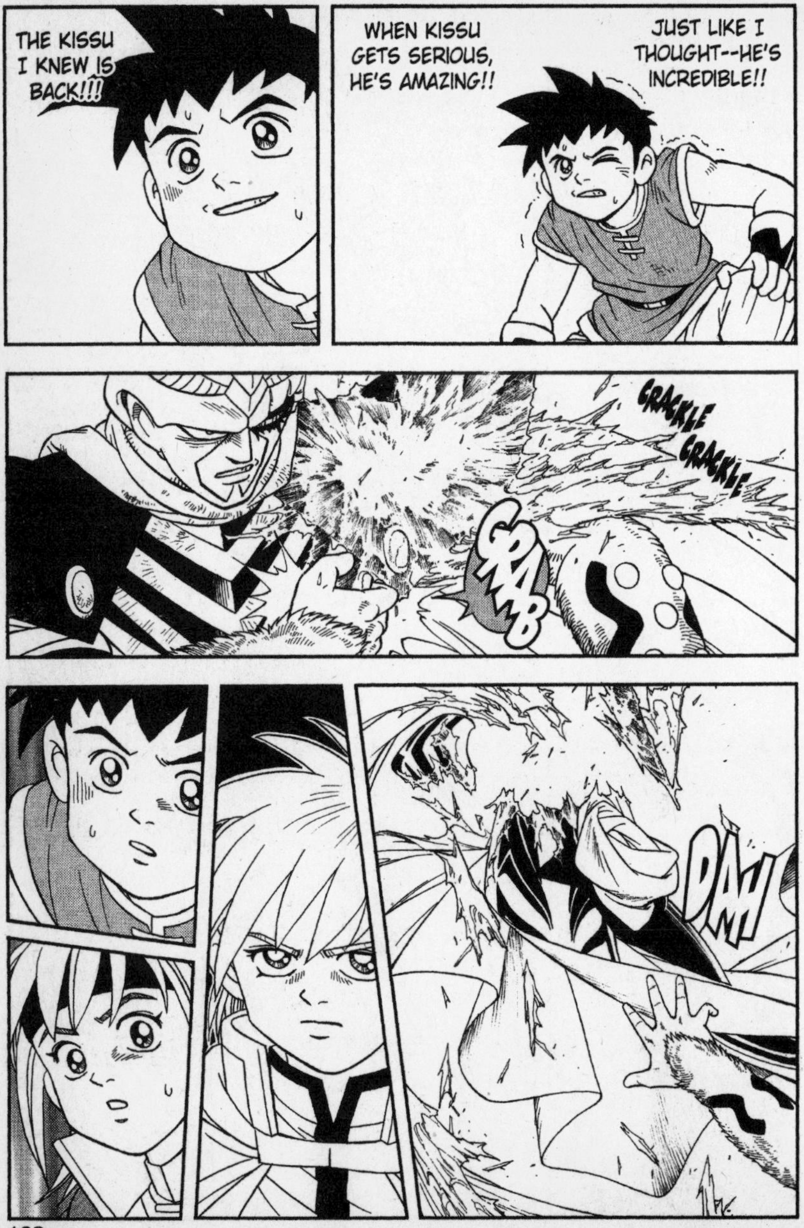
JUST LIKE I THOUGHT--HE'S INCREDIBLE!!
WHEN KISSU GETS SERIOUS, HE'S AMAZING!!
THE KISSU I KNEW IS BACK!!!
CRACKLE
CRACKLE
GRAB
DAM

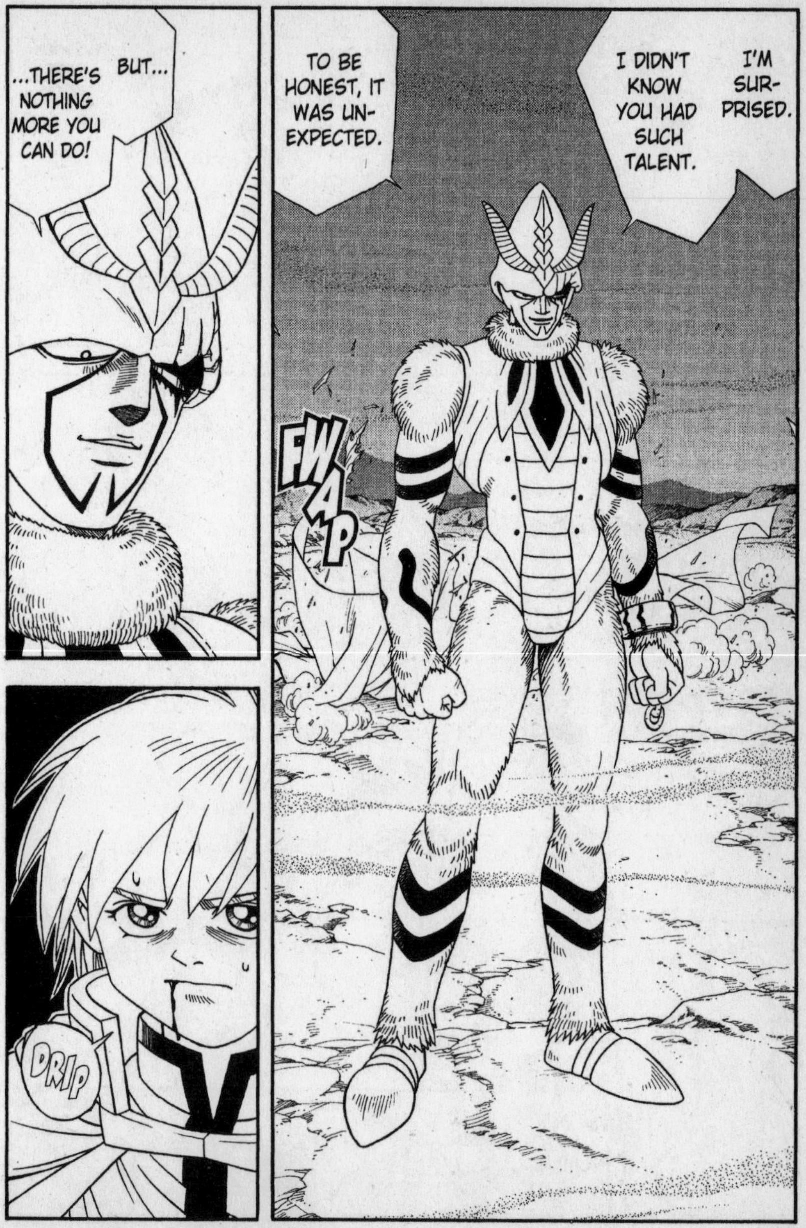
I'M SUR-PRISED.
I DIDN'T KNOW YOU HAD SUCH TALENT.
TO BE HONEST, IT WAS UN-EXPECTED.
FWAP
BUT...
...THERE'S NOTHING MORE YOU CAN DO!
DRIP

READ THIS WAY

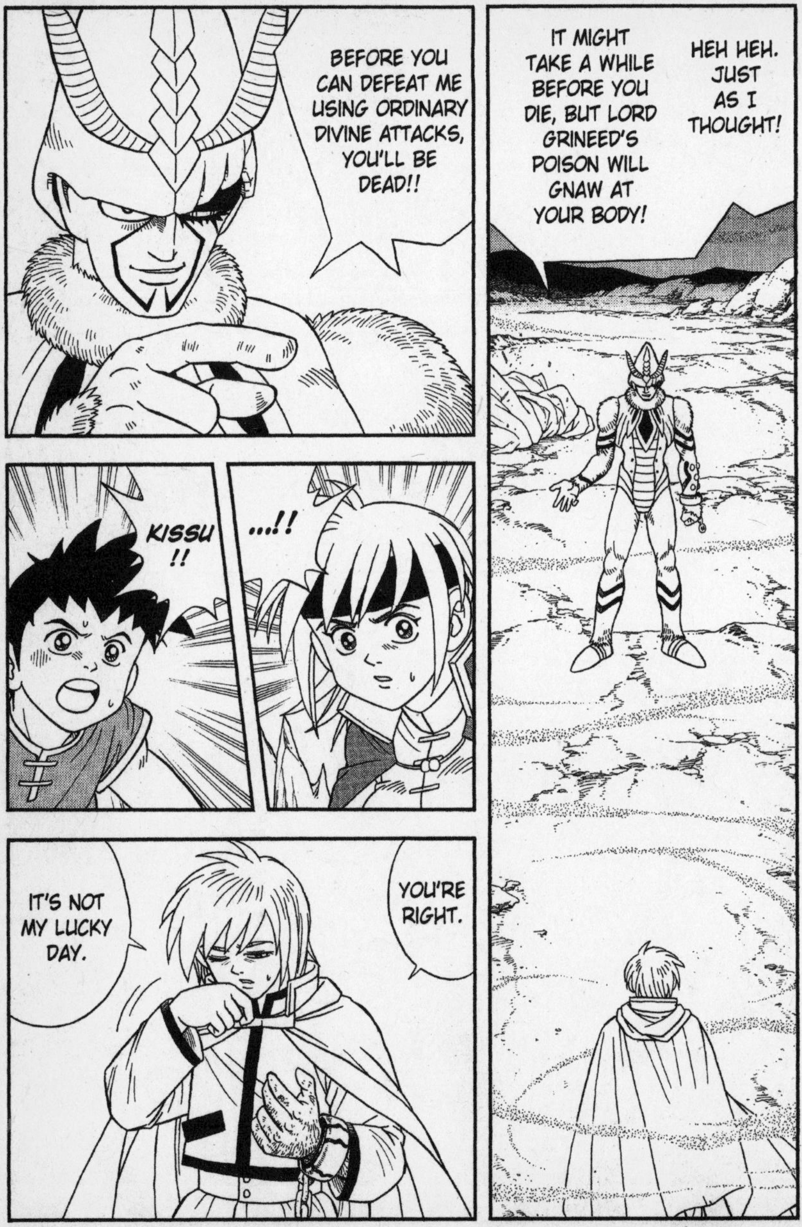
HEH HEH. JUST AS I THOUGHT!
IT MIGHT TAKE A WHILE BEFORE YOU DIE, BUT LORD GRINEED'S POISON WILL GNAW AT YOUR BODY!
BEFORE YOU CAN DEFEAT ME USING ORDINARY DIVINE ATTACKS, YOU'LL BE DEAD!!
...!!
KISSU !!
YOU'RE RIGHT.
IT'S NOT MY LUCKY DAY.

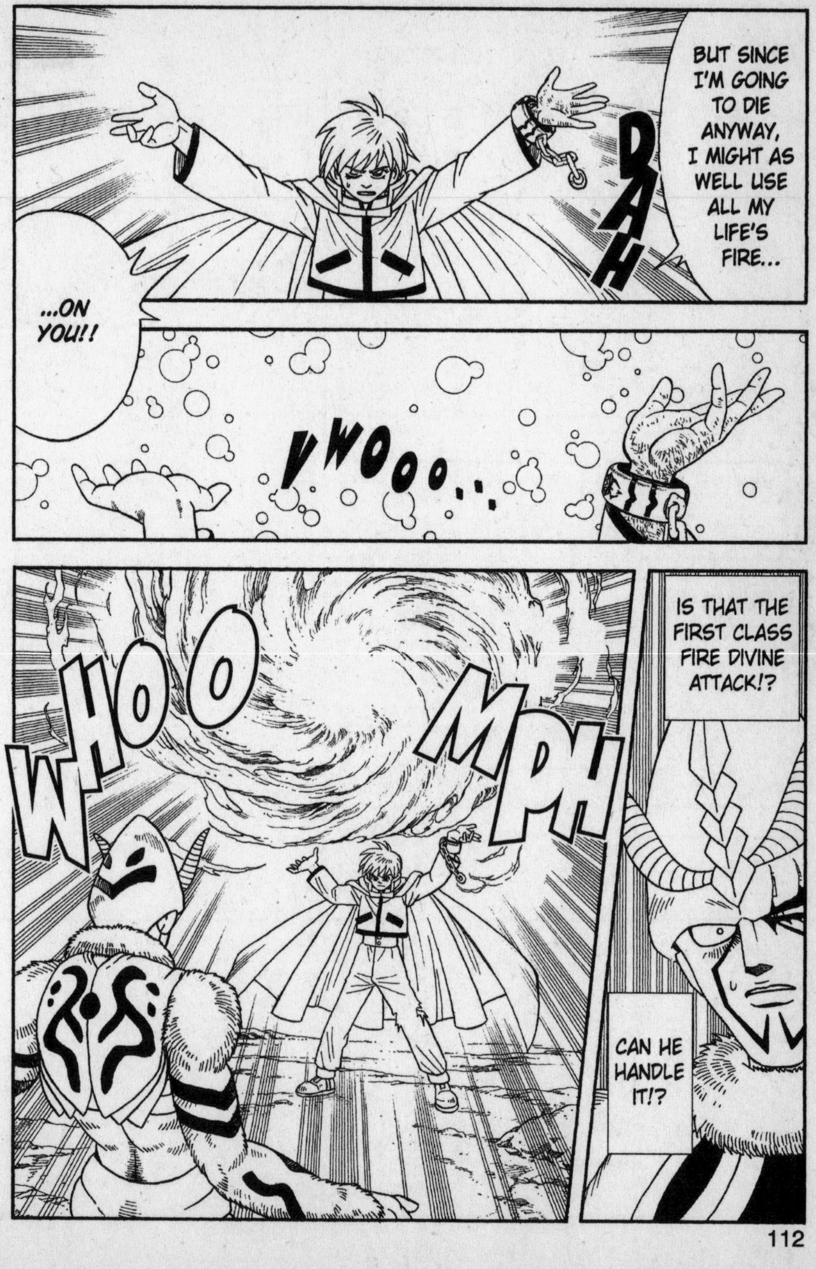
BUT SINCE I'M GOING TO DIE ANYWAY, I MIGHT AS WELL USE ALL MY LIFE'S FIRE...
DAH
...ON YOU!!
VWOOO...
IS THAT THE FIRST CLASS FIRE DIVINE ATTACK!?
CAN HE HANDLE IT!?
WHOOMPH

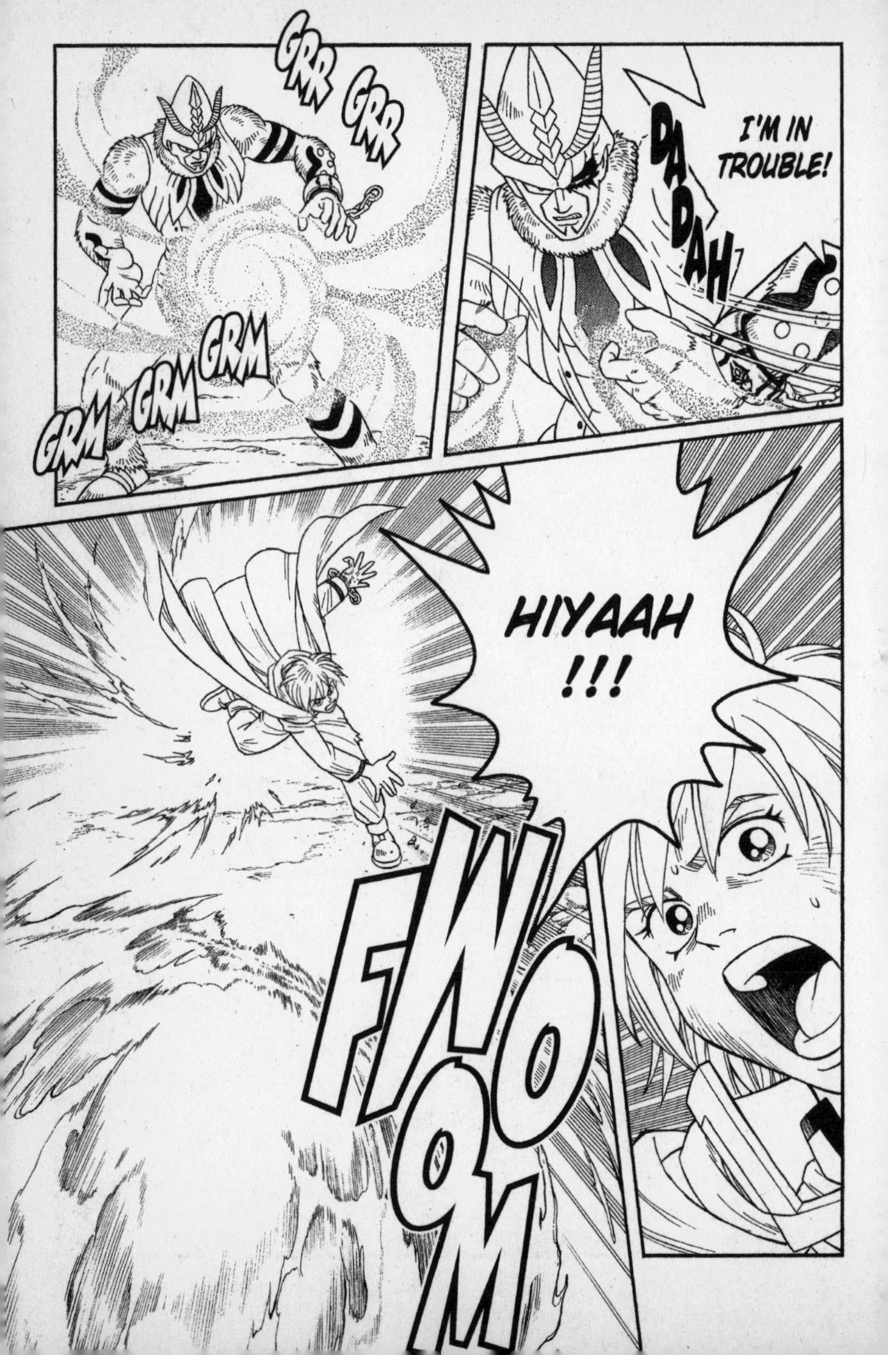
DADAH
I'M IN TROUBLE!
GRR GRR
GRM GRM GRM
HIYAAH !!!
FWOOM

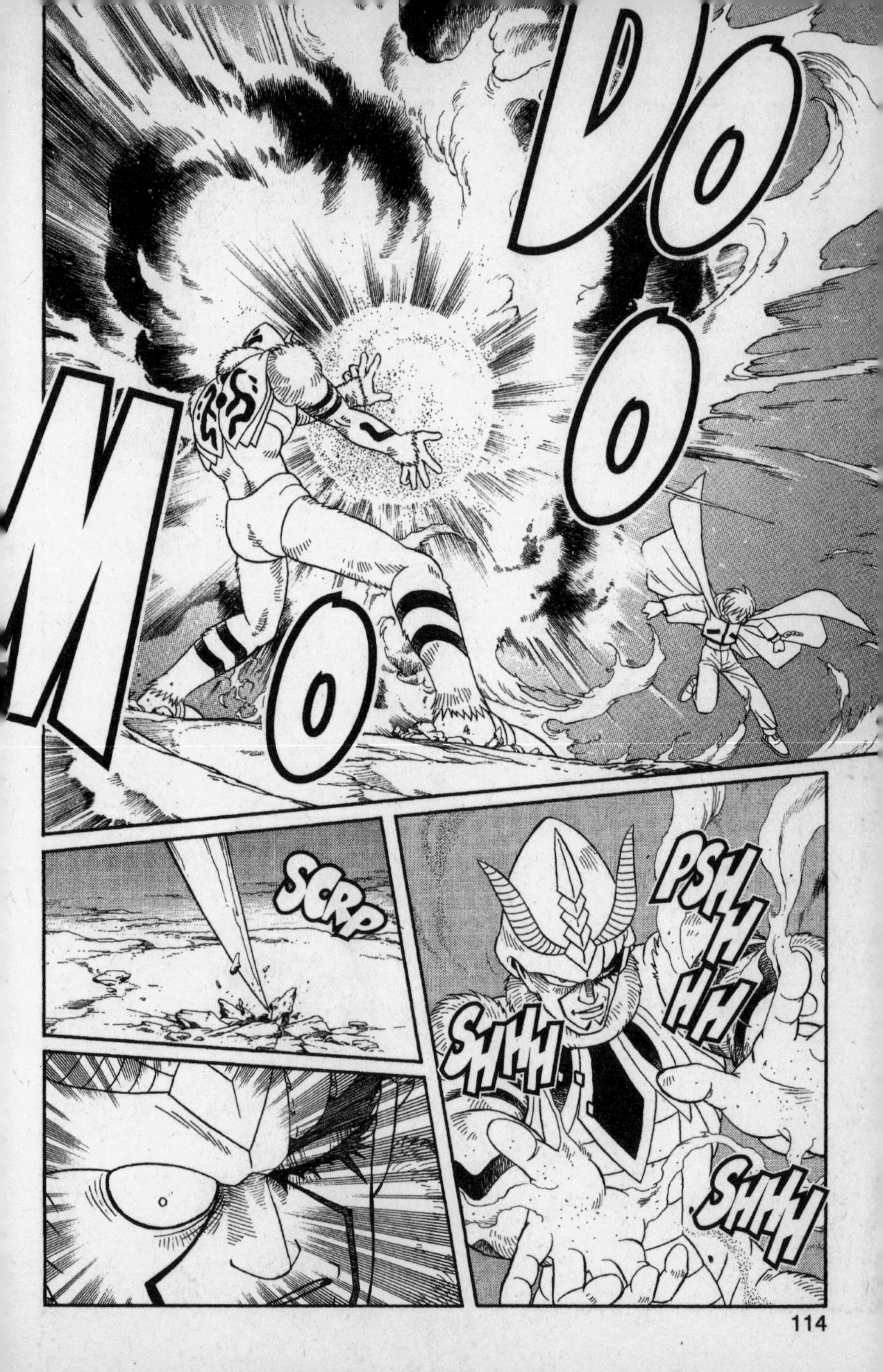
DOOOM
PSHHHHH
SHHH
SHHH
SCRP

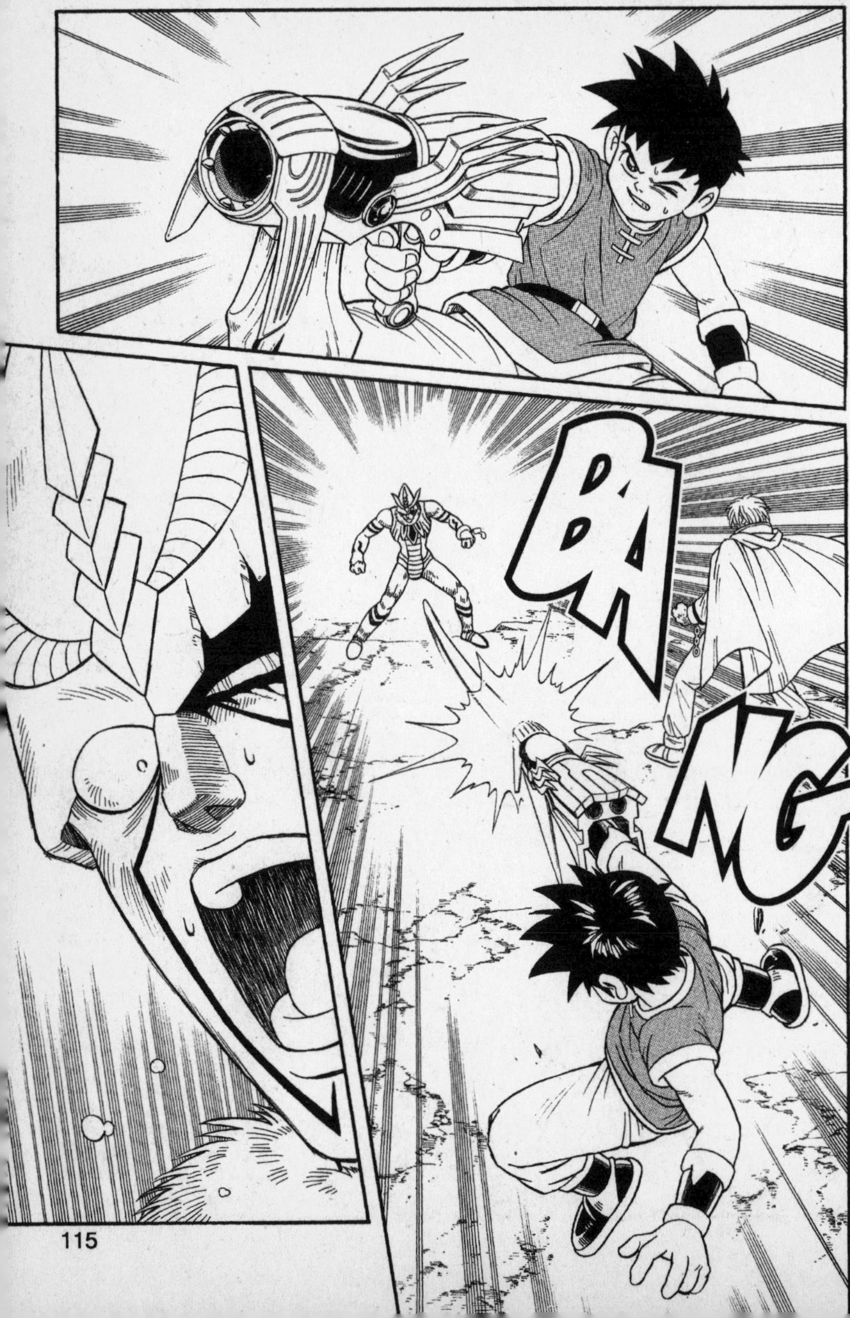
BANG

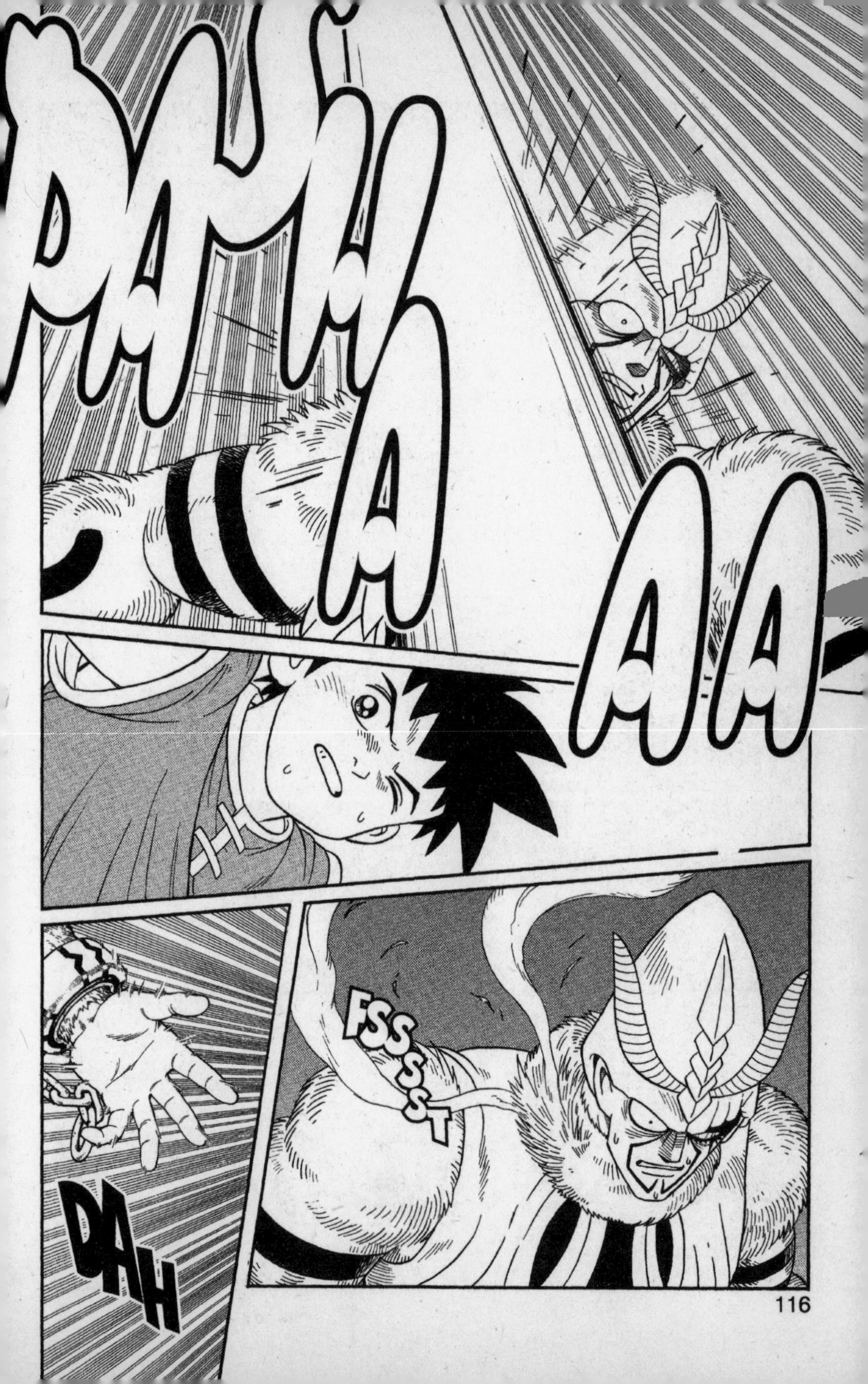
PAAAAAA
FSSSST
DAH

READ THIS WAY

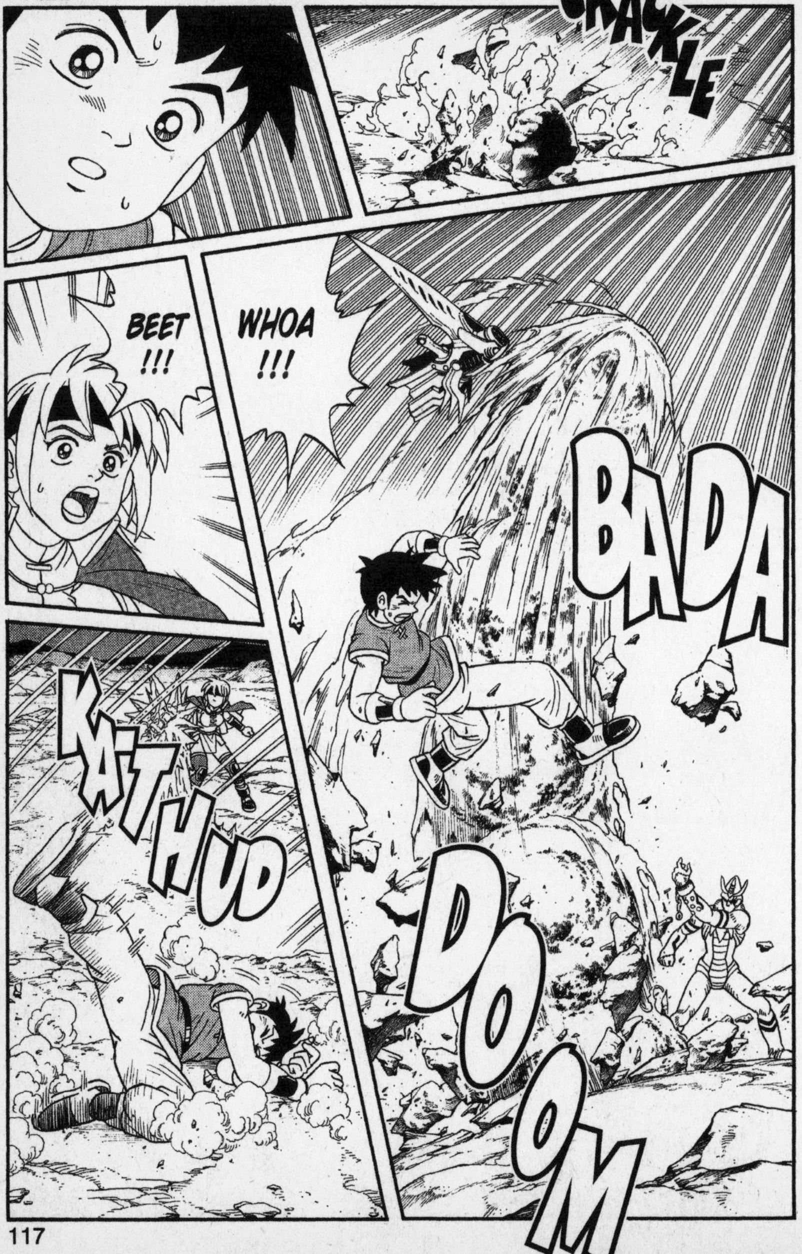

CRACKLE
WHOA !!!
BADA
DOOOM
BEET !!!
KA-THUD

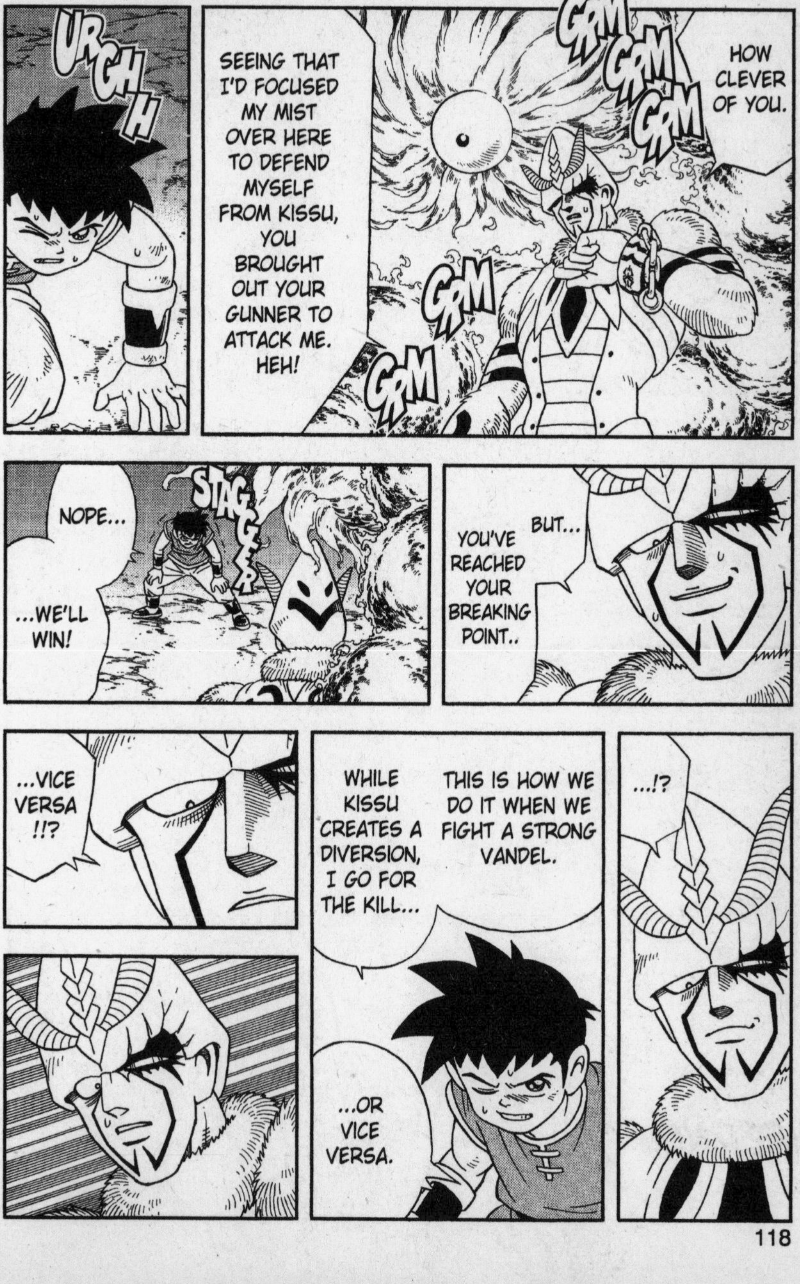
HOW CLEVER OF YOU.
GRM GRM GRM
SEEING THAT I'D FOCUSED MY MIST OVER HERE TO DEFEND MYSELF FROM KISSU, YOU BROUGHT OUT YOUR GUNNER TO ATTACK ME. HEH!
GRM
GRM
URGHH
BUT...
YOU'VE REACHED YOUR BREAKING POINT..
NOPE...
...WE'LL WIN!
STAGGER
...!?
THIS IS HOW WE DO IT WHEN WE FIGHT A STRONG VANDEL.
WHILE KISSU CREATES A DIVERSION, I GO FOR THE KILL...
...OR VICE VERSA.
...VICE VERSA !!?

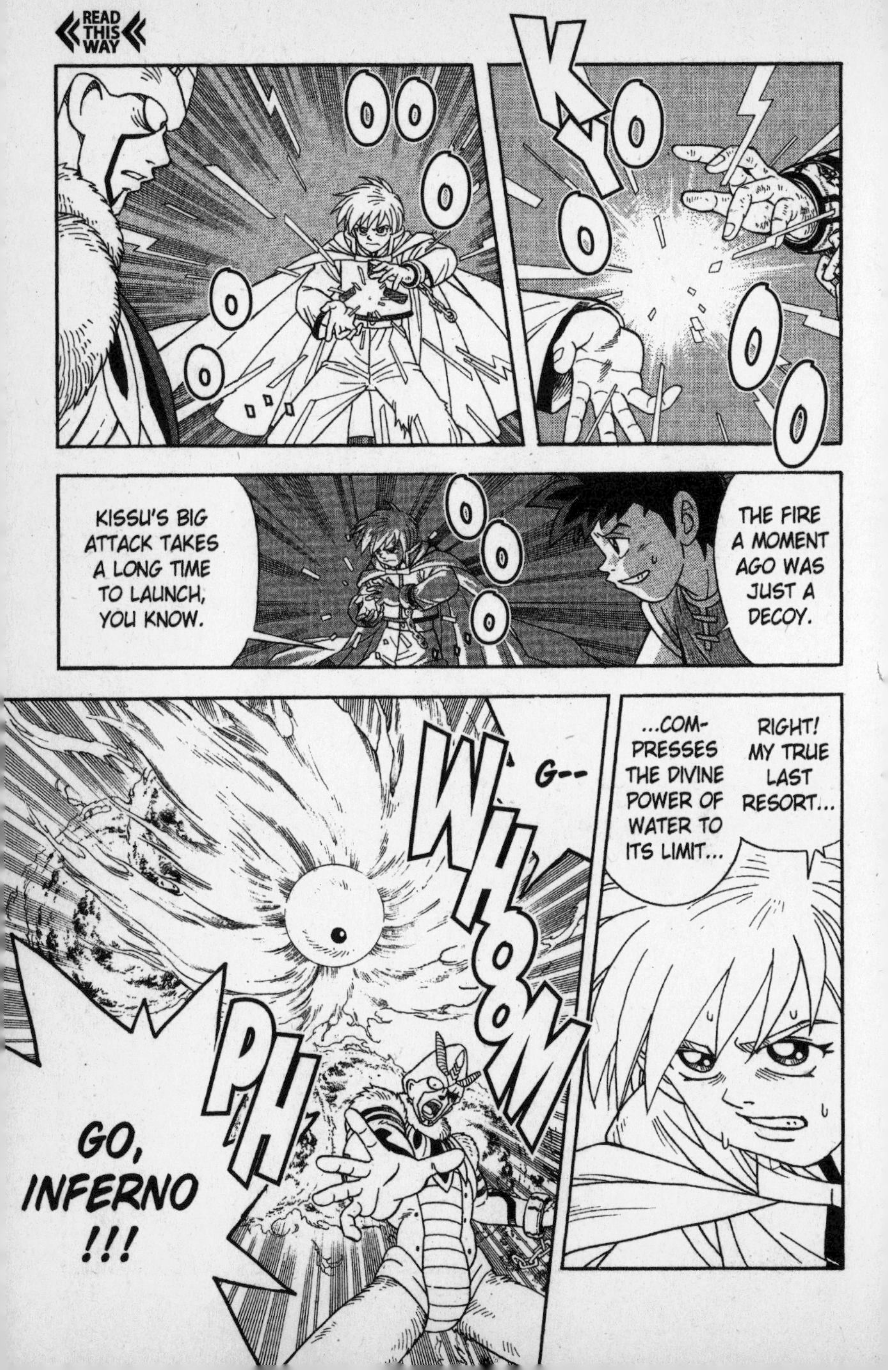
READ THIS WAY
KYOOO
OOOOO
THE FIRE A MOMENT AGO WAS JUST A DECOY.
KISSU'S BIG ATTACK TAKES A LONG TIME TO LAUNCH, YOU KNOW.
RIGHT! MY TRUE LAST RESORT...
...COMPRESSES THE DIVINE POWER OF WATER TO ITS LIMIT...
G--
WHOOM
PH
GO, INFERNO !!!

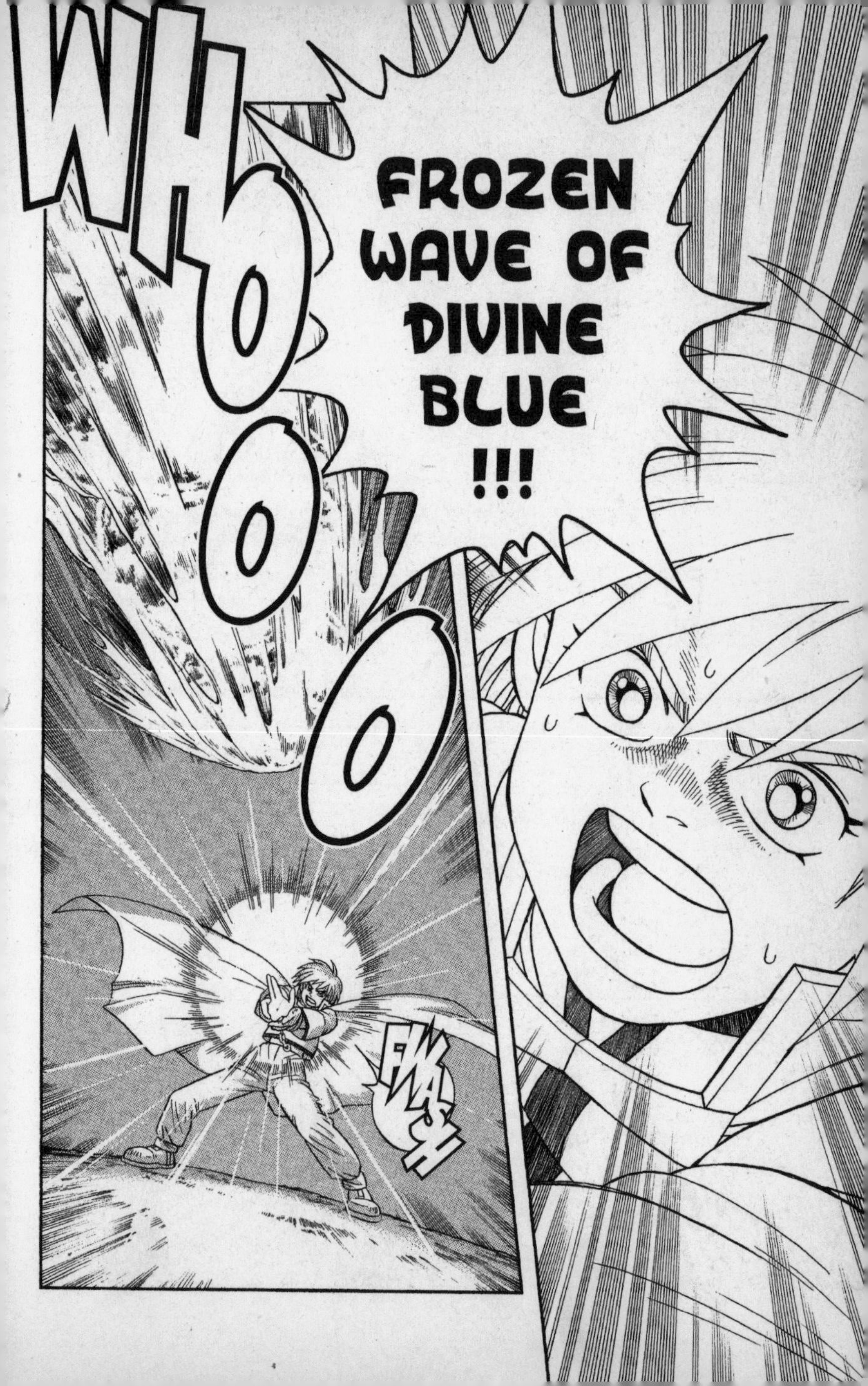
FROZEN WAVE OF DIVINE BLUE !!!
WHOOOO
FWASH

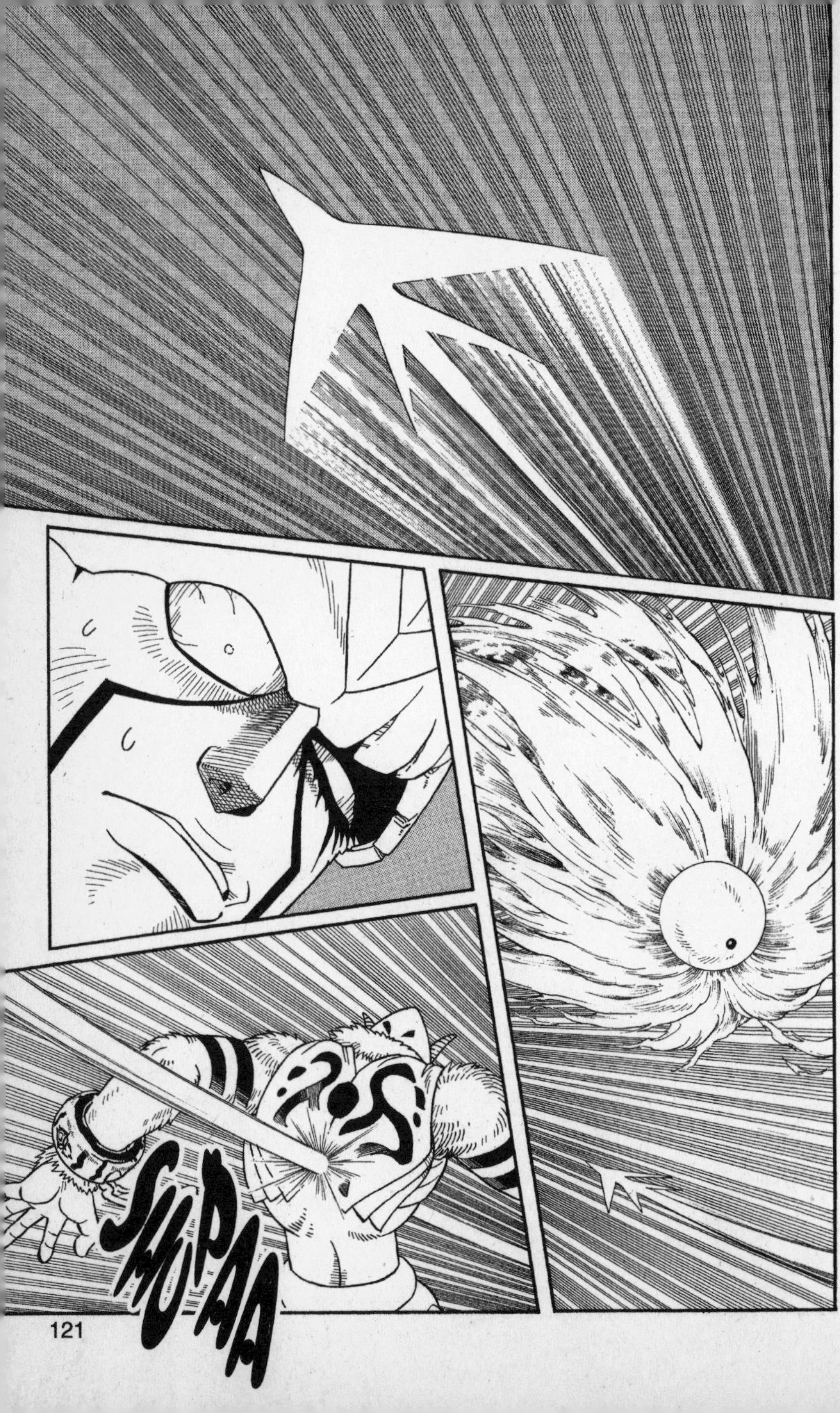
SHUPAA

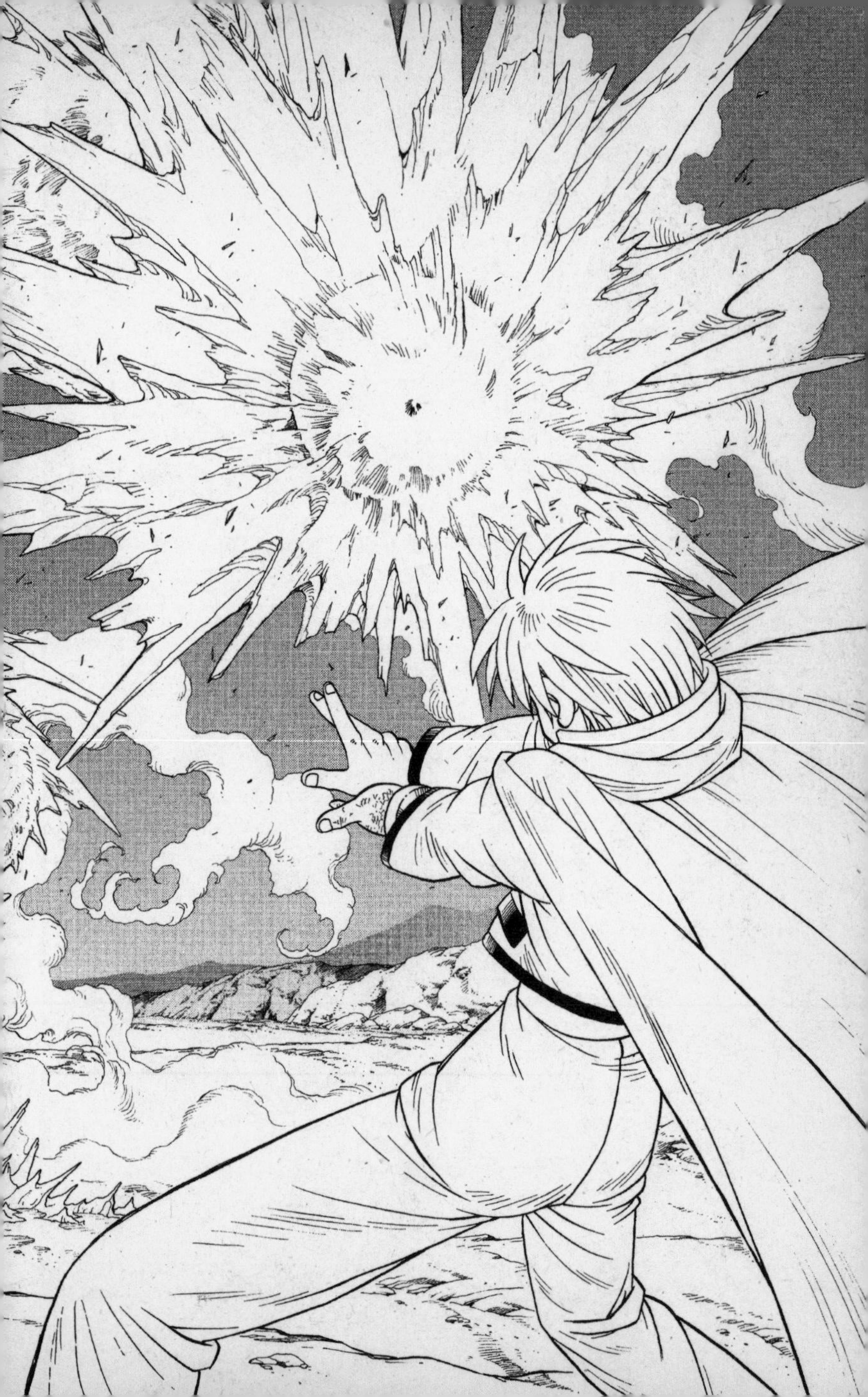

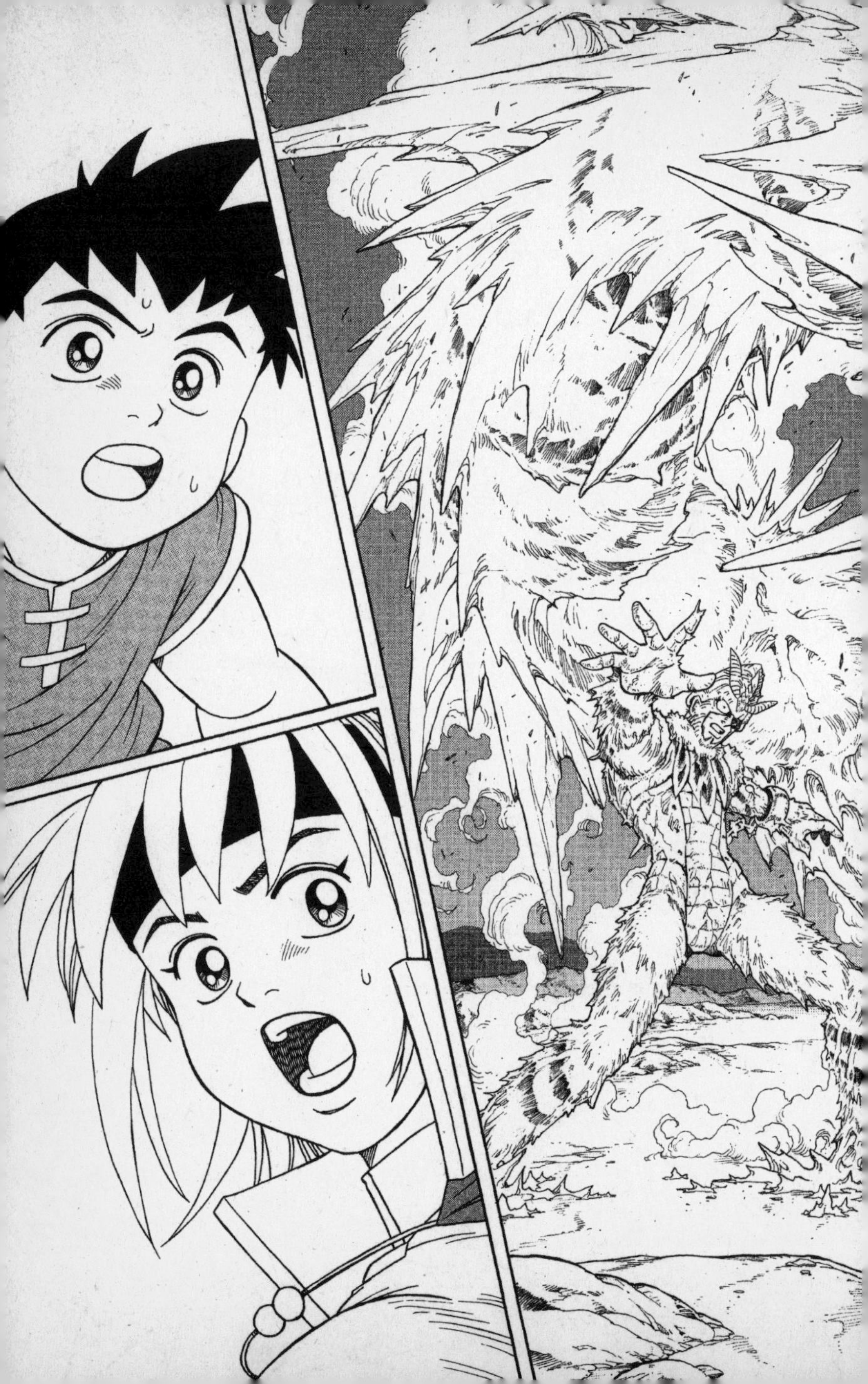

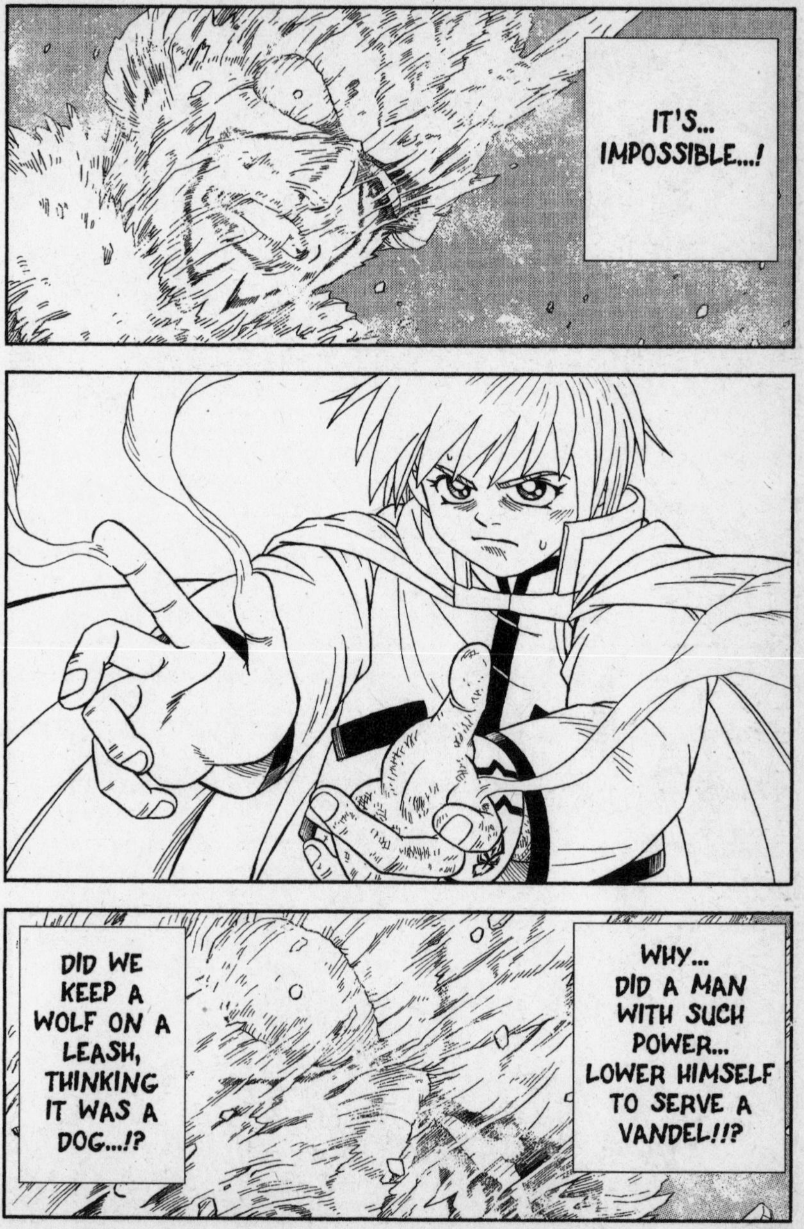
IT'S... IMPOSSIBLE...!
WHY... DID A MAN WITH SUCH POWER... LOWER HIMSELF TO SERVE A VANDEL!!?
DID WE KEEP A WOLF ON A LEASH, THINKING IT WAS A DOG...!?

READ THIS WAY

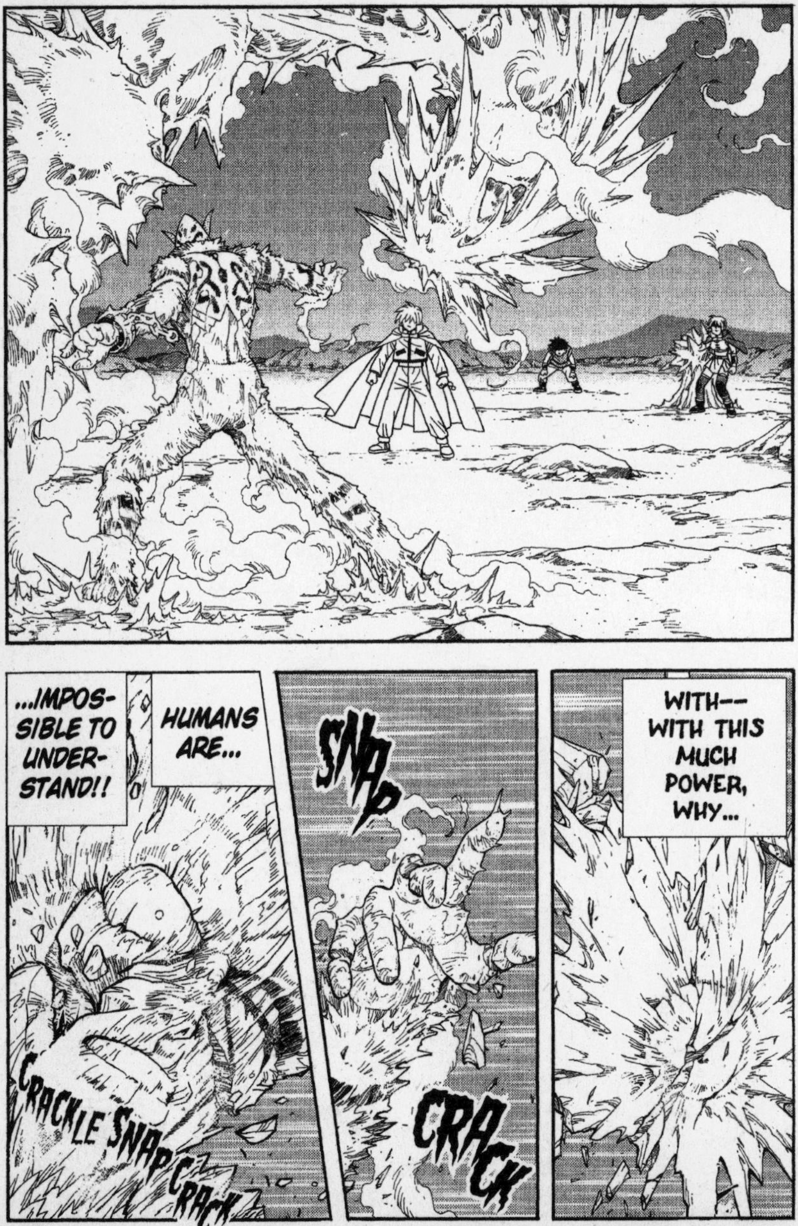
WITH-- WITH THIS MUCH POWER, WHY...
SNAP
CRACK
HUMANS ARE...
...IMPOSSIBLE TO UNDERSTAND!!
CRACKLE SNAP CRACK

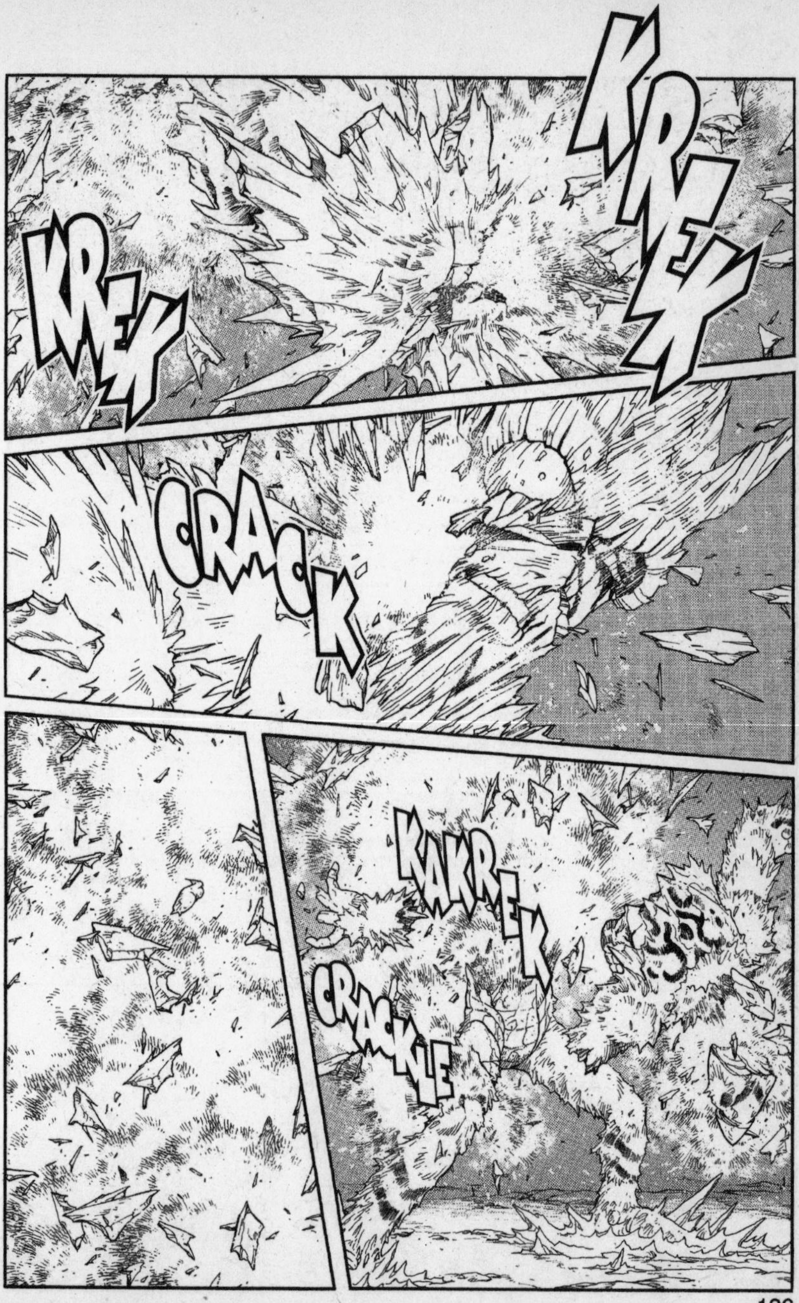
KREK
KREK
CRACK
KAKREK
CRACKLE

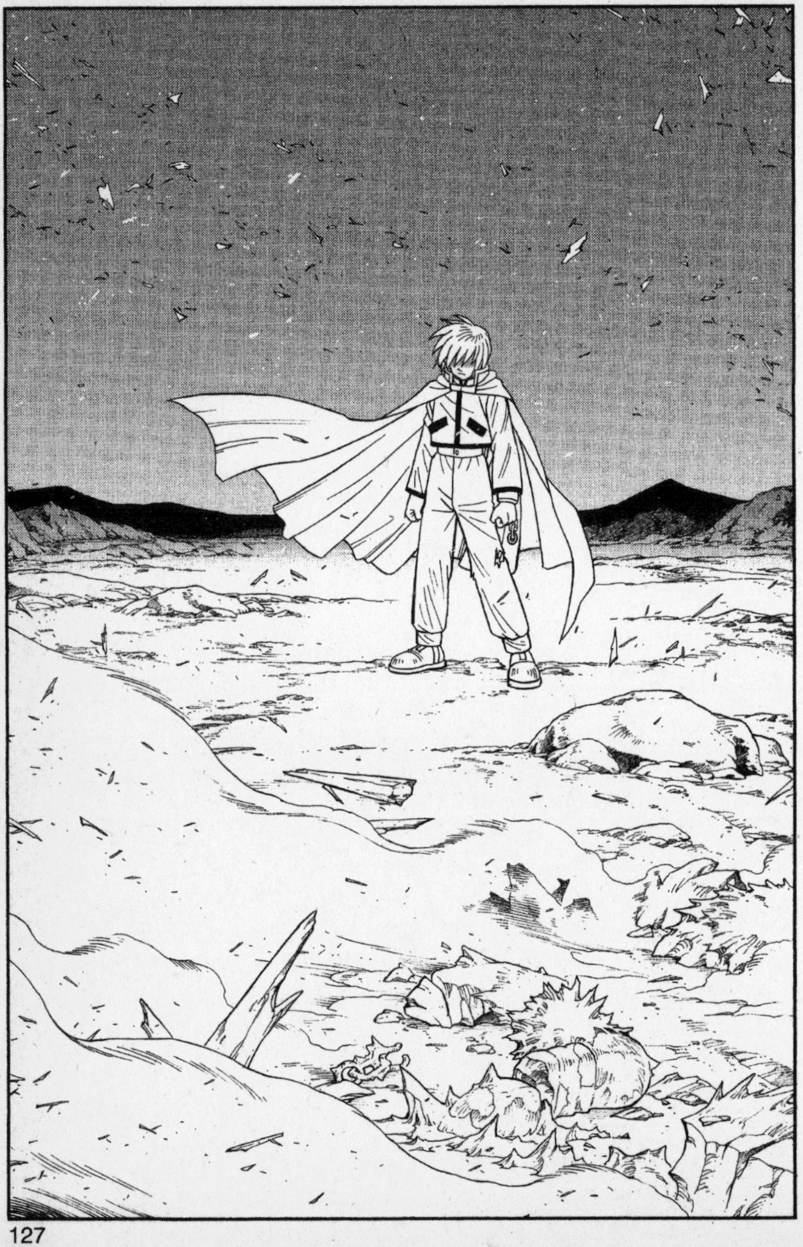

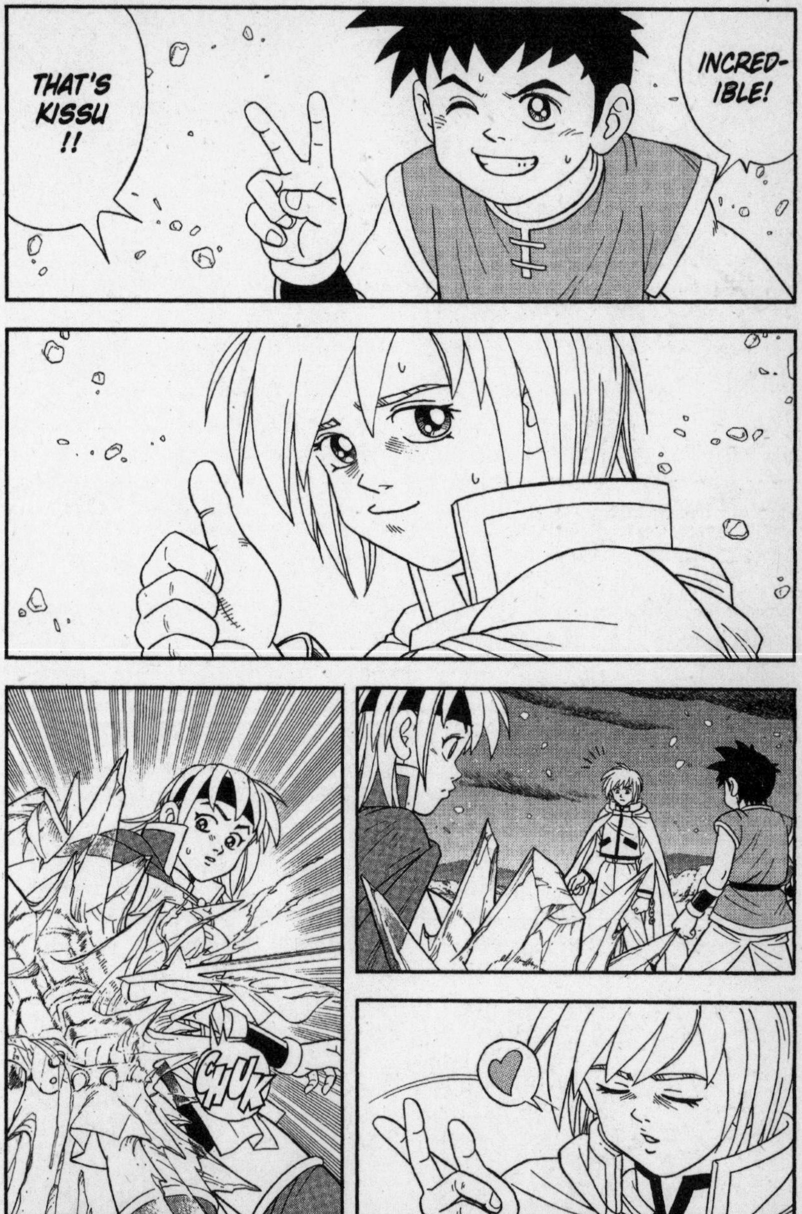
INCRED-IBLE!
THAT'S KISSU !!
CHUK

READ THIS WAY

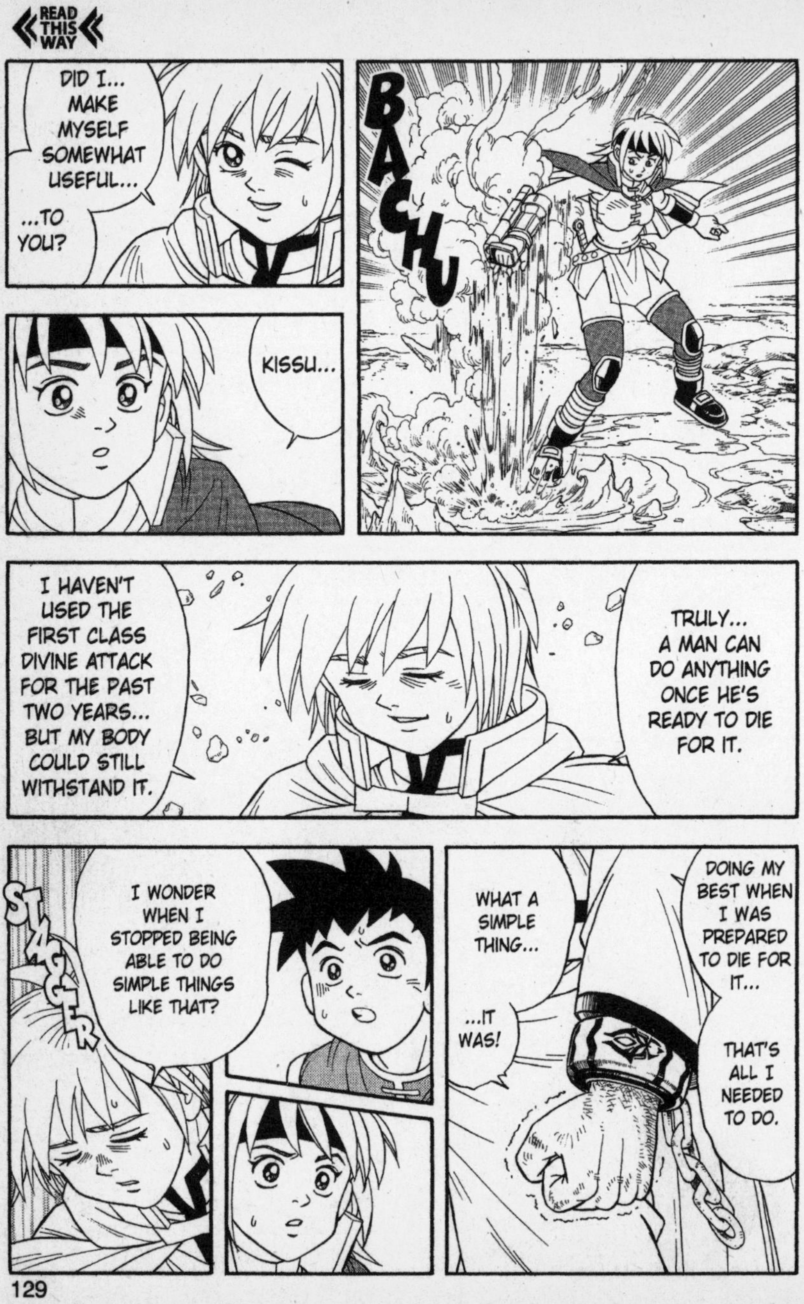
BACHU
DID I... MAKE MYSELF SOMEWHAT USEFUL...
...TO YOU?
KISSU...
I HAVEN'T USED THE FIRST CLASS DIVINE ATTACK FOR THE PAST TWO YEARS... BUT MY BODY COULD STILL WITHSTAND IT.
TRULY... A MAN CAN DO ANYTHING ONCE HE'S READY TO DIE FOR IT.
DOING MY BEST WHEN I WAS PREPARED TO DIE FOR IT...
WHAT A SIMPLE THING...
...IT WAS!
THAT'S ALL I NEEDED TO DO.
I WONDER WHEN I STOPPED BEING ABLE TO DO SIMPLE THINGS LIKE THAT?
STAGGER

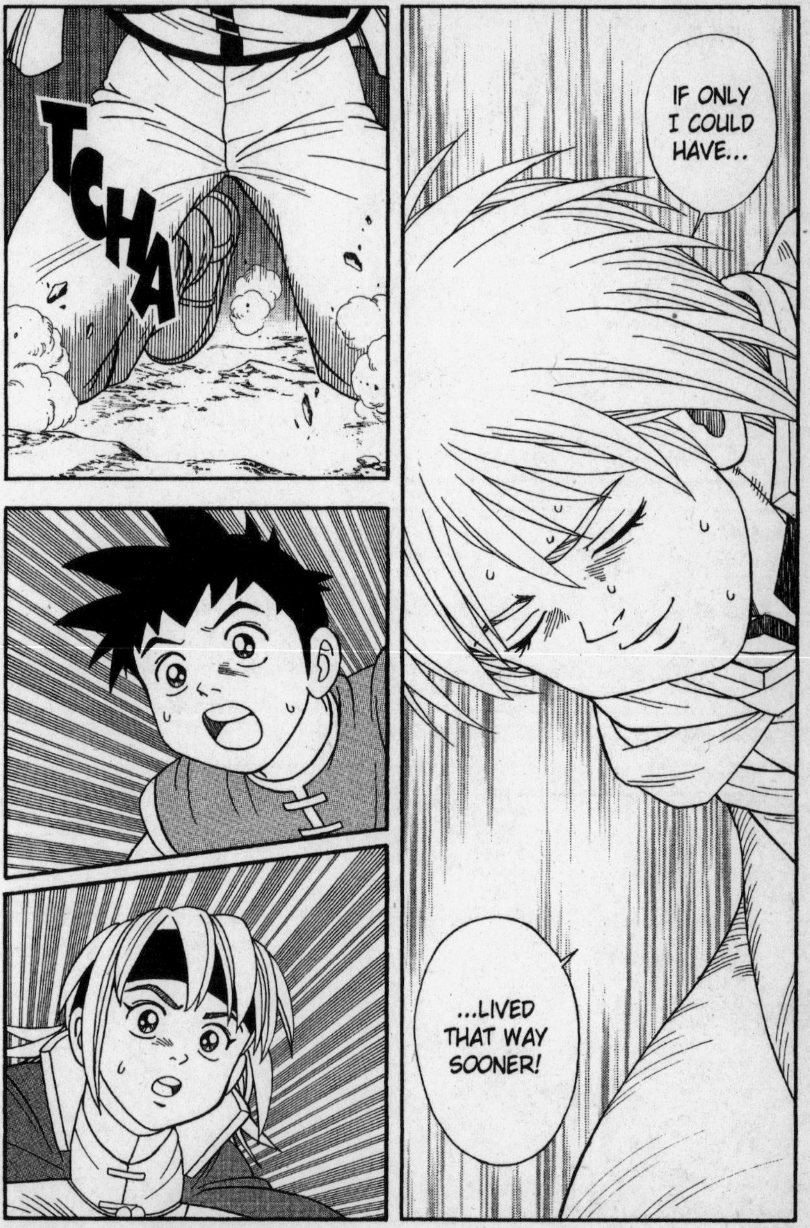
IF ONLY I COULD HAVE...
...LIVED THAT WAY SOONER!
TCHA

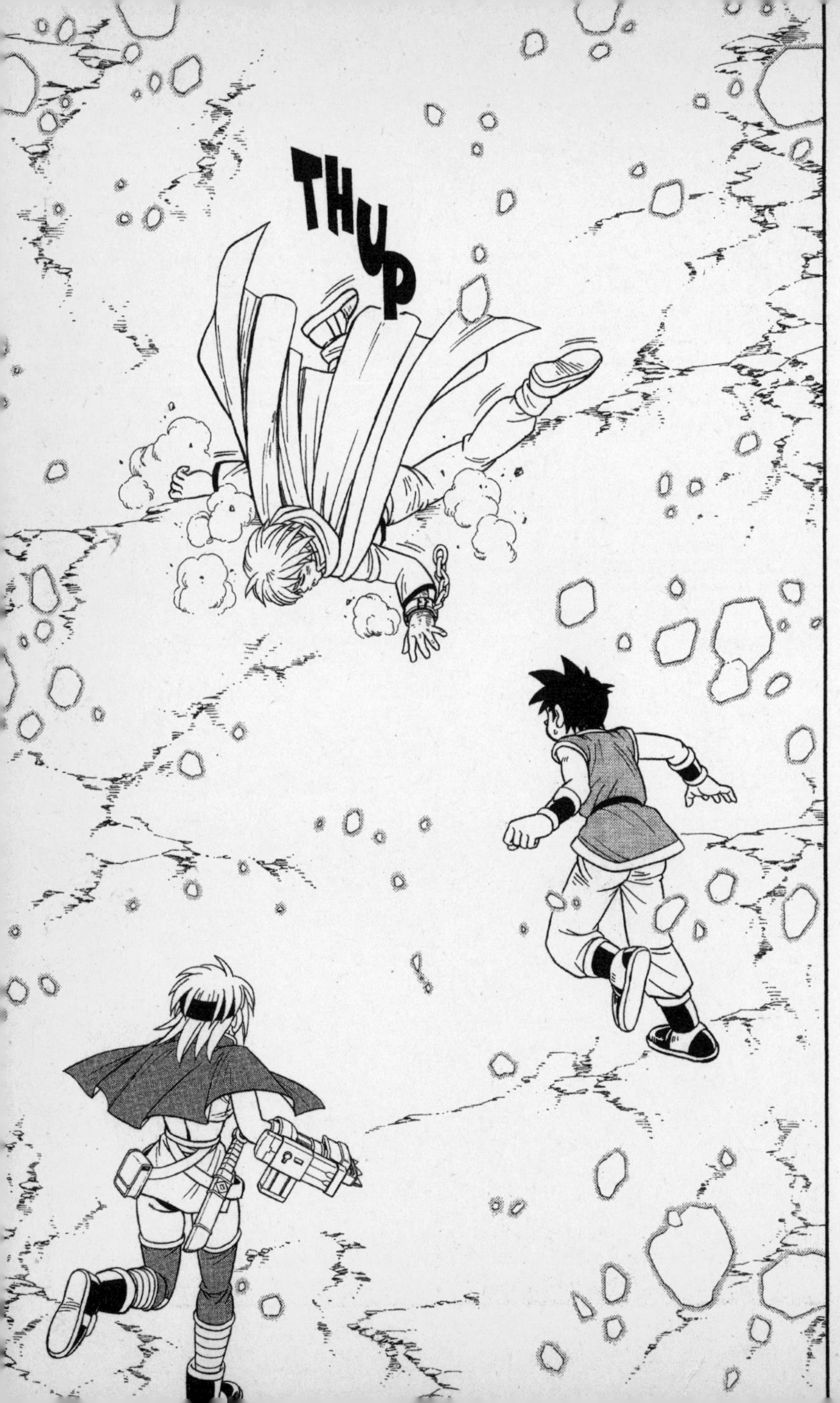
THUP

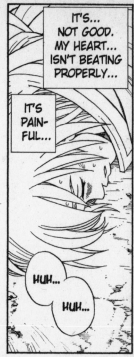

IT'S...
NOT GOOD.
MY HEART...
ISN'T BEATING
PROPERLY...

IT'S
PAIN-
FUL...

HUH...

HUH...

HUH...

HUH...

HUH...

HUH...

...!!

...BEET...

HUH...

HUH...

I GUESS
I'M DYING...

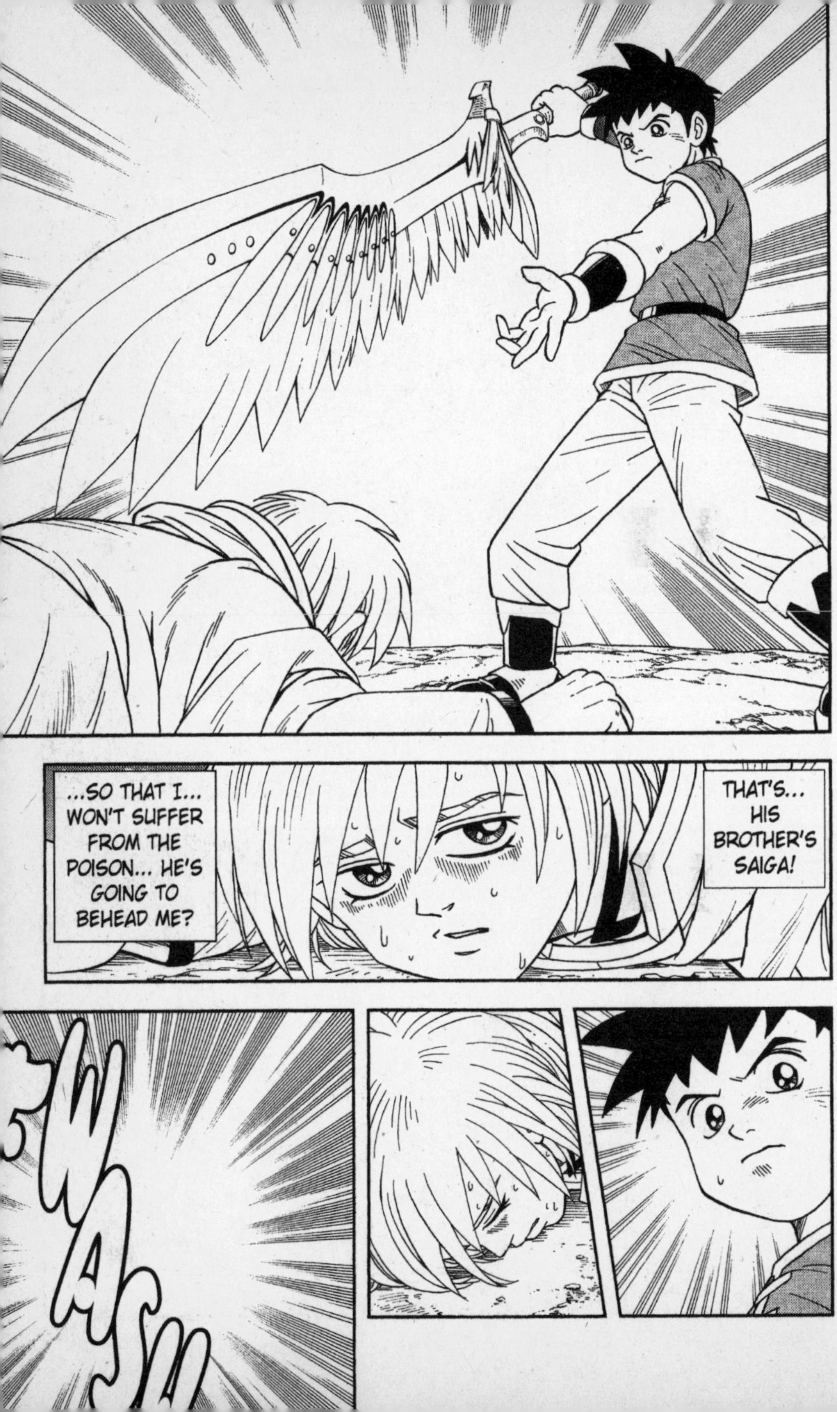
THAT'S... HIS BROTHER'S SAIGA!
...SO THAT I... WON'T SUFFER FROM THE POISON... HE'S GOING TO BEHEAD ME?
SWASH

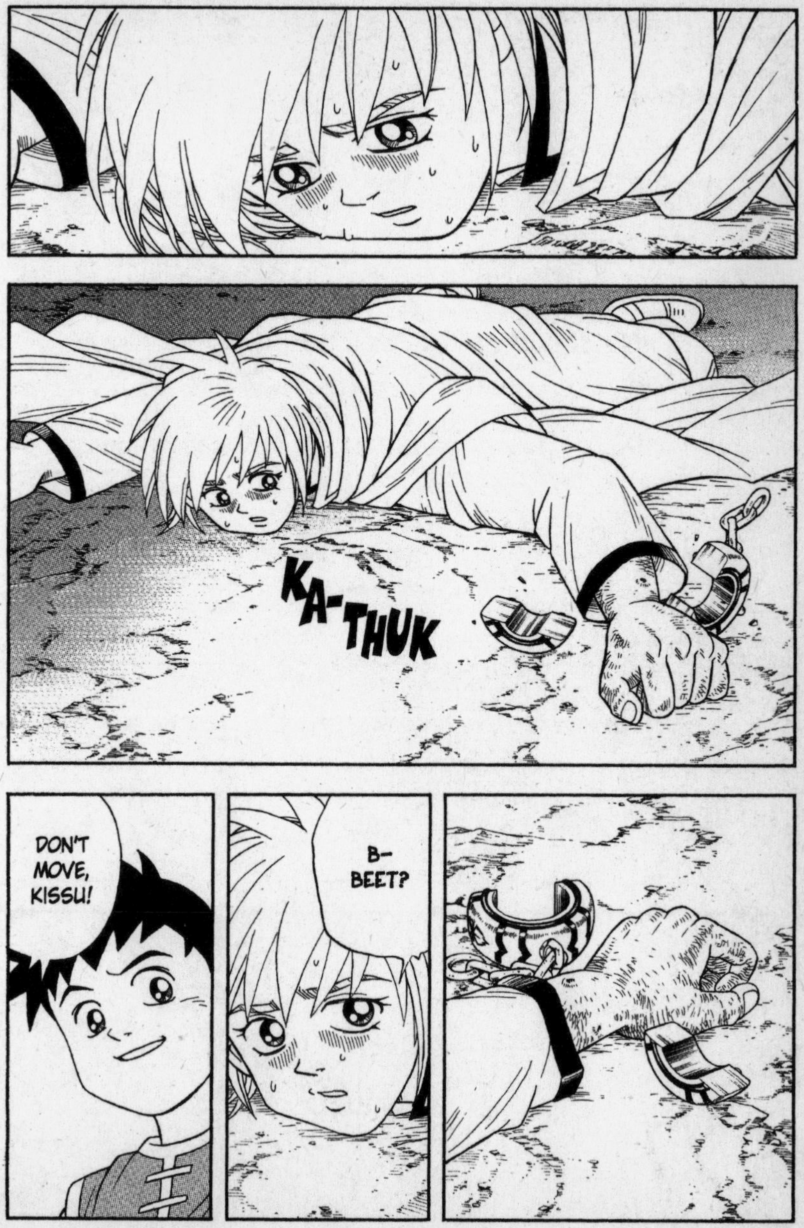
KA-THUK
B-
BEET?
DON'T
MOVE,
KISSU!

READ THIS WAY

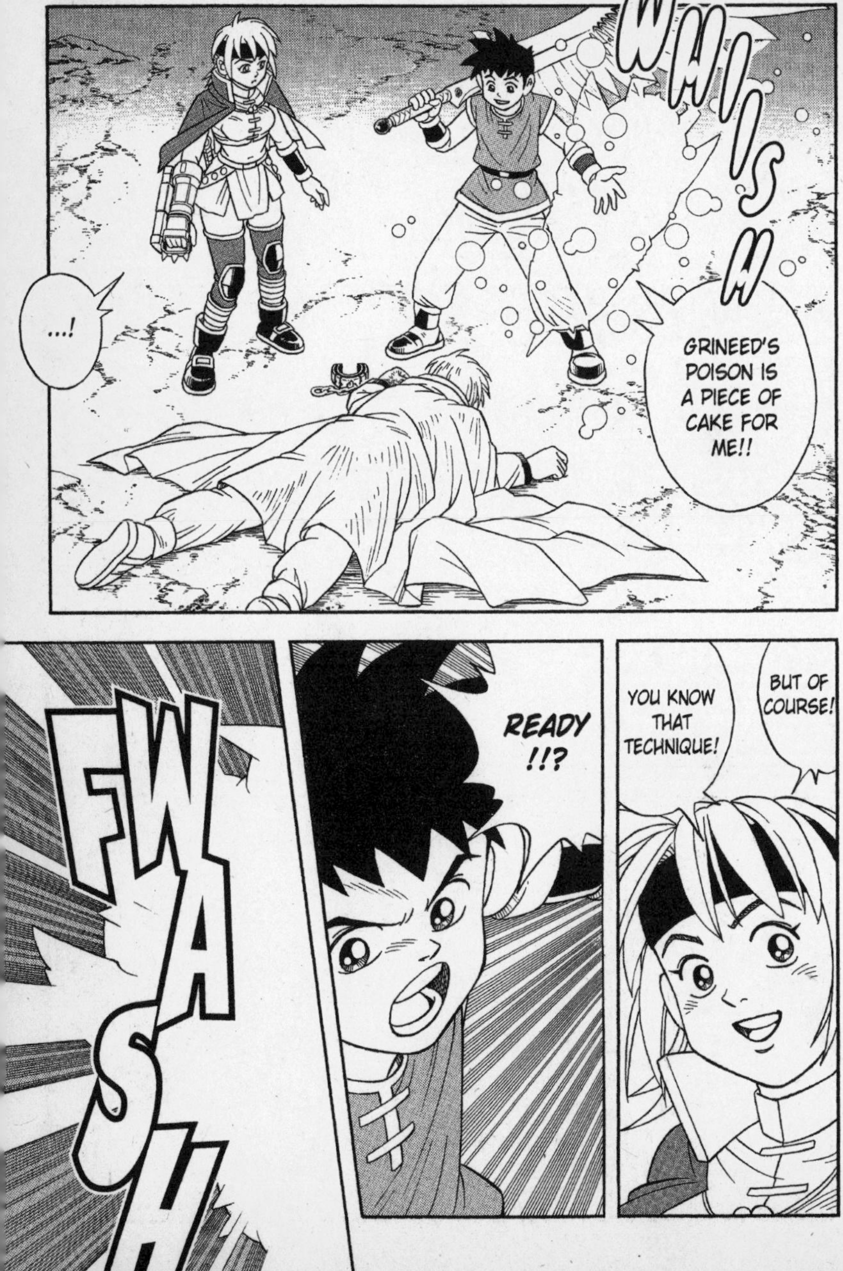
WHIISH
GRINEED'S POISON IS A PIECE OF CAKE FOR ME!!
...!
BUT OF COURSE!
YOU KNOW THAT TECHNIQUE!
READY!!?
FWASH

THE CROWN SHIELD'S ANTIDOTE POWER...

...IS A TECHNIQUE I RECENTLY LEARNED!!

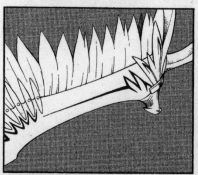

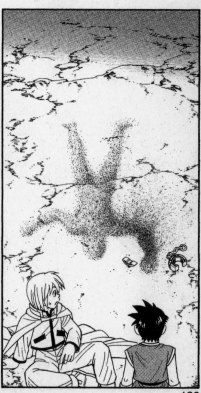

READ THIS WAY

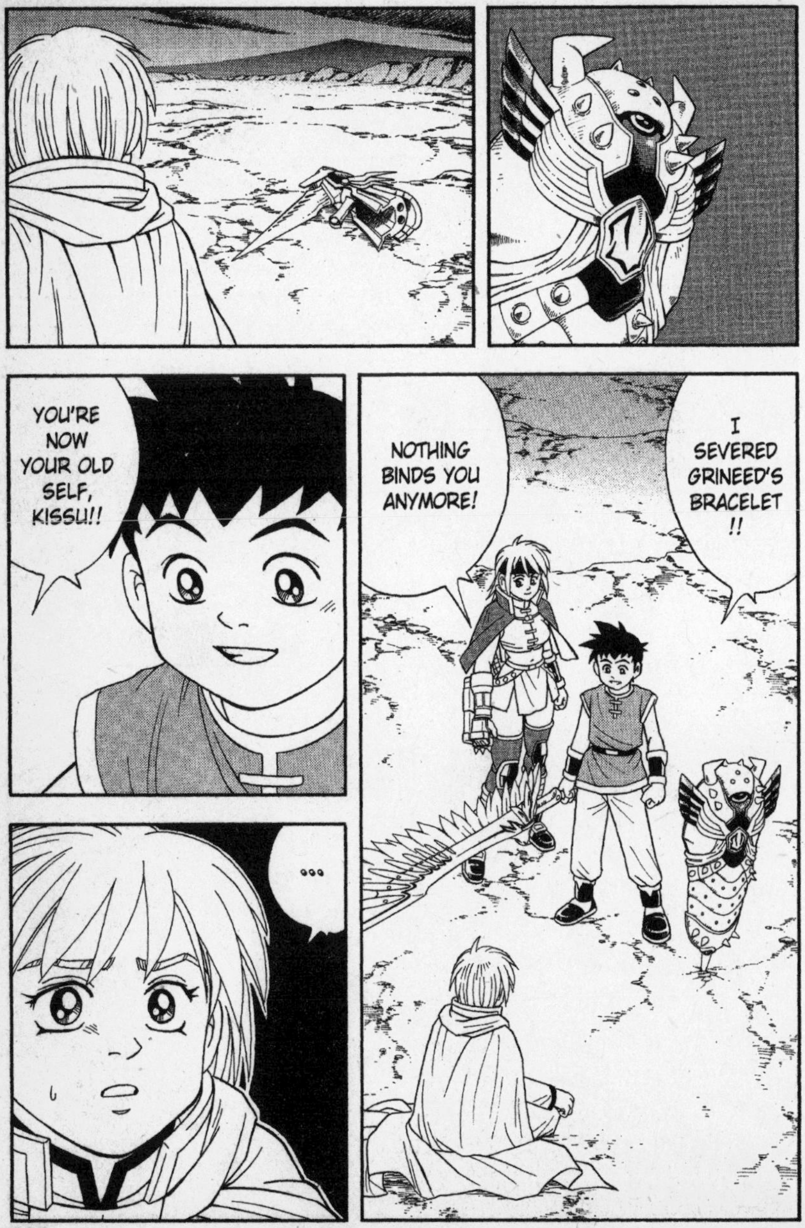

I SEVERED GRINEED'S BRACELET!!
NOTHING BINDS YOU ANYMORE!
YOU'RE NOW YOUR OLD SELF, KISSU!!
...

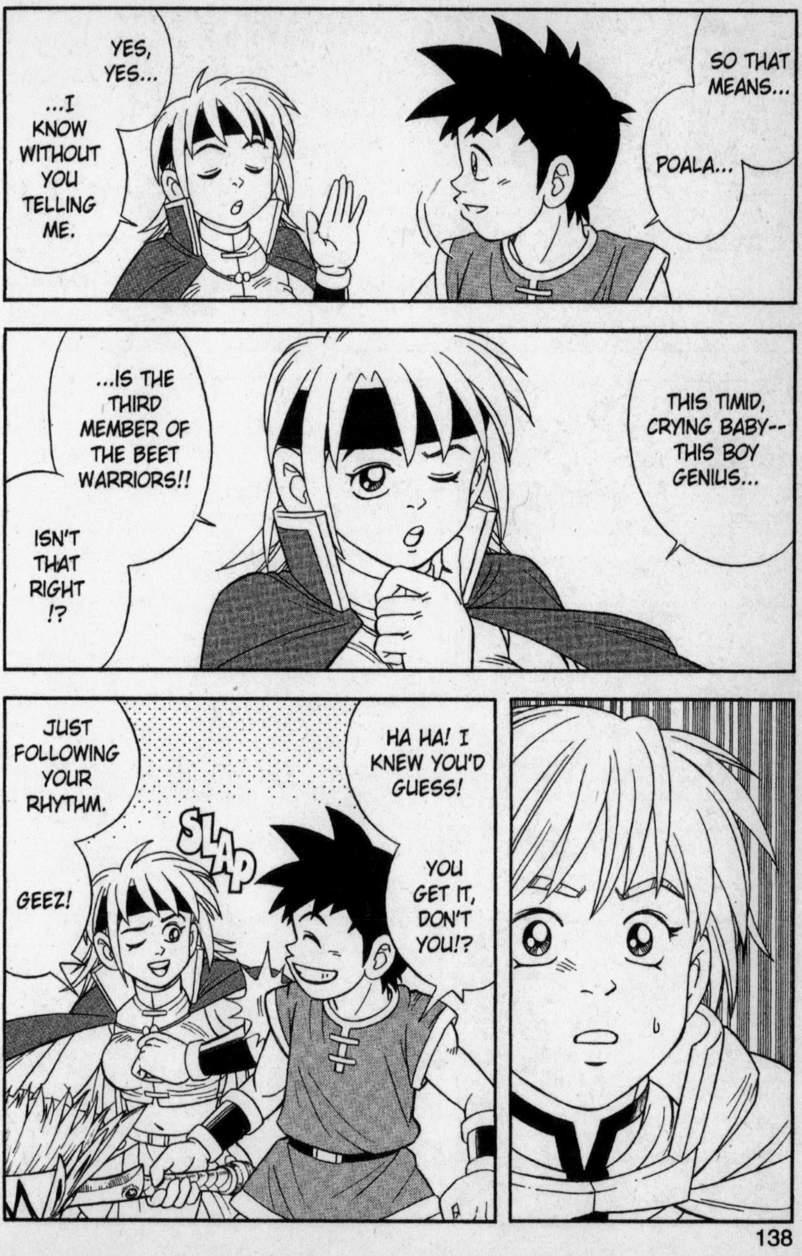
SO THAT MEANS...
POALA...
YES, YES...
...I KNOW WITHOUT YOU TELLING ME.
THIS TIMID, CRYING BABY-- THIS BOY GENIUS...
...IS THE THIRD MEMBER OF THE BEET WARRIORS!!
ISN'T THAT RIGHT !?
HA HA! I KNEW YOU'D GUESS!
JUST FOLLOWING YOUR RHYTHM.
SLAP
YOU GET IT, DON'T YOU!?
GEEZ!

READ THIS WAY

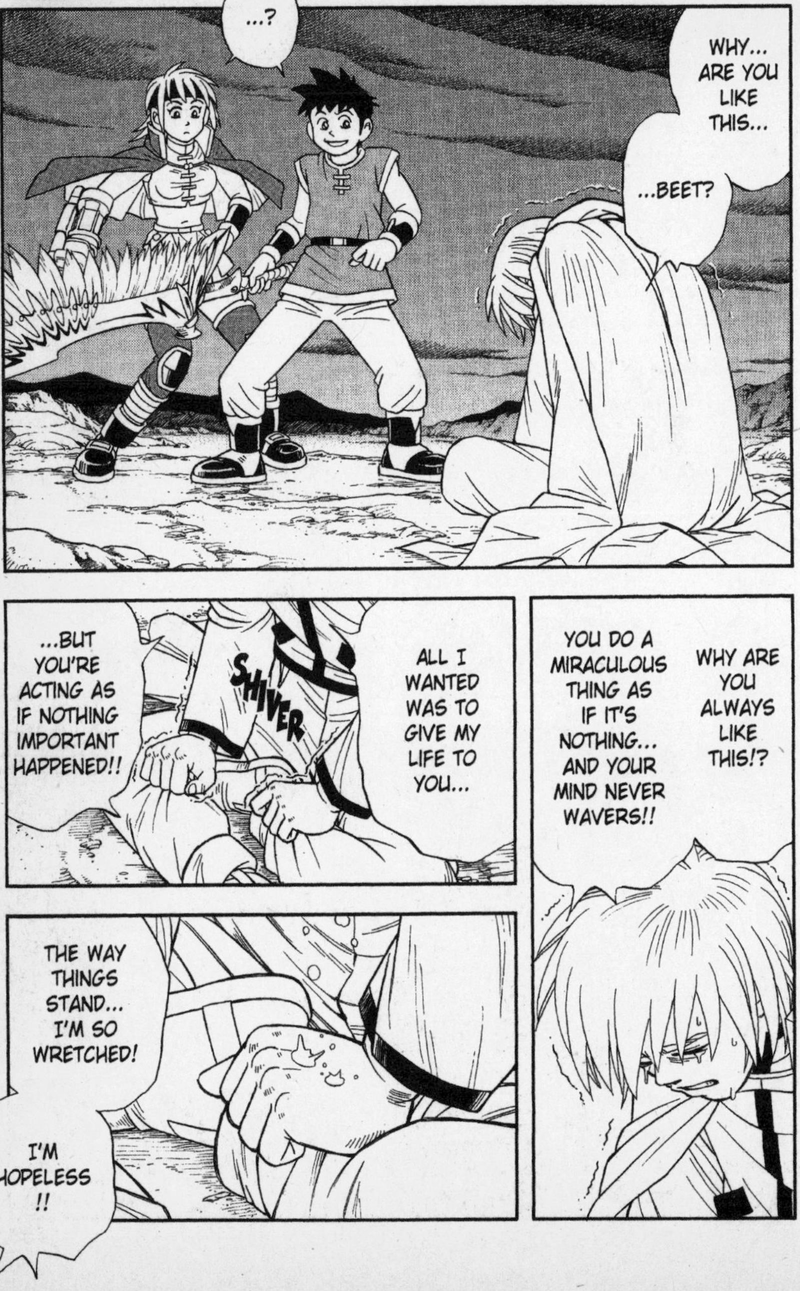
WHY... ARE YOU LIKE THIS...
...BEET?
...?
WHY ARE YOU ALWAYS LIKE THIS!?
YOU DO A MIRACULOUS THING AS IF IT'S NOTHING... AND YOUR MIND NEVER WAVERS!!
ALL I WANTED WAS TO GIVE MY LIFE TO YOU...
...BUT YOU'RE ACTING AS IF NOTHING IMPORTANT HAPPENED!!
SHIVER
THE WAY THINGS STAND... I'M SO WRETCHED!
I'M HOPELESS !!

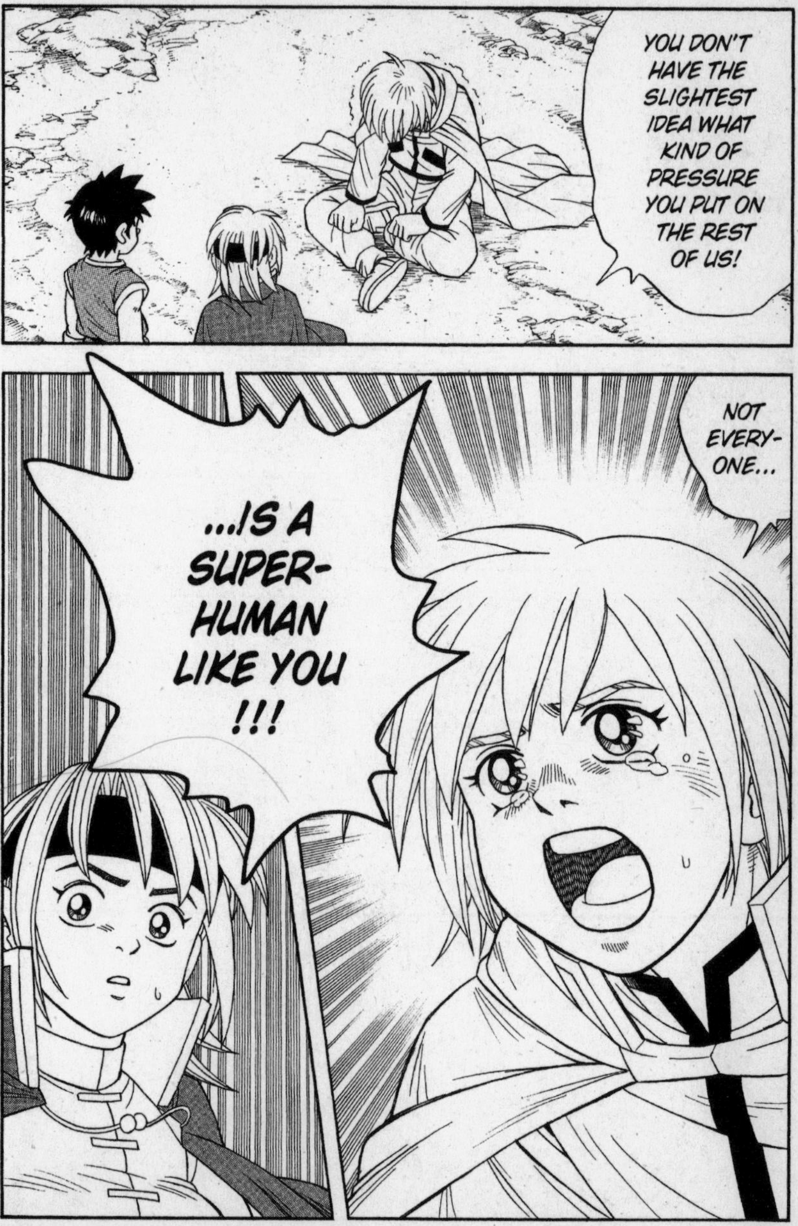
YOU DON'T HAVE THE SLIGHTEST IDEA WHAT KIND OF PRESSURE YOU PUT ON THE REST OF US!
NOT EVERY-ONE...
...IS A SUPER-HUMAN LIKE YOU !!!

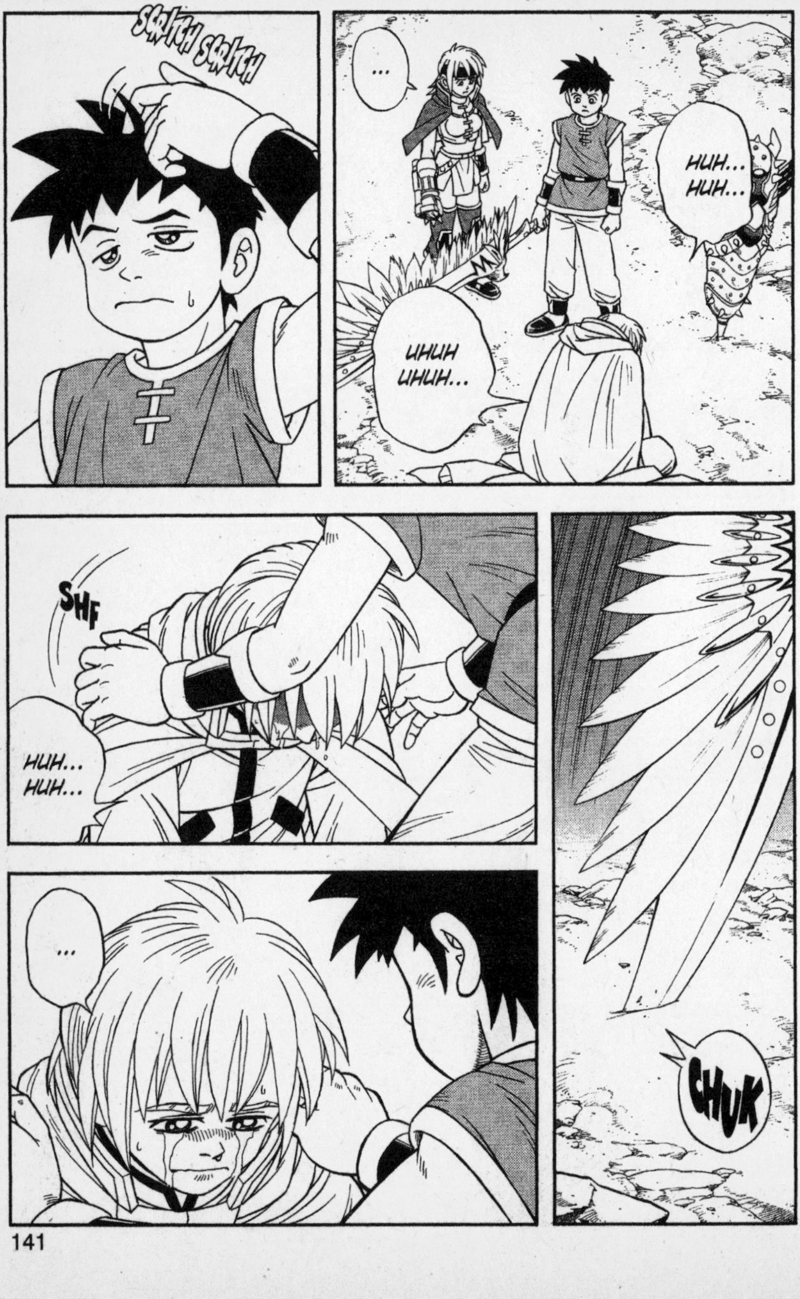
...
HUH... HUH...
UHUH UHUH...
SCRITCH SCRITCH
CHUK
SHF
HUH... HUH...
...

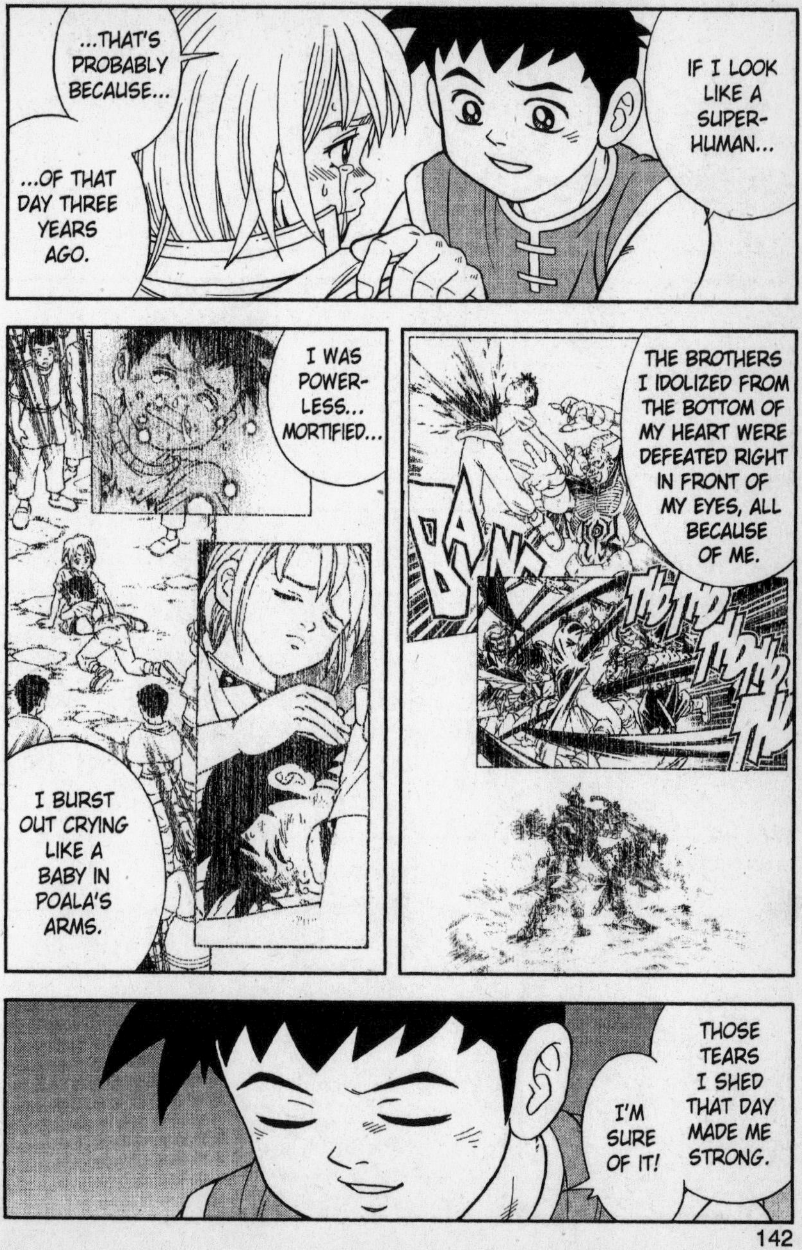
IF I LOOK LIKE A SUPER-HUMAN...
...THAT'S PROBABLY BECAUSE...
...OF THAT DAY THREE YEARS AGO.
THE BROTHERS I IDOLIZED FROM THE BOTTOM OF MY HEART WERE DEFEATED RIGHT IN FRONT OF MY EYES, ALL BECAUSE OF ME.
I WAS POWER-LESS... MORTIFIED...
I BURST OUT CRYING LIKE A BABY IN POALA'S ARMS.
THOSE TEARS I SHED THAT DAY MADE ME STRONG.
I'M SURE OF IT!

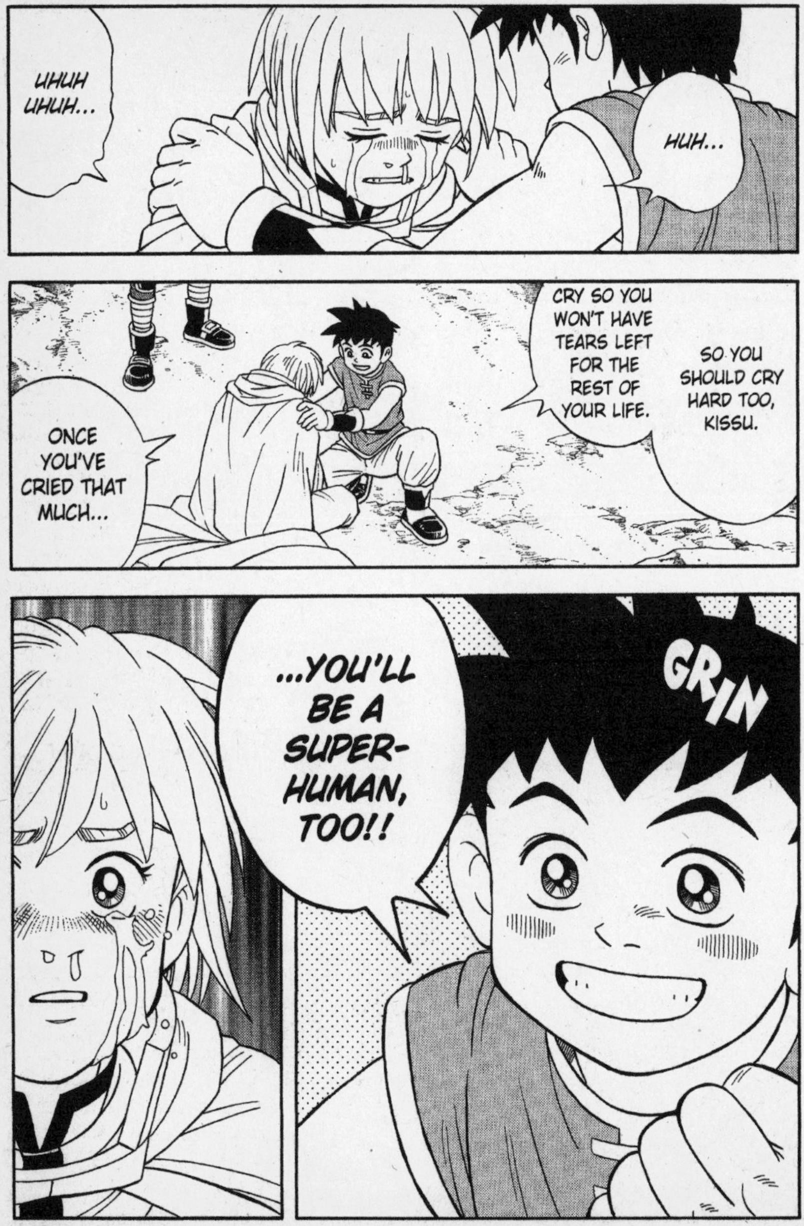
HUH...
UHUH UHUH...
SO YOU SHOULD CRY HARD TOO, KISSU.
CRY SO YOU WON'T HAVE TEARS LEFT FOR THE REST OF YOUR LIFE.
ONCE YOU'VE CRIED THAT MUCH...
GRIN
...YOU'LL BE A SUPER-HUMAN, TOO!!

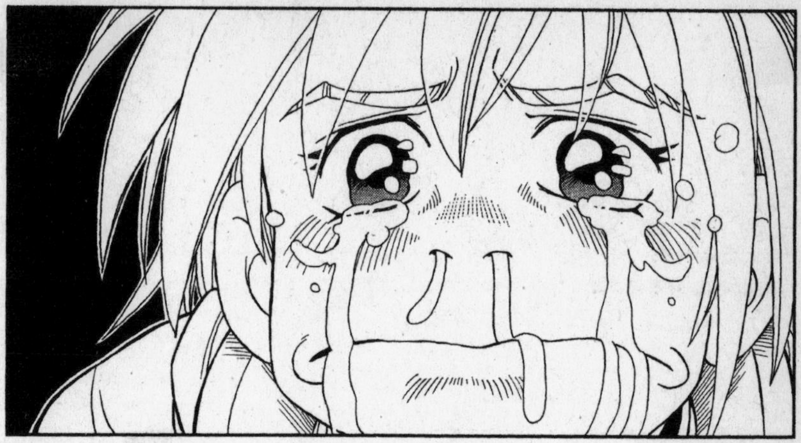

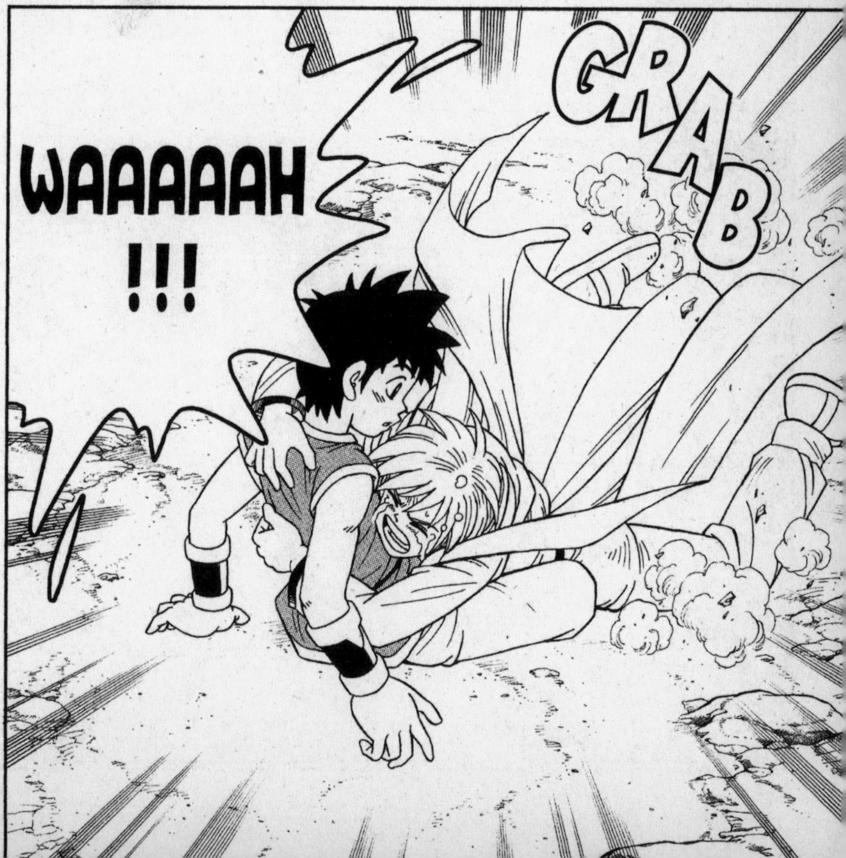
GRAB
WAAAAAH!!!

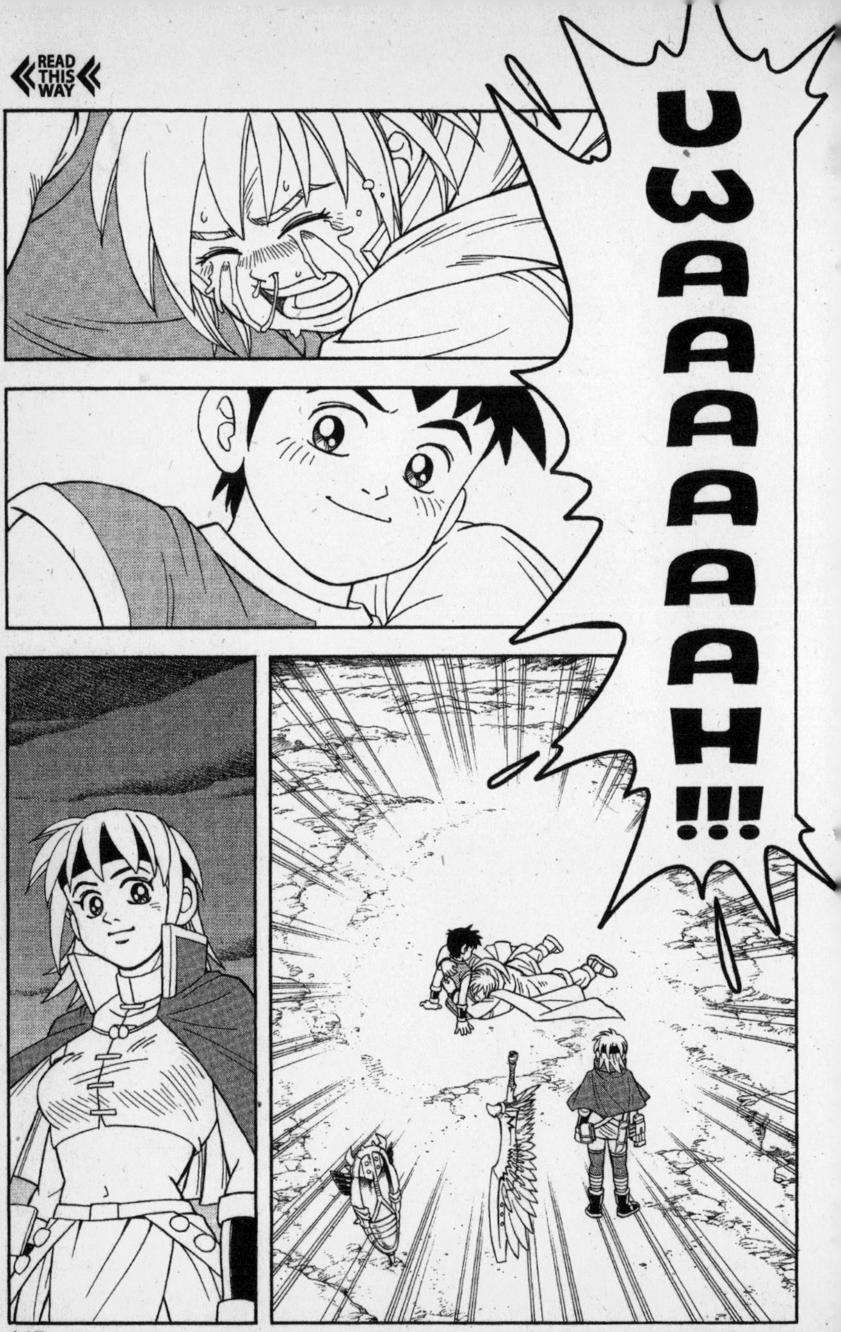
READ THIS WAY
UWAAAAAAH!!!

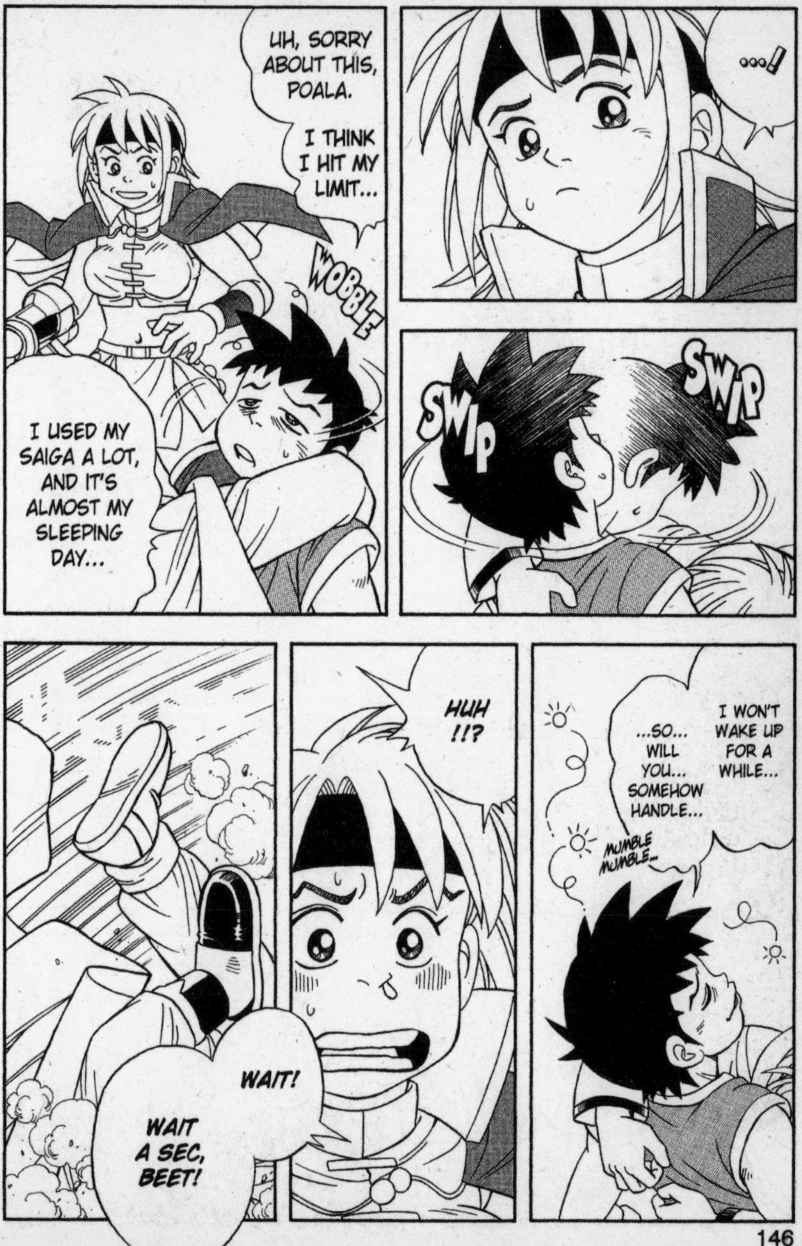
...!
SWIP
SWIP
UH, SORRY ABOUT THIS, POALA.
I THINK I HIT MY LIMIT...
WOBBLE
I USED MY SAIGA A LOT, AND IT'S ALMOST MY SLEEPING DAY...
I WON'T WAKE UP FOR A WHILE...
...SO... WILL YOU... SOMEHOW HANDLE...
MUMBLE MUMBLE...
HUH !!?
WAIT!
WAIT A SEC, BEET!

READ THIS WAY

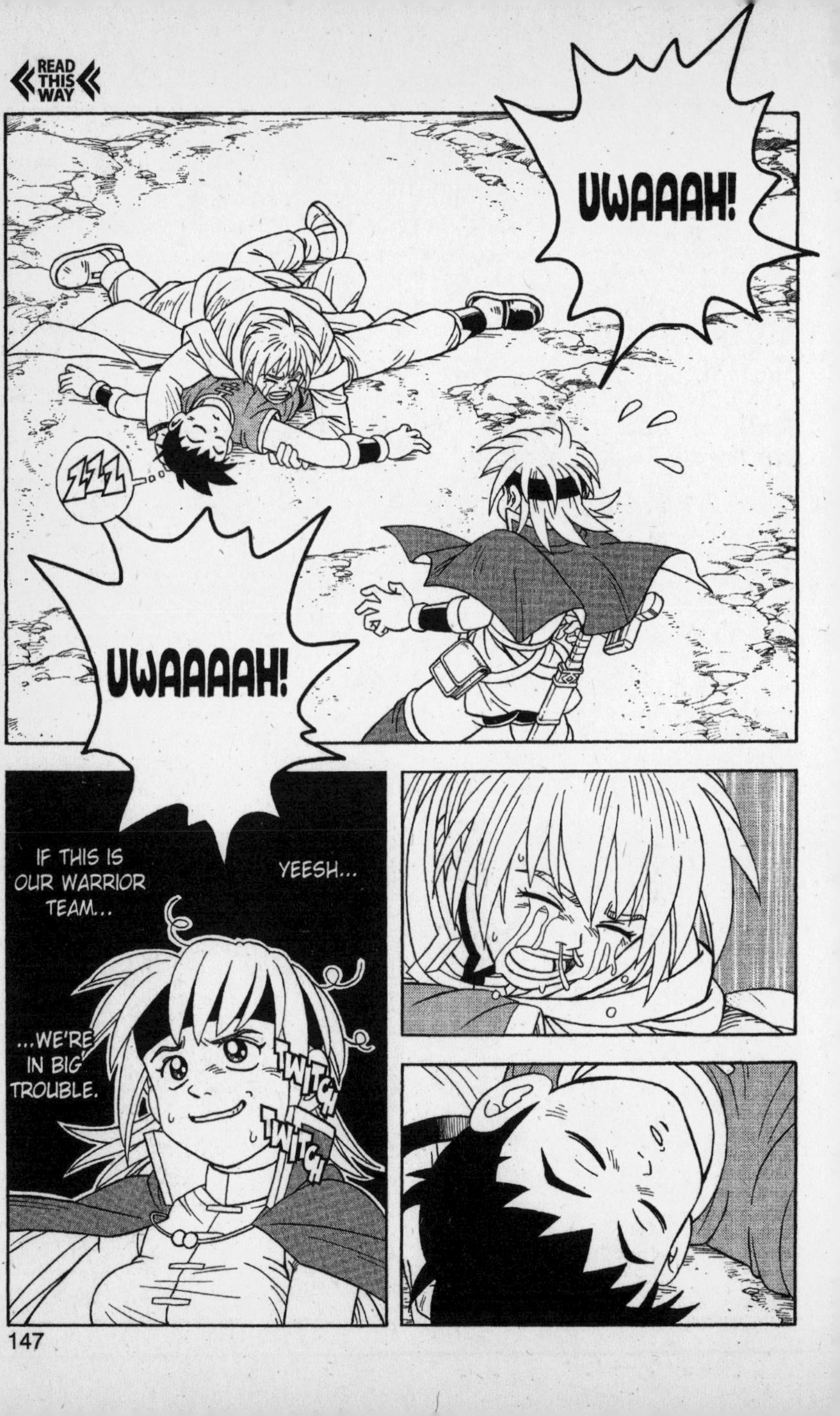

UWAAAH!
ZZZ
UWAAAAH!
YEESH...
IF THIS IS OUR WARRIOR TEAM...
...WE'RE IN BIG TROUBLE.
TWITCH
TWITCH

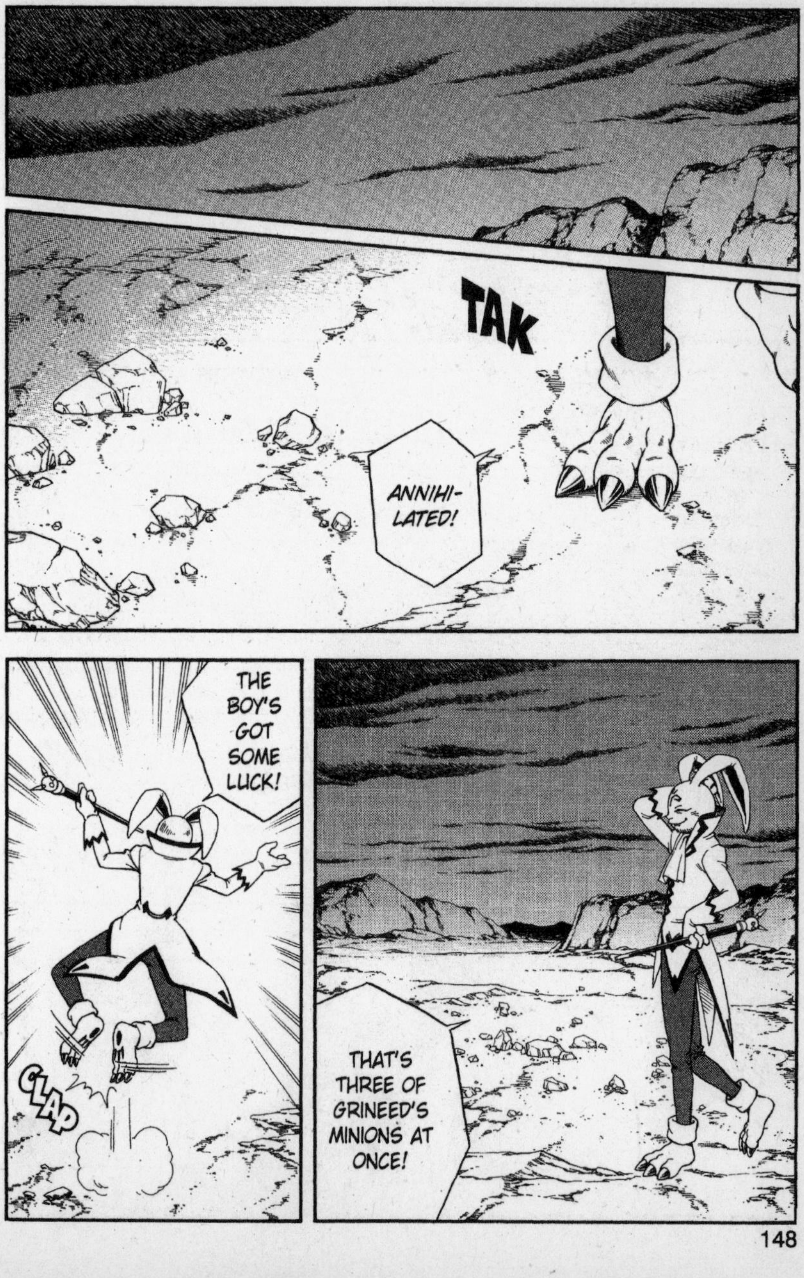

TAK
ANNIHI-LATED!
THAT'S THREE OF GRINEED'S MINIONS AT ONCE!
THE BOY'S GOT SOME LUCK!
CLAP

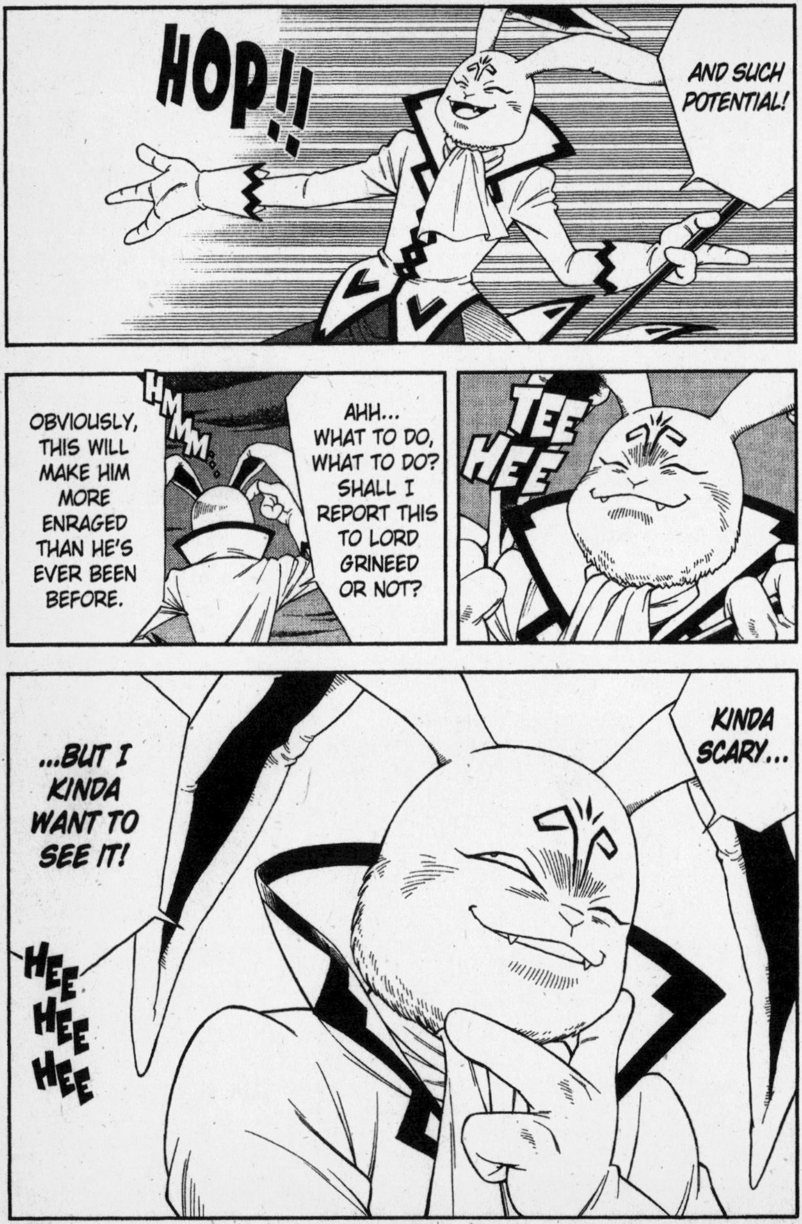
AND SUCH POTENTIAL!
HOP!!
TEE HEE
AHH... WHAT TO DO, WHAT TO DO? SHALL I REPORT THIS TO LORD GRINEED OR NOT?
HMMM
OBVIOUSLY, THIS WILL MAKE HIM MORE ENRAGED THAN HE'S EVER BEEN BEFORE.
KINDA SCARY...
...BUT I KINDA WANT TO SEE IT!
HEE HEE HEE

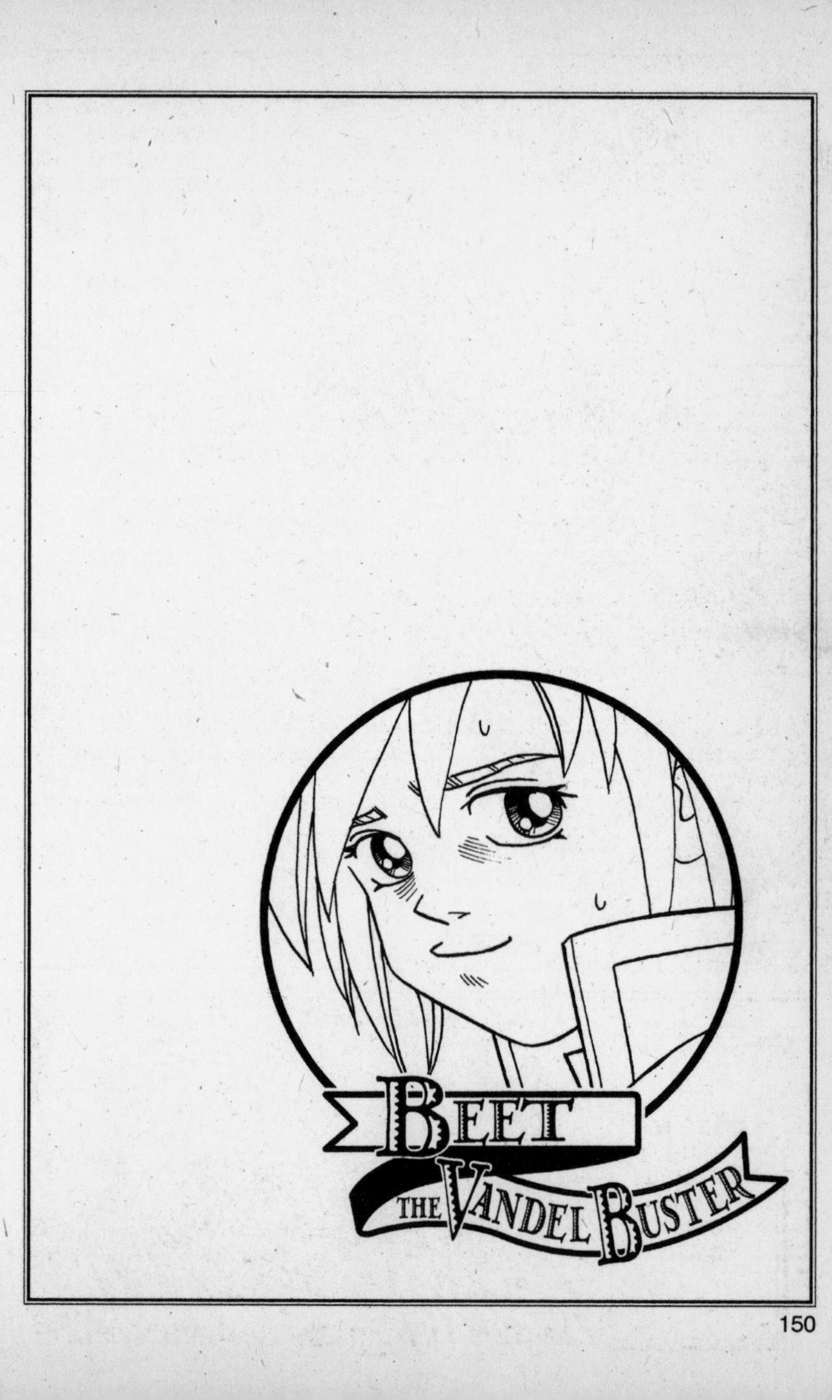
BEET
THE VANDEL BUSTER

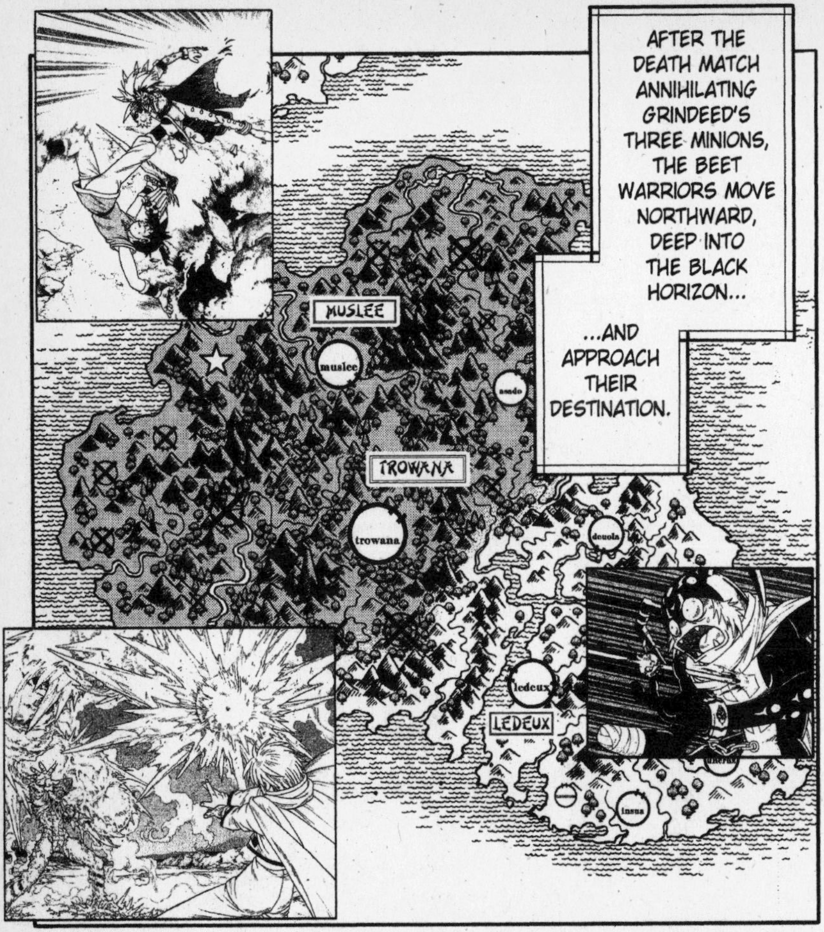
AFTER THE DEATH MATCH ANNIHILATING GRINDEED'S THREE MINIONS, THE BEET WARRIORS MOVE NORTHWARD, DEEP INTO THE BLACK HORIZON...
...AND APPROACH THEIR DESTINATION.
MUSLEE
muslee
TROWANA
trowana
deuola
ledeux
LEDEUX
insna

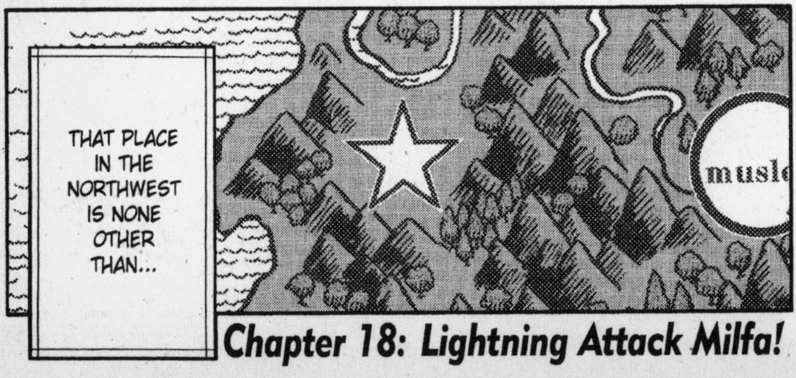
THAT PLACE IN THE NORTHWEST IS NONE OTHER THAN...
musle

Chapter 18: Lightning Attack Milfa!

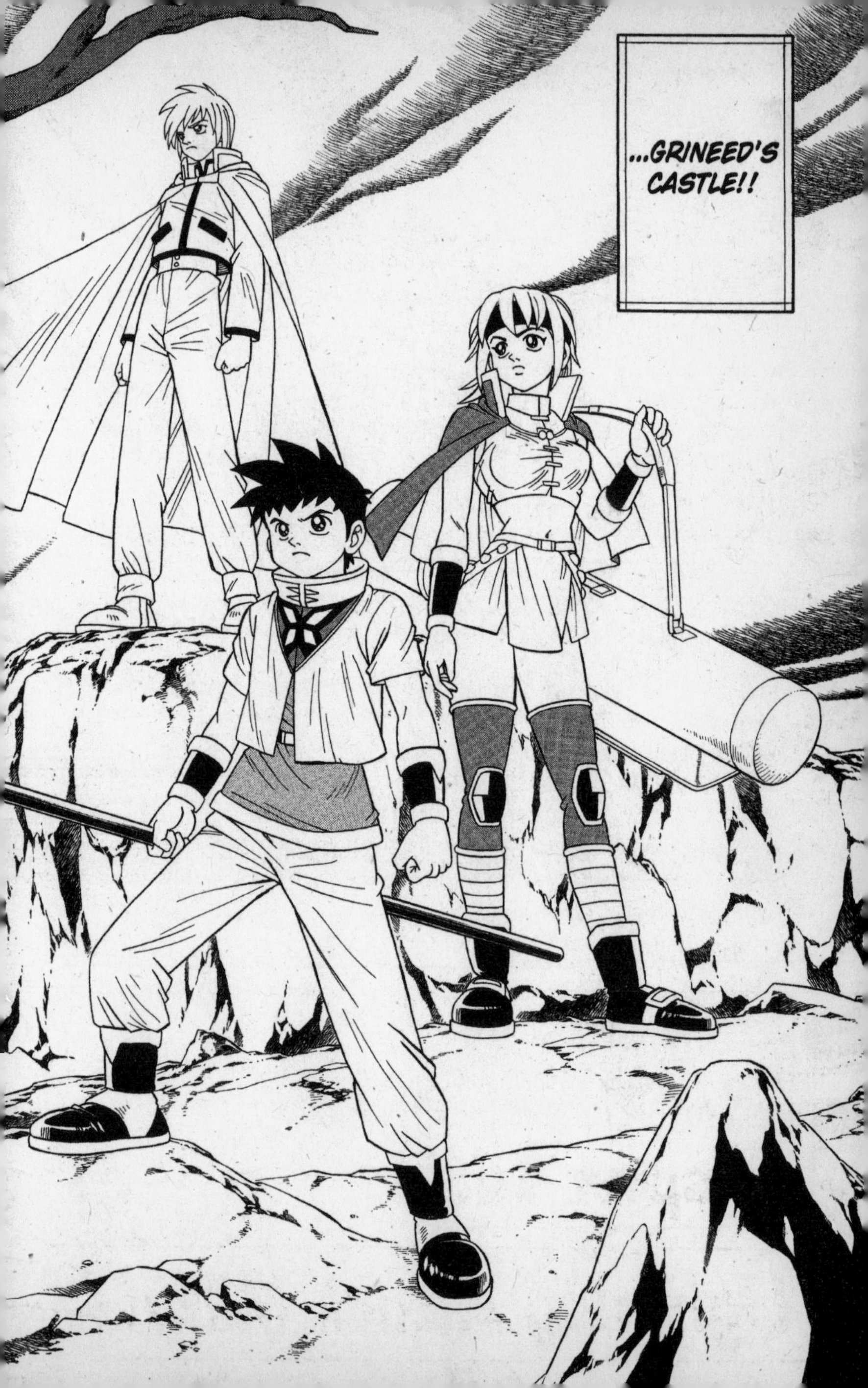
...GRINEED'S CASTLE!!

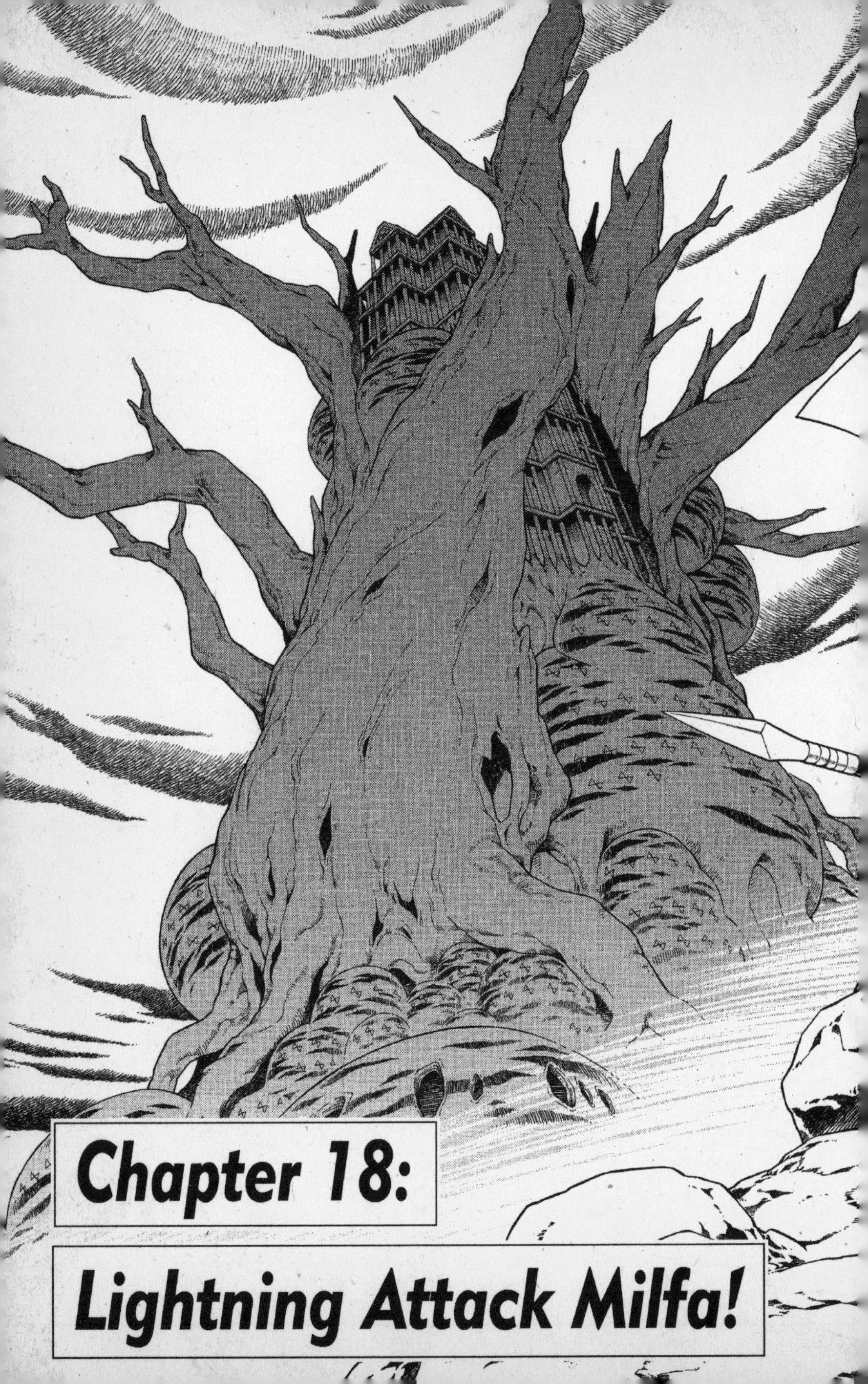
Chapter 18:
Lightning Attack Milfa!

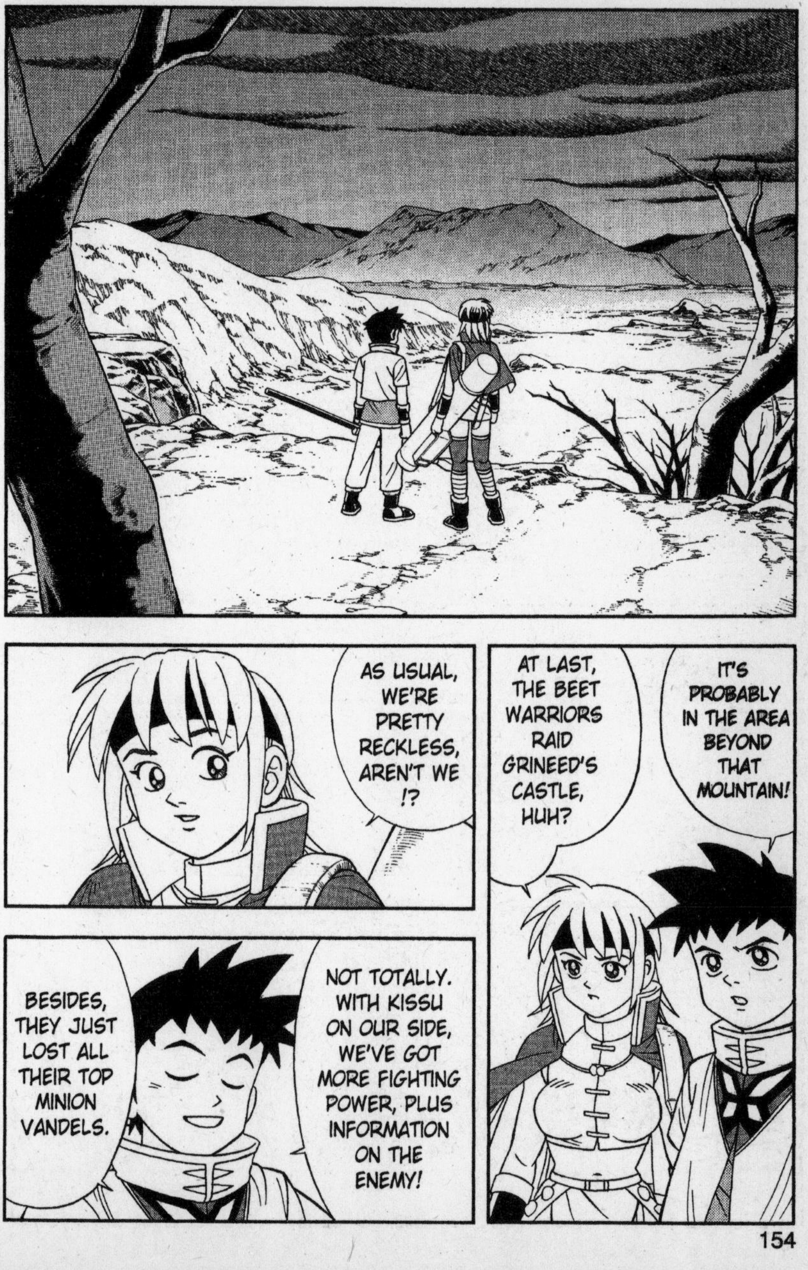
IT'S PROBABLY IN THE AREA BEYOND THAT MOUNTAIN!
AT LAST, THE BEET WARRIORS RAID GRINEED'S CASTLE, HUH?
AS USUAL, WE'RE PRETTY RECKLESS, AREN'T WE !?
NOT TOTALLY. WITH KISSU ON OUR SIDE, WE'VE GOT MORE FIGHTING POWER, PLUS INFORMATION ON THE ENEMY!
BESIDES, THEY JUST LOST ALL THEIR TOP MINION VANDELS.

READ THIS WAY

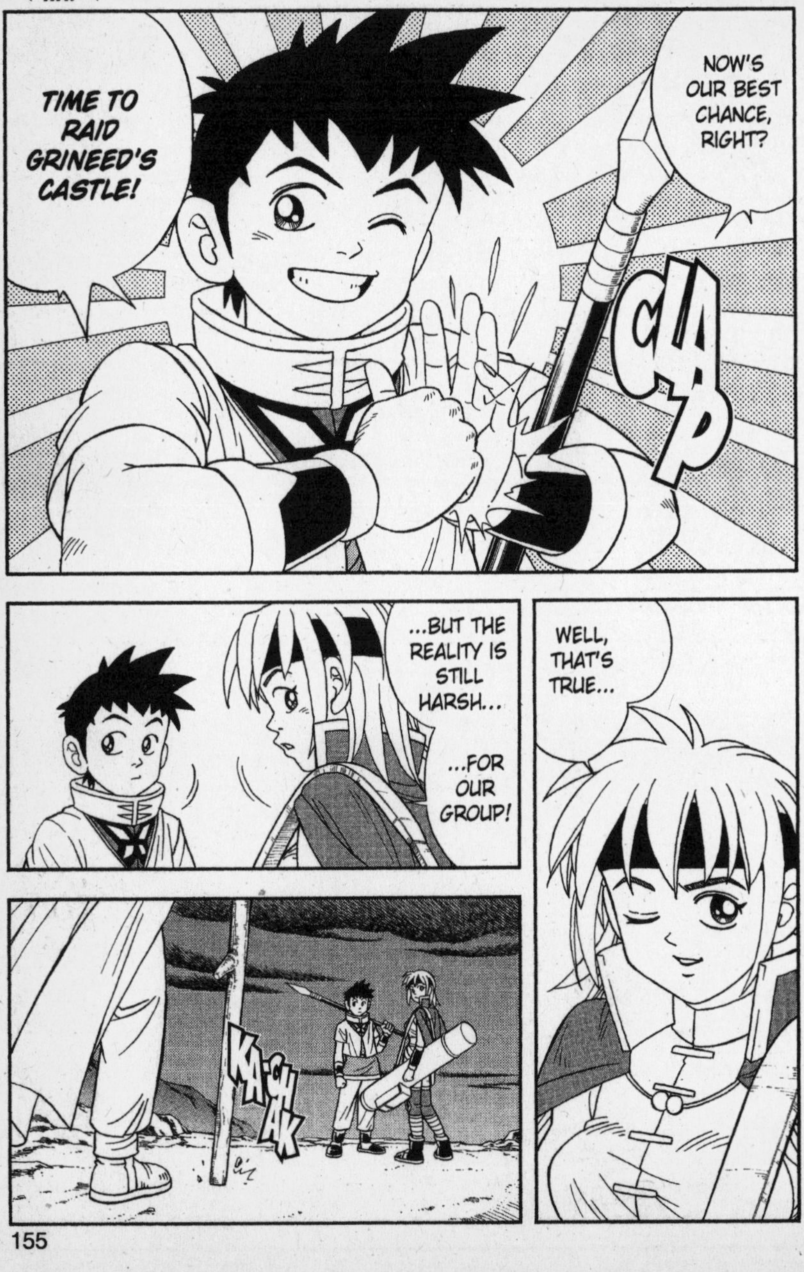
NOW'S OUR BEST CHANCE, RIGHT?
TIME TO RAID GRINEED'S CASTLE!
CLAP
WELL, THAT'S TRUE...
...BUT THE REALITY IS STILL HARSH...
...FOR OUR GROUP!
KA-CHAK

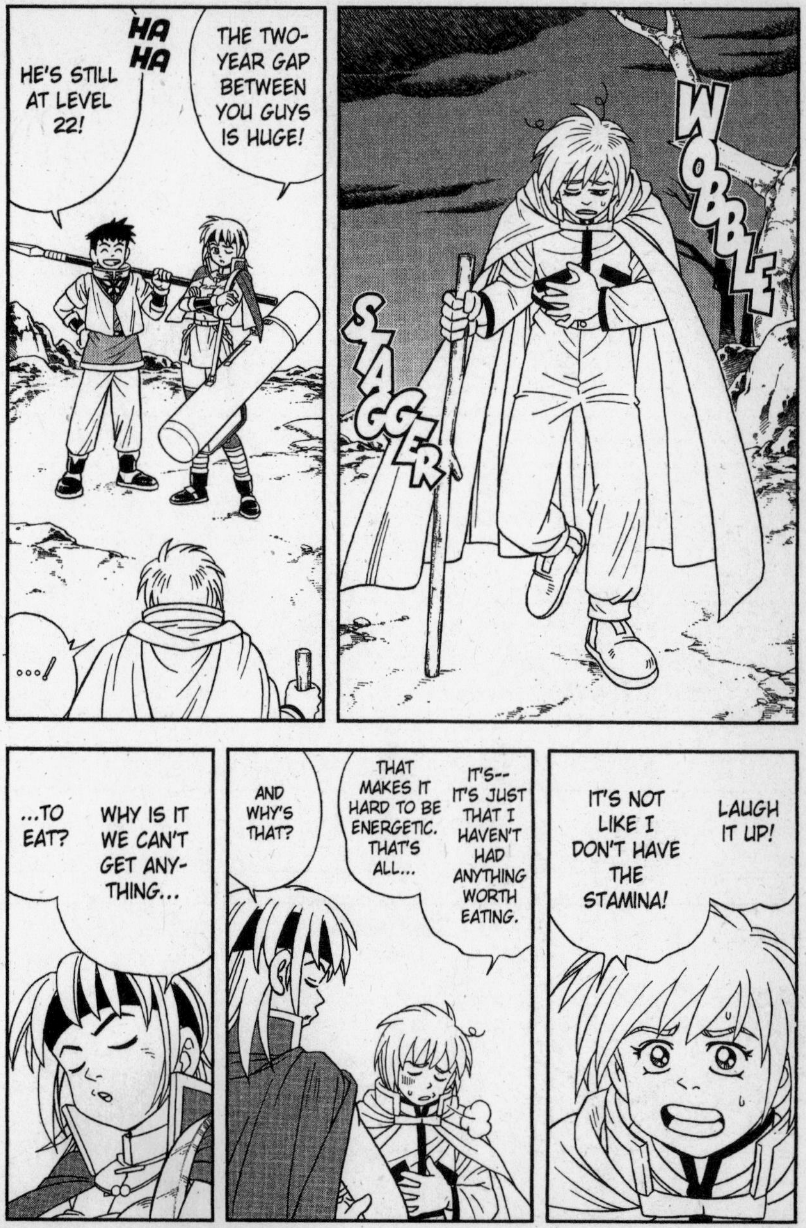
WOBBLE
STAGGER
THE TWO-YEAR GAP BETWEEN YOU GUYS IS HUGE!
HA HA
HE'S STILL AT LEVEL 22!
...!
LAUGH IT UP!
IT'S NOT LIKE I DON'T HAVE THE STAMINA!
IT'S-- IT'S JUST THAT I HAVEN'T HAD ANYTHING WORTH EATING.
THAT MAKES IT HARD TO BE ENERGETIC. THAT'S ALL...
AND WHY'S THAT?
WHY IS IT WE CAN'T GET ANYTHING...
...TO EAT?

READ THIS WAY

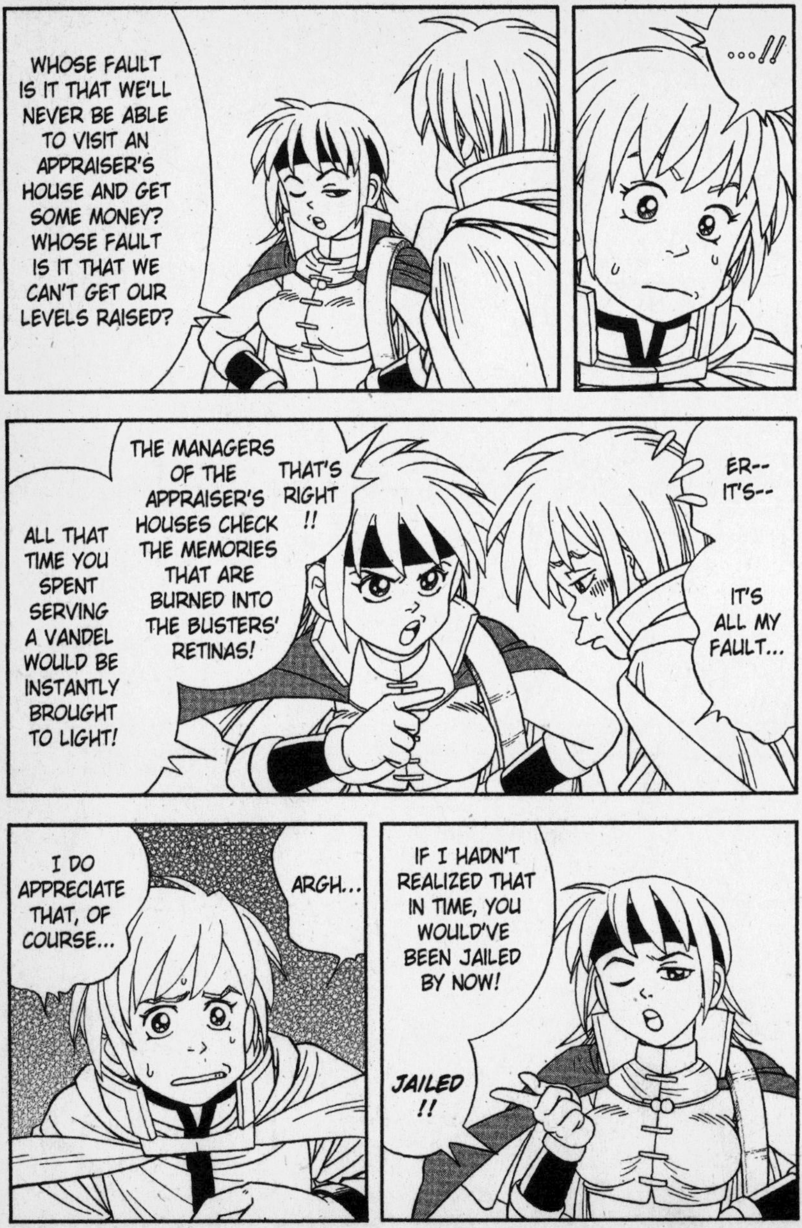
...!!
WHOSE FAULT IS IT THAT WE'LL NEVER BE ABLE TO VISIT AN APPRAISER'S HOUSE AND GET SOME MONEY? WHOSE FAULT IS IT THAT WE CAN'T GET OUR LEVELS RAISED?
ER-- IT'S--
IT'S ALL MY FAULT...
THAT'S RIGHT !!
THE MANAGERS OF THE APPRAISER'S HOUSES CHECK THE MEMORIES THAT ARE BURNED INTO THE BUSTERS' RETINAS!
ALL THAT TIME YOU SPENT SERVING A VANDEL WOULD BE INSTANTLY BROUGHT TO LIGHT!
IF I HADN'T REALIZED THAT IN TIME, YOU WOULD'VE BEEN JAILED BY NOW!
JAILED !!
ARGH...
I DO APPRECIATE THAT, OF COURSE...

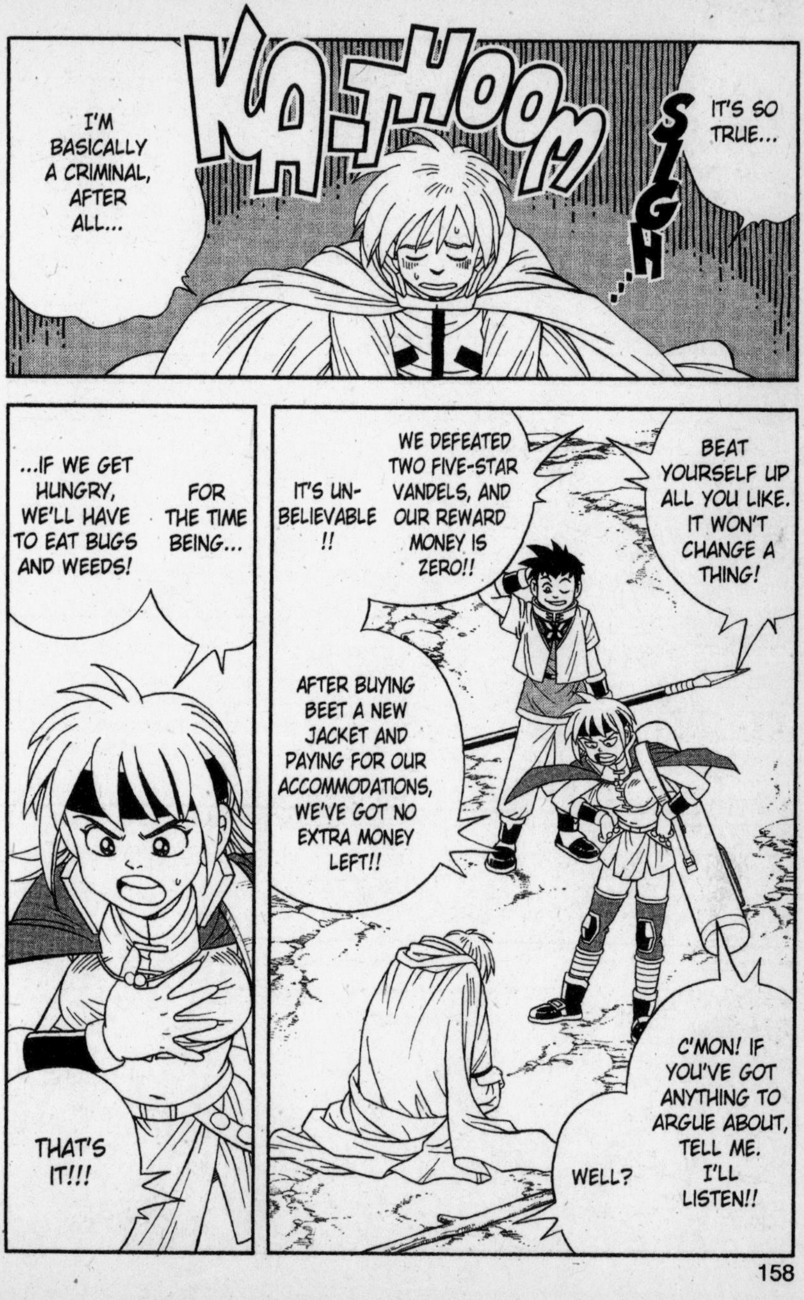
IT'S SO TRUE...
SIGH...
KA-THOOM
I'M BASICALLY A CRIMINAL, AFTER ALL...
BEAT YOURSELF UP ALL YOU LIKE. IT WON'T CHANGE A THING!
WE DEFEATED TWO FIVE-STAR VANDELS, AND OUR REWARD MONEY IS ZERO!!
IT'S UN-BELIEVABLE !!
AFTER BUYING BEET A NEW JACKET AND PAYING FOR OUR ACCOMMODATIONS, WE'VE GOT NO EXTRA MONEY LEFT!!
C'MON! IF YOU'VE GOT ANYTHING TO ARGUE ABOUT, TELL ME. I'LL LISTEN!!
WELL?
FOR THE TIME BEING...
...IF WE GET HUNGRY, WE'LL HAVE TO EAT BUGS AND WEEDS!
THAT'S IT!!!

READ THIS WAY

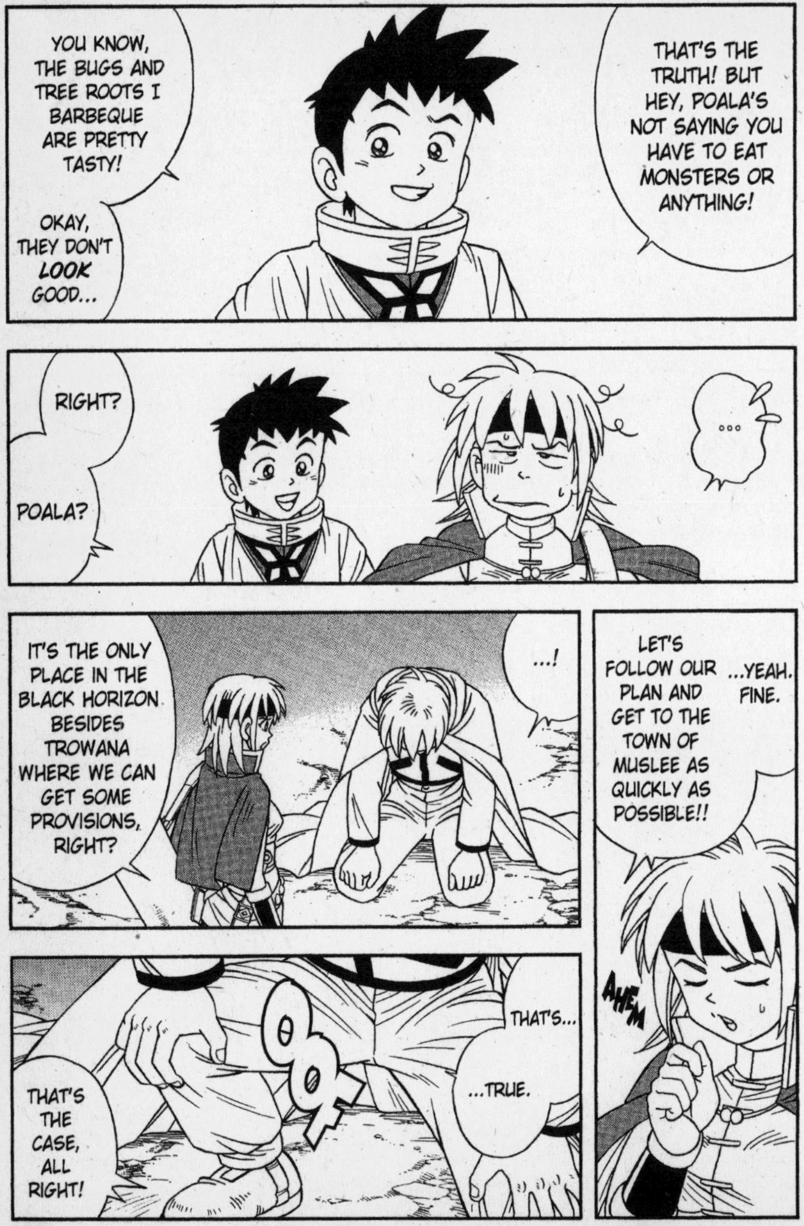

THAT'S THE TRUTH! BUT HEY, POALA'S NOT SAYING YOU HAVE TO EAT MONSTERS OR ANYTHING!
YOU KNOW, THE BUGS AND TREE ROOTS I BARBEQUE ARE PRETTY TASTY!
OKAY, THEY DON'T *LOOK* GOOD...
...
RIGHT?
POALA?
LET'S FOLLOW OUR PLAN AND GET TO THE TOWN OF MUSLEE AS QUICKLY AS POSSIBLE!!
...YEAH. FINE.
AHEM
...!
IT'S THE ONLY PLACE IN THE BLACK HORIZON BESIDES TROWANA WHERE WE CAN GET SOME PROVISIONS, RIGHT?
THAT'S...
...TRUE.
THAT'S THE CASE, ALL RIGHT!

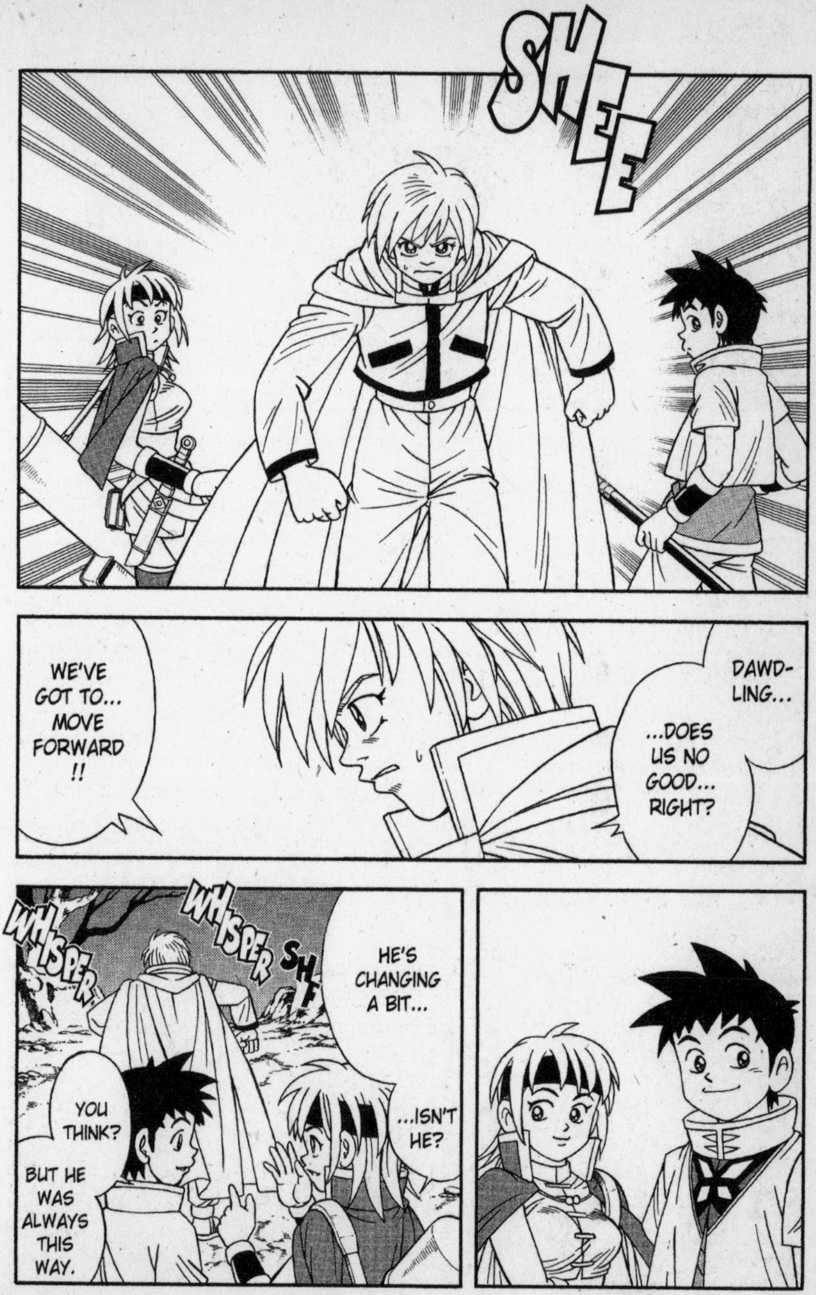
SHEE
DAWD-LING... ...DOES US NO GOOD... RIGHT?
WE'VE GOT TO... MOVE FORWARD !!
HE'S CHANGING A BIT...
...ISN'T HE?
SHF
WHISPER
WHISPER
YOU THINK?
BUT HE WAS ALWAYS THIS WAY.

READ THIS WAY

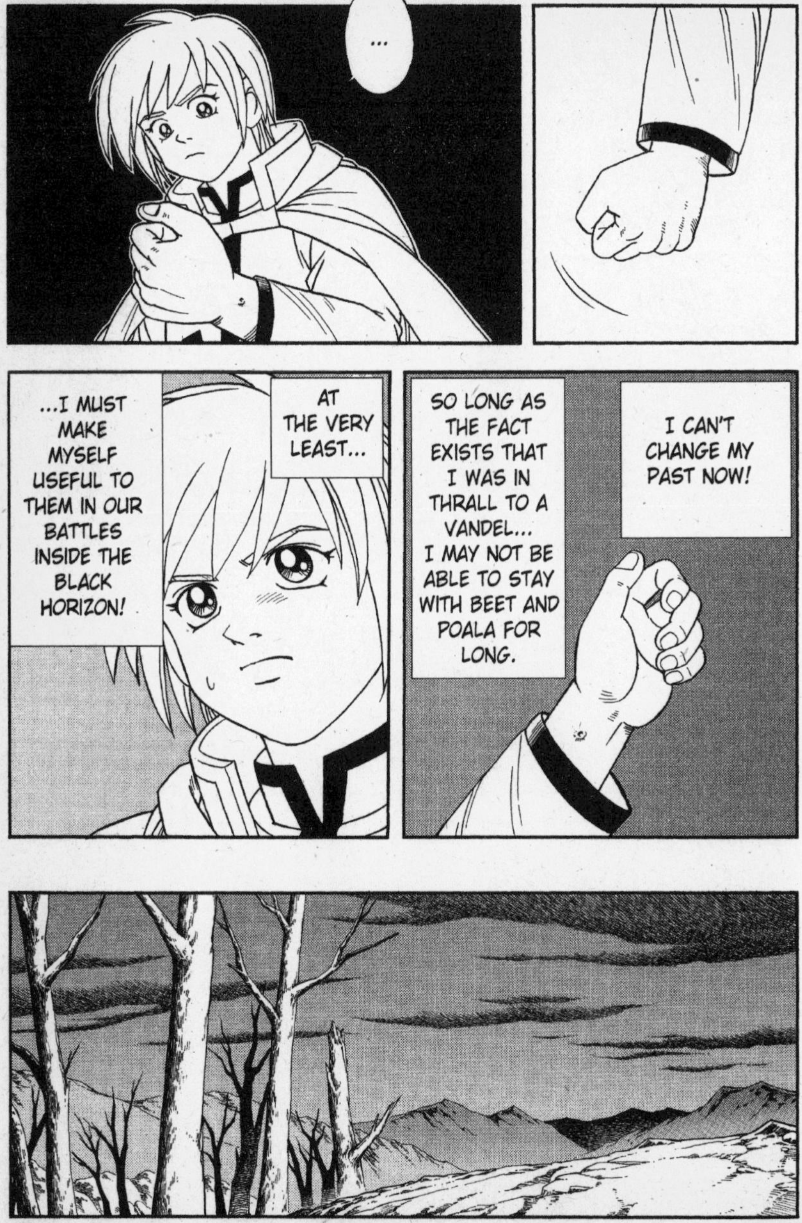
...
I CAN'T CHANGE MY PAST NOW!
SO LONG AS THE FACT EXISTS THAT I WAS IN THRALL TO A VANDEL... I MAY NOT BE ABLE TO STAY WITH BEET AND POALA FOR LONG.
AT THE VERY LEAST...
...I MUST MAKE MYSELF USEFUL TO THEM IN OUR BATTLES INSIDE THE BLACK HORIZON!

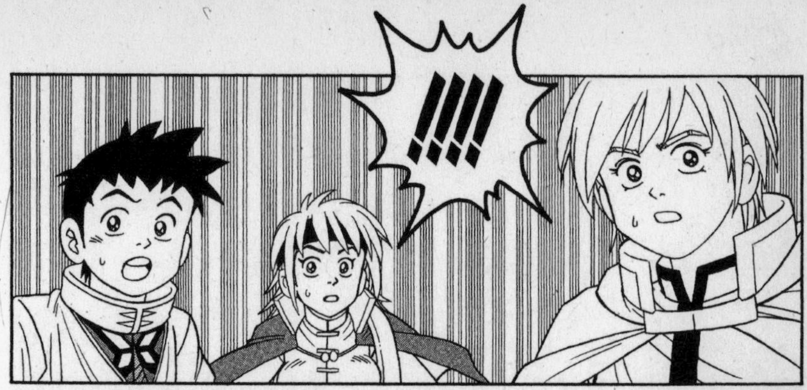
!!!!!
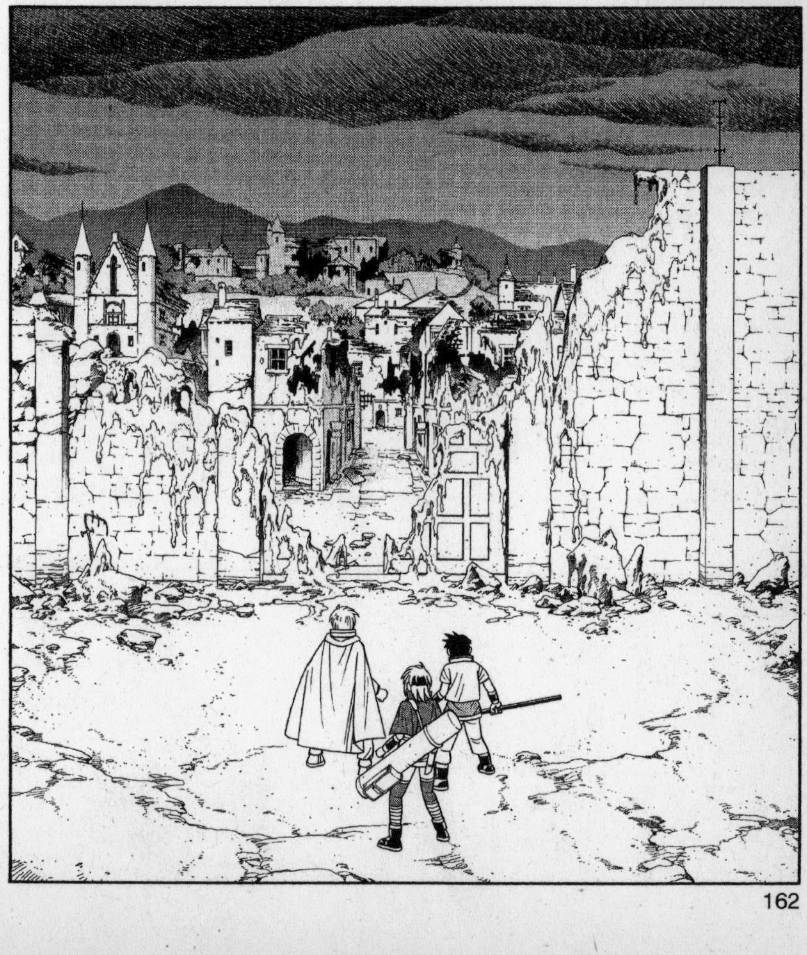

READ THIS WAY

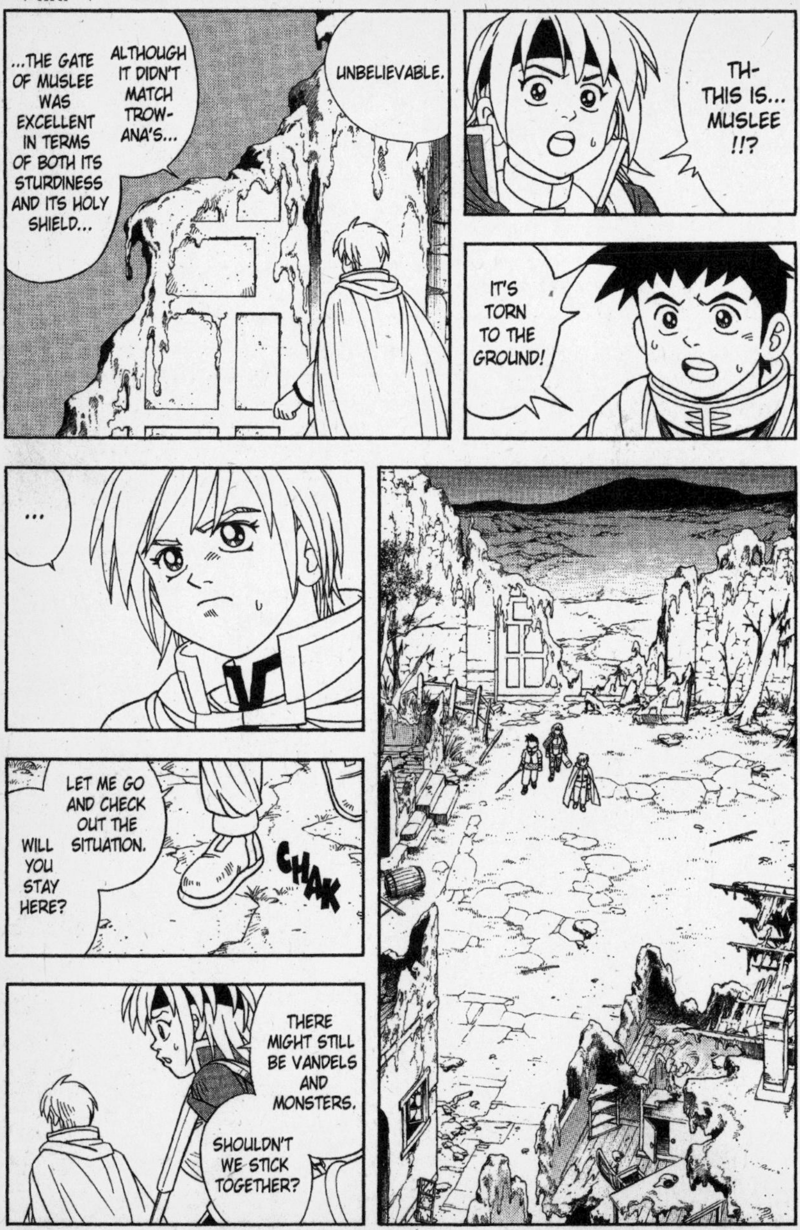
TH- THIS IS... MUSLEE !!?
IT'S TORN TO THE GROUND!
UNBELIEVABLE.
ALTHOUGH IT DIDN'T MATCH TROW-ANA'S...
...THE GATE OF MUSLEE WAS EXCELLENT IN TERMS OF BOTH ITS STURDINESS AND ITS HOLY SHIELD...
...
LET ME GO AND CHECK OUT THE SITUATION.
WILL YOU STAY HERE?
CHAK
THERE MIGHT STILL BE VANDELS AND MONSTERS.
SHOULDN'T WE STICK TOGETHER?

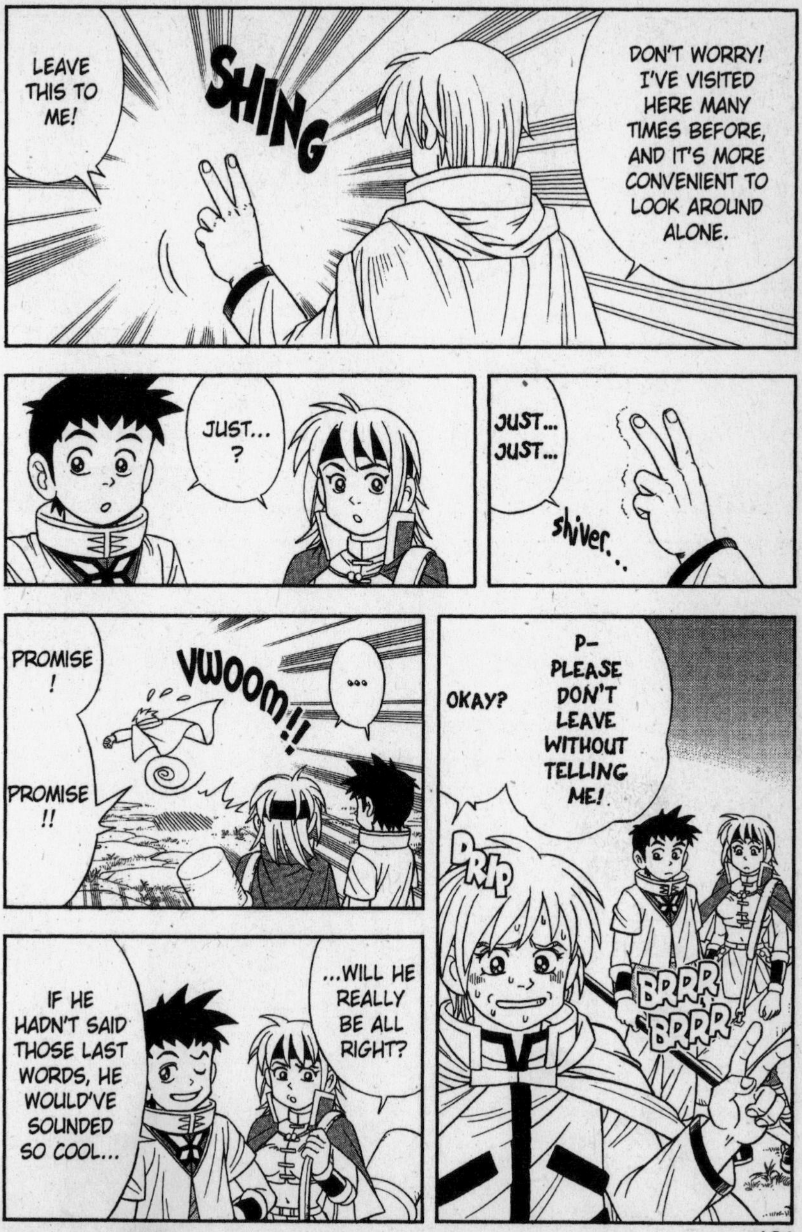
DON'T WORRY! I'VE VISITED HERE MANY TIMES BEFORE, AND IT'S MORE CONVENIENT TO LOOK AROUND ALONE.
SHING
LEAVE THIS TO ME!
JUST... JUST...
shiver...
JUST... ?
P- PLEASE DON'T LEAVE WITHOUT TELLING ME!
OKAY?
DRIP
BRRR BRRR
...
VWOOM!!
PROMISE !
PROMISE !!
...WILL HE REALLY BE ALL RIGHT?
IF HE HADN'T SAID THOSE LAST WORDS, HE WOULD'VE SOUNDED SO COOL...

READ THIS WAY

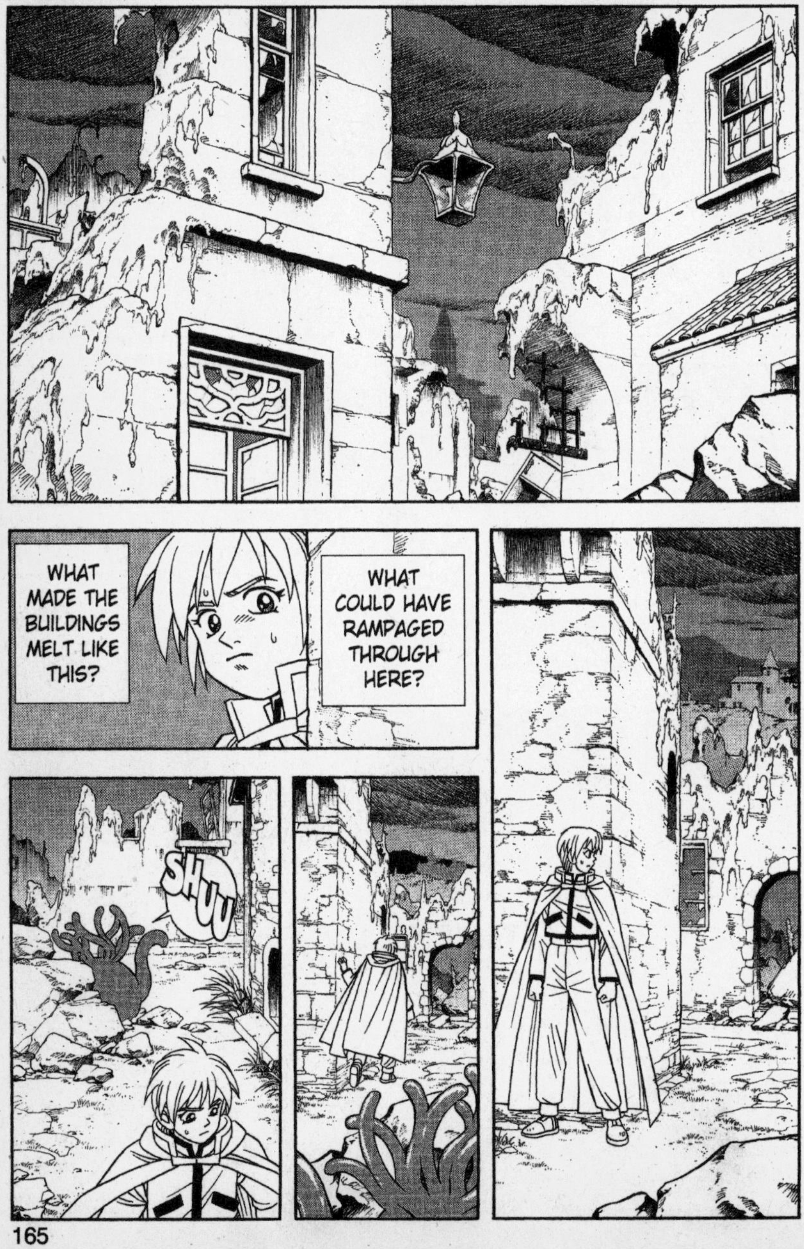
WHAT COULD HAVE RAMPAGED THROUGH HERE?
WHAT MADE THE BUILDINGS MELT LIKE THIS?
SHUU

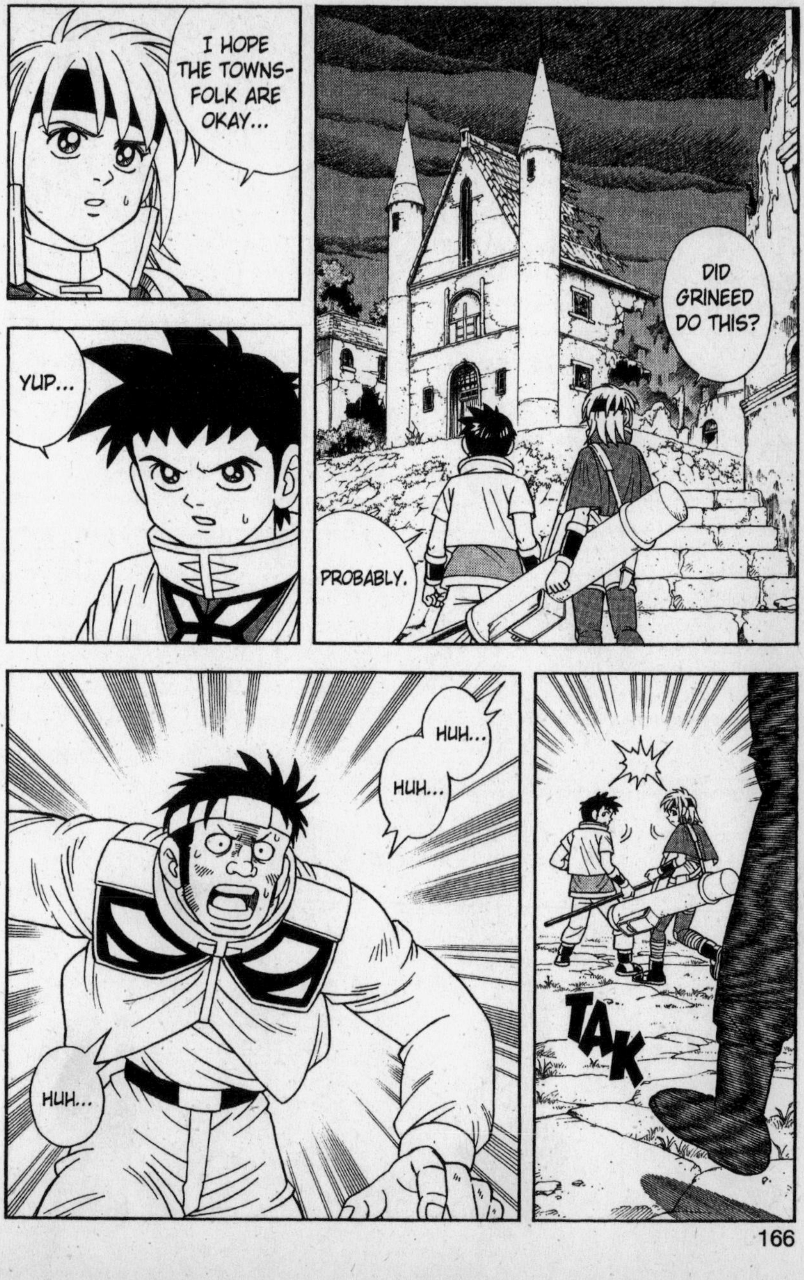
DID GRINEED DO THIS?
PROBABLY.
I HOPE THE TOWNS-FOLK ARE OKAY...
YUP...
TAK
HUH...
HUH...
HUH...

READ THIS WAY

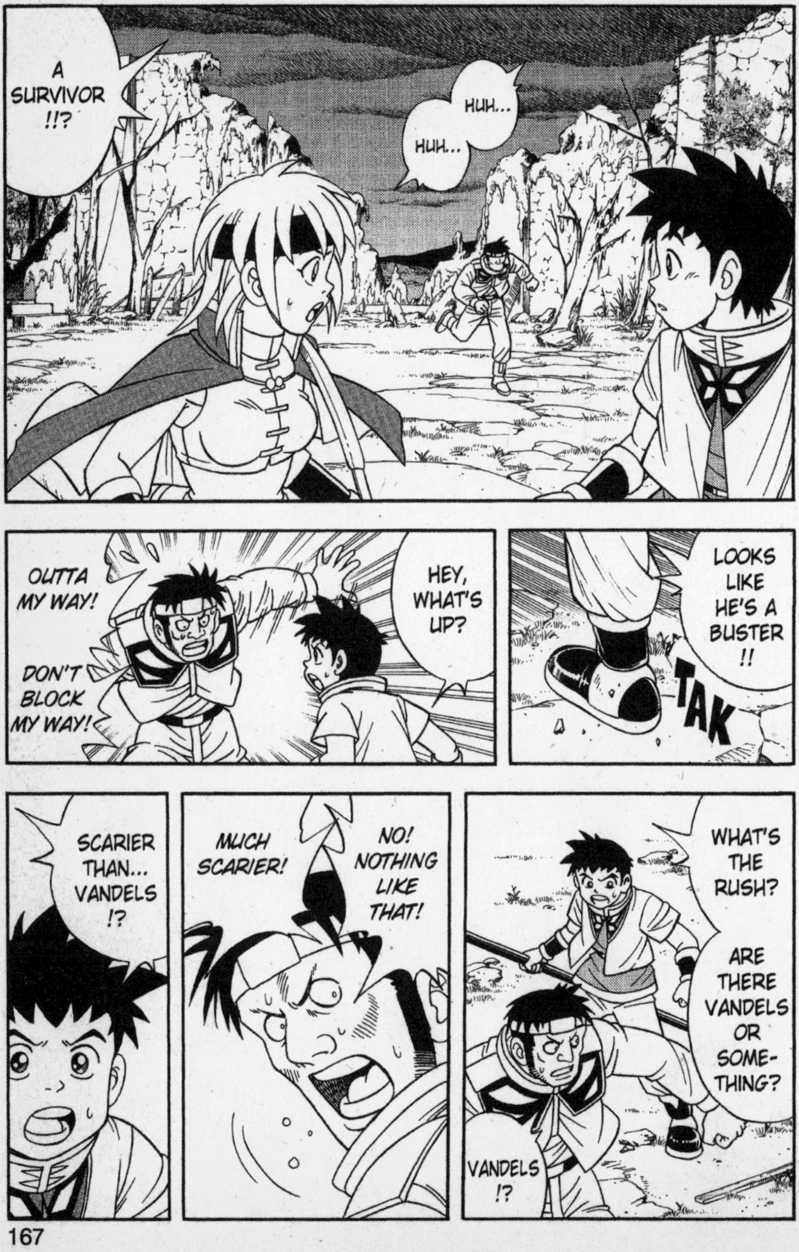

HUH... HUH...
A SURVIVOR !!?
LOOKS LIKE HE'S A BUSTER !!
TAK
HEY, WHAT'S UP?
OUTTA MY WAY!
DON'T BLOCK MY WAY!
WHAT'S THE RUSH?
ARE THERE VANDELS OR SOME-THING?
VANDELS !?
NO! NOTHING LIKE THAT!
MUCH SCARIER!
SCARIER THAN... VANDELS !?

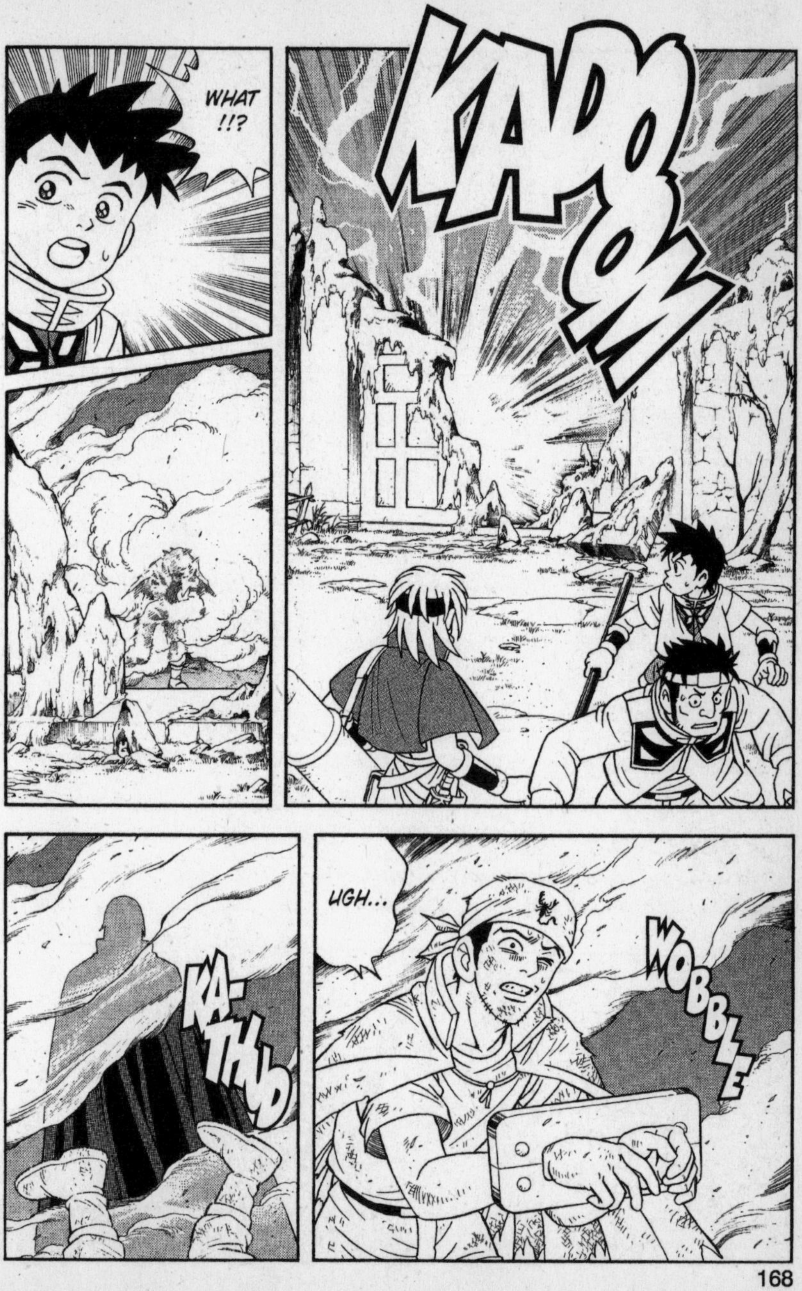
KADOOM
WHAT !!?
UGH...
WOBBLE
KA-THUD

READ THIS WAY

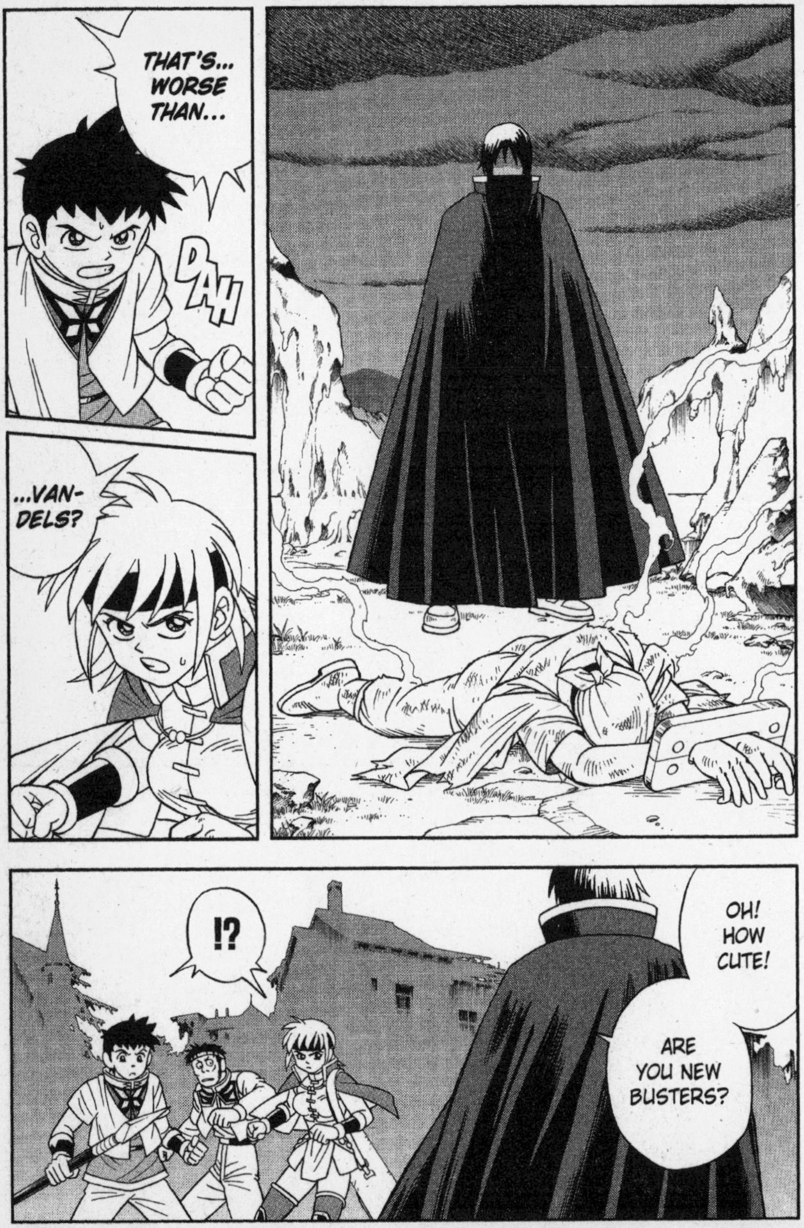
THAT'S... WORSE THAN...
DAH
...VAN-DELS?
OH! HOW CUTE!
ARE YOU NEW BUSTERS?
!?

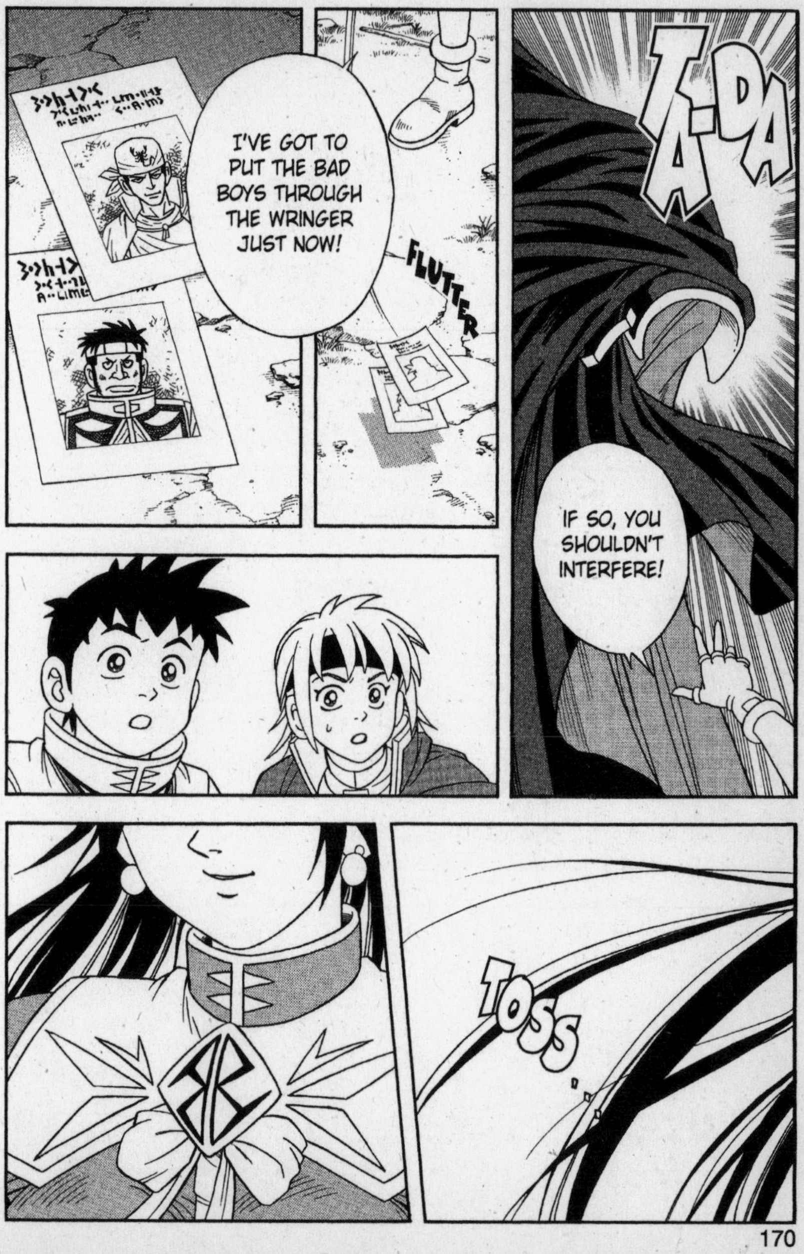
TA-DA
IF SO, YOU SHOULDN'T INTERFERE!
I'VE GOT TO PUT THE BAD BOYS THROUGH THE WRINGER JUST NOW!
FLUTTER
TOSS

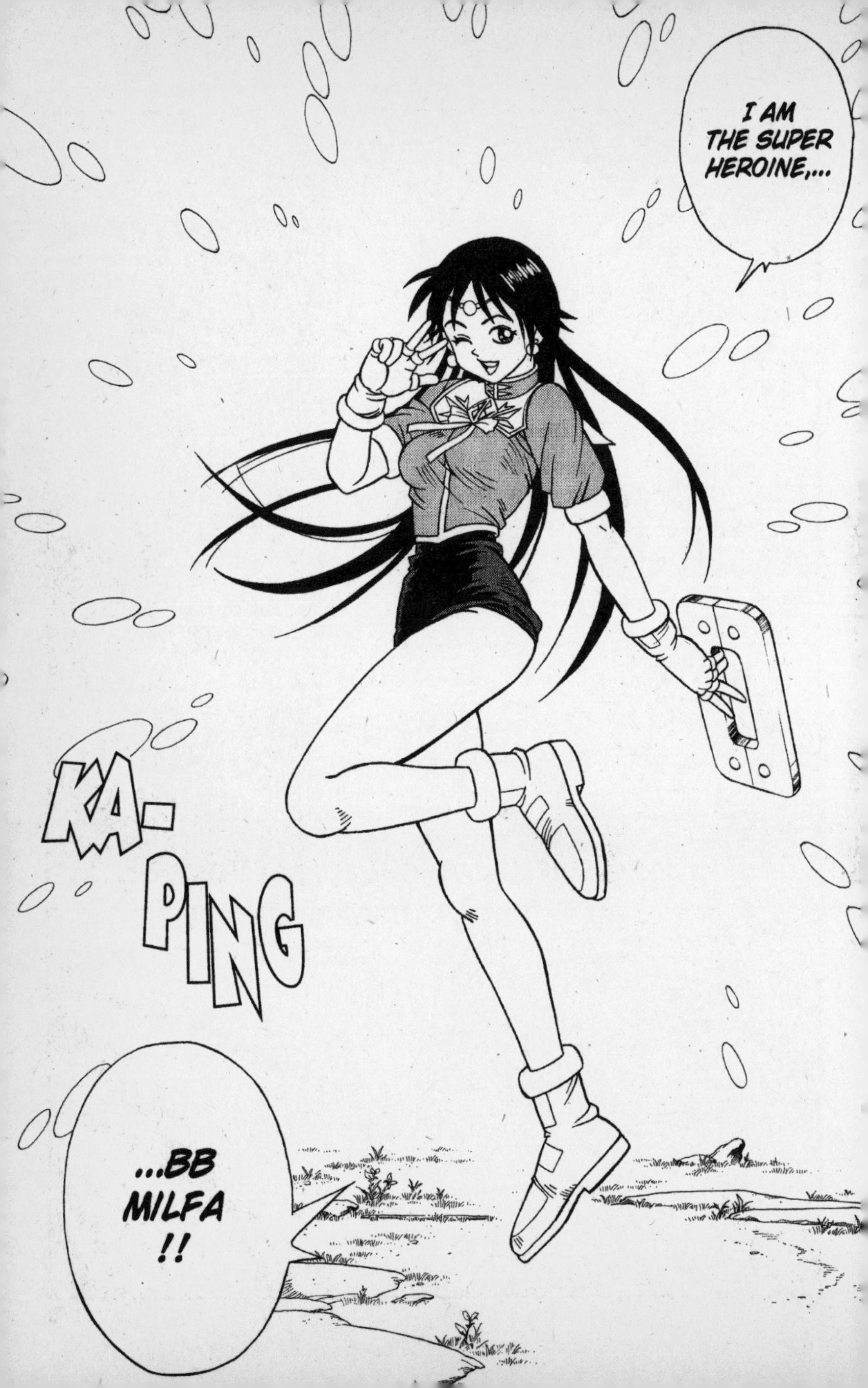
I AM THE SUPER HEROINE,...
KA-PING
...BB MILFA !!

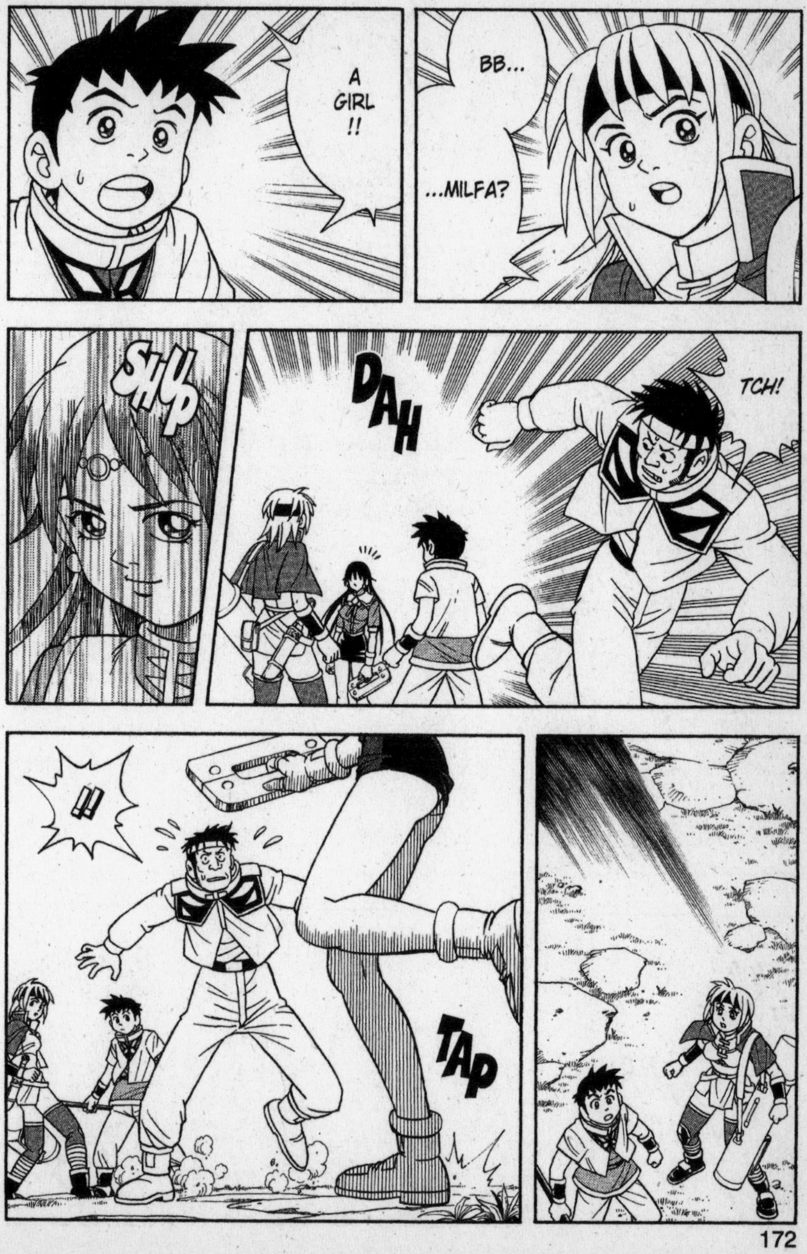
BB...
...MILFA?
A GIRL !!
TCH!
DAH
SHUP
!!
TAP

READ THIS WAY

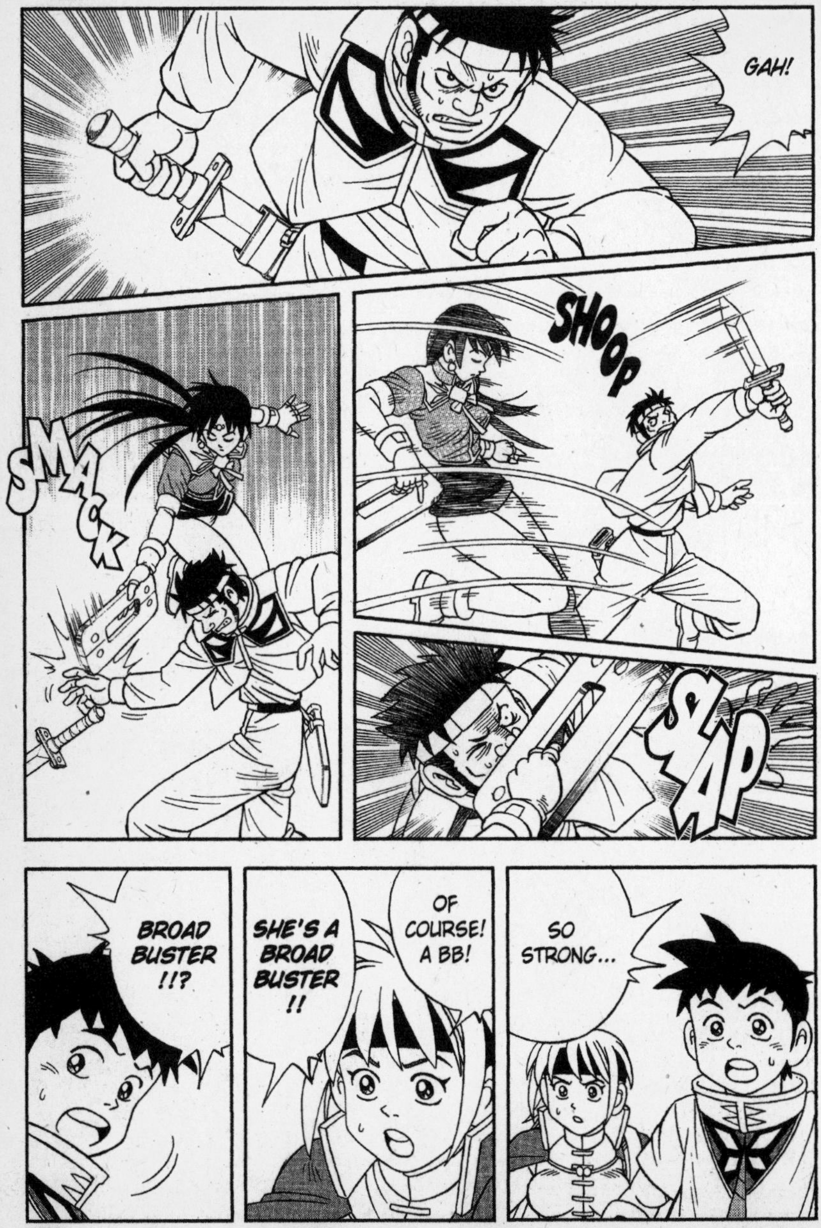
GAH!
SHOOP
SLAP
SMACK
SO STRONG...
OF COURSE! A BB!
SHE'S A BROAD BUSTER !!
BROAD BUSTER !!?

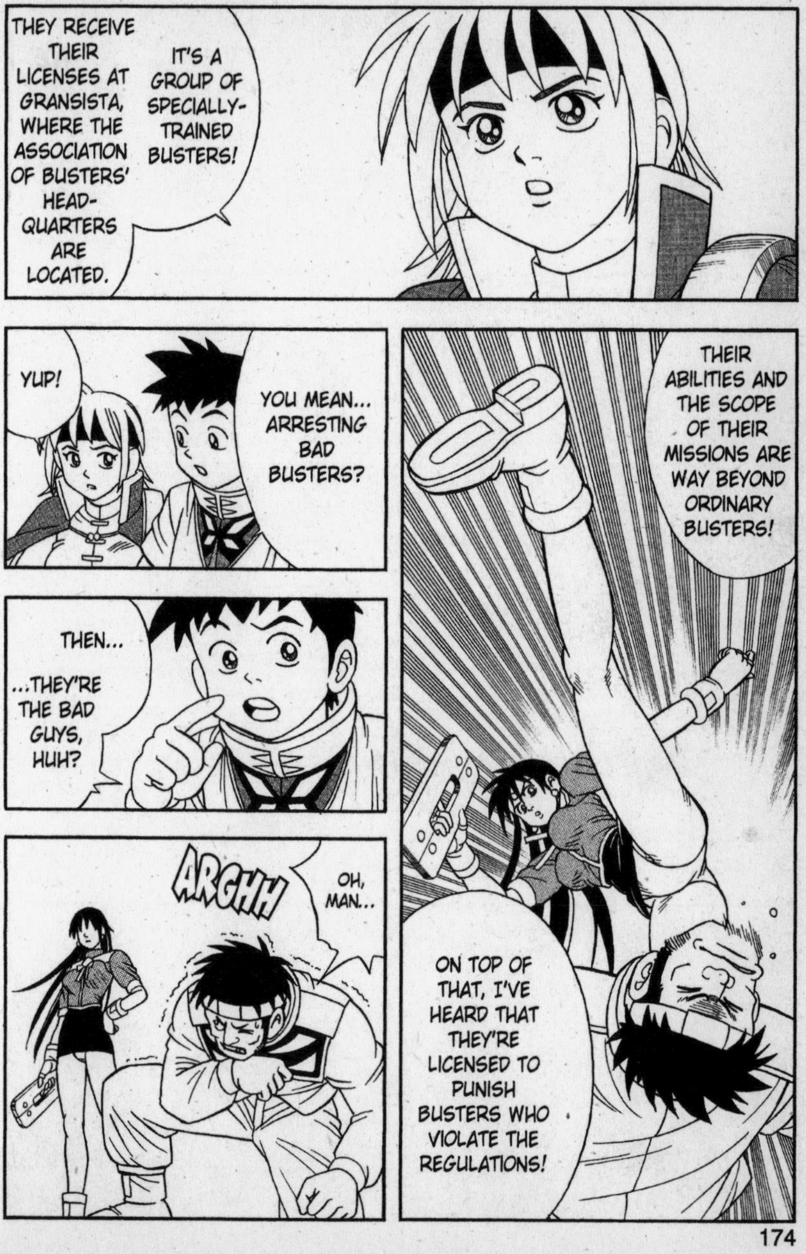
IT'S A GROUP OF SPECIALLY-TRAINED BUSTERS!
THEY RECEIVE THEIR LICENSES AT GRANSISTA, WHERE THE ASSOCIATION OF BUSTERS' HEAD-QUARTERS ARE LOCATED.
THEIR ABILITIES AND THE SCOPE OF THEIR MISSIONS ARE WAY BEYOND ORDINARY BUSTERS!
ON TOP OF THAT, I'VE HEARD THAT THEY'RE LICENSED TO PUNISH BUSTERS WHO VIOLATE THE REGULATIONS!
YOU MEAN... ARRESTING BAD BUSTERS?
YUP!
THEN...
...THEY'RE THE BAD GUYS, HUH?
OH, MAN...
ARGHH

READ THIS WAY

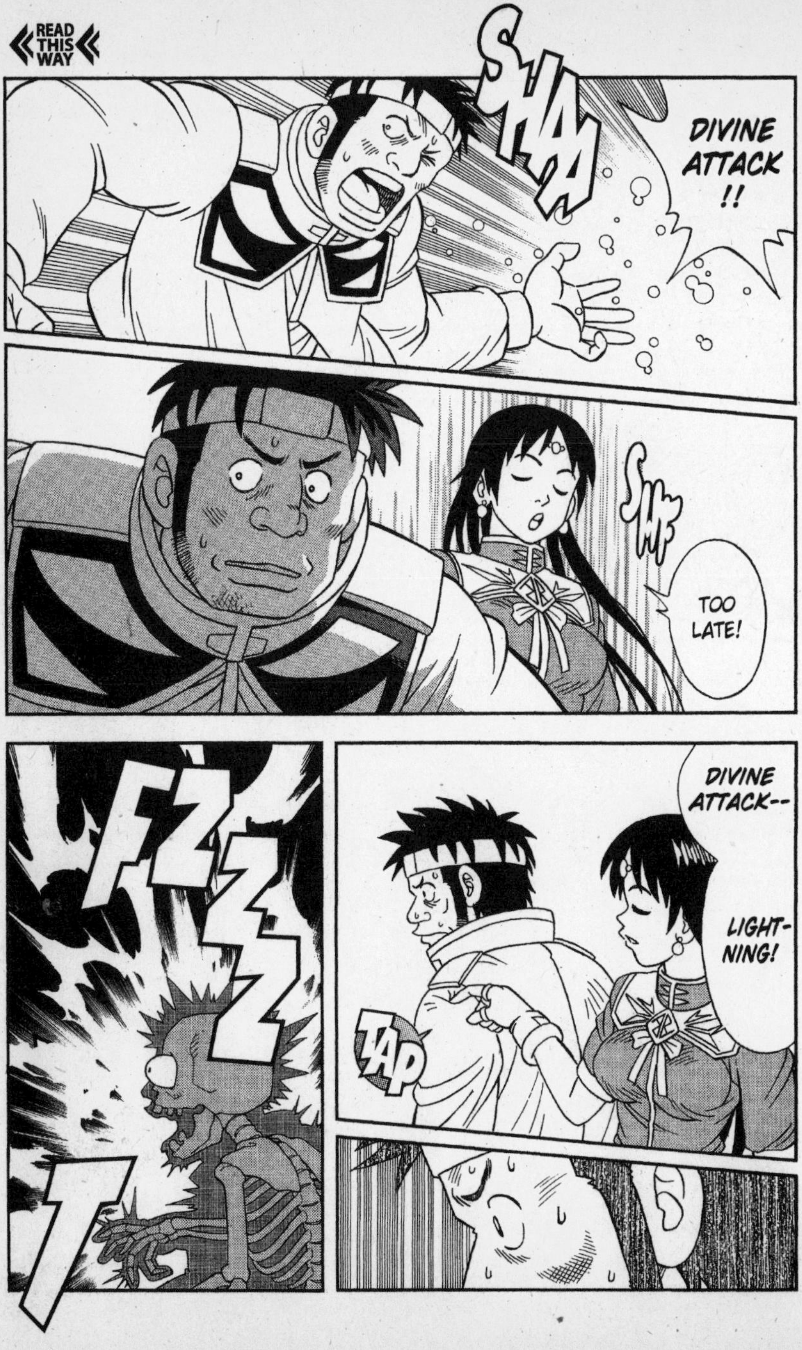
SHAA
DIVINE ATTACK!!
SHF
TOO LATE!
DIVINE ATTACK--
LIGHT-NING!
TAP
FZZT

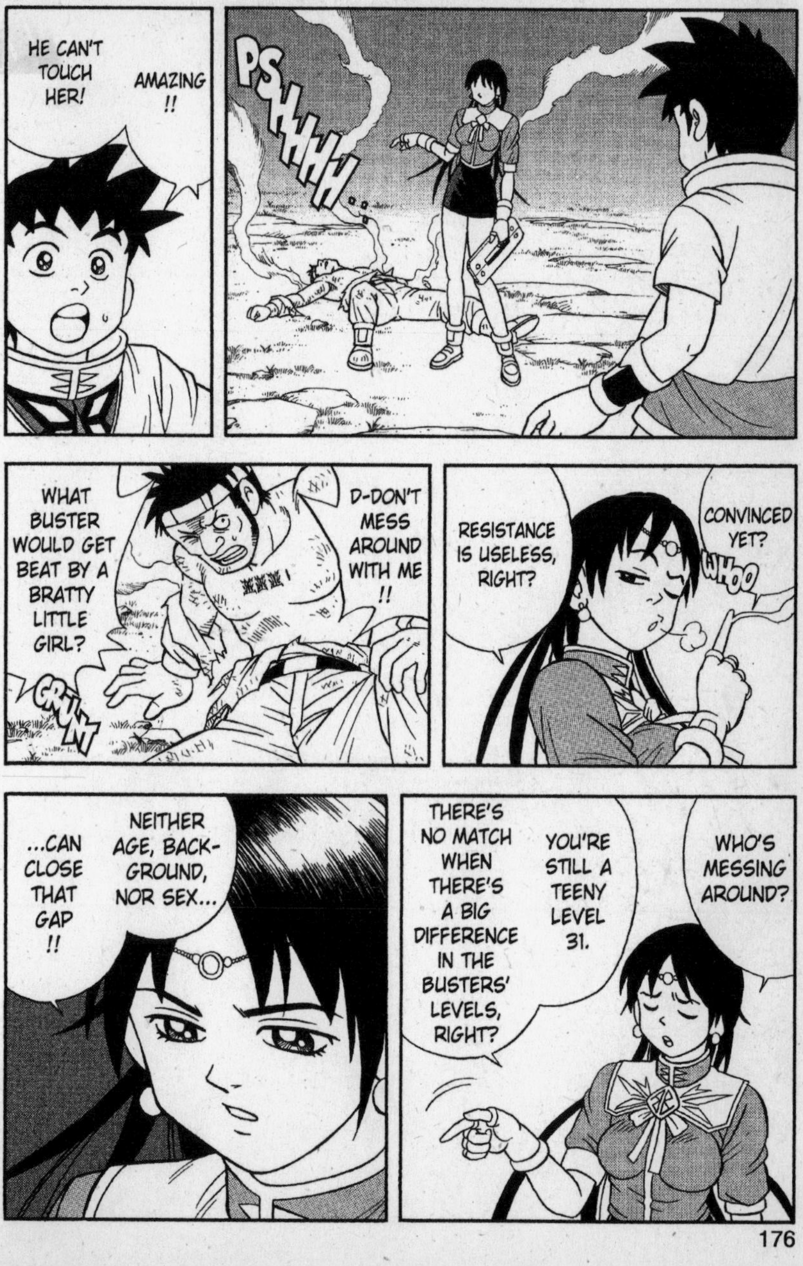
PSHHHH..
AMAZING !!
HE CAN'T TOUCH HER!
CONVINCED YET?
WHOO
RESISTANCE IS USELESS, RIGHT?
D-DON'T MESS AROUND WITH ME !!
WHAT BUSTER WOULD GET BEAT BY A BRATTY LITTLE GIRL?
GRUNT
WHO'S MESSING AROUND?
YOU'RE STILL A TEENY LEVEL 31.
THERE'S NO MATCH WHEN THERE'S A BIG DIFFERENCE IN THE BUSTERS' LEVELS, RIGHT?
NEITHER AGE, BACK-GROUND, NOR SEX...
...CAN CLOSE THAT GAP !!

READ THIS WAY

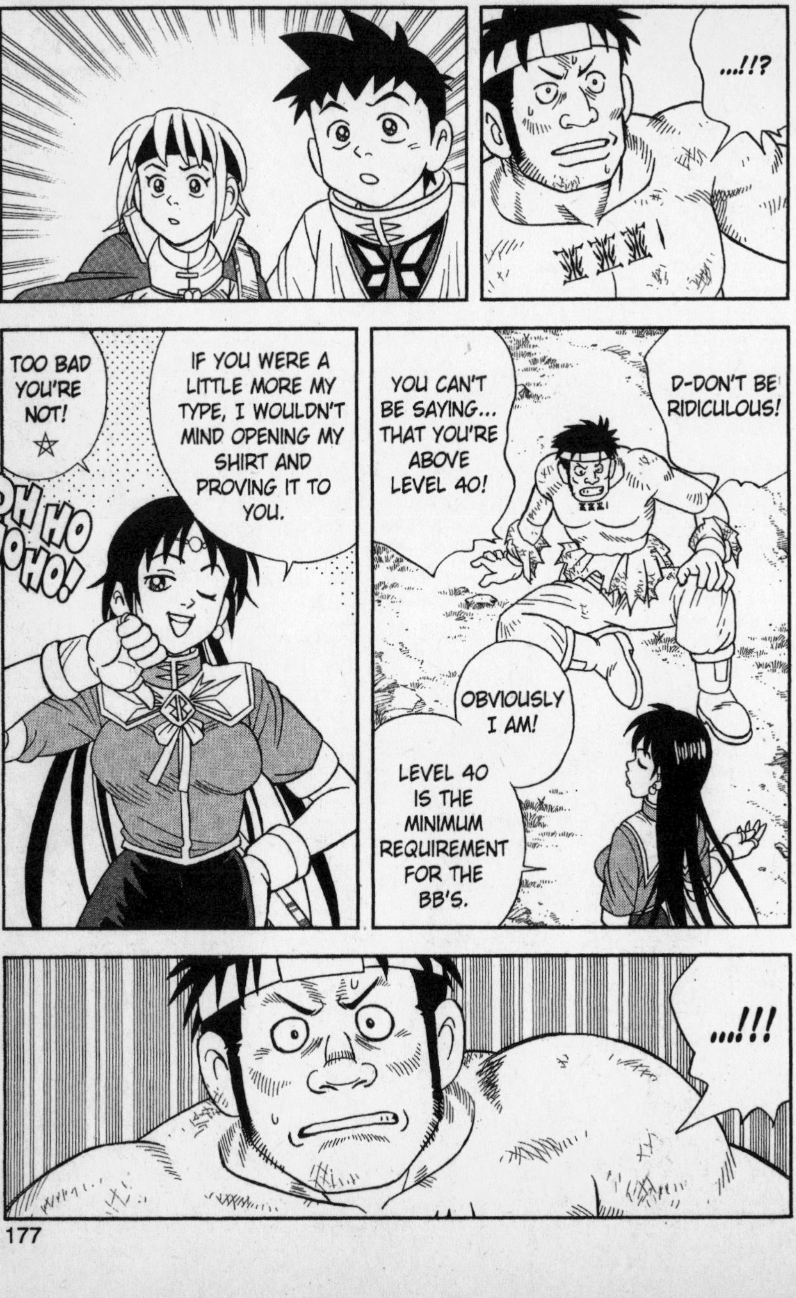

...!!?
D-DON'T BE RIDICULOUS!
YOU CAN'T BE SAYING... THAT YOU'RE ABOVE LEVEL 40!
OBVIOUSLY I AM!
LEVEL 40 IS THE MINIMUM REQUIREMENT FOR THE BB'S.
IF YOU WERE A LITTLE MORE MY TYPE, I WOULDN'T MIND OPENING MY SHIRT AND PROVING IT TO YOU.
TOO BAD YOU'RE NOT! ☆
OH HO HO HO!
...!!!

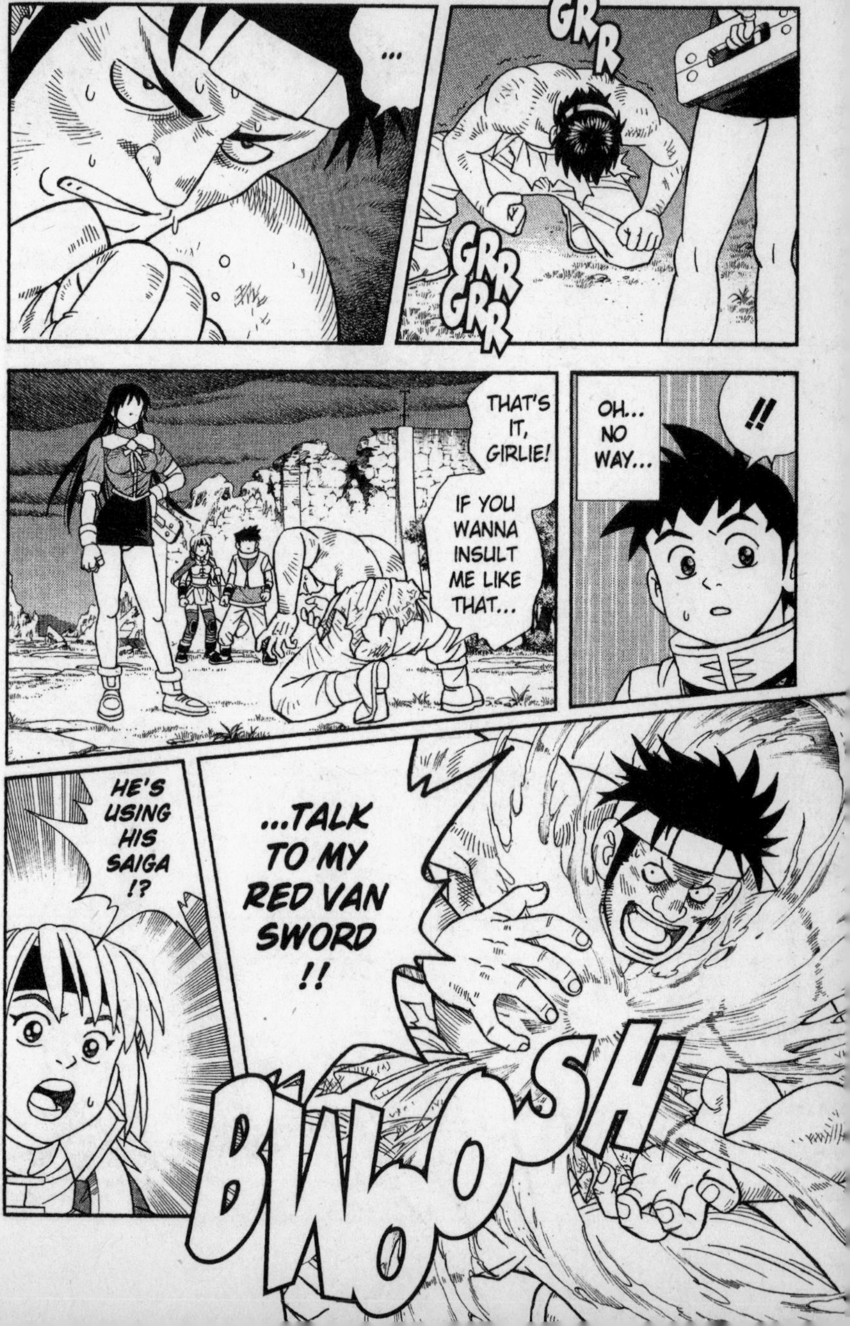
GRR
GRR
GRR
...
!!
OH... NO WAY...
THAT'S IT, GIRLIE!
IF YOU WANNA INSULT ME LIKE THAT...
...TALK TO MY RED VAN SWORD !!
BWOOSH
HE'S USING HIS SAIGA !?

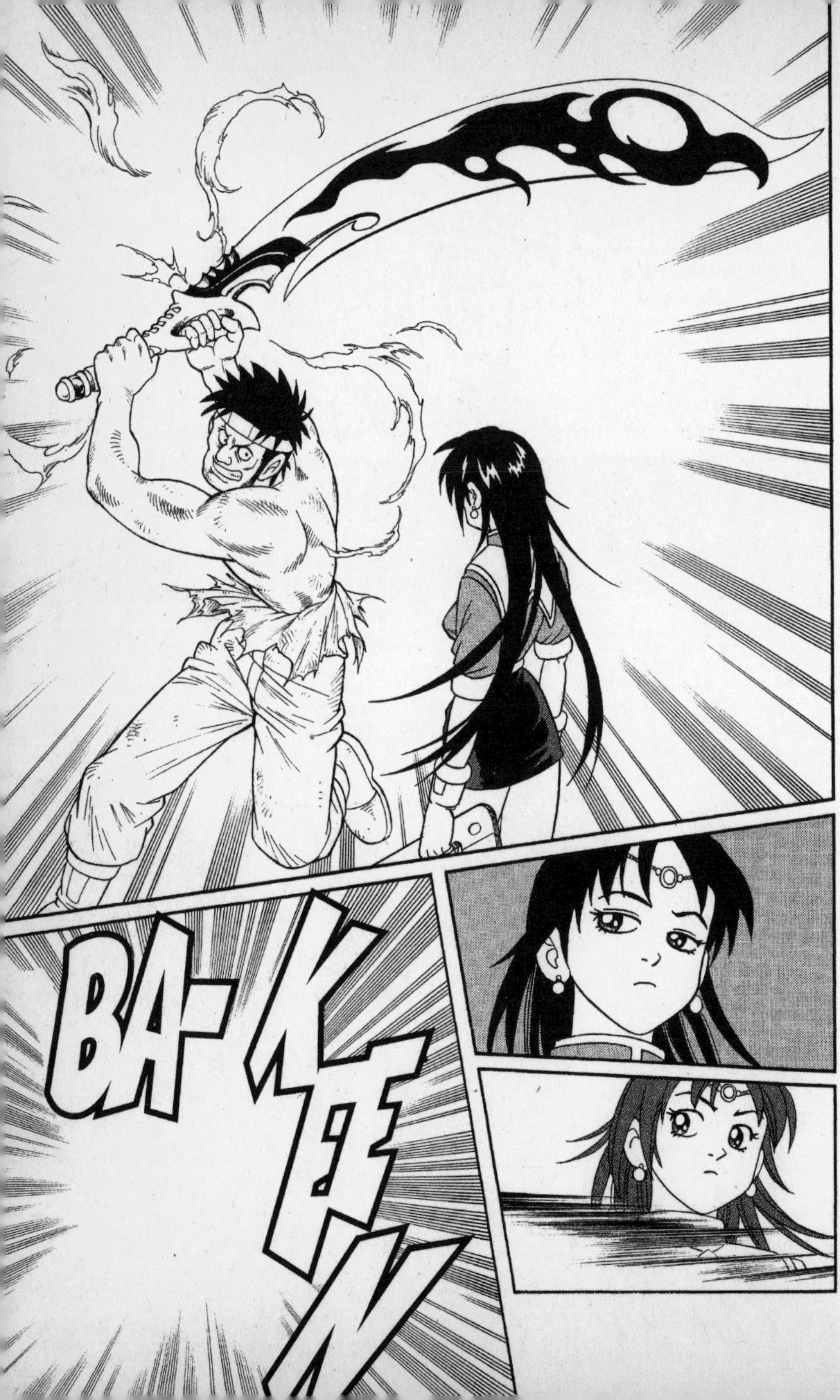
BA-KEEN

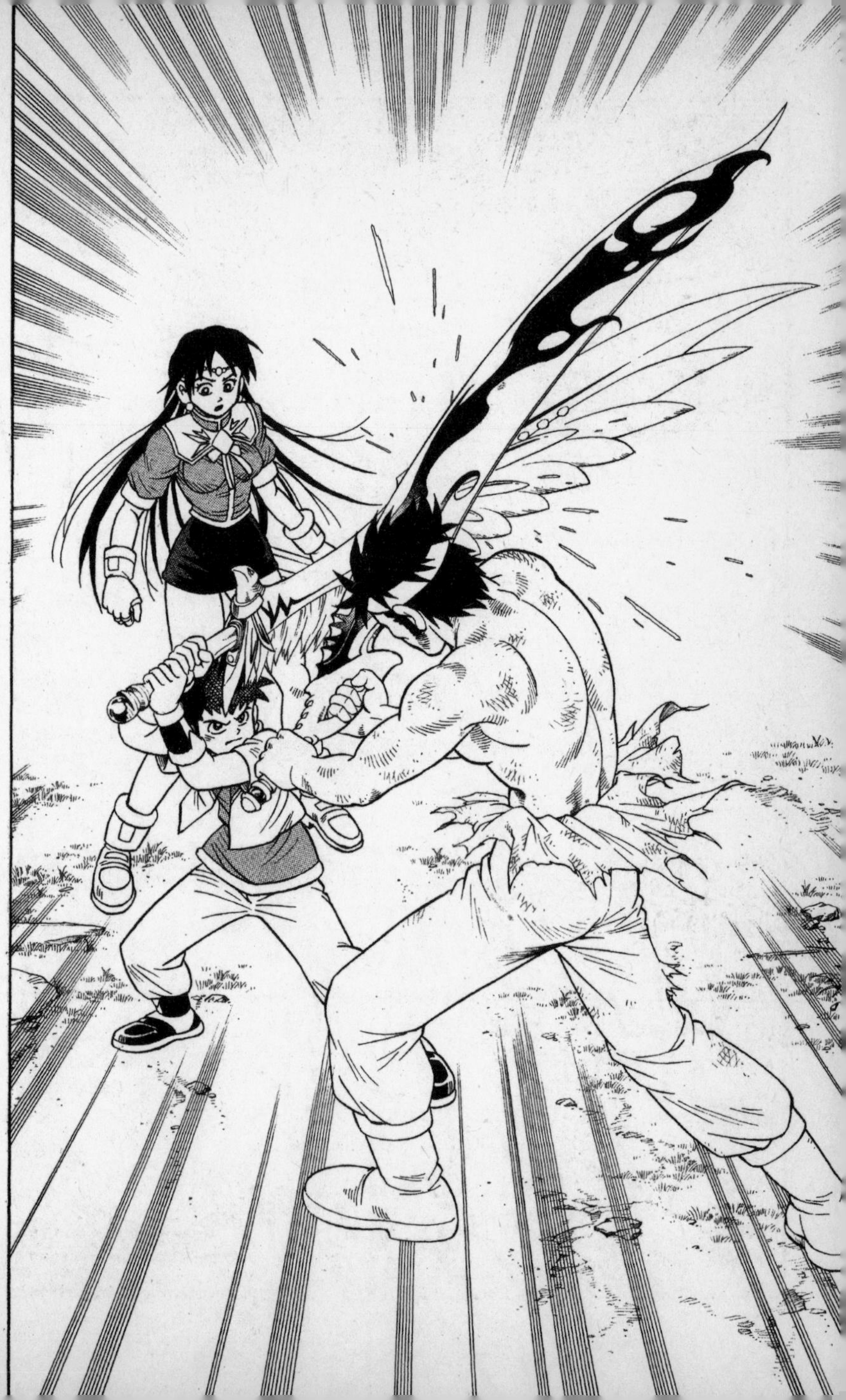

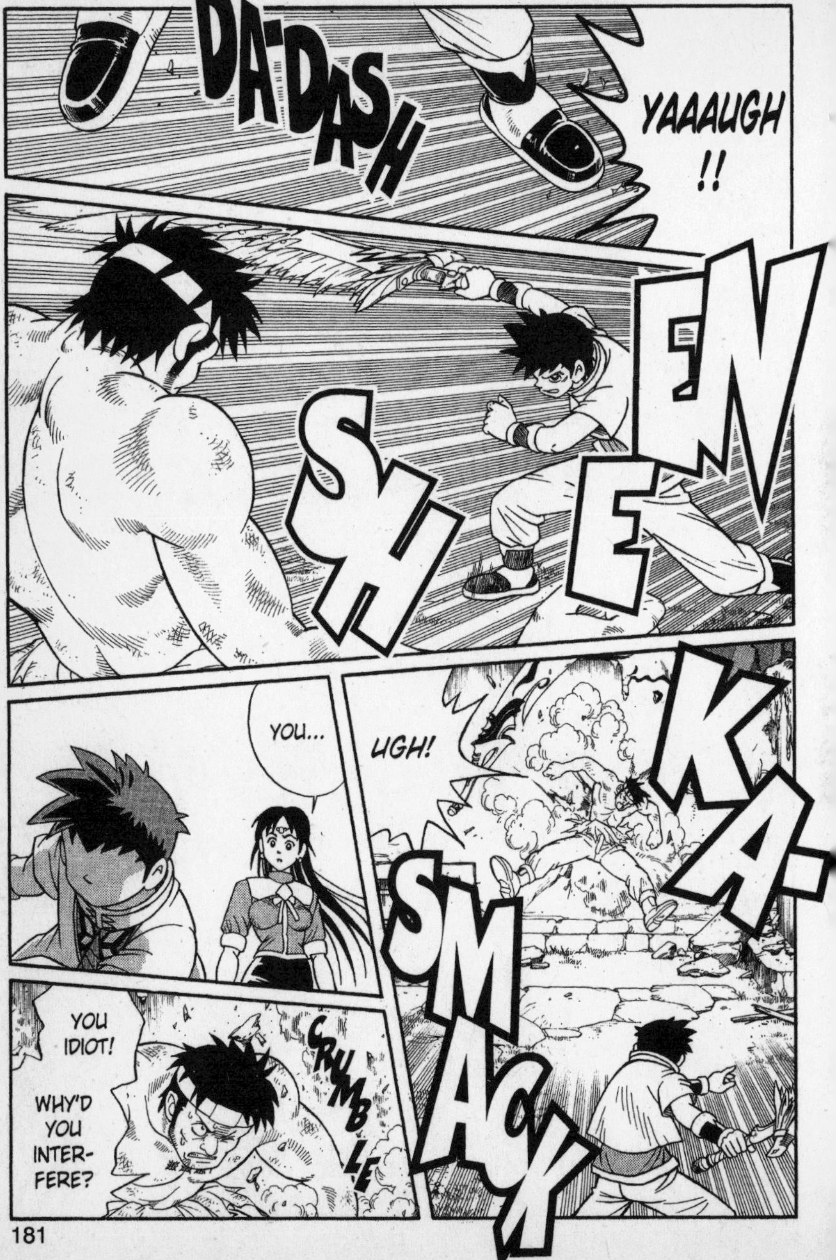
YAAAUGH !!
DA-DASH
SHEEN
KA-SMACK
UGH!
YOU...
CRUMBLE
YOU IDIOT!
WHY'D YOU INTER-FERE?

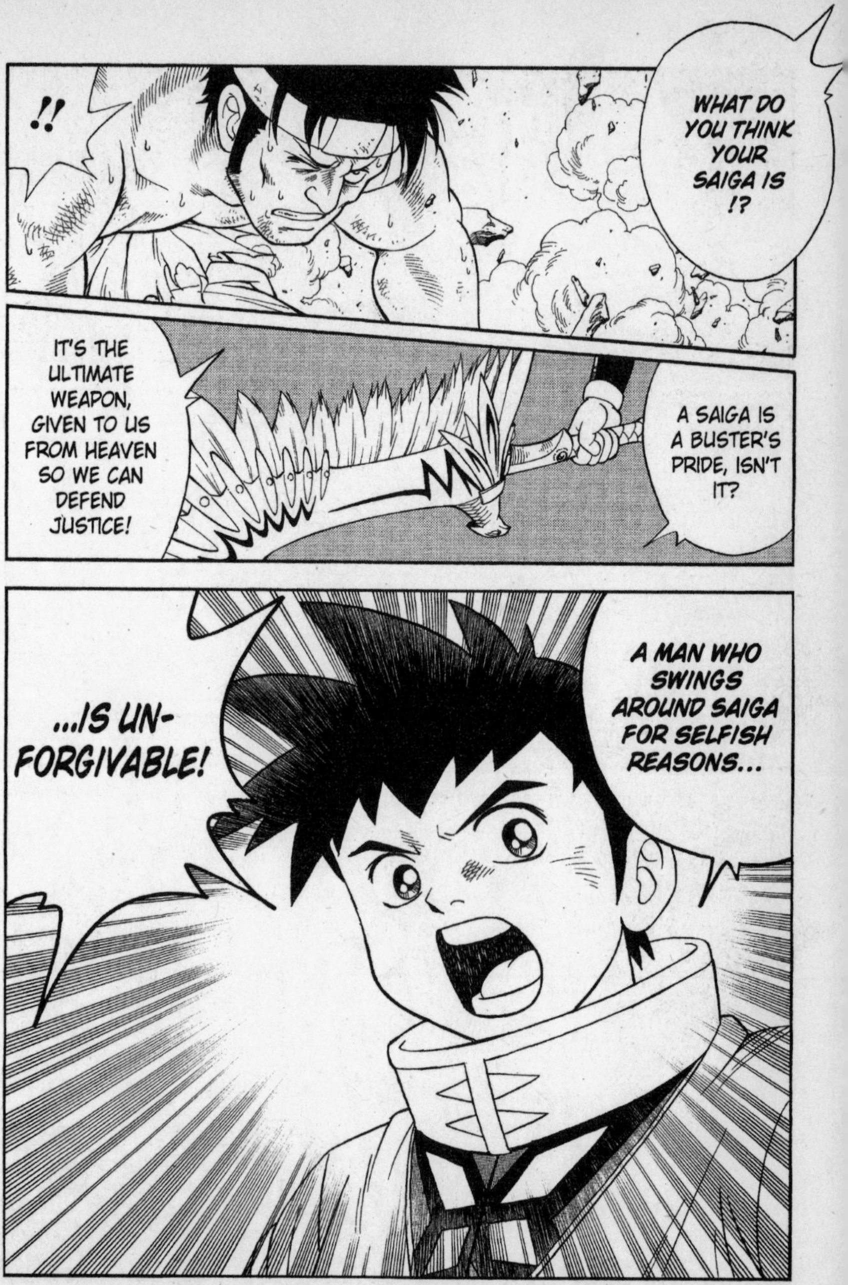
WHAT DO YOU THINK YOUR SAIGA IS !?
!!
A SAIGA IS A BUSTER'S PRIDE, ISN'T IT?
IT'S THE ULTIMATE WEAPON, GIVEN TO US FROM HEAVEN SO WE CAN DEFEND JUSTICE!
A MAN WHO SWINGS AROUND SAIGA FOR SELFISH REASONS...
...IS UN-FORGIVABLE!

READ THIS WAY

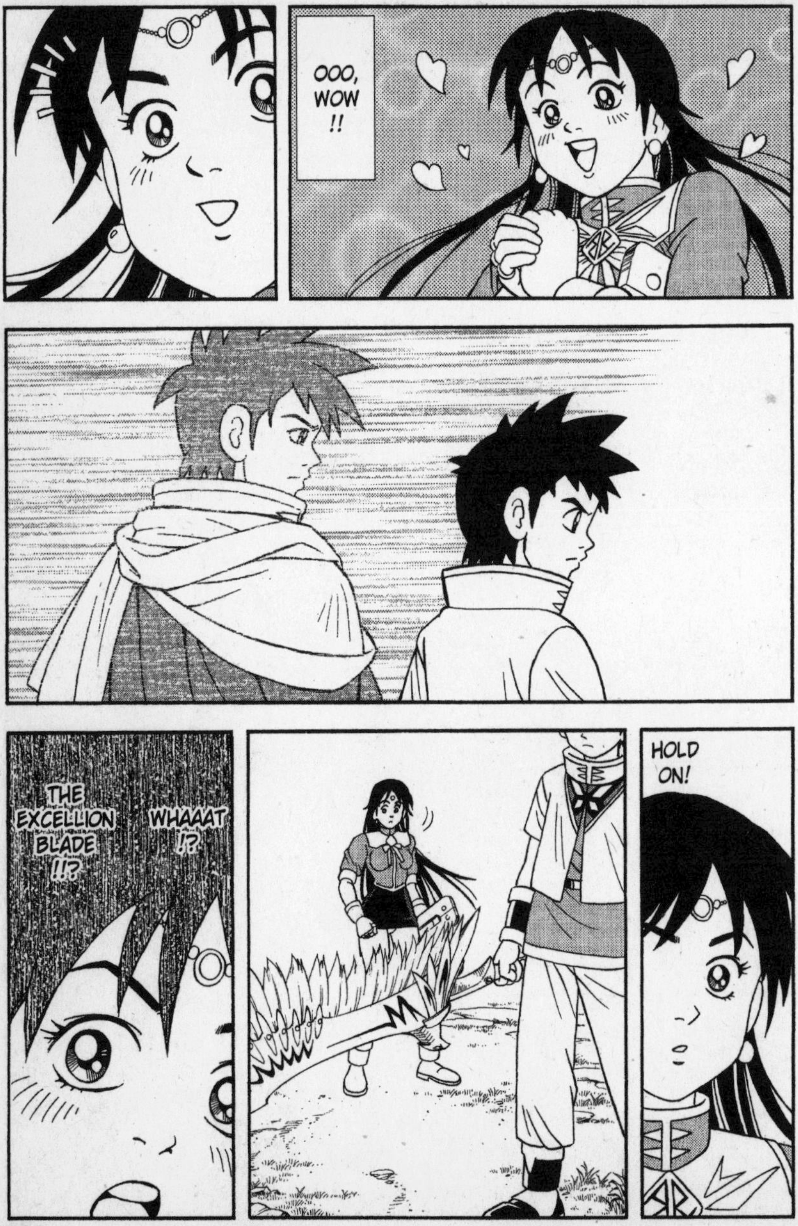
OOO, WOW !!
HOLD ON!
WHAAAT !?
THE EXCELLION BLADE !!?

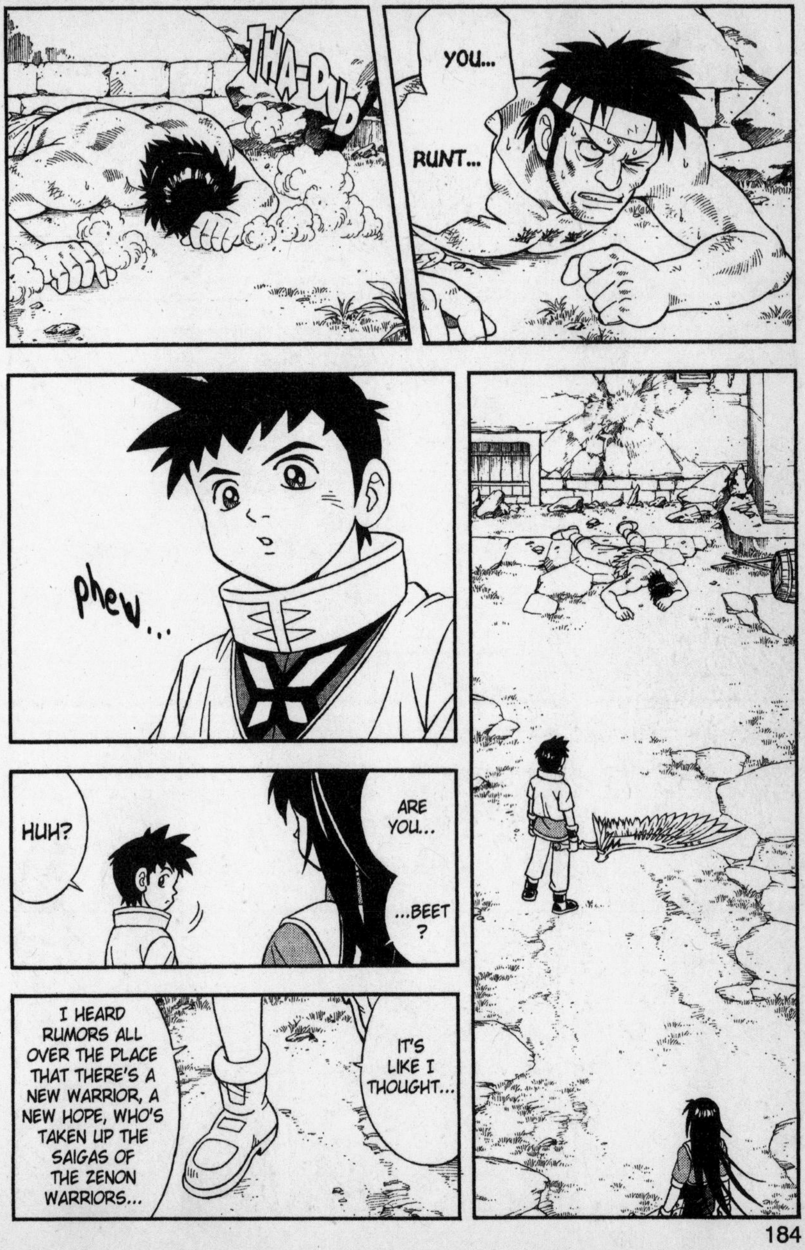
YOU...
RUNT...
THA-DUD
phew...
ARE YOU...
...BEET?
HUH?
IT'S LIKE I THOUGHT...
I HEARD RUMORS ALL OVER THE PLACE THAT THERE'S A NEW WARRIOR, A NEW HOPE, WHO'S TAKEN UP THE SAIGAS OF THE ZENON WARRIORS...

READ THIS WAY

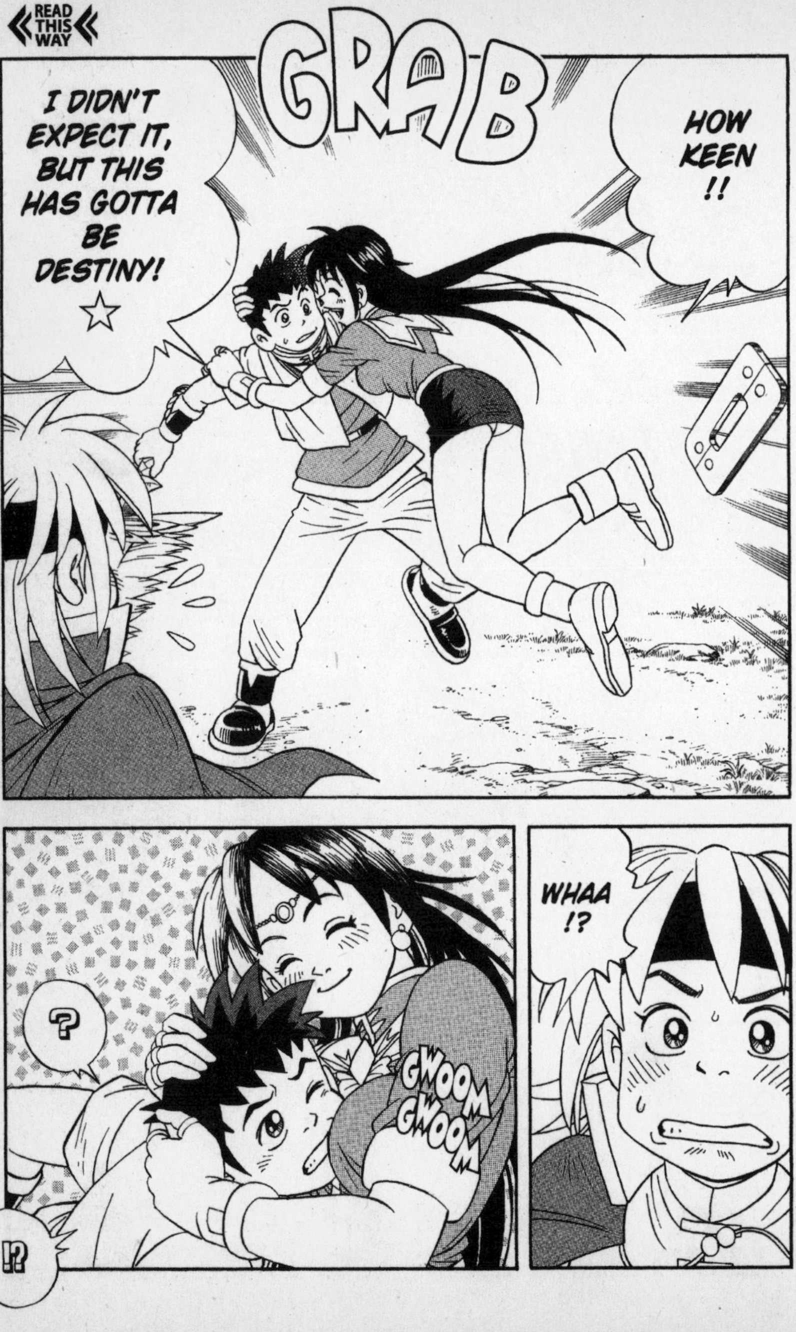
GRAB
HOW KEEN !!
I DIDN'T EXPECT IT, BUT THIS HAS GOTTA BE DESTINY! ☆
WHAA !?
?
GWOOM GWOOM
!?

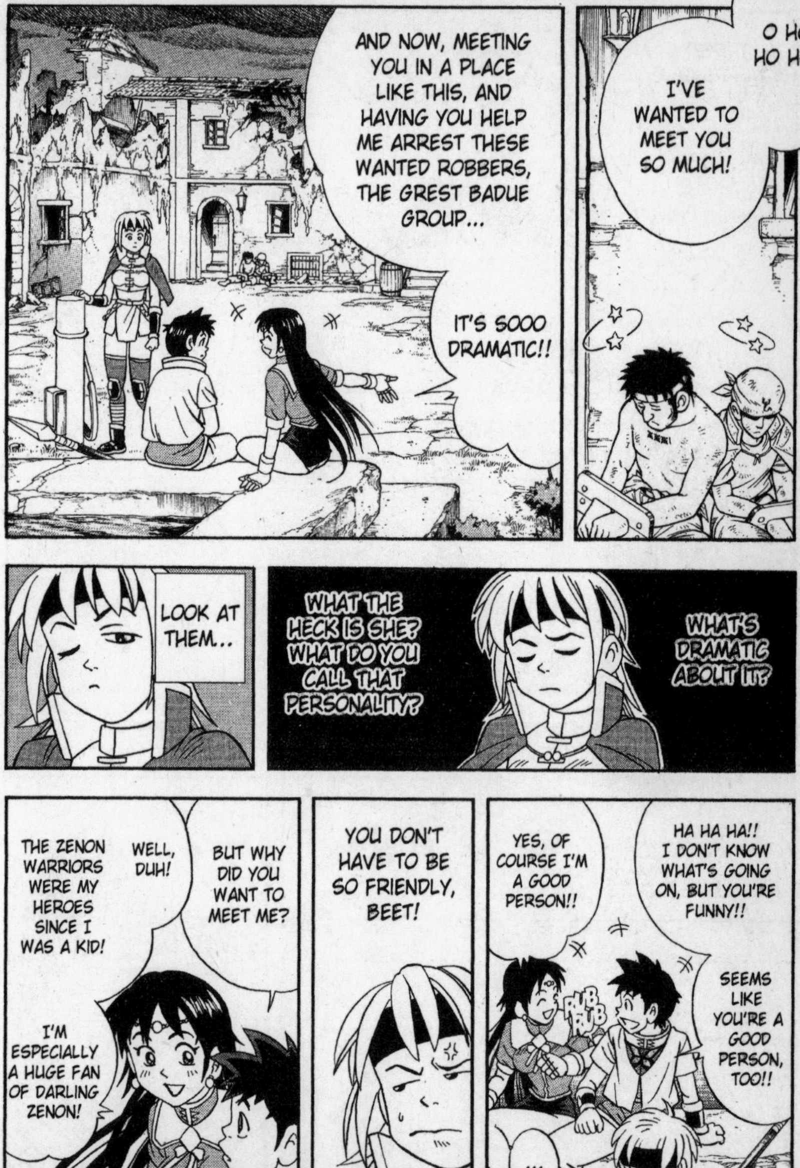

O HO HO HO!
I'VE WANTED TO MEET YOU SO MUCH!
AND NOW, MEETING YOU IN A PLACE LIKE THIS, AND HAVING YOU HELP ME ARREST THESE WANTED ROBBERS, THE GREST BADUE GROUP...
IT'S SOOO DRAMATIC!!
WHAT'S DRAMATIC ABOUT IT?
WHAT THE HECK IS SHE? WHAT DO YOU CALL THAT PERSONALITY?
LOOK AT THEM...
HA HA HA!! I DON'T KNOW WHAT'S GOING ON, BUT YOU'RE FUNNY!!
SEEMS LIKE YOU'RE A GOOD PERSON, TOO!!
YES, OF COURSE I'M A GOOD PERSON!!
RUB RUB
...
YOU DON'T HAVE TO BE SO FRIENDLY, BEET!
BUT WHY DID YOU WANT TO MEET ME?
WELL, DUH!
THE ZENON WARRIORS WERE MY HEROES SINCE I WAS A KID!
I'M ESPECIALLY A HUGE FAN OF DARLING ZENON!

READ THIS WAY

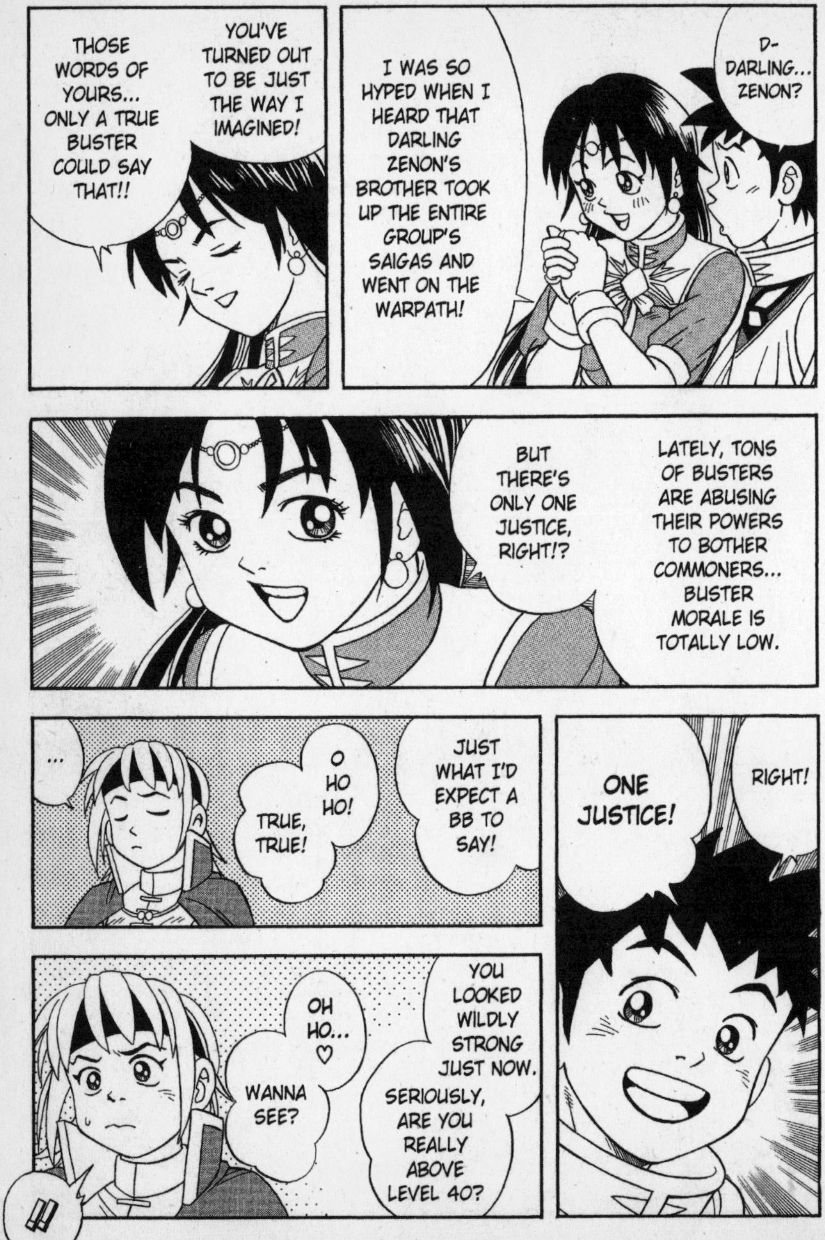
D-DARLING... ZENON?
I WAS SO HYPED WHEN I HEARD THAT DARLING ZENON'S BROTHER TOOK UP THE ENTIRE GROUP'S SAIGAS AND WENT ON THE WARPATH!
YOU'VE TURNED OUT TO BE JUST THE WAY I IMAGINED!
THOSE WORDS OF YOURS... ONLY A TRUE BUSTER COULD SAY THAT!!
LATELY, TONS OF BUSTERS ARE ABUSING THEIR POWERS TO BOTHER COMMONERS... BUSTER MORALE IS TOTALLY LOW.
BUT THERE'S ONLY ONE JUSTICE, RIGHT!?
RIGHT!
ONE JUSTICE!
JUST WHAT I'D EXPECT A BB TO SAY!
O HO HO!
TRUE, TRUE!
...
YOU LOOKED WILDLY STRONG JUST NOW.
SERIOUSLY, ARE YOU REALLY ABOVE LEVEL 40?
OH HO... ♡
WANNA SEE?
!!

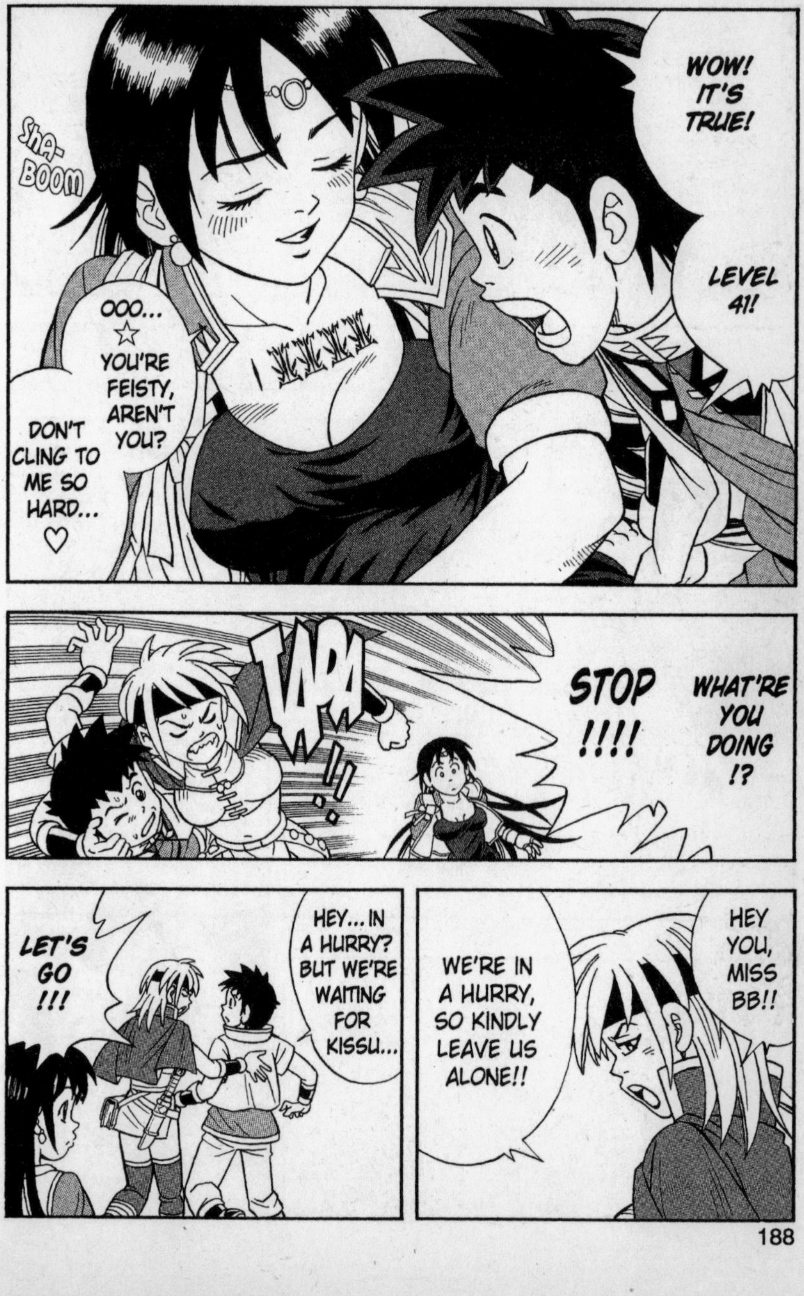
WOW! IT'S TRUE!
LEVEL 41!
SHA-BOOM
OOO... ☆ YOU'RE FEISTY, AREN'T YOU?
DON'T CLING TO ME SO HARD... ♡
WHAT'RE YOU DOING !?
STOP !!!!
TAPA
!!
HEY YOU, MISS BB!!
WE'RE IN A HURRY, SO KINDLY LEAVE US ALONE!!
HEY... IN A HURRY? BUT WE'RE WAITING FOR KISSU...
LET'S GO !!!

READ THIS WAY

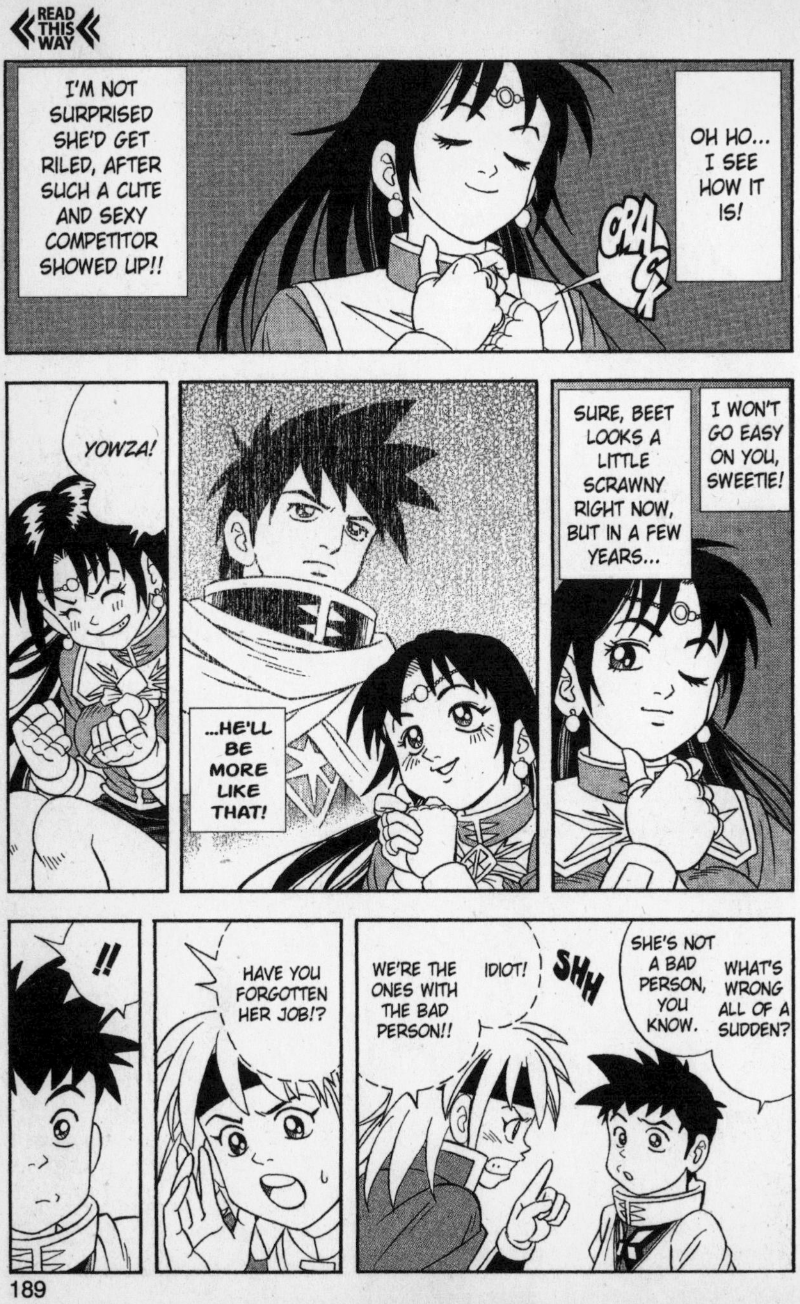
OH HO... I SEE HOW IT IS!
CRACK
I'M NOT SURPRISED SHE'D GET RILED, AFTER SUCH A CUTE AND SEXY COMPETITOR SHOWED UP!!
I WON'T GO EASY ON YOU, SWEETIE!
SURE, BEET LOOKS A LITTLE SCRAWNY RIGHT NOW, BUT IN A FEW YEARS...
...HE'LL BE MORE LIKE THAT!
YOWZA!
WHAT'S WRONG ALL OF A SUDDEN?
SHE'S NOT A BAD PERSON, YOU KNOW.
SHH
IDIOT!
WE'RE THE ONES WITH THE BAD PERSON!!
HAVE YOU FORGOTTEN HER JOB!?
!!

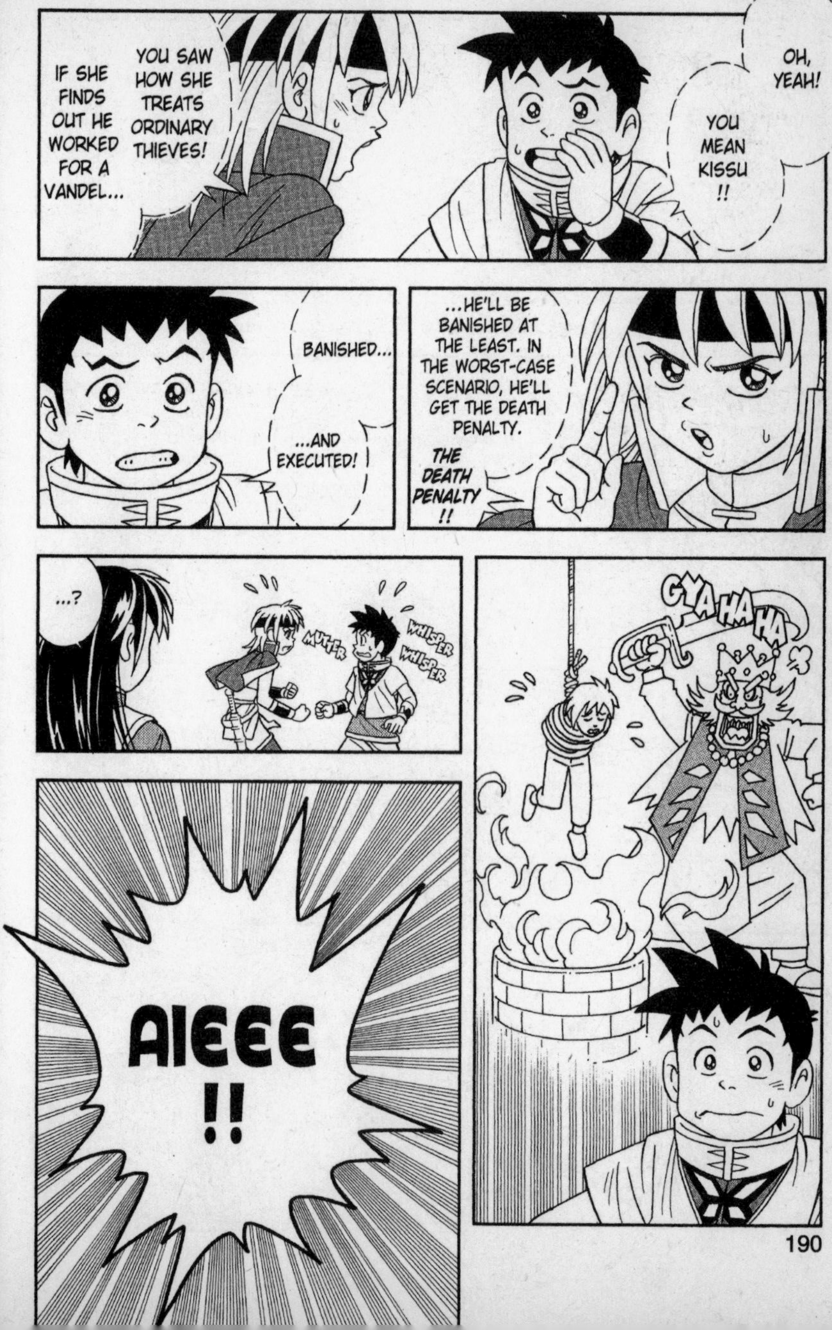
OH, YEAH!
YOU MEAN KISSU !!
YOU SAW HOW SHE TREATS ORDINARY THIEVES!
IF SHE FINDS OUT HE WORKED FOR A VANDEL...
...HE'LL BE BANISHED AT THE LEAST. IN THE WORST-CASE SCENARIO, HE'LL GET THE DEATH PENALTY.
THE DEATH PENALTY !!
BANISHED...
...AND EXECUTED!
GYAHAHA
WHISPER WHISPER
MUTTER
...?
AIEEE !!

READ THIS WAY

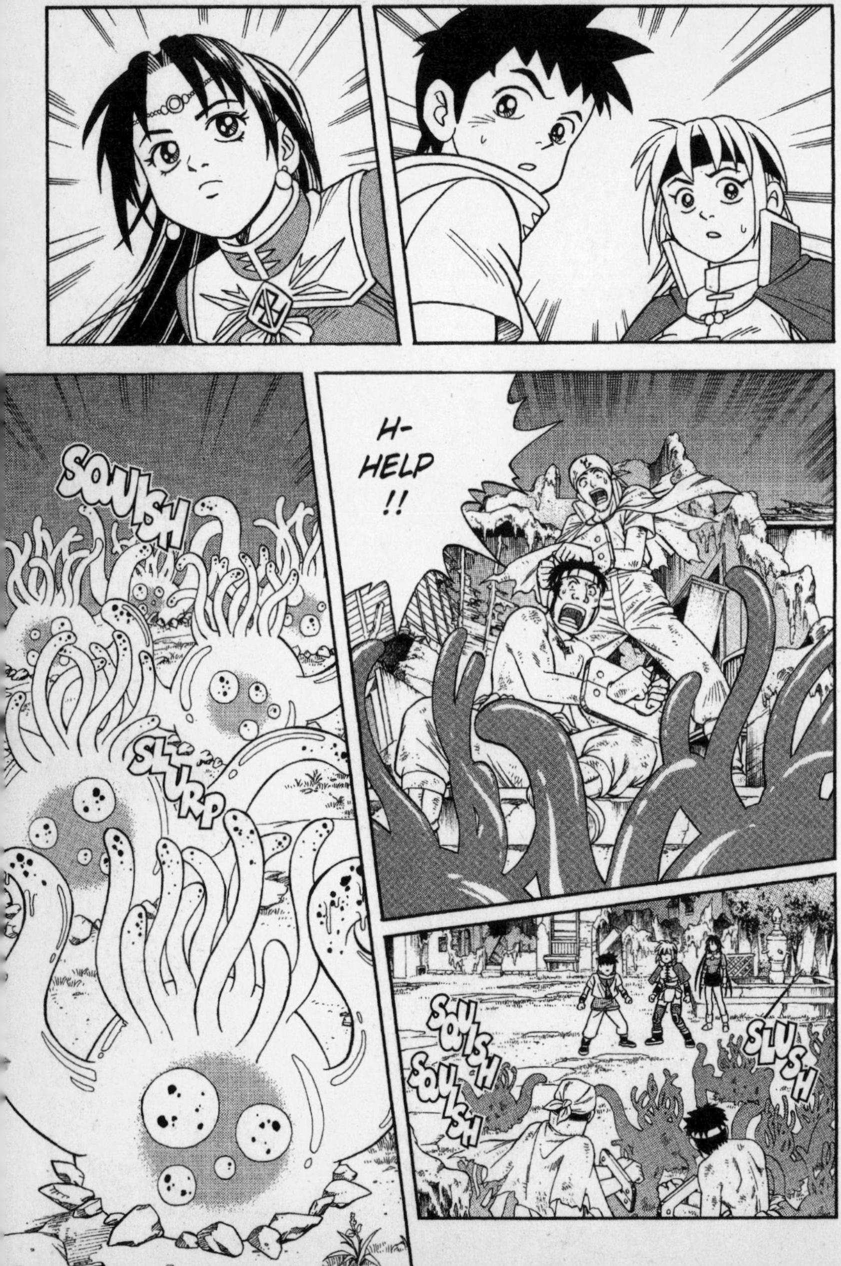

H-HELP!!
SLUSH
SQUISH
SQUISH
SQUISH
SLURP

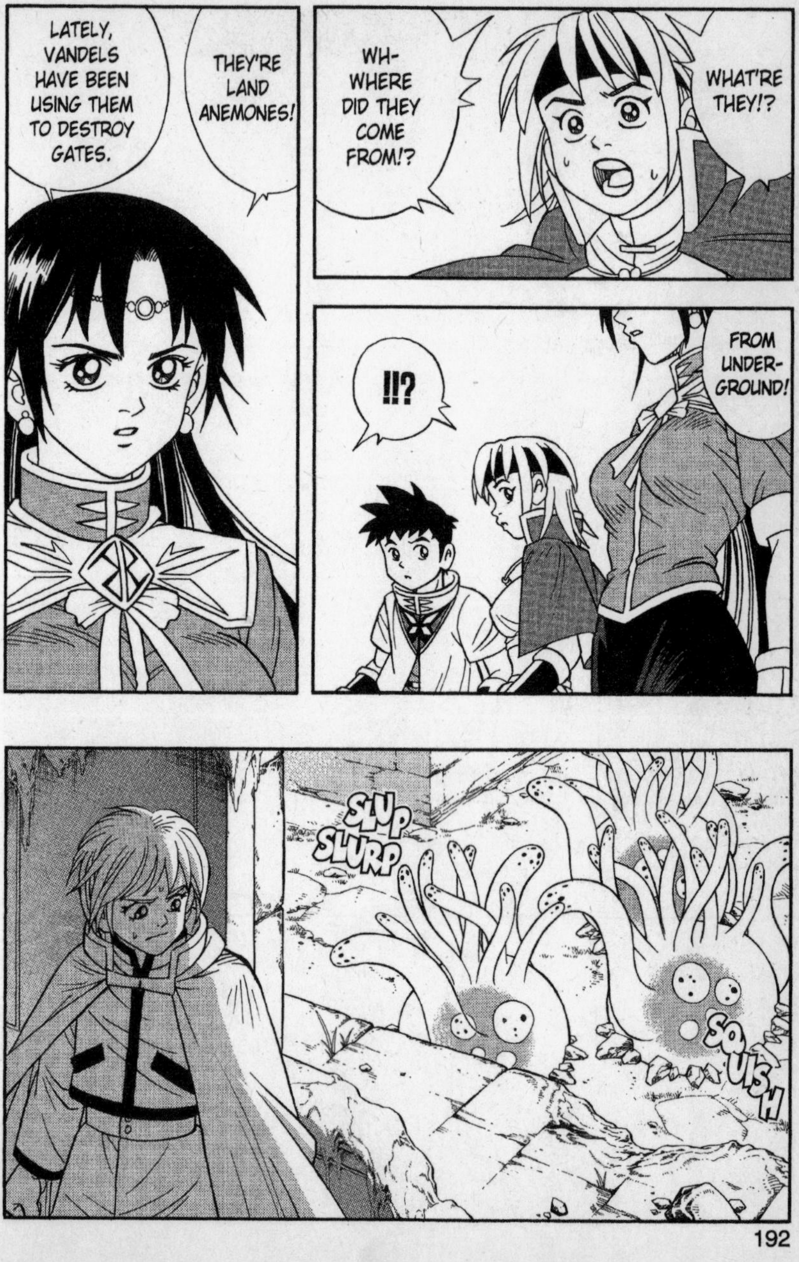
WHAT'RE THEY!?
WH- WHERE DID THEY COME FROM!?
FROM UNDER-GROUND!
!!?
THEY'RE LAND ANEMONES!
LATELY, VANDELS HAVE BEEN USING THEM TO DESTROY GATES.
SLUP SLURP
SQUISH

READ THIS WAY

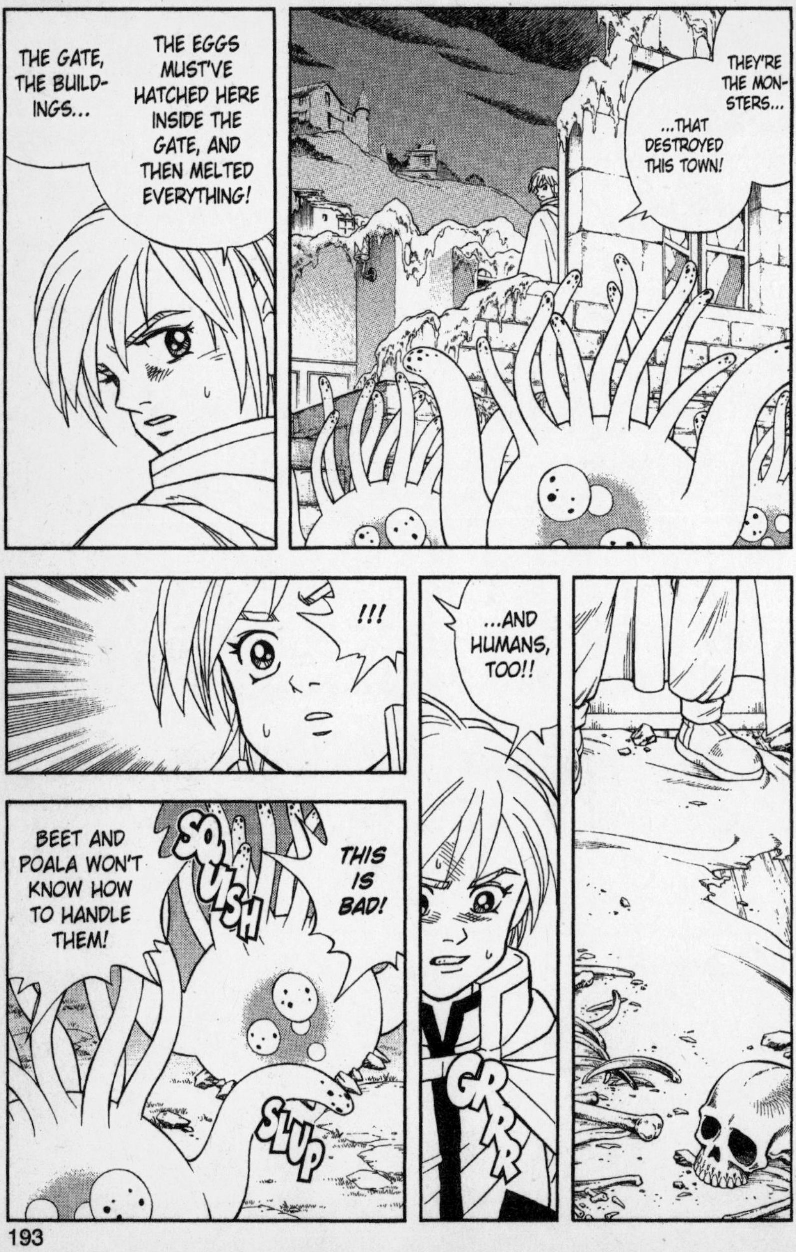
THEY'RE THE MON-STERS...
...THAT DESTROYED THIS TOWN!
THE EGGS MUST'VE HATCHED HERE INSIDE THE GATE, AND THEN MELTED EVERYTHING!
THE GATE, THE BUILD-INGS...
...AND HUMANS, TOO!!
GRRR
!!!
THIS IS BAD!
SQUISH
BEET AND POALA WON'T KNOW HOW TO HANDLE THEM!
SLUP

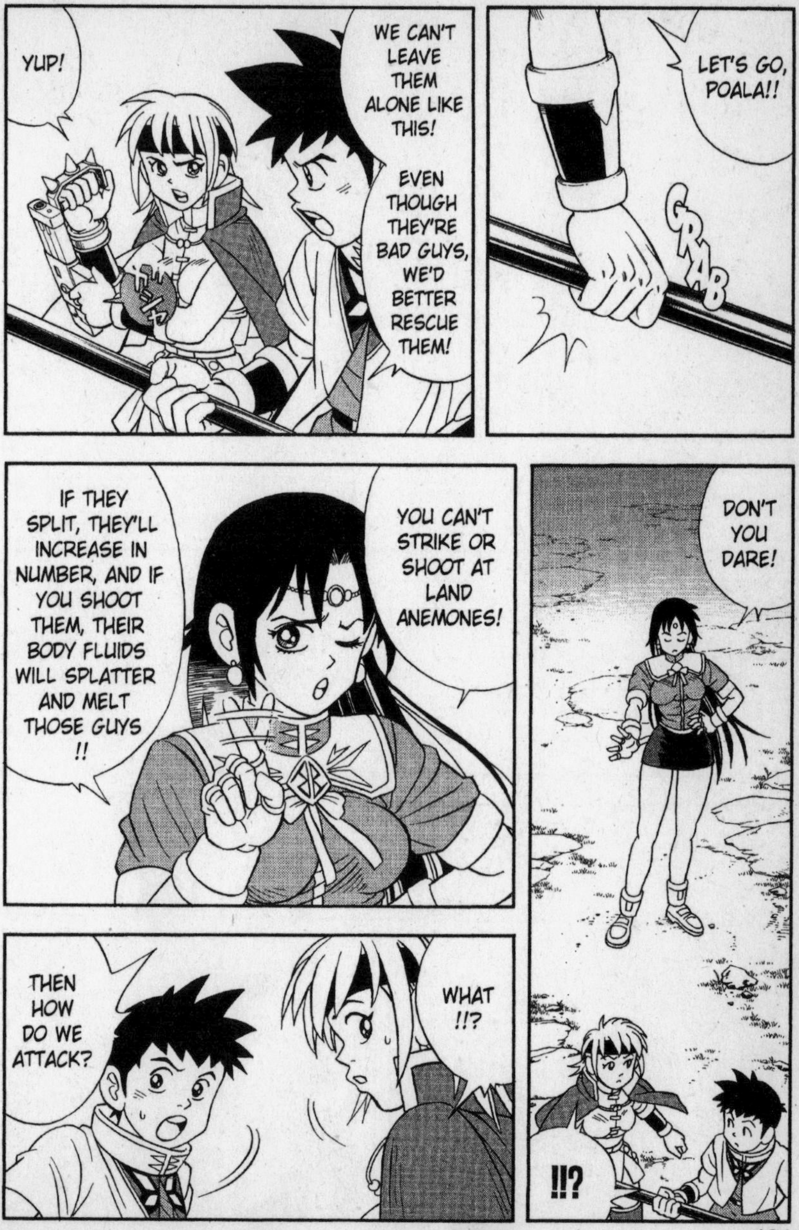
LET'S GO, POALA!!
GRAB
WE CAN'T LEAVE THEM ALONE LIKE THIS!
EVEN THOUGH THEY'RE BAD GUYS, WE'D BETTER RESCUE THEM!
YUP!
DON'T YOU DARE!
!!?
YOU CAN'T STRIKE OR SHOOT AT LAND ANEMONES!
IF THEY SPLIT, THEY'LL INCREASE IN NUMBER, AND IF YOU SHOOT THEM, THEIR BODY FLUIDS WILL SPLATTER AND MELT THOSE GUYS !!
WHAT !!?
THEN HOW DO WE ATTACK?

READ THIS WAY

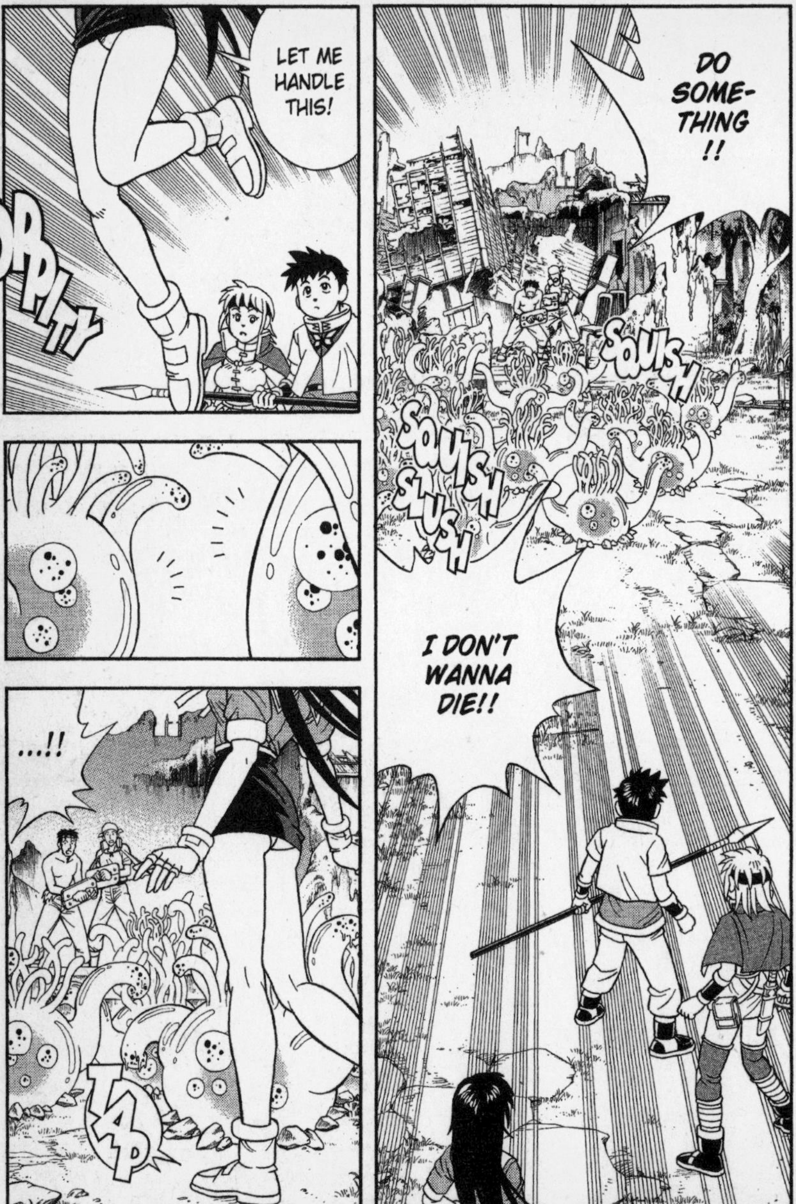

DO SOME-THING!!
SQUISH
SQUISH
SLUSH
I DON'T WANNA DIE!!
LET ME HANDLE THIS!
HOPPITY
...!!
TAP

YOO HOO!
I'M A WHOLE LOT TASTIER THAN THOSE ICKY MEN, AREN'T I?
OH HO
COME ON OVER AND GET ME!
SQUOSH
SLUP
SLURP
SQUASH
SLUUURP
SLUUURP
SLUUURP

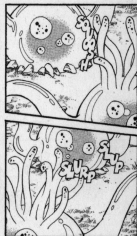

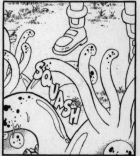

READ THIS WAY

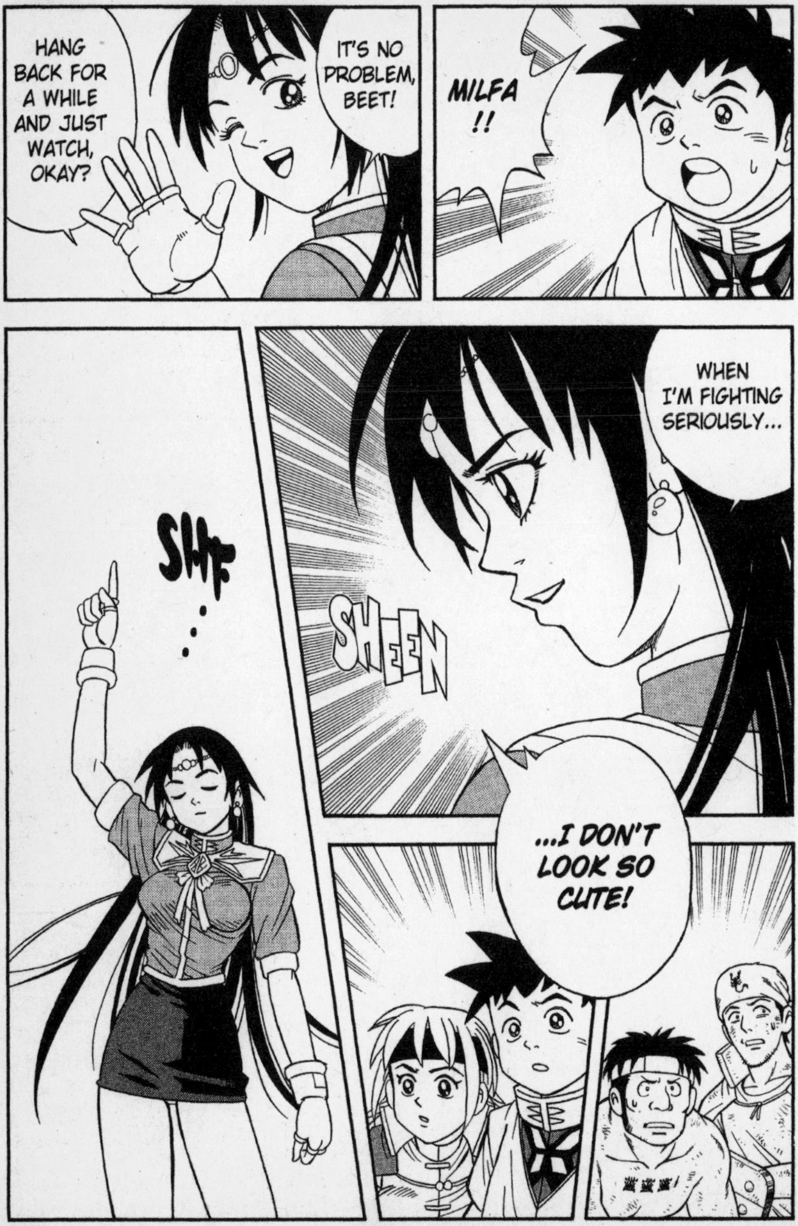
MILFA !!
IT'S NO PROBLEM, BEET!
HANG BACK FOR A WHILE AND JUST WATCH, OKAY?
WHEN I'M FIGHTING SERIOUSLY...
SHEEN
...I DON'T LOOK SO CUTE!
SHF
...

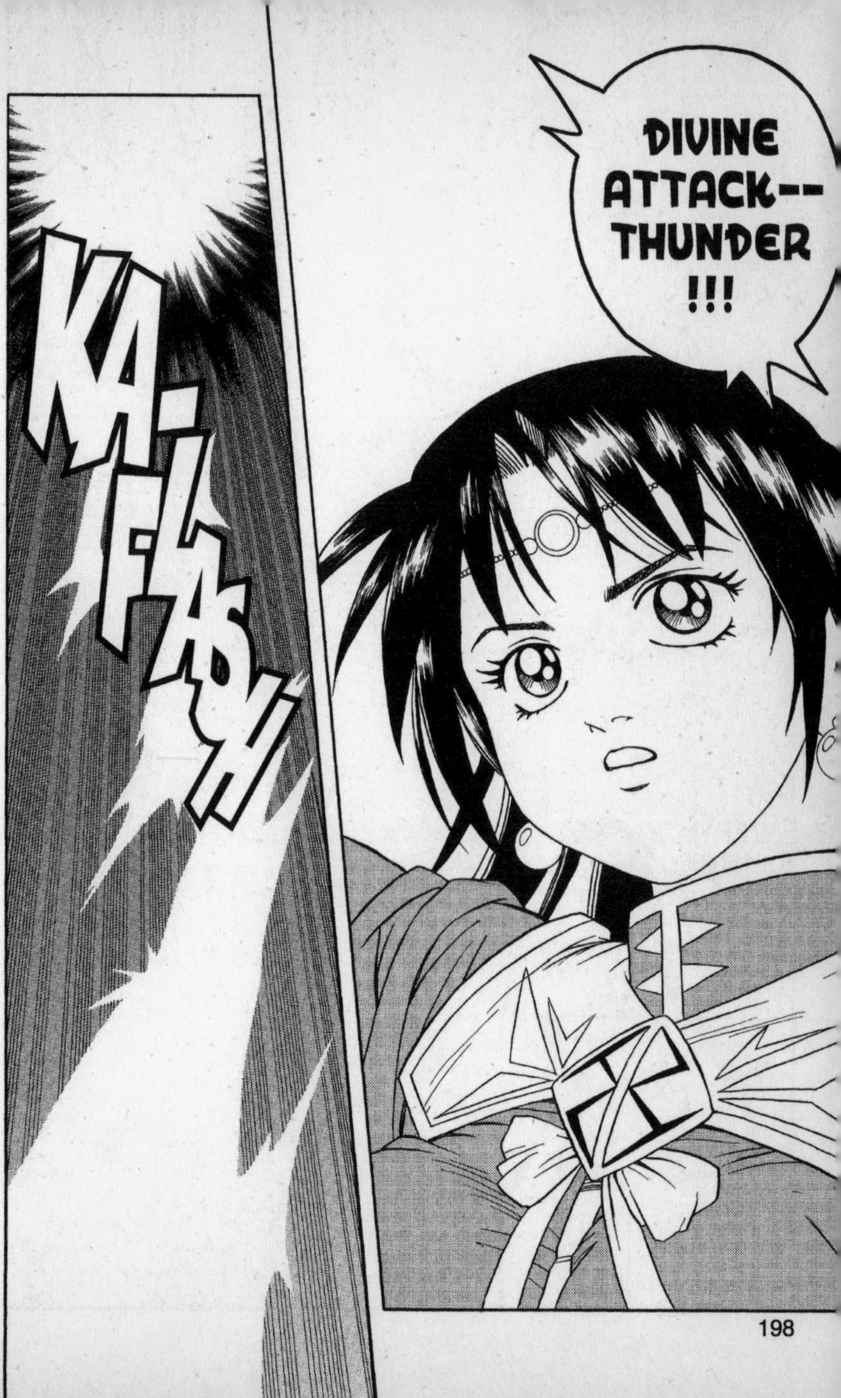
DIVINE ATTACK-- THUNDER !!!
KA-F-FLASH

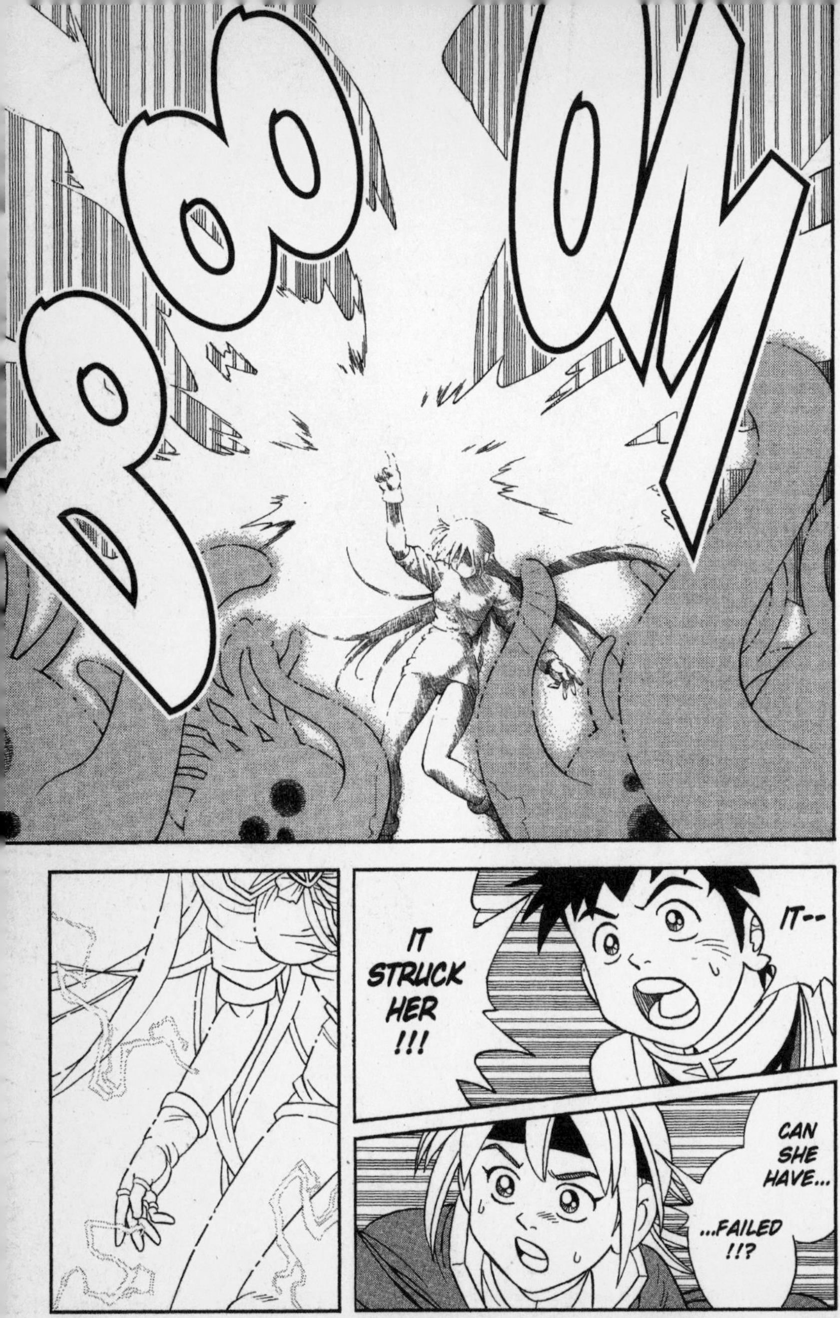
IT--
IT STRUCK HER!!!
CAN SHE HAVE...
...FAILED!!?

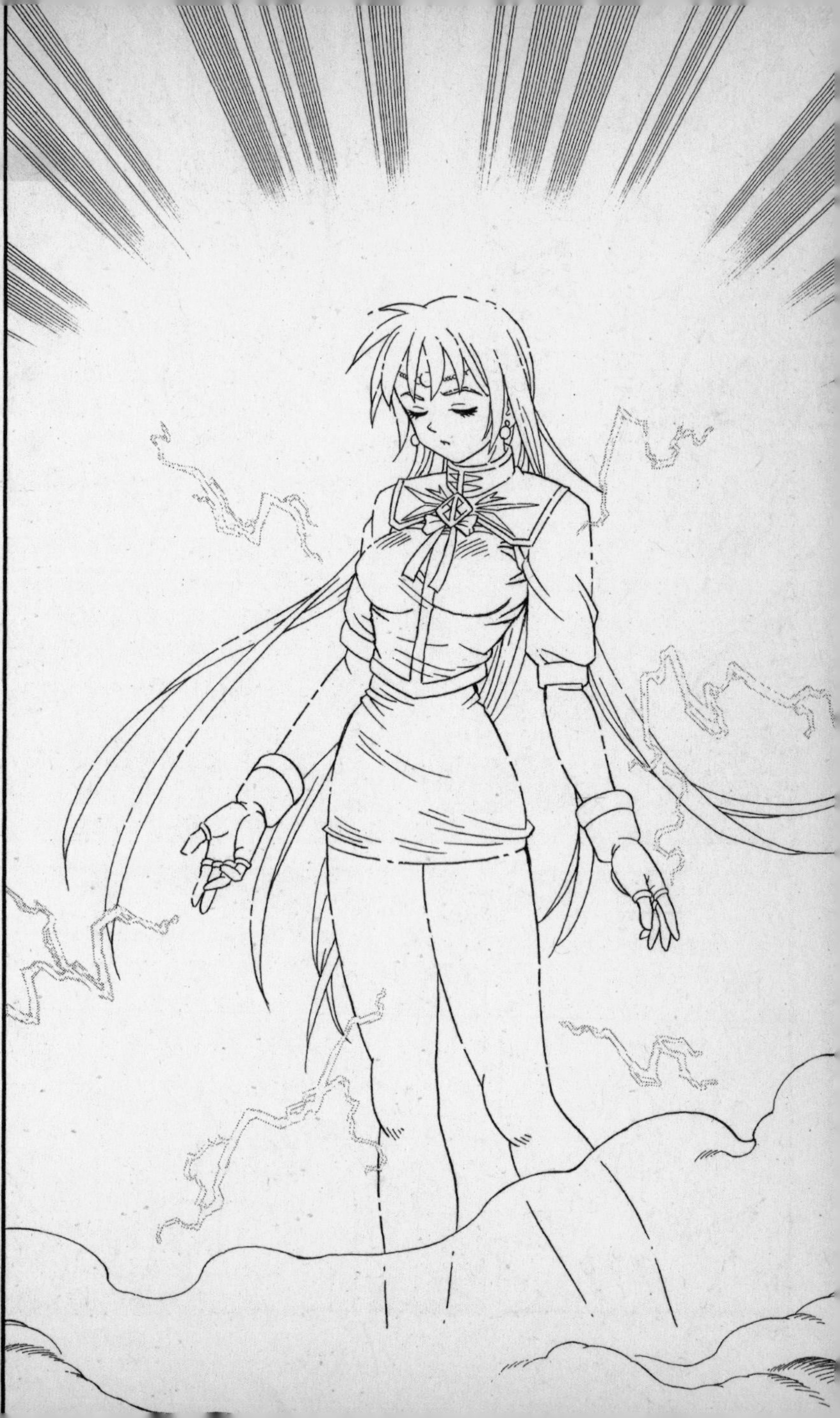

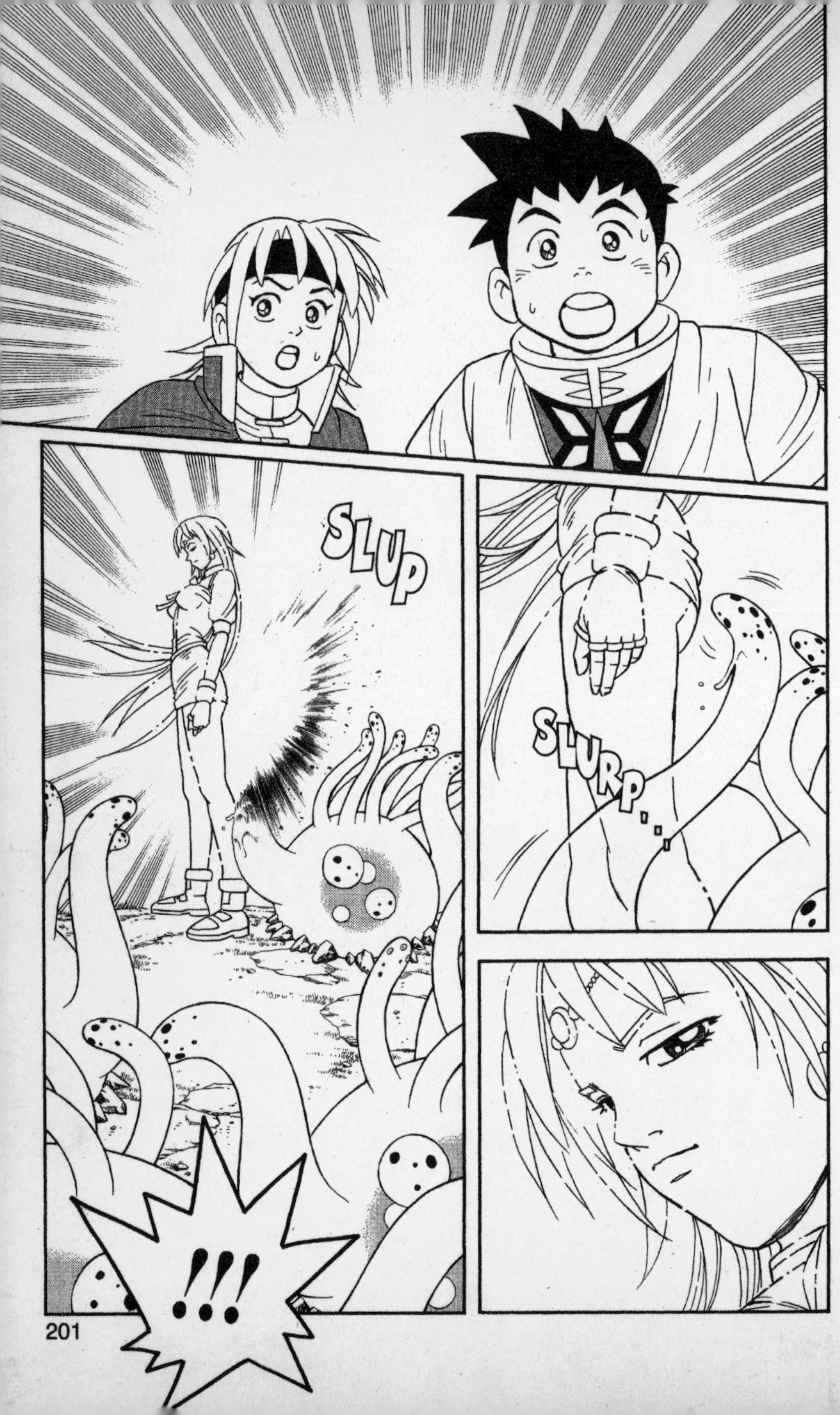
SLURP...
SLUP
!!!

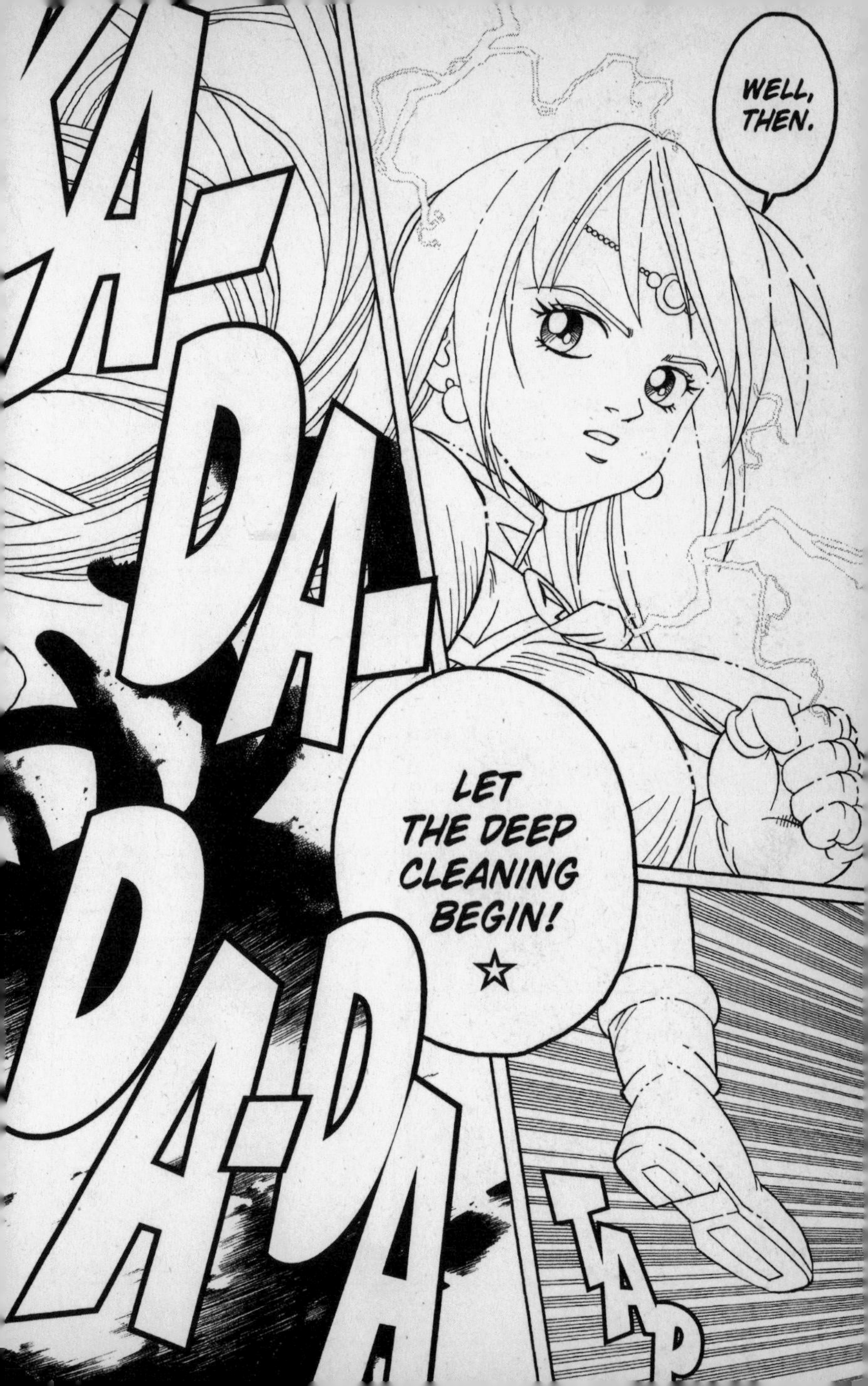
WELL, THEN.
LET THE DEEP CLEANING BEGIN! ☆
KA-DA-DA-DA
TAP

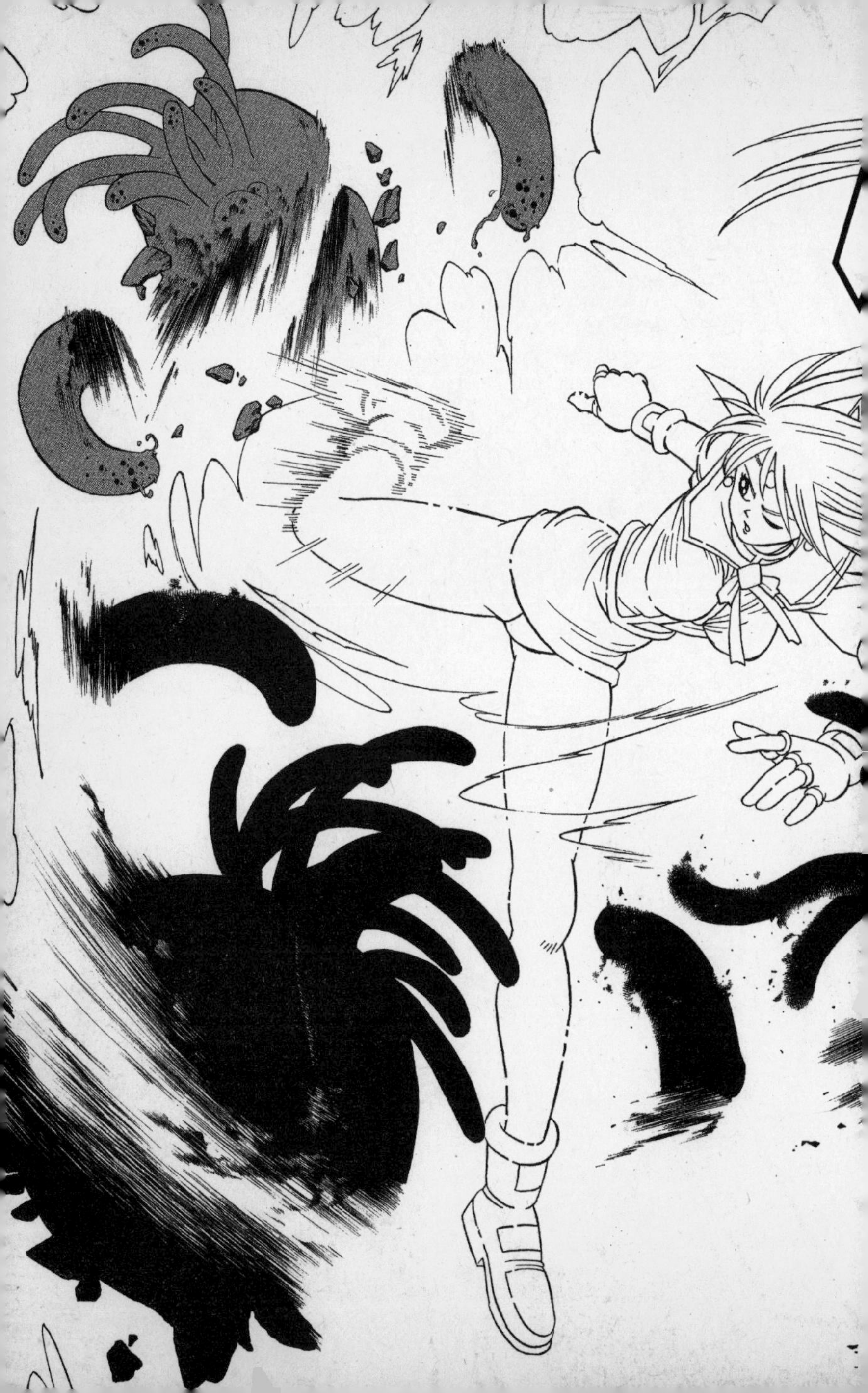

Coming Next Volume...

Beet, Poala, and Kissu skip town, hoping Broad Buster Milfa will stay in the dark about Kissu's shadowed past. But Milfa is a professional, and even her crush on Kissu won't keep her from tracking him down and delivering him to justice! The Beet Warriors escape further into the Black Horizon, and arrive at Grineed's castle just in time to get caught up in his sinister new plan—the Great Undertaking of the Century! Do the Beet Warriors stand a chance against the threat of Grineed's unlimited power?

Available in August 2005!

DRAGON BALL Z™
MEET THE NEW GENERATION... GOTEN AND TRUNKS!
Vol. 1-20 on sale now!
Only $7.95 Each!
SHONEN JUMP™ GRAPHIC NOVELS
On sale at:
www.shonenjump.com
Also available at your local bookstore, comic store and Suncoast Motion Picture Company.
COMIC SHOP LOCATOR SERVICE
888-COMIC-BOOK
888-266-4226
VIZ
DRAGON BALL ©1984 by BIRD STUDIO / SHUEISHA Inc.

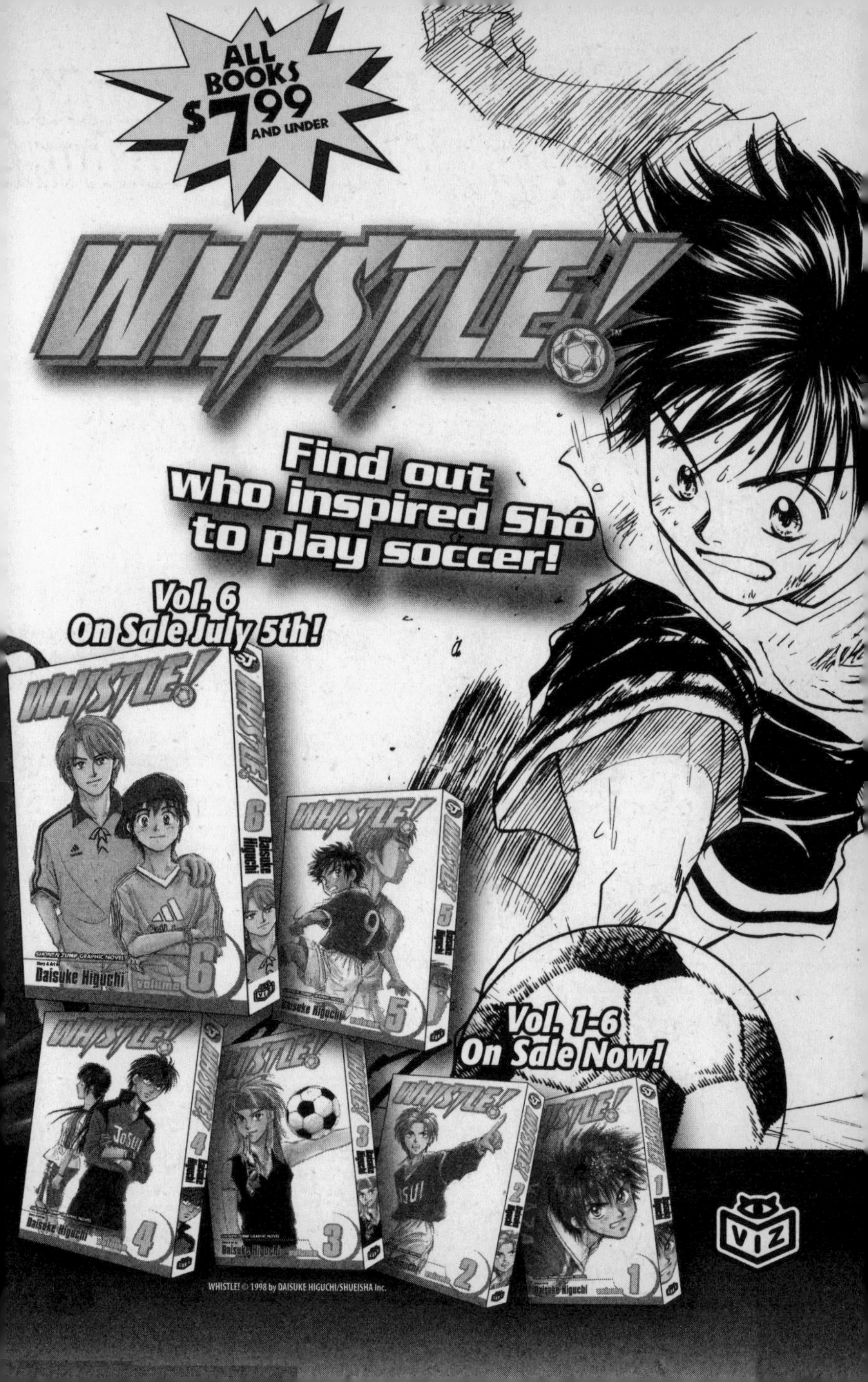
ALL BOOKS $7.99 AND UNDER
WHISTLE!
Find out who inspired Shô to play soccer!
Vol. 6 On Sale July 5th!
Vol. 1-6 On Sale Now!
Daisuke Higuchi
VIZ
WHISTLE! © 1998 by DAISUKE HIGUCHI/SHUEISHA Inc.

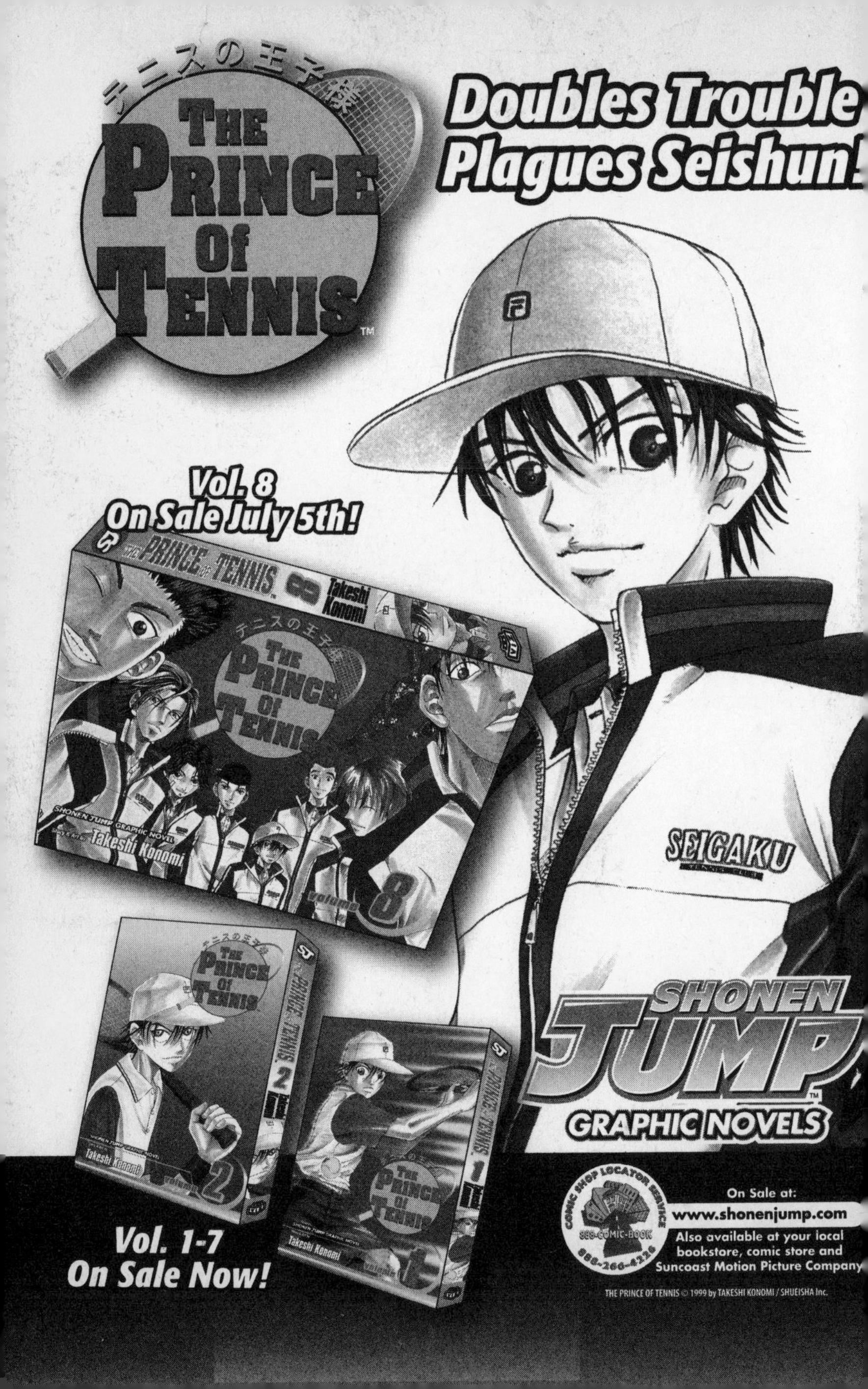

テニスの王子様
THE PRINCE OF TENNIS
Doubles Trouble Plagues Seishun!
Vol. 8
On Sale July 5th!
Vol. 1-7
On Sale Now!
SHONEN JUMP
GRAPHIC NOVELS
On Sale at:
www.shonenjump.com
Also available at your local bookstore, comic store and Suncoast Motion Picture Company
THE PRINCE OF TENNIS © 1999 by TAKESHI KONOMI / SHUEISHA Inc.

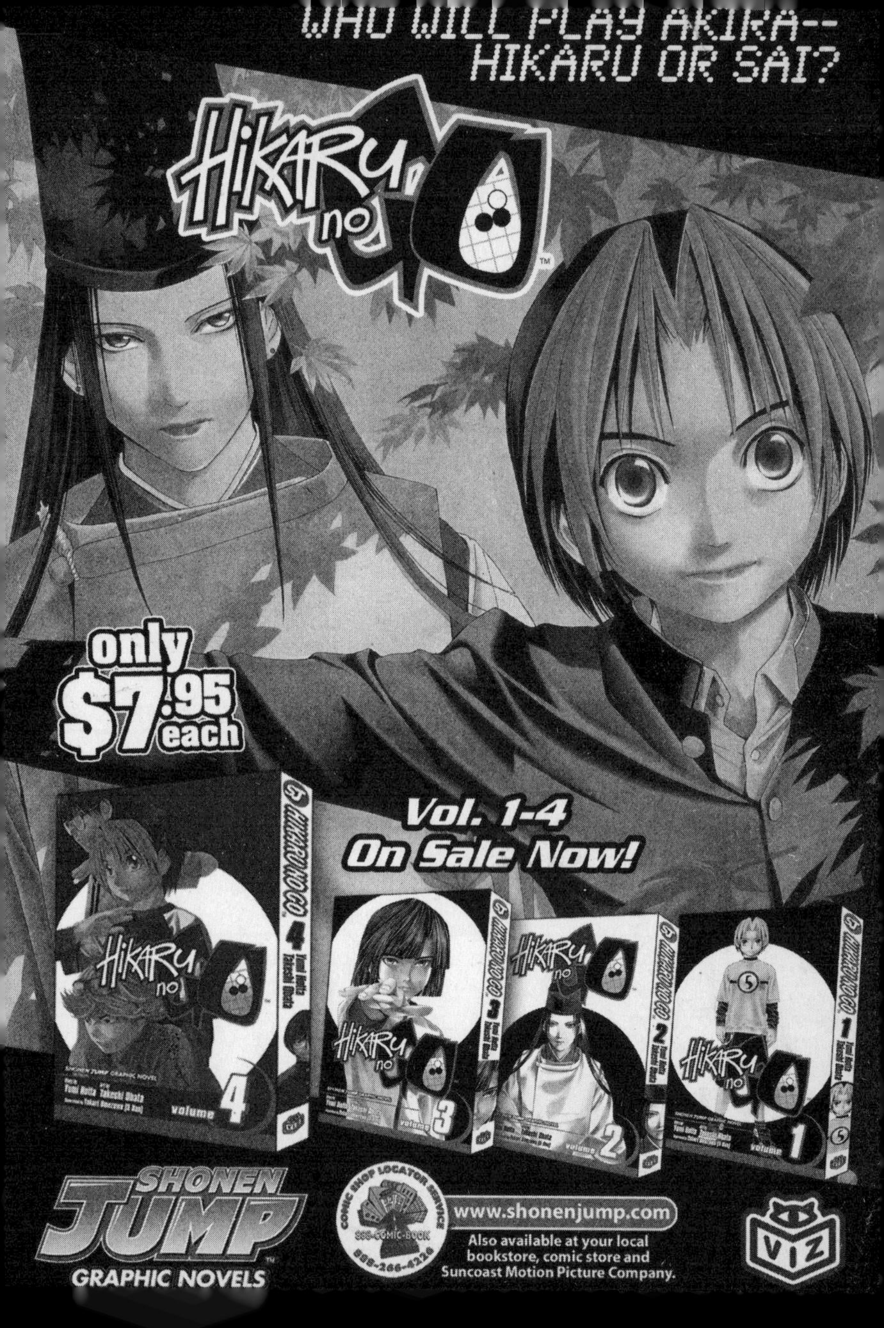
WHO WILL PLAY AKIRA--
HIKARU OR SAI?
HIKARU no GO™
only $7.95 each
Vol. 1-4
On Sale Now!
SHONEN JUMP
GRAPHIC NOVELS
COMIC SHOP LOCATOR SERVICE
888-COMIC-BOOK
888-266-4226
www.shonenjump.com
Also available at your local
bookstore, comic store and
Suncoast Motion Picture Company.
VIZ

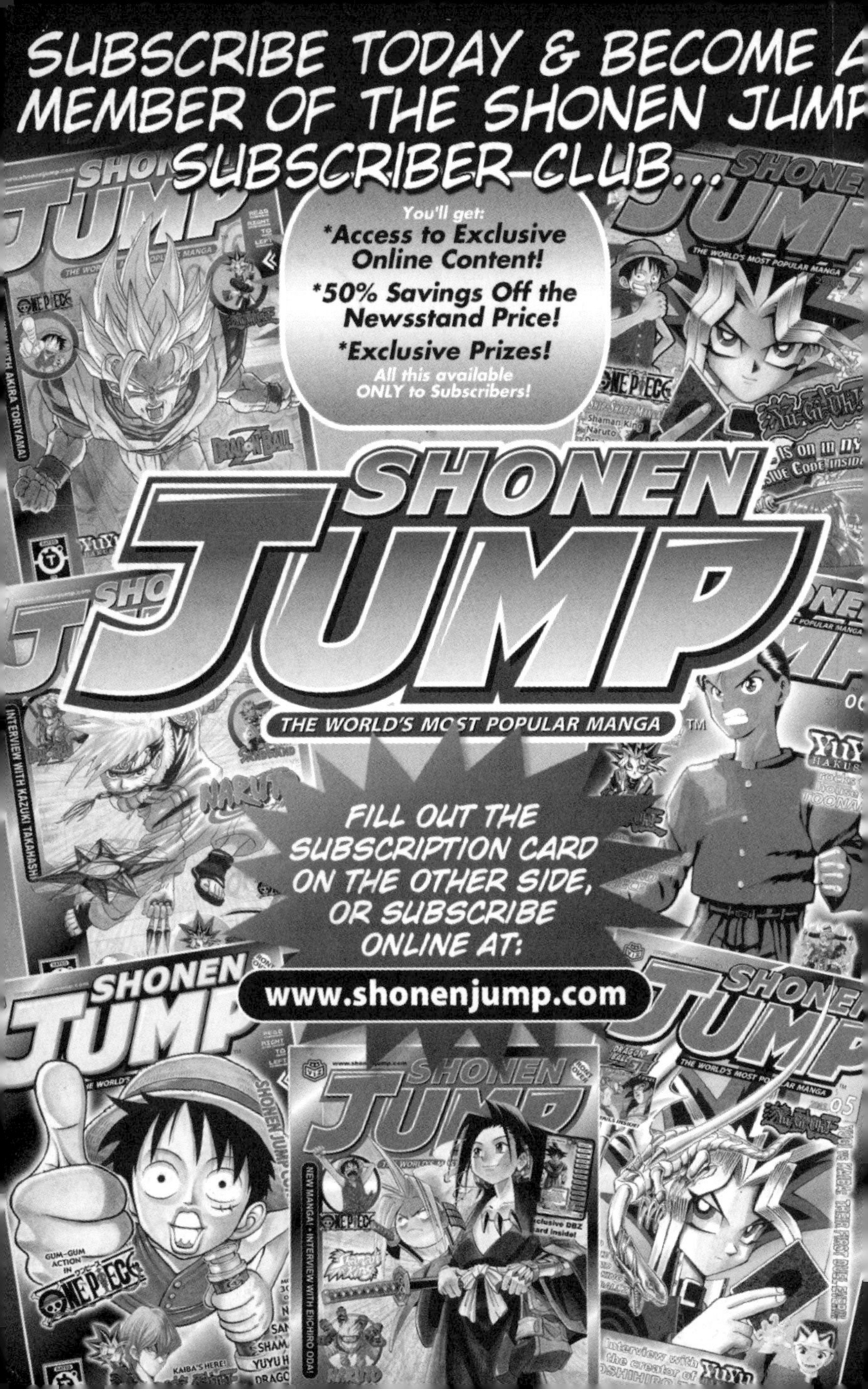
SUBSCRIBE TODAY & BECOME A MEMBER OF THE SHONEN JUMP SUBSCRIBER CLUB...
You'll get:
*Access to Exclusive Online Content!
*50% Savings Off the Newsstand Price!
*Exclusive Prizes!
All this available ONLY to Subscribers!
SHONEN JUMP
THE WORLD'S MOST POPULAR MANGA
FILL OUT THE SUBSCRIPTION CARD ON THE OTHER SIDE, OR SUBSCRIBE ONLINE AT:
www.shonenjump.com

COMPLETE OUR SURVEY AND LET US KNOW WHAT YOU THINK!

☐ Please do NOT send me information about VIZ and SHONEN JUMP products, news and events, special offers, or other information.

☐ Please do NOT send me information from VIZ's trusted business partners.

Name: _____

Address: _____

City: _____ State: _____ Zip: _____

E-mail: _____

☐ Male ☐ Female   Date of Birth (mm/dd/yyyy): ___ / ___ / ___   (Under 13? Parental consent required)

① Do you purchase SHONEN JUMP Magazine?

☐ Yes   ☐ No (if no, skip the next two questions)

If **YES**, do you subscribe?

☐ Yes   ☐ No

If **NO**, how often do you purchase SHONEN JUMP Magazine?

☐ 1-3 issues a year

☐ 4-6 issues a year

☐ more than 7 issues a year

② Which SHONEN JUMP Graphic Novel did you purchase? (please check one)

☐ Beet the Vandel Buster   ☐ Bleach   ☐ Dragon Ball

☐ Dragon Ball Z   ☐ Hikaru no Go   ☐ Knights of the Zodiac

☐ Naruto   ☐ One Piece   ☐ Rurouni Kenshin

☐ Shaman King   ☐ The Prince of Tennis   ☐ Ultimate Muscle

☐ Whistle!   ☐ Yu-Gi-Oh!   ☐ YuYu Hakusho

☐ Other _____

Will you purchase subsequent volumes?

☐ Yes   ☐ No

③ How did you learn about this title? (check all that apply)

☐ Favorite title   ☐ Advertisement   ☐ Article

☐ Gift   ☐ Read excerpt in SHONEN JUMP Magazine

☐ Recommendation   ☐ Special offer   ☐ Through TV animation

☐ Website   ☐ Other _____

4 **Of the ti**[…]**urchased the Graphic**[…]

- [ ] Yes

If **YES**, wh[…]

- [ ] Dragon Ball Z
- [ ] Hikaru no Go
- [ ] Naruto
- [ ] One Piece
- [ ] Shaman King
- [ ] Yu-Gi-Oh!
- [ ] YuYu Hakusho

If **YES**, what were your reasons for purchasing? (please pick up to 3)

- [ ] A favorite title
- [ ] A favorite creator/artist
- [ ] I want to read it in one go
- [ ] I want to read it over and over again
- [ ] There are extras that aren't in the magazine
- [ ] The quality of printing is better than the magazine
- [ ] Recommendation
- [ ] Special offer
- [ ] Other

If **NO**, why did/would you not purchase it?

- [ ] I'm happy just reading it in the magazine
- [ ] It's not worth buying the graphic novel
- [ ] All the manga pages are in black and white unlike the magazine
- [ ] There are other graphic novels that I prefer
- [ ] There are too many to collect for each title
- [ ] It's too small
- [ ] Other ____________________

5 **Of the titles NOT serialized in the Magazine, which ones have you purchased? (check all that apply)**

- [ ] Beet the Vandel Buster
- [ ] Bleach
- [ ] Dragon Ball
- [ ] Knights of the Zodiac
- [ ] The Prince of Tennis
- [ ] Rurouni Kenshin
- [ ] Whistle!
- [ ] Other ____________
- [ ] None

If you did purchase any of the above, what were your reasons for purchase?

- [ ] A favorite title
- [ ] A favorite creator/artist
- [ ] Read a preview in SHONEN JUMP Magazine and wanted to read the rest of the story
- [ ] Recommendation
- [ ] Other

Will you purchase subsequent volumes?

- [ ] Yes
- [ ] No

6 **What race/ethnicity do you consider yourself? (please check one)**

- [ ] Asian/Pacific Islander
- [ ] Black/African American
- [ ] Hispanic/Latino
- [ ] Native American/Alaskan Native
- [ ] White/Caucasian
- [ ] Other

THANK YOU! Please send the completed form to:

VIZ Survey
42 Catharine St.
Poughkeepsie, NY 12601

All information provided will be used for internal purposes only. We promise not to sell or otherwise divulge your information.